W9-ADX-767

1

Hina matsuri

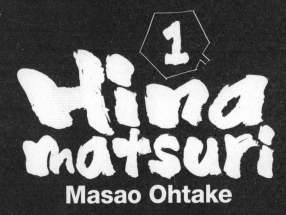

Masao Ohtake

HINA MATSURI Vol.1

CONTENTS

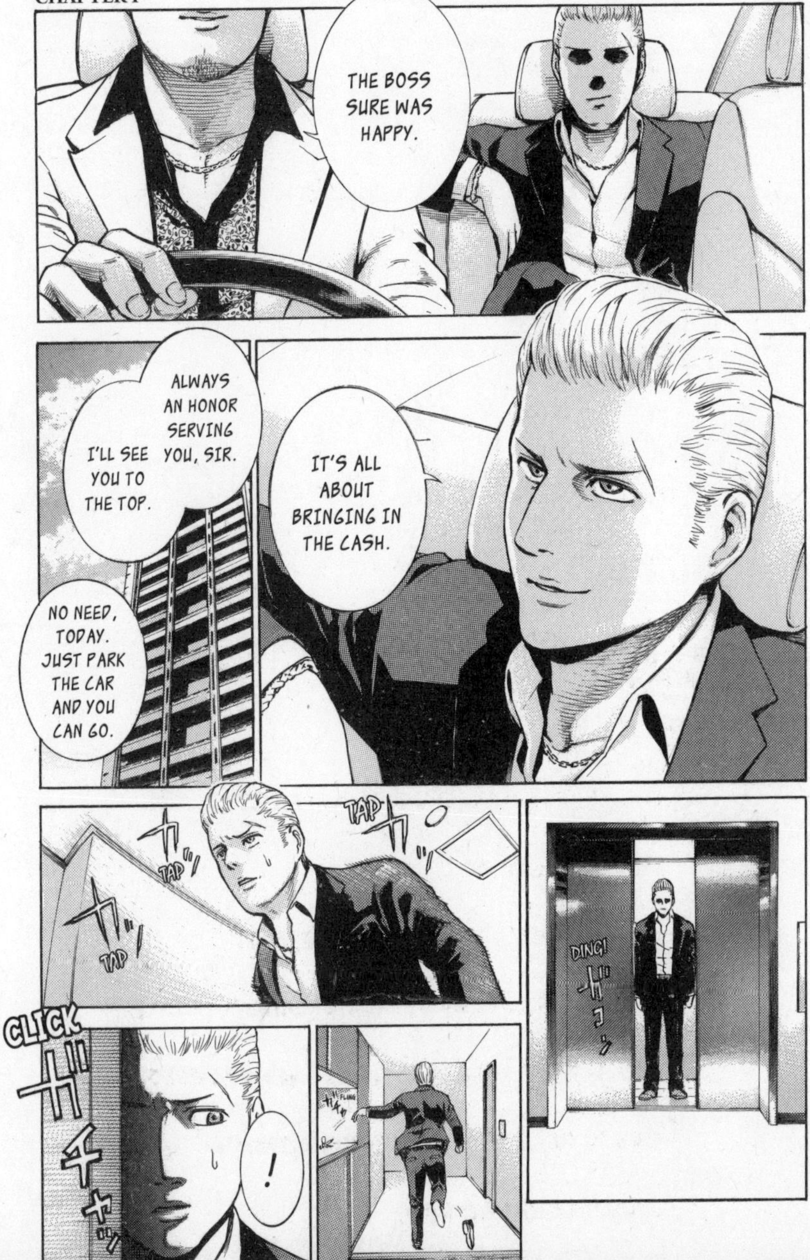
THE BOSS SURE WAS HAPPY.
IT'S ALL ABOUT BRINGING IN THE CASH.
ALWAYS AN HONOR SERVING YOU, SIR.
I'LL SEE YOU TO THE TOP.
NO NEED, TODAY. JUST PARK THE CAR AND YOU CAN GO.
DING!
TAP
TAP
TAP
FLING
CLICK
!

CHAPTER 1
THE PSYCHOKINETIC GIRL APPEARS!

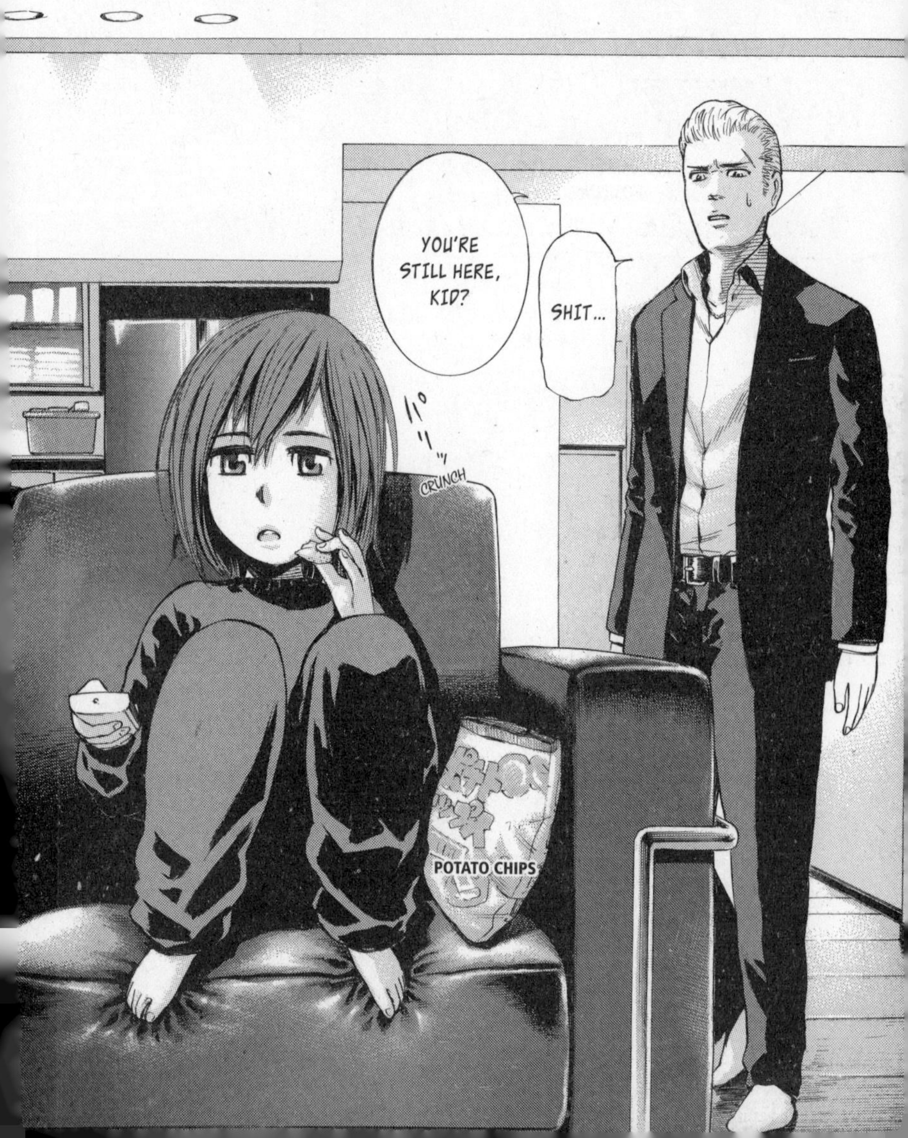
SHIT...
YOU'RE STILL HERE, KID?
CRUNCH
POTATO CHIPS

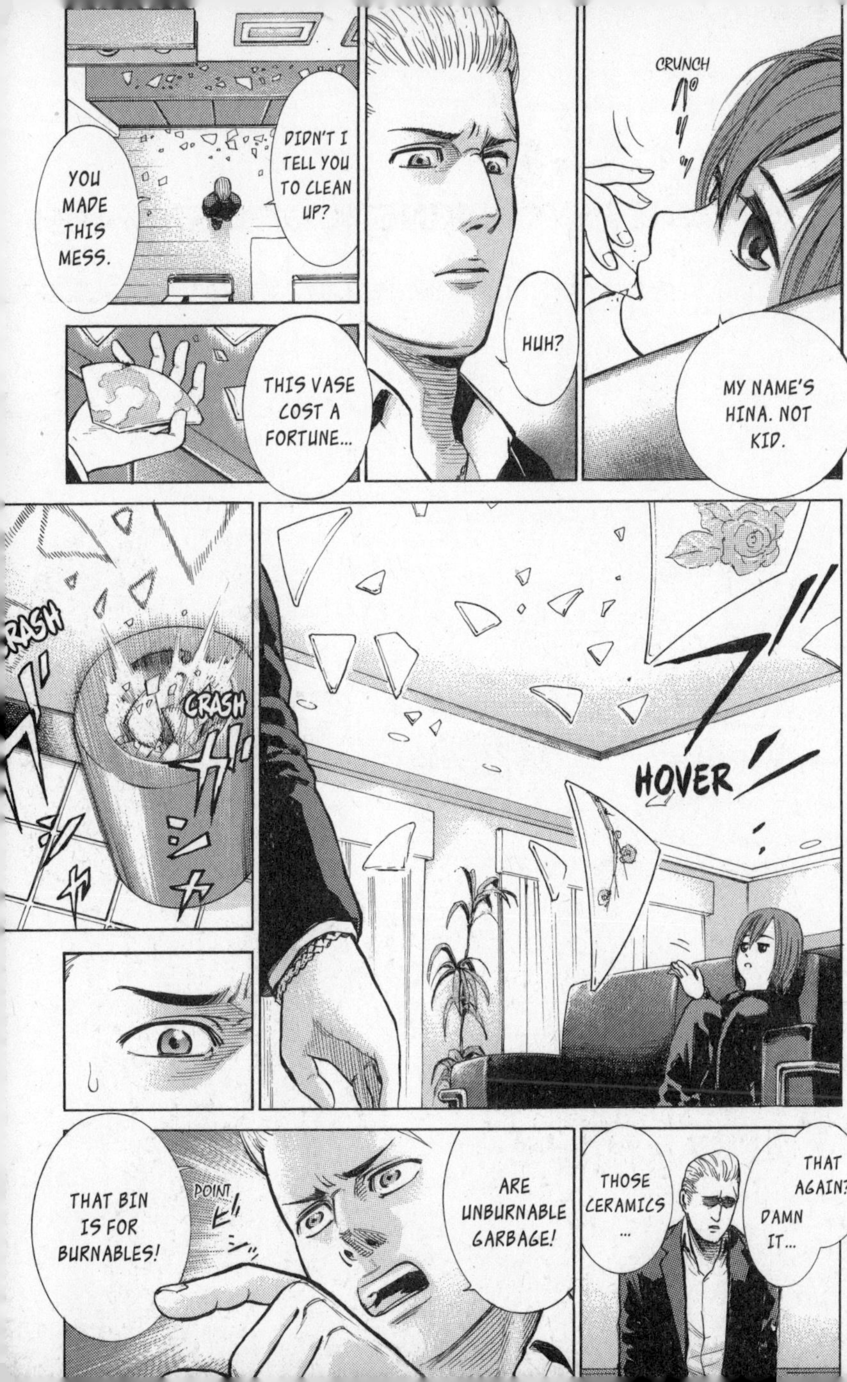
CRUNCH
MY NAME'S HINA. NOT KID.
HUH?
DIDN'T I TELL YOU TO CLEAN UP?
YOU MADE THIS MESS.
THIS VASE COST A FORTUNE...
HOVER
CRASH
CRASH
THAT AGAIN? DAMN IT...
THOSE CERAMICS ...
ARE UNBURNABLE GARBAGE!
POINT
THAT BIN IS FOR BURNABLES!

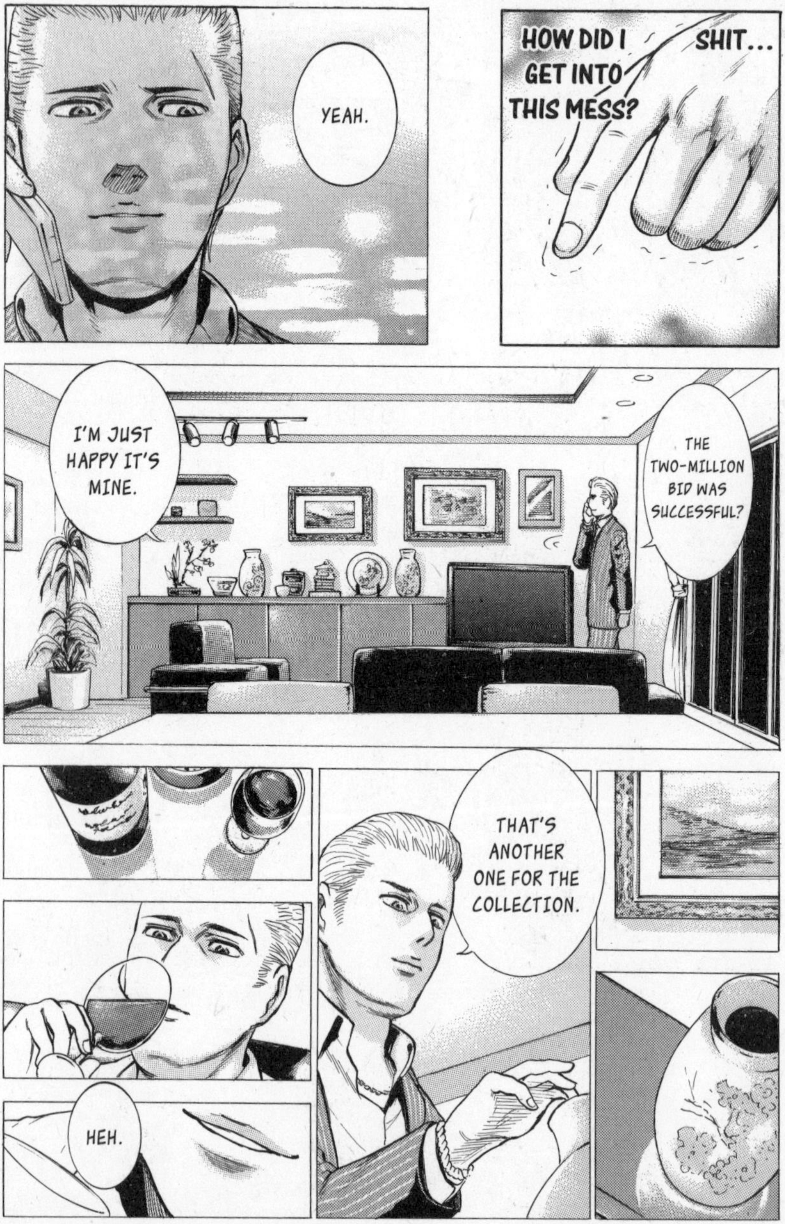
SHIT...
HOW DID I GET INTO THIS MESS?
YEAH.
THE TWO-MILLION BID WAS SUCCESSFUL?
I'M JUST HAPPY IT'S MINE.
THAT'S ANOTHER ONE FOR THE COLLECTION.
HEH.

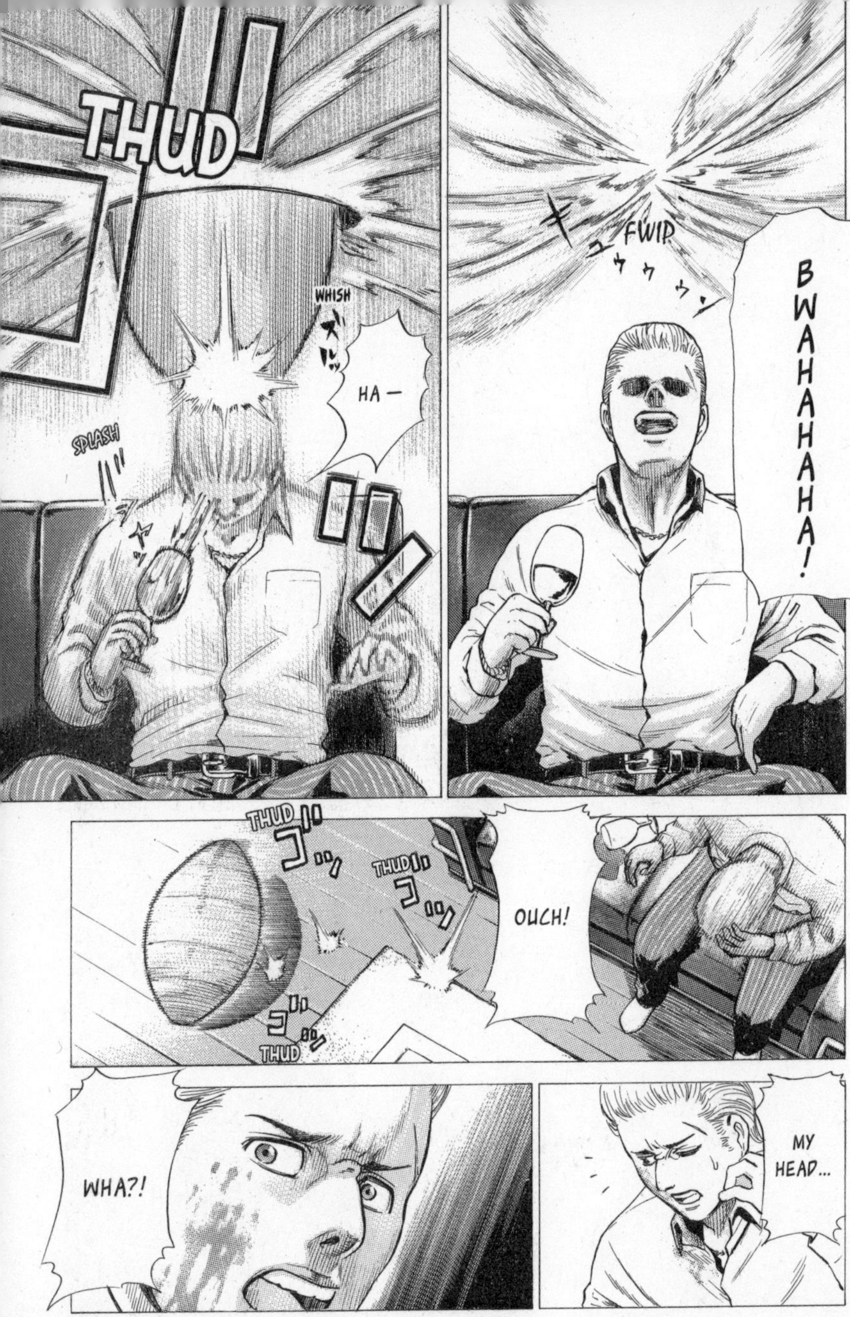
FWIP
BWAHAHAHAHA!
THUD
WHISH
HA—
SPLASH
THUD
THUD
OUCH!
THUD
MY HEAD...
WHA?!

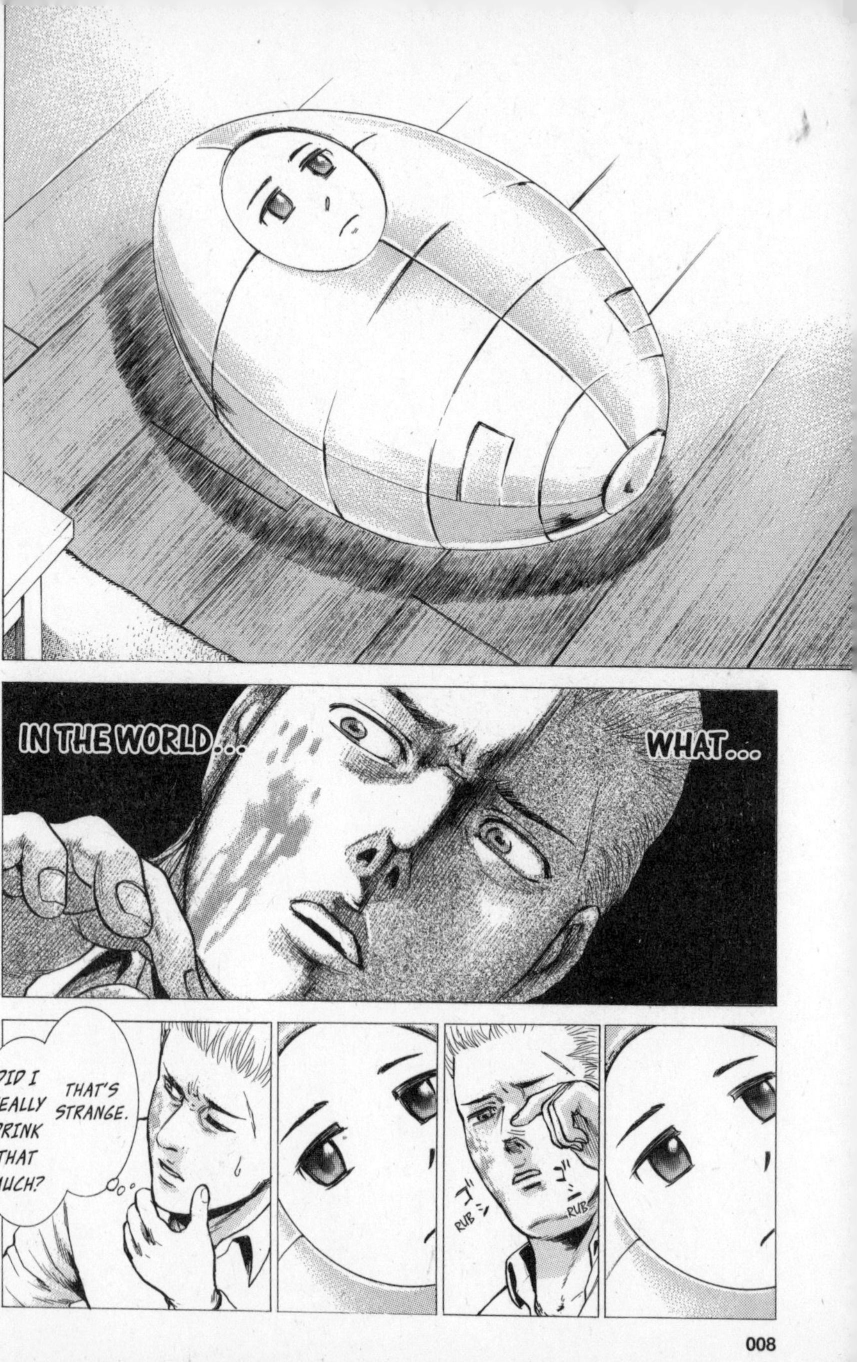
WHAT...
IN THE WORLD...
RUB
RUB
THAT'S STRANGE.
DID I REALLY DRINK THAT MUCH?

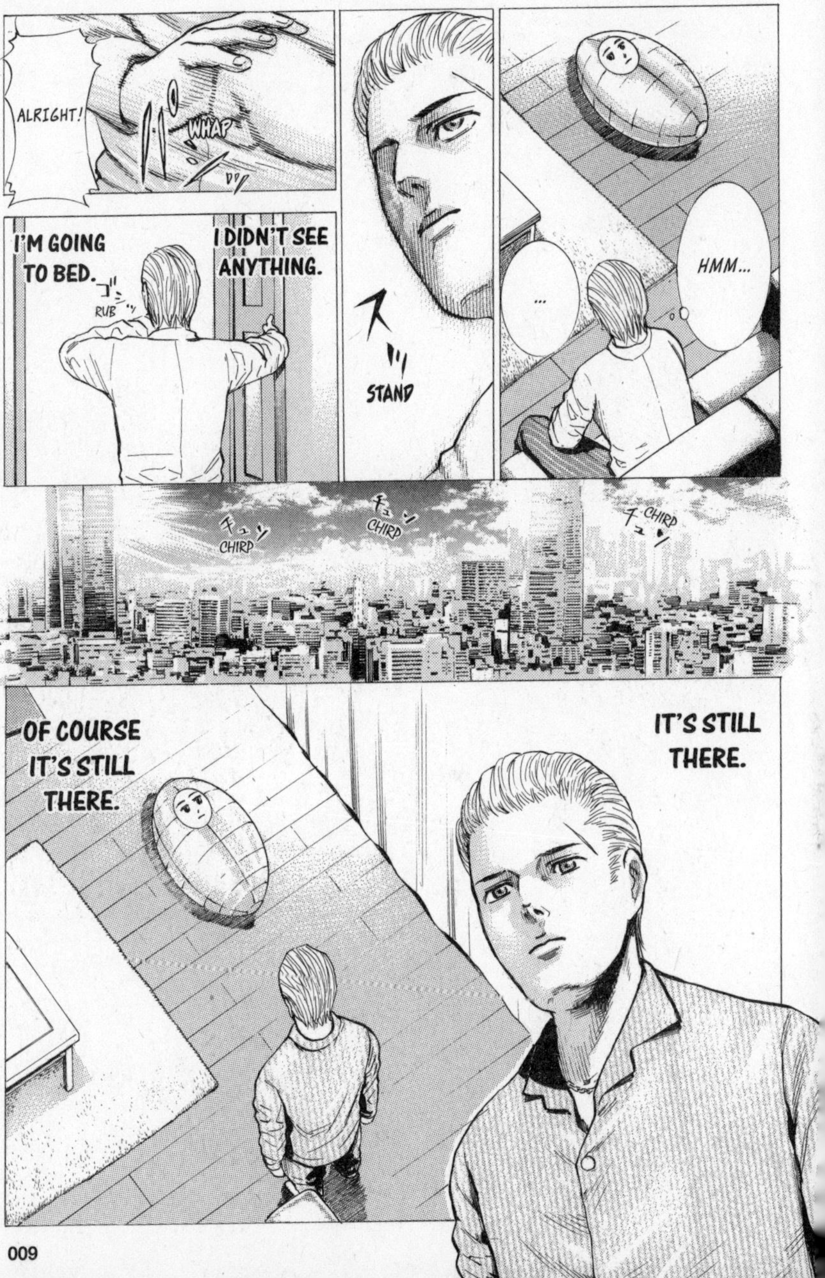
HMM...
...
STAND
ALRIGHT!
WHAP
I DIDN'T SEE ANYTHING.
I'M GOING TO BED.
RUB
CHIRP
CHIRP
CHIRP
IT'S STILL THERE.
OF COURSE IT'S STILL THERE.

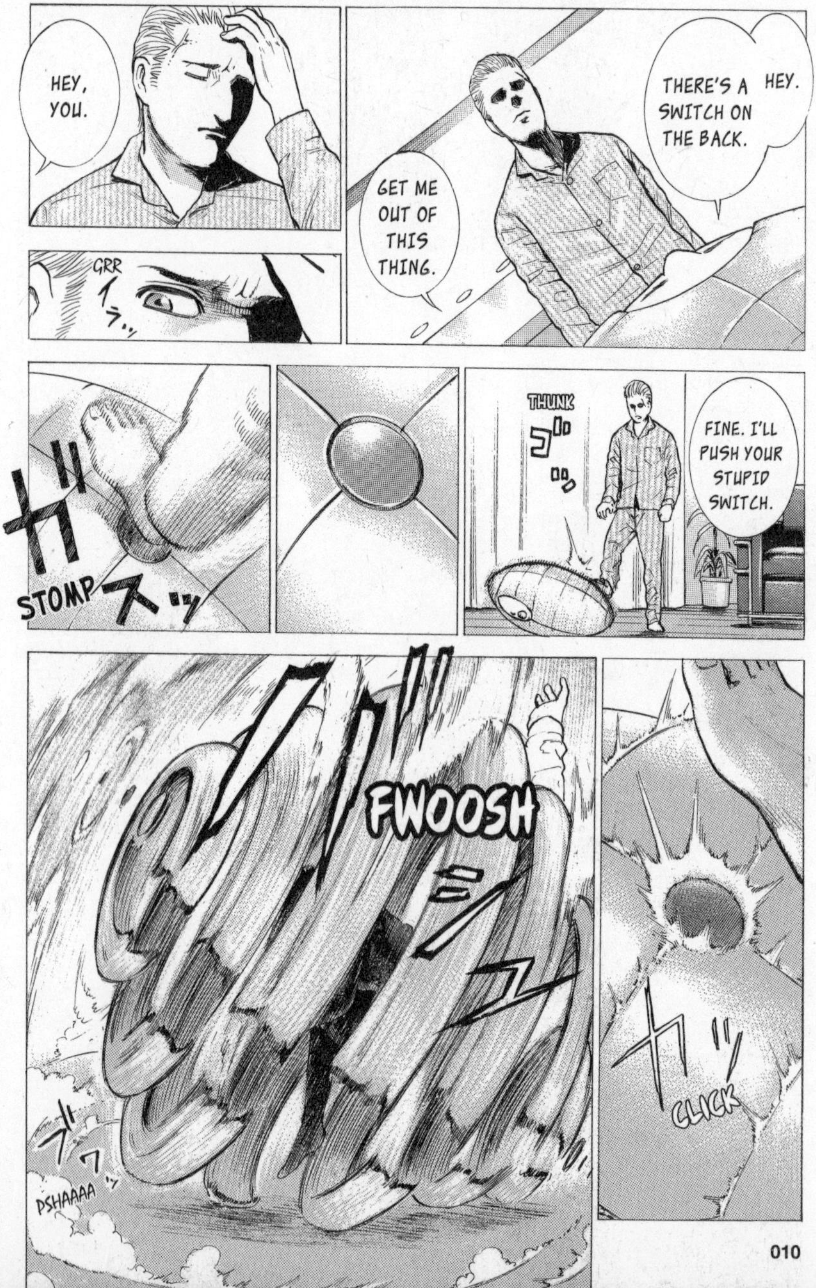
HEY.
THERE'S A SWITCH ON THE BACK.
GET ME OUT OF THIS THING.
HEY, YOU.
GRR
FINE. I'LL PUSH YOUR STUPID SWITCH.
THUNK
STOMP
CLICK
FWOOSH
PSHAAAA

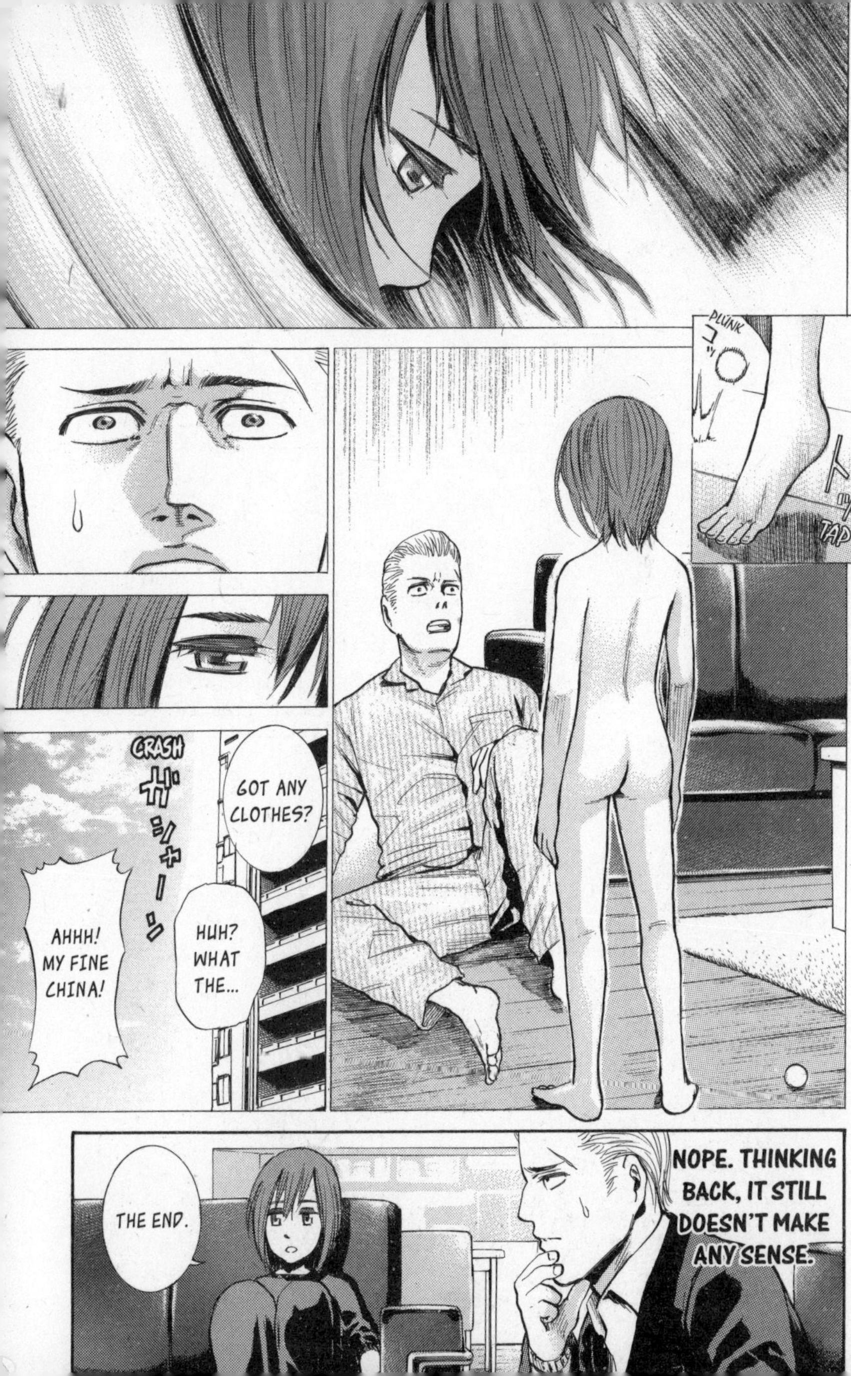
PLUNK
TAP
CRASH
GOT ANY CLOTHES?
HUH? WHAT THE...
AHHH! MY FINE CHINA!
NOPE. THINKING BACK, IT STILL DOESN'T MAKE ANY SENSE.
THE END.

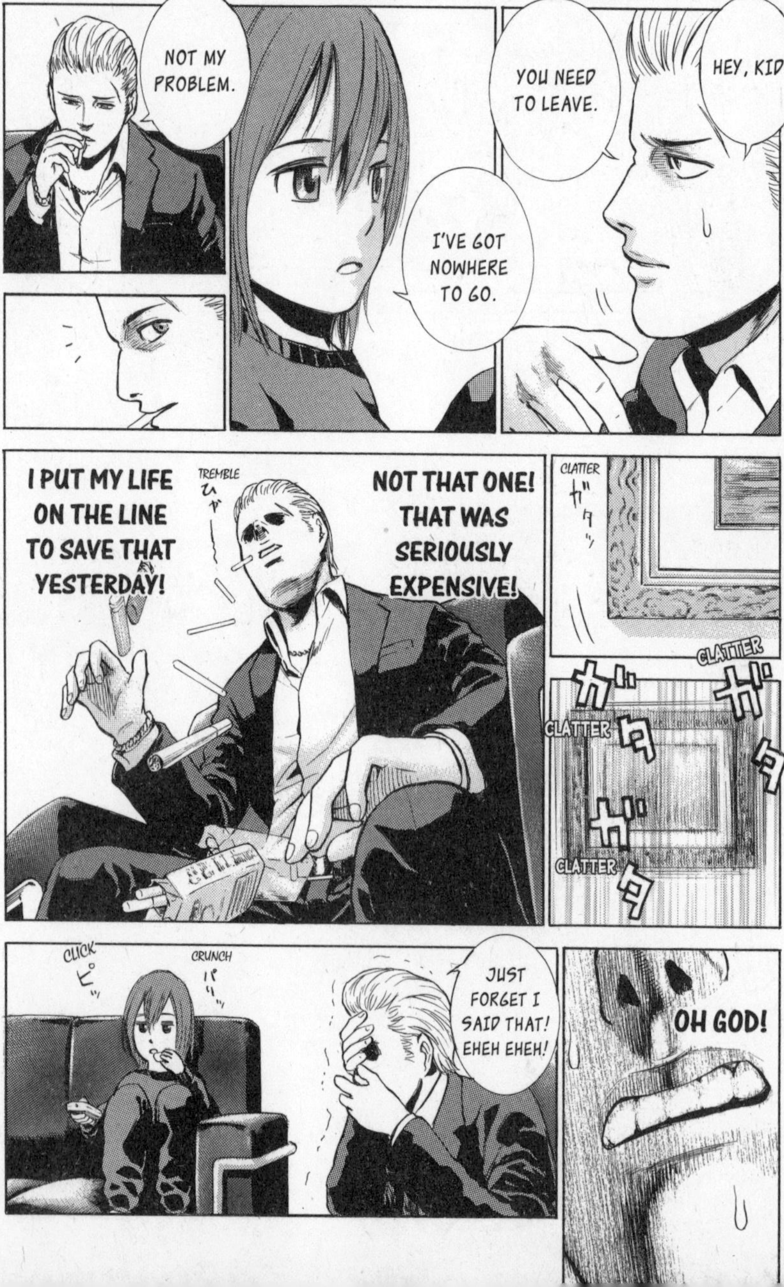
HEY, KID.
YOU NEED TO LEAVE.
I'VE GOT NOWHERE TO GO.
NOT MY PROBLEM.
CLATTER
ガタッ
CLATTER
ガタ
CLATTER
ガタ
CLATTER
ガタ
NOT THAT ONE! THAT WAS SERIOUSLY EXPENSIVE!
TREMBLE
I PUT MY LIFE ON THE LINE TO SAVE THAT YESTERDAY!
OH GOD!
JUST FORGET I SAID THAT! EHEH EHEH!
CRUNCH
CLICK

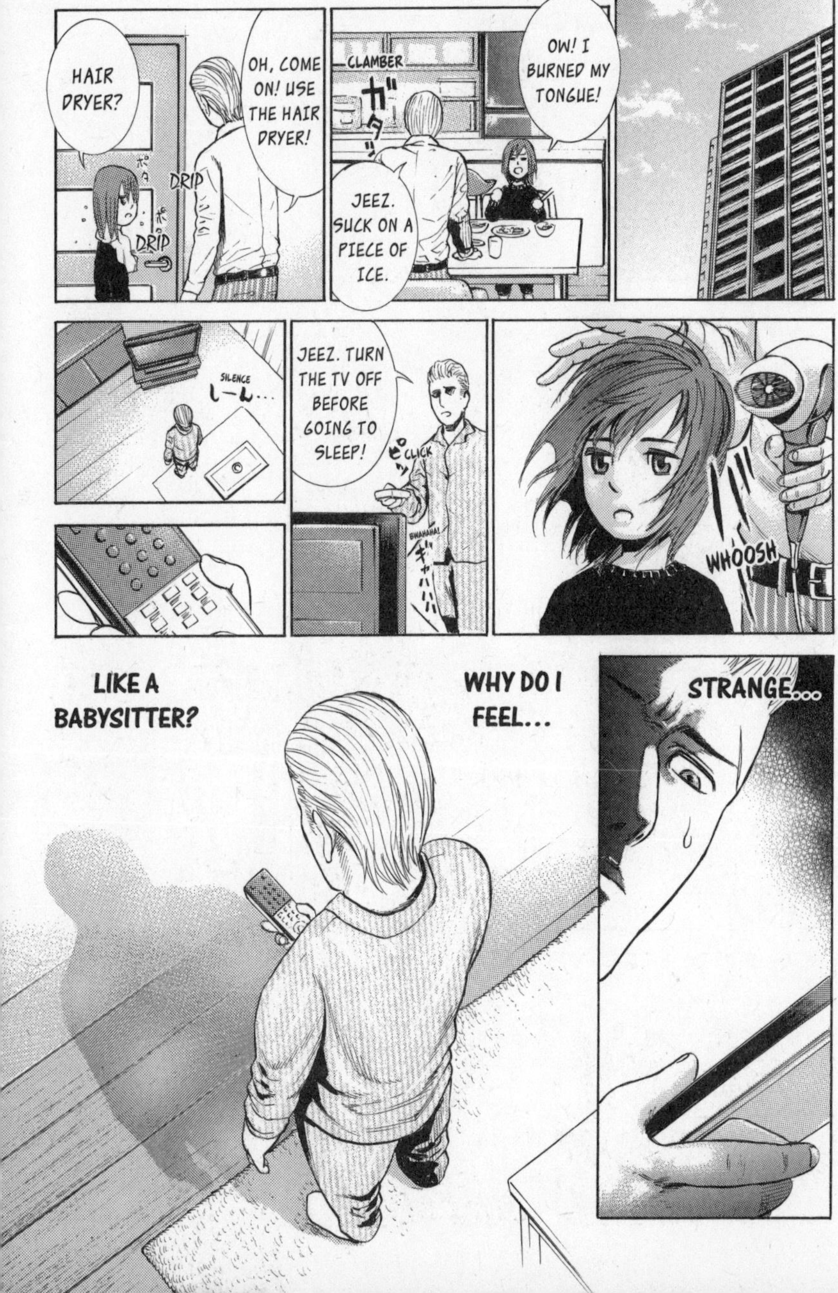
OW! I BURNED MY TONGUE!
CLAMBER
ガタッ
JEEZ. SUCK ON A PIECE OF ICE.
OH, COME ON! USE THE HAIR DRYER!
HAIR DRYER?
DRIP
DRIP
WHOOSH
JEEZ. TURN THE TV OFF BEFORE GOING TO SLEEP!
CLICK
BWAHAHA!
SILENCE
しーん…
STRANGE...
WHY DO I FEEL...
LIKE A BABYSITTER?

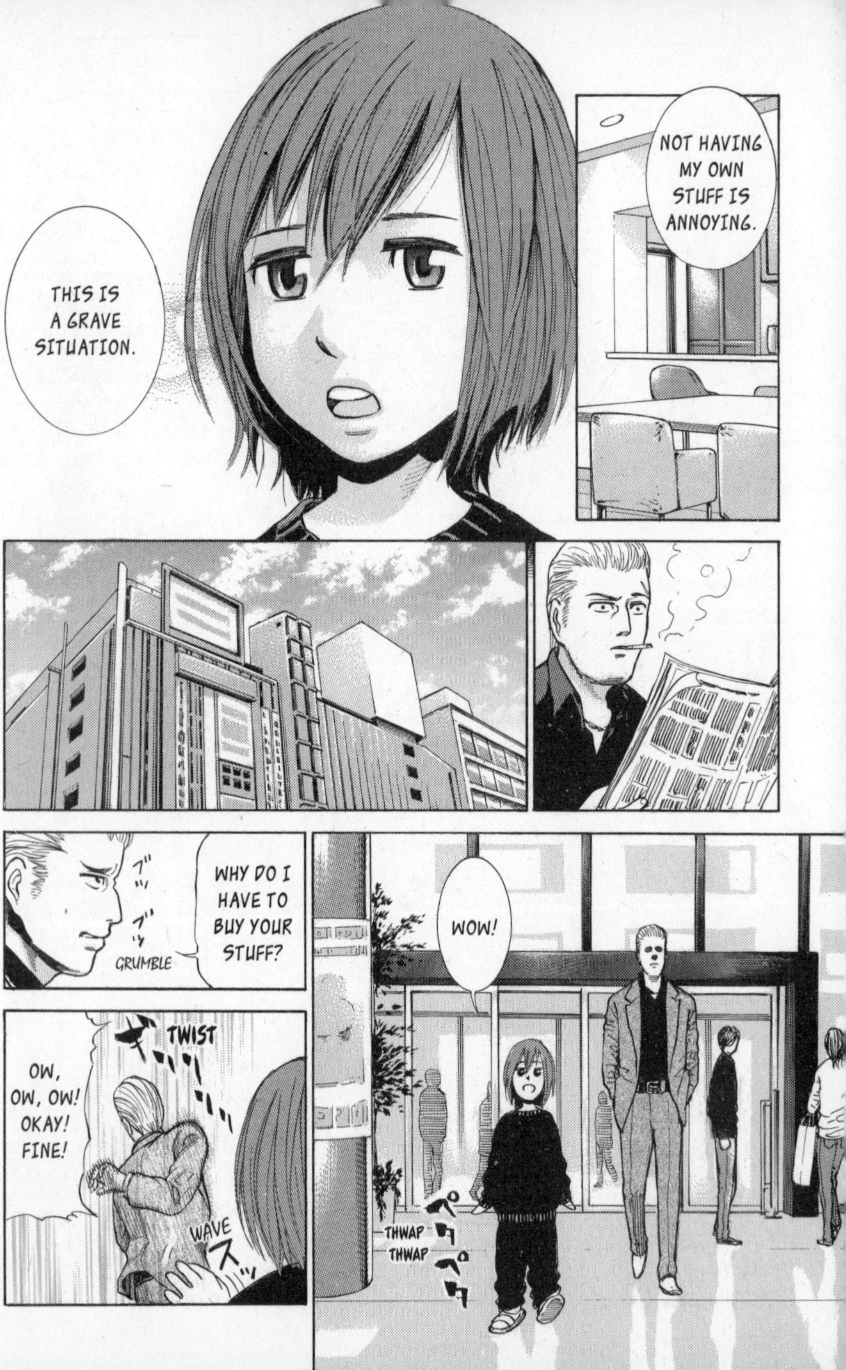

NOT HAVING MY OWN STUFF IS ANNOYING.
THIS IS A GRAVE SITUATION.
WOW!
THWAP THWAP
GRUMBLE
WHY DO I HAVE TO BUY YOUR STUFF?
TWIST
OW, OW, OW! OKAY! FINE!
WAVE

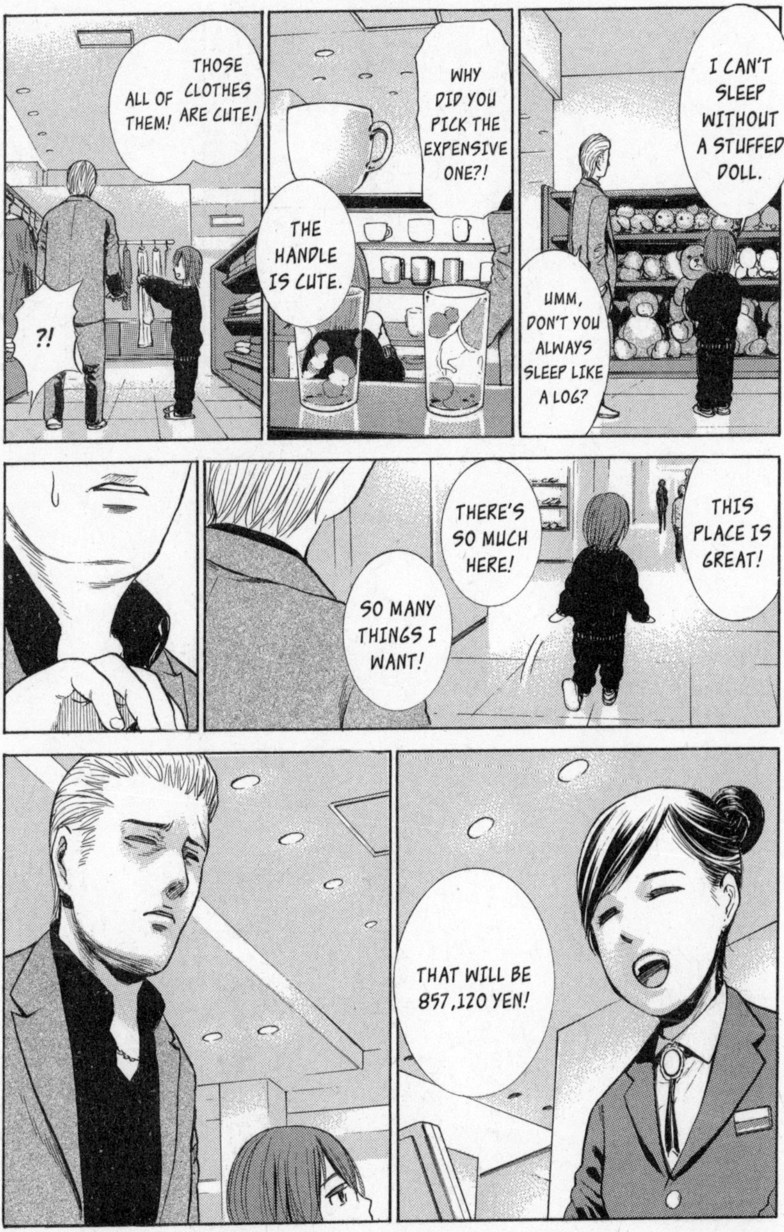
I CAN'T SLEEP WITHOUT A STUFFED DOLL.
UMM, DON'T YOU ALWAYS SLEEP LIKE A LOG?
WHY DID YOU PICK THE EXPENSIVE ONE?!
THE HANDLE IS CUTE.
THOSE CLOTHES ARE CUTE!
ALL OF THEM!
?!
THIS PLACE IS GREAT!
THERE'S SO MUCH HERE!
SO MANY THINGS I WANT!
THAT WILL BE 857,120 YEN!

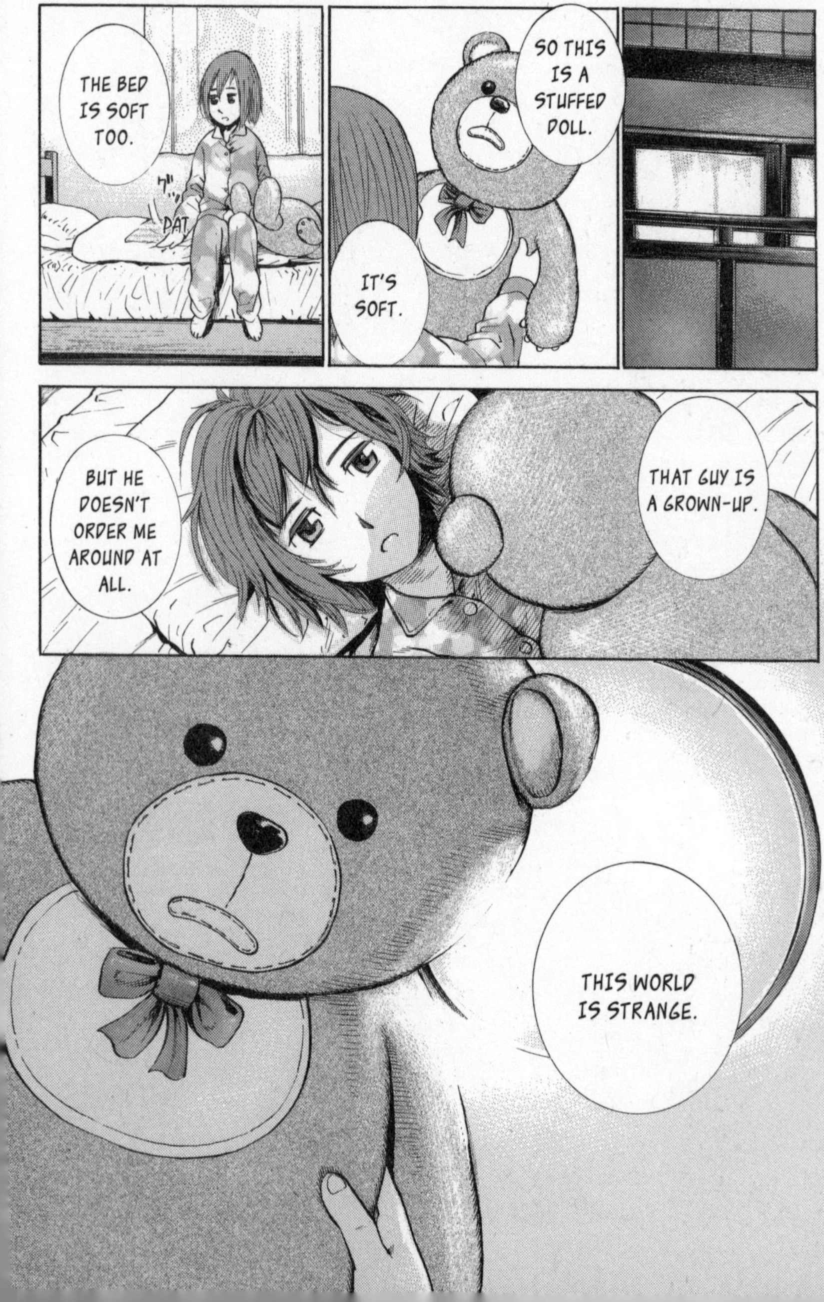
SO THIS IS A STUFFED DOLL.
IT'S SOFT.
THE BED IS SOFT TOO.
PAT
THAT GUY IS A GROWN-UP.
BUT HE DOESN'T ORDER ME AROUND AT ALL.
THIS WORLD IS STRANGE.

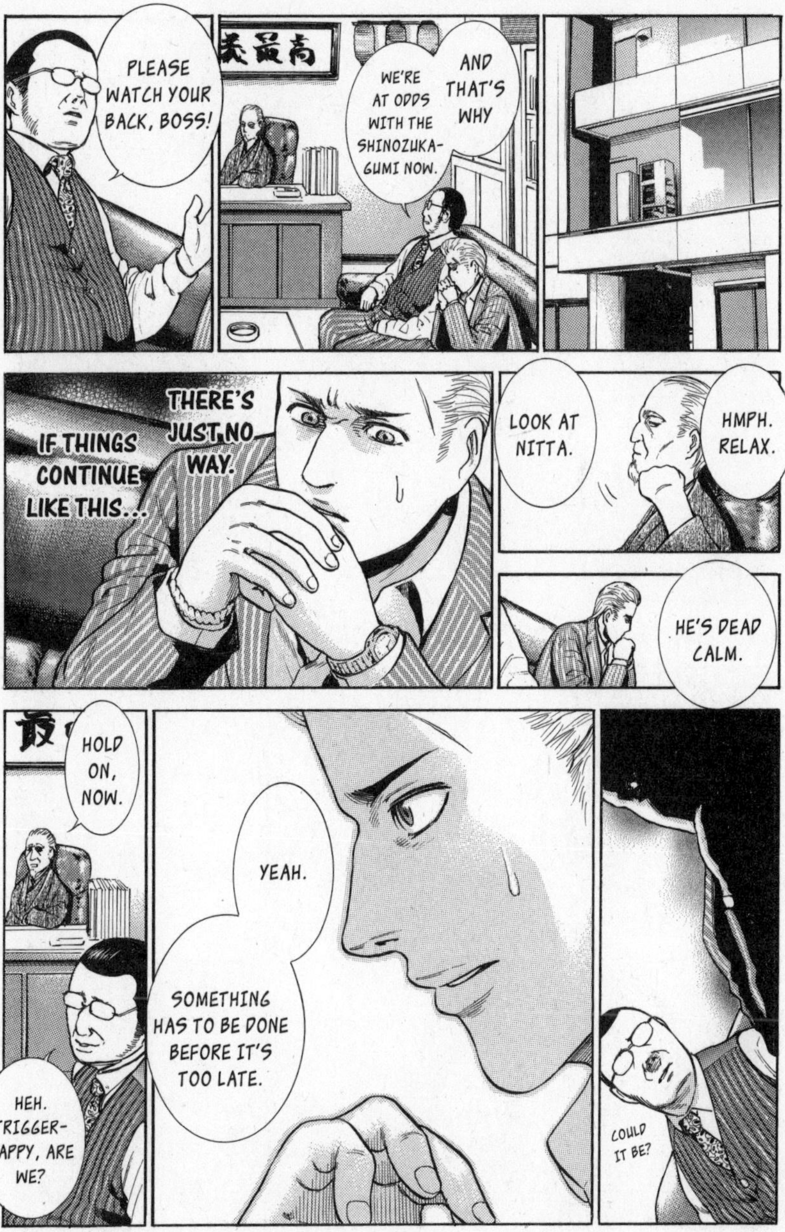
AND THAT'S WHY
WE'RE AT ODDS WITH THE SHINOZUKA-GUMI NOW.
PLEASE WATCH YOUR BACK, BOSS!
HMPH. RELAX.
LOOK AT NITTA.
HE'S DEAD CALM.
THERE'S JUST NO WAY.
IF THINGS CONTINUE LIKE THIS...
COULD IT BE?
YEAH.
SOMETHING HAS TO BE DONE BEFORE IT'S TOO LATE.
HOLD ON, NOW.
HEH. TRIGGER-HAPPY, ARE WE?

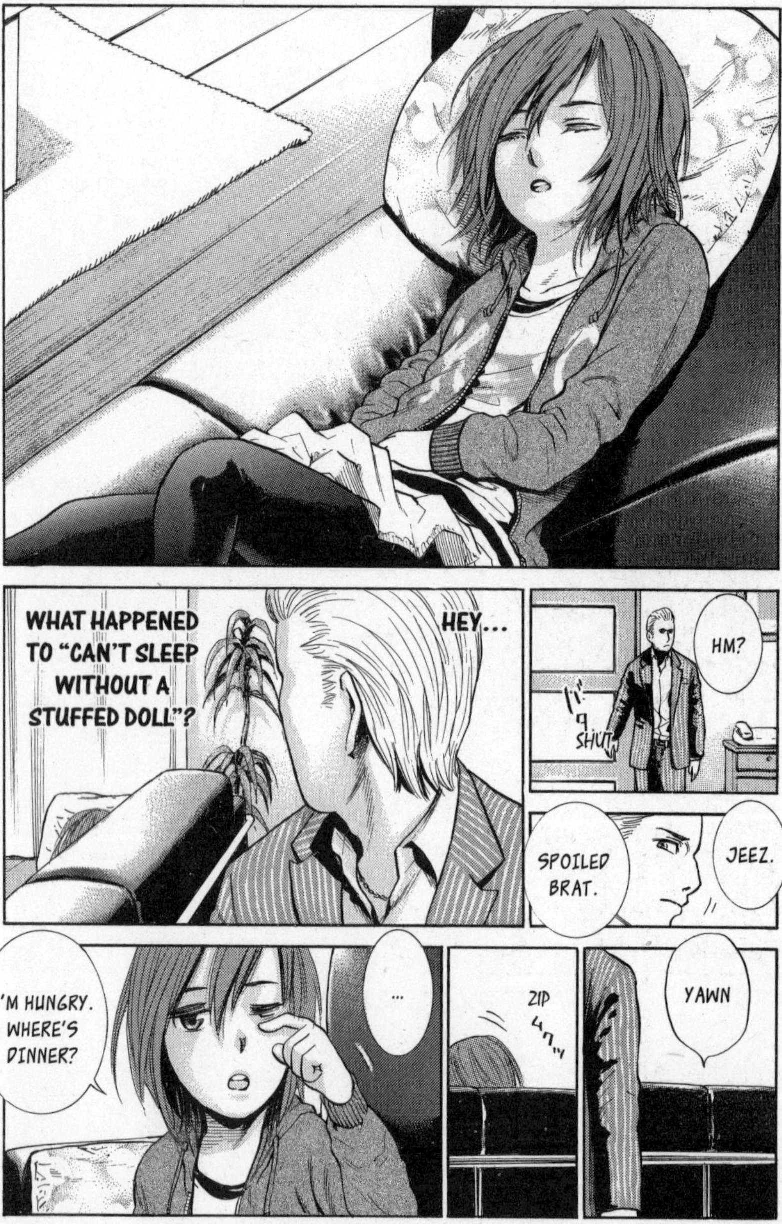
HM?
SHUT
JEEZ.
SPOILED BRAT.
HEY...
WHAT HAPPENED TO "CAN'T SLEEP WITHOUT A STUFFED DOLL"?
YAWN
ZIP
...
I'M HUNGRY. WHERE'S DINNER?

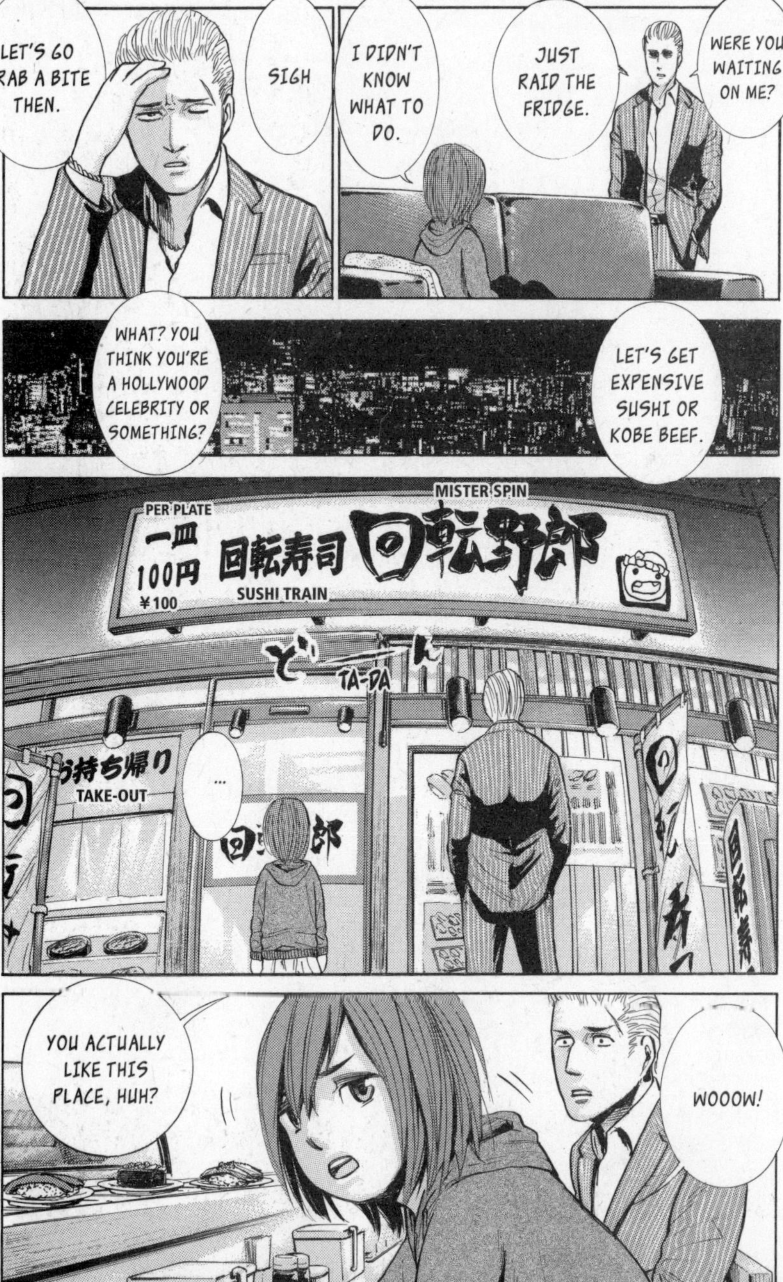
WERE YOU WAITING ON ME?
JUST RAID THE FRIDGE.
I DIDN'T KNOW WHAT TO DO.
SIGH
LET'S GO GRAB A BITE THEN.
LET'S GET EXPENSIVE SUSHI OR KOBE BEEF.
WHAT? YOU THINK YOU'RE A HOLLYWOOD CELEBRITY OR SOMETHING?
MISTER SPIN
回転野郎
回転寿司
SUSHI TRAIN
一皿
100円
PER PLATE
¥100
ど——ん
TA-DA
持ち帰り
TAKE-OUT
...
WOOOW!
YOU ACTUALLY LIKE THIS PLACE, HUH?

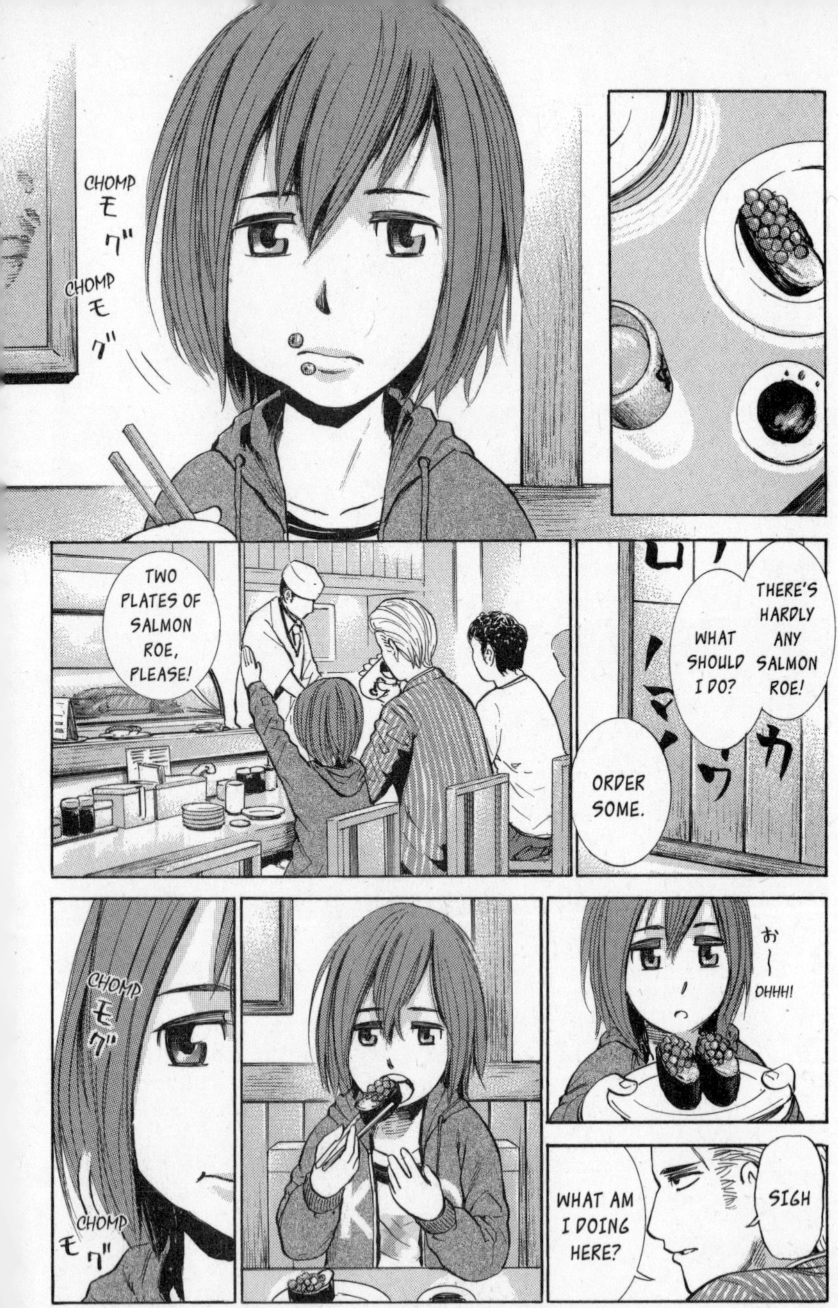
CHOMP
モグ
CHOMP
モグ
THERE'S HARDLY ANY SALMON ROE!
WHAT SHOULD I DO?
ORDER SOME.
TWO PLATES OF SALMON ROE, PLEASE!
おー
OHHH!
SIGH
WHAT AM I DOING HERE?
CHOMP
モグ
CHOMP
モグ

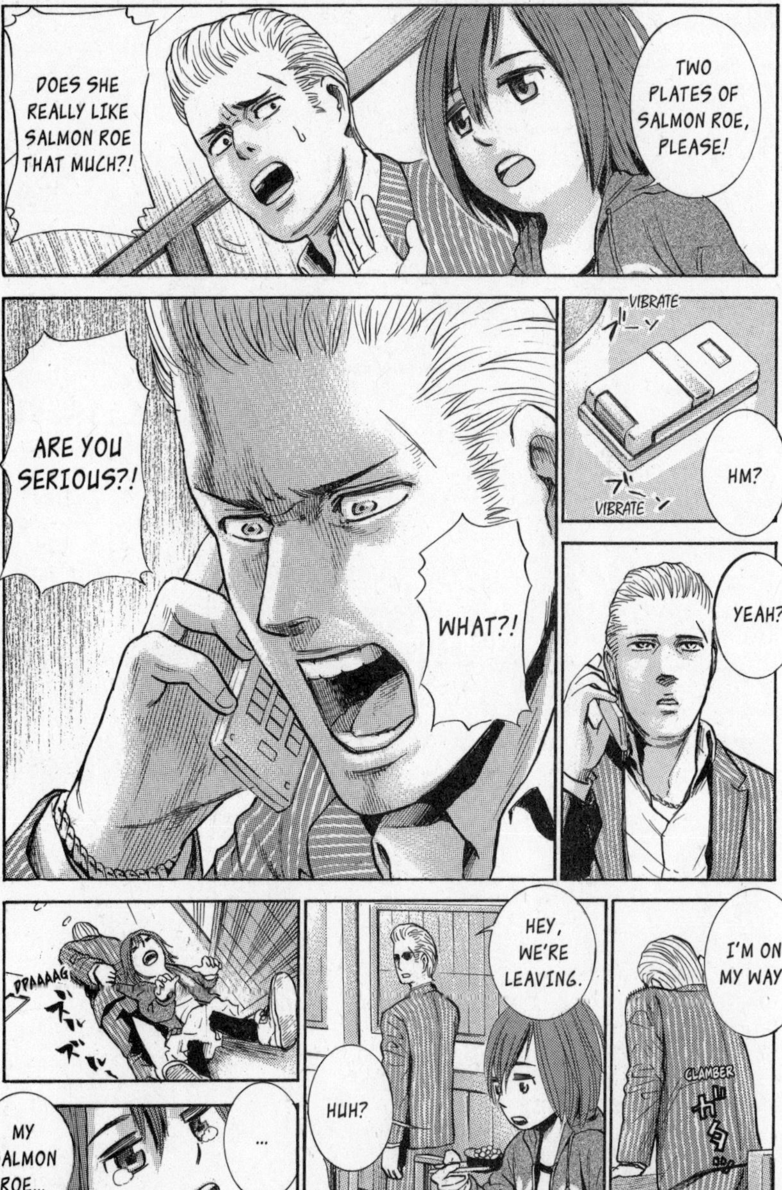

TWO PLATES OF SALMON ROE, PLEASE!
DOES SHE REALLY LIKE SALMON ROE THAT MUCH?!
VIBRATE
VIBRATE
HM?
YEAH?
WHAT?!
ARE YOU SERIOUS?!
I'M ON MY WAY!
CLAMBER
HEY, WE'RE LEAVING.
HUH?
DRAAAAG
...
MY SALMON ROE...

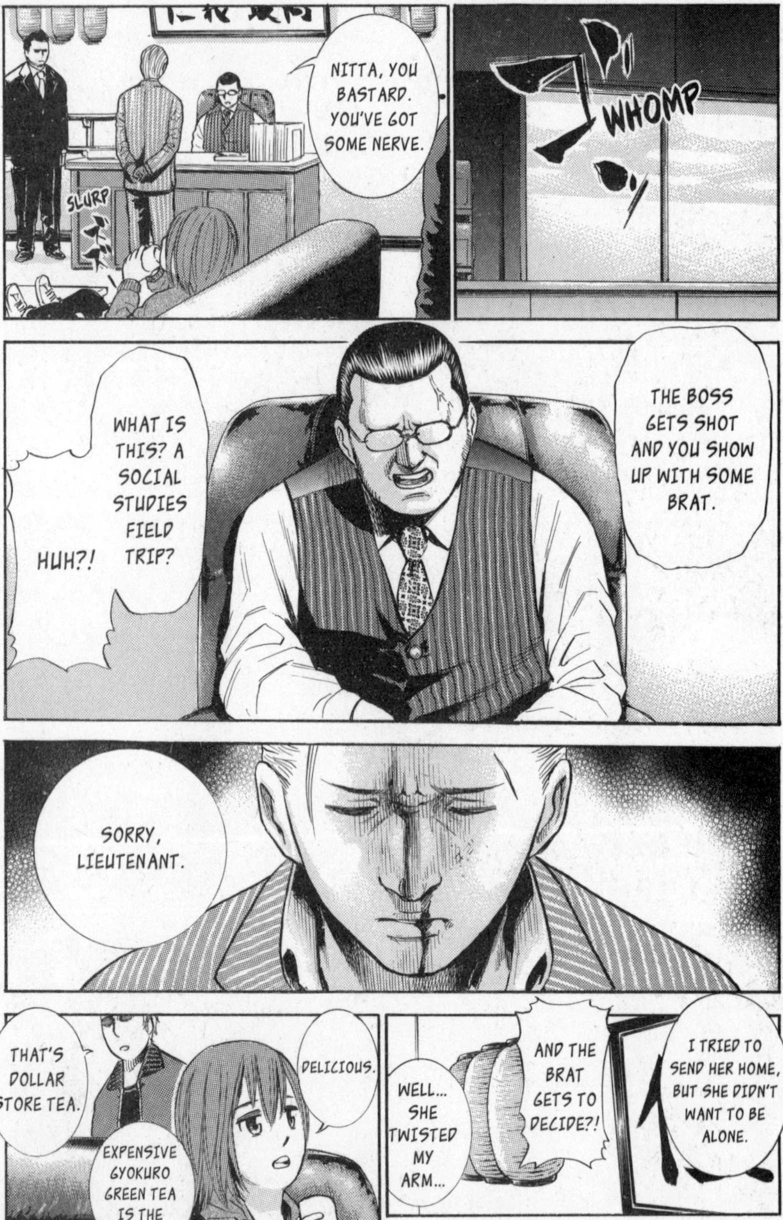
WHOMP
NITTA, YOU BASTARD. YOU'VE GOT SOME NERVE.
SLURP
THE BOSS GETS SHOT AND YOU SHOW UP WITH SOME BRAT.
WHAT IS THIS? A SOCIAL STUDIES FIELD TRIP?
HUH?!
SORRY, LIEUTENANT.
I TRIED TO SEND HER HOME, BUT SHE DIDN'T WANT TO BE ALONE.
AND THE BRAT GETS TO DECIDE?!
WELL... SHE TWISTED MY ARM...
DELICIOUS.
THAT'S DOLLAR STORE TEA.
EXPENSIVE GYOKURO GREEN TEA IS THE BEST.

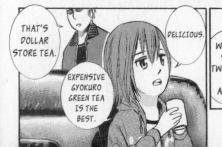

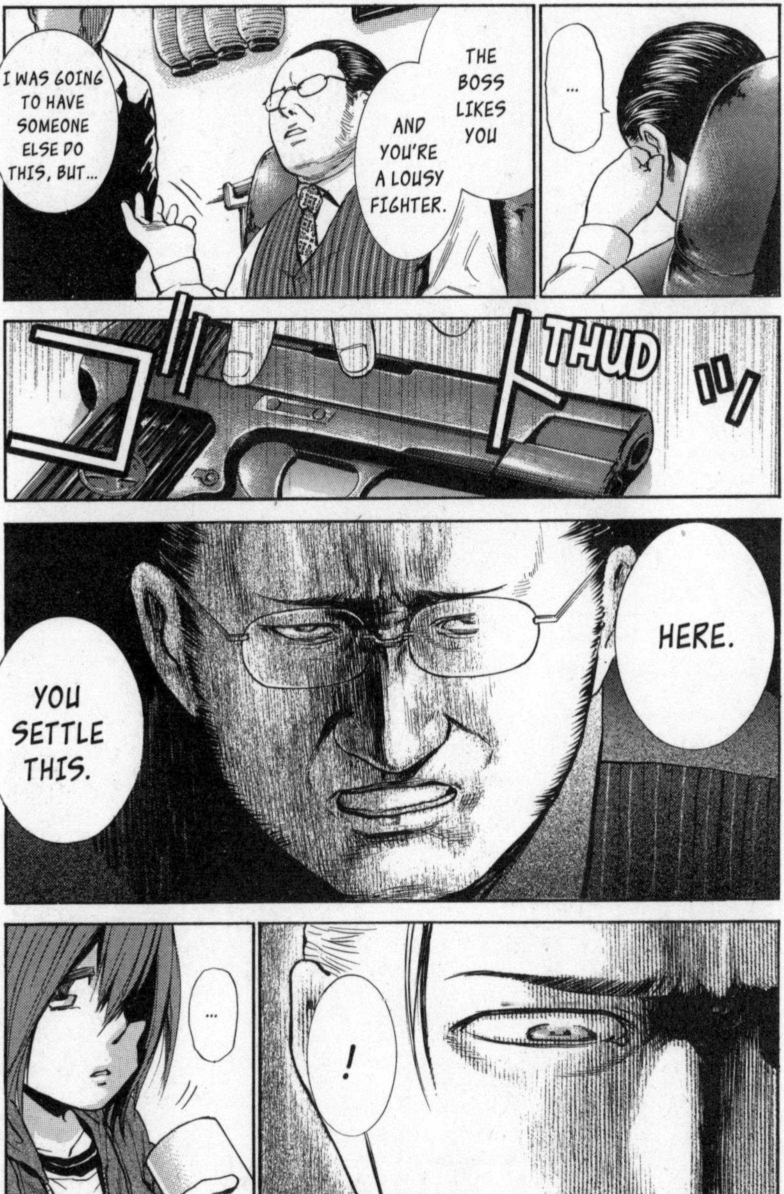
...
THE BOSS LIKES YOU
AND YOU'RE A LOUSY FIGHTER.
I WAS GOING TO HAVE SOMEONE ELSE DO THIS, BUT...
THUD
HERE.
YOU SETTLE THIS.
!
...

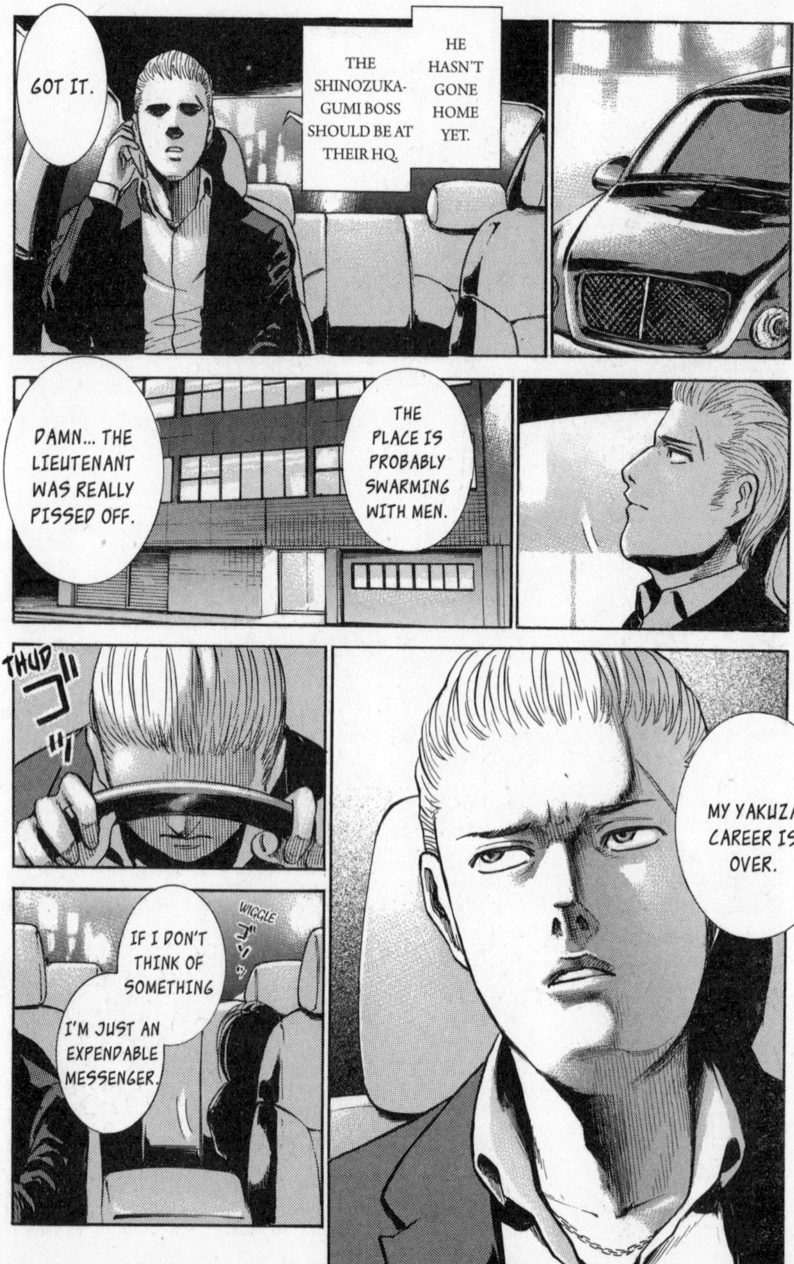
THE SHINOZUKA-GUMI BOSS SHOULD BE AT THEIR HQ.
HE HASN'T GONE HOME YET.
GOT IT.
THE PLACE IS PROBABLY SWARMING WITH MEN.
DAMN... THE LIEUTENANT WAS REALLY PISSED OFF.
MY YAKUZA CAREER IS OVER.
THUD
WIGGLE
IF I DON'T THINK OF SOMETHING
I'M JUST AN EXPENDABLE MESSENGER.

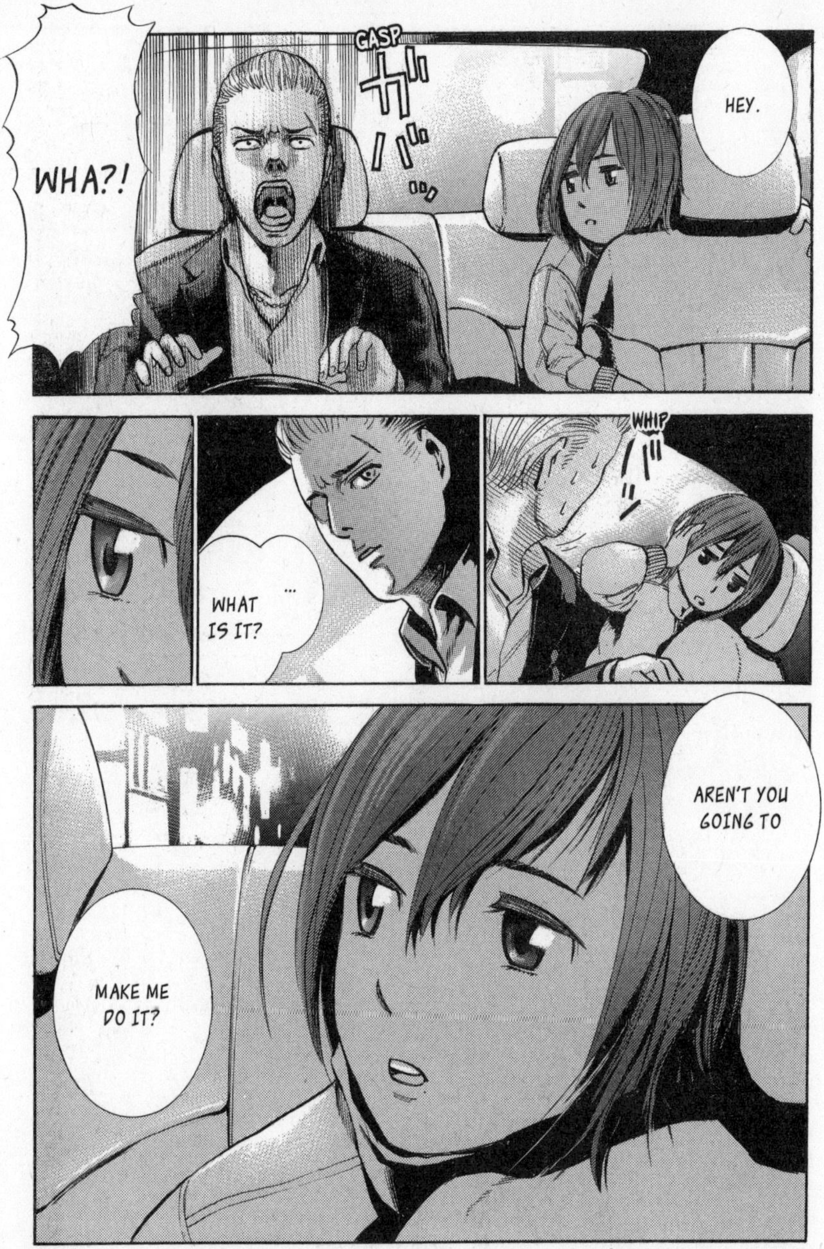
HEY.
GASP
WHA?!
WHIP
... WHAT IS IT?
AREN'T YOU GOING TO
MAKE ME DO IT?

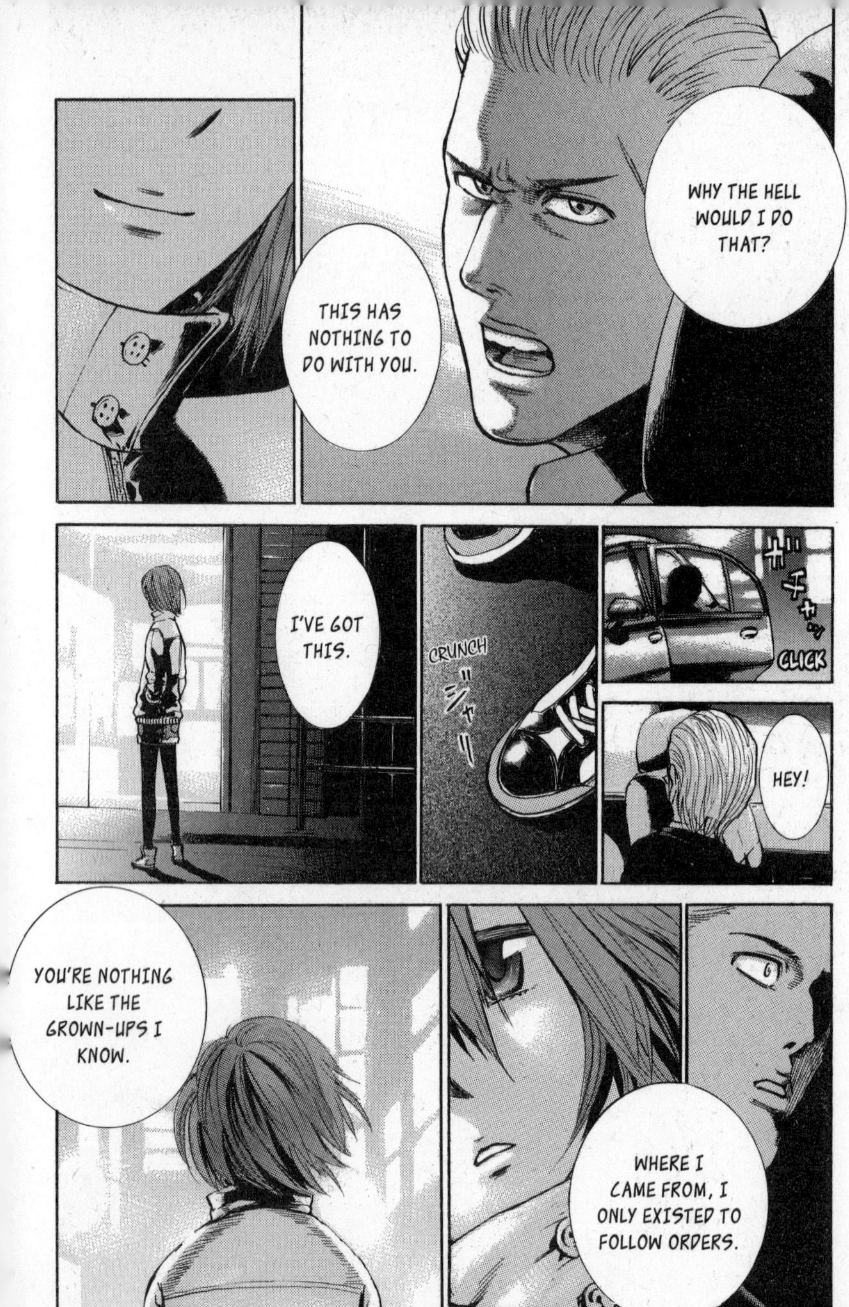
WHY THE HELL WOULD I DO THAT?
THIS HAS NOTHING TO DO WITH YOU.
ガチャッ
CLICK
HEY!
CRUNCH
ジャリ
I'VE GOT THIS.
WHERE I CAME FROM, I ONLY EXISTED TO FOLLOW ORDERS.
YOU'RE NOTHING LIKE THE GROWN-UPS I KNOW.

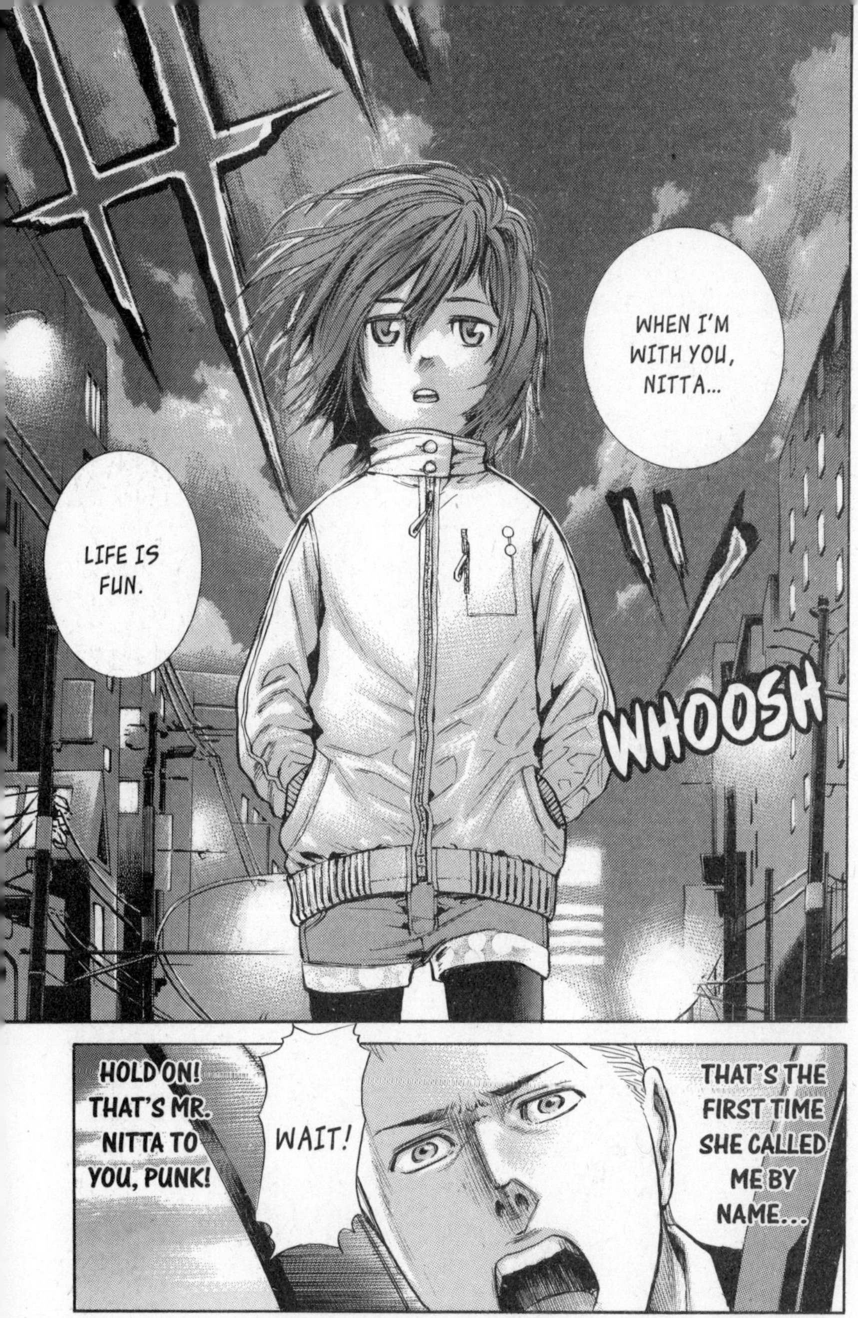
WHEN I'M WITH YOU, NITTA...
LIFE IS FUN.
WHOOSH
THAT'S THE FIRST TIME SHE CALLED ME BY NAME...
WAIT!
HOLD ON! THAT'S MR. NITTA TO YOU, PUNK!

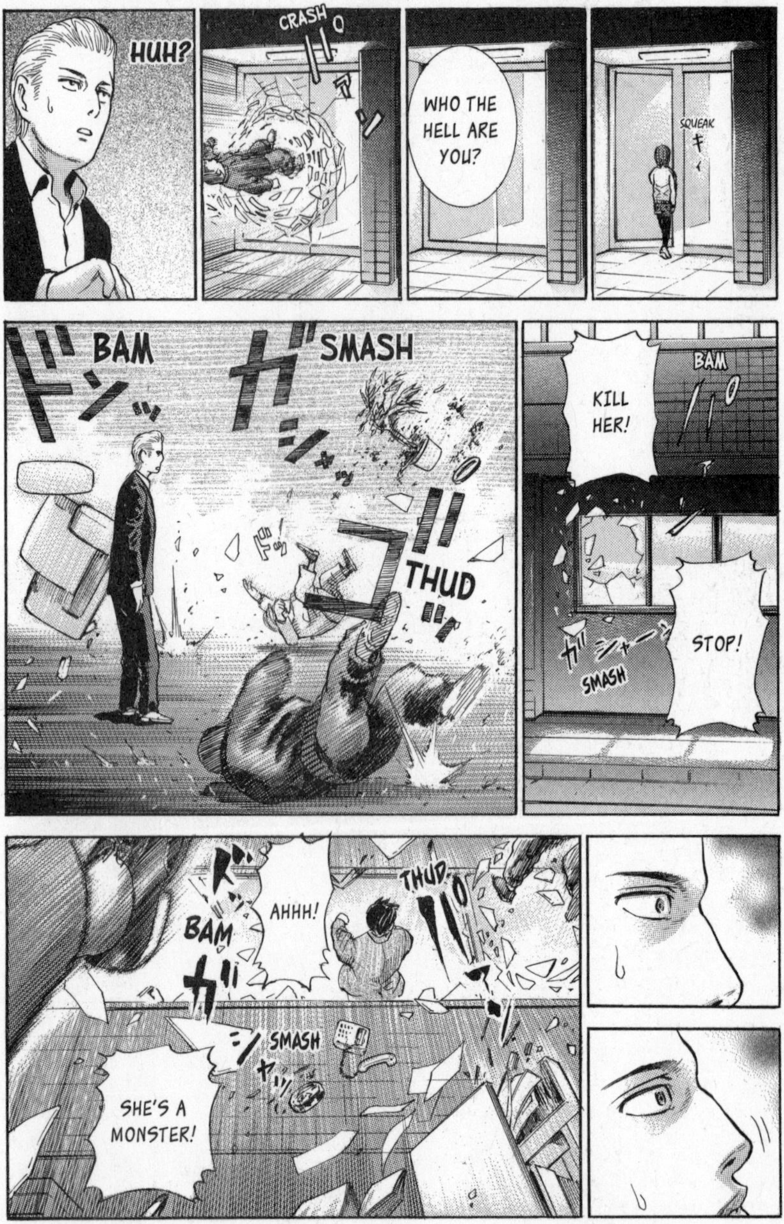
SQUEAK
WHO THE HELL ARE YOU?
CRASH
HUH?
KILL HER!
BAM
SMASH
STOP!
SMASH
BAM
THUD
THUD
AHHH!
BAM
SMASH
SHE'S A MONSTER!

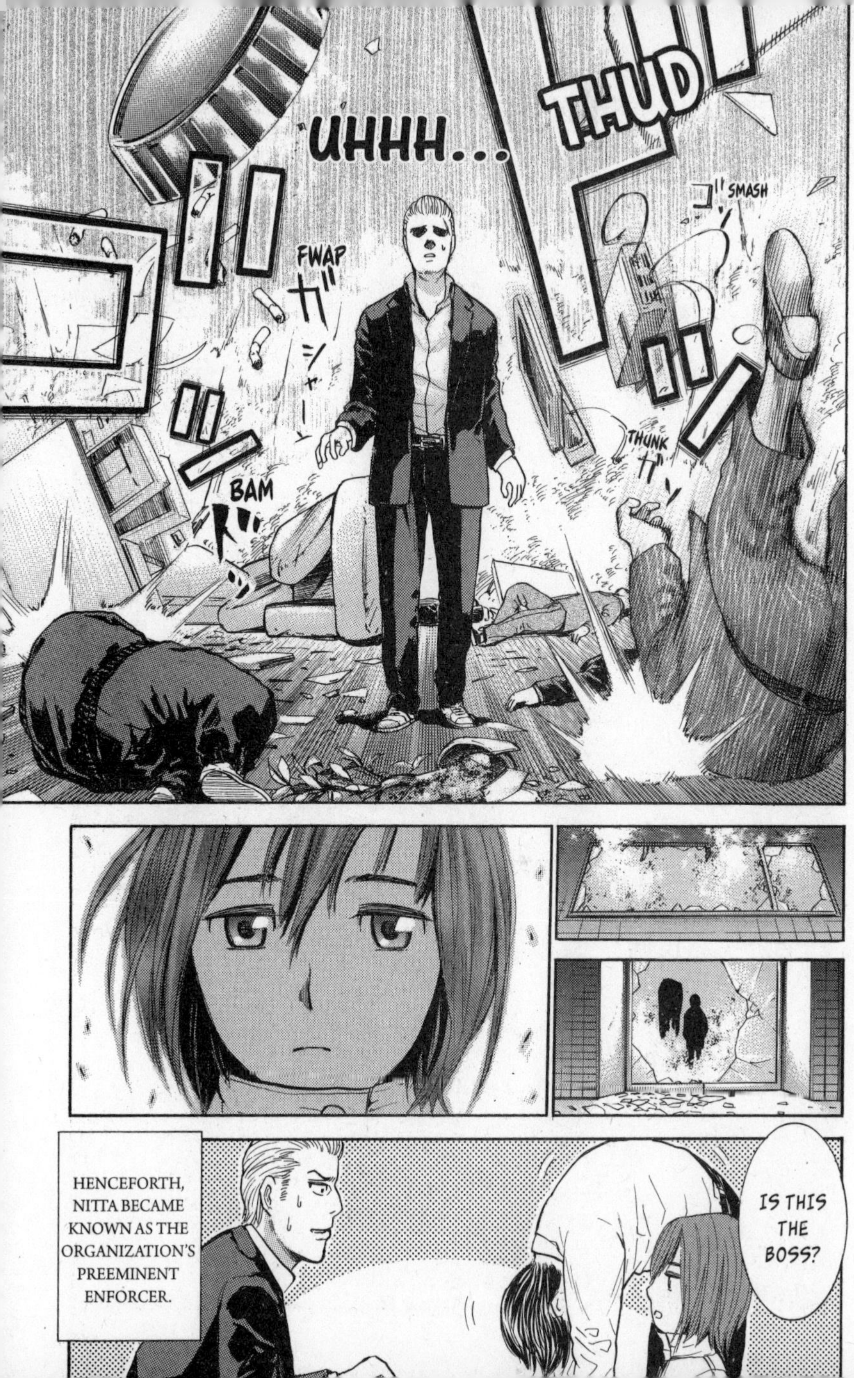
THUD
SMASH
THUNK
UHHH...
FWAP
BAM
IS THIS THE BOSS?
HENCEFORTH, NITTA BECAME KNOWN AS THE ORGANIZATION'S PREEMINENT ENFORCER.

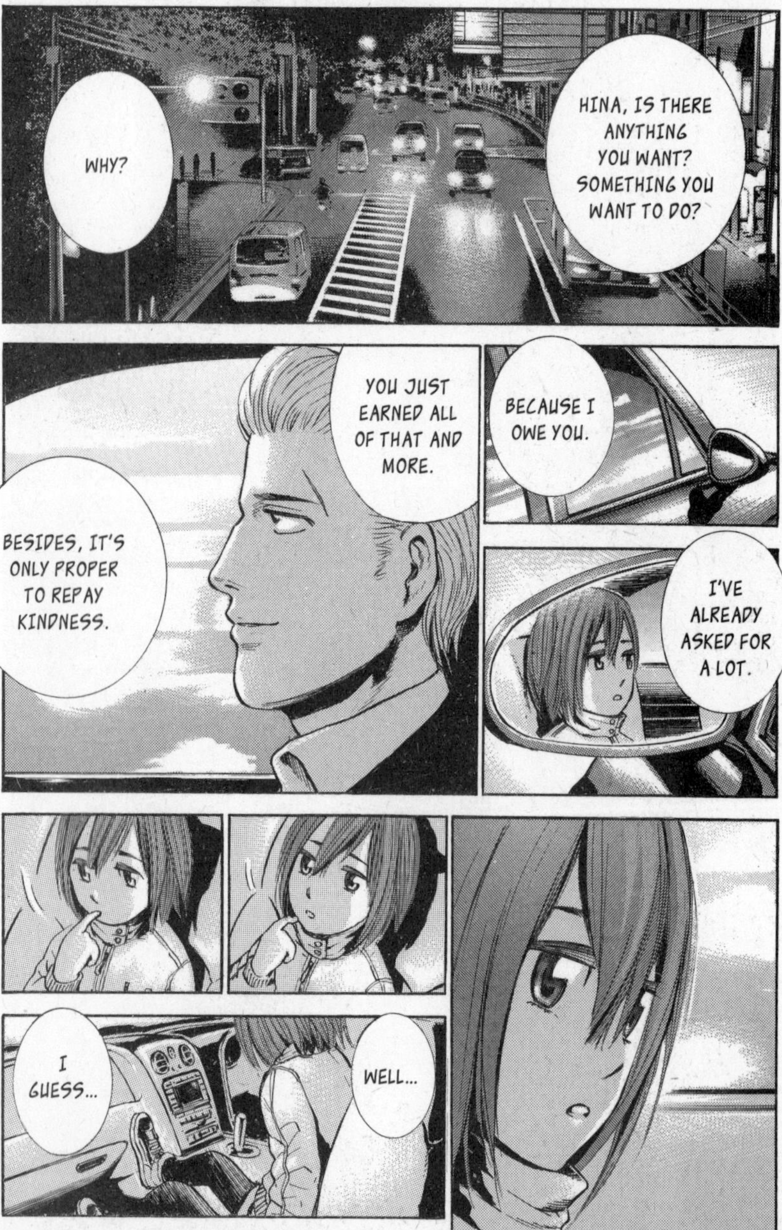
HINA, IS THERE ANYTHING YOU WANT? SOMETHING YOU WANT TO DO?
WHY?
BECAUSE I OWE YOU.
I'VE ALREADY ASKED FOR A LOT.
YOU JUST EARNED ALL OF THAT AND MORE.
BESIDES, IT'S ONLY PROPER TO REPAY KINDNESS.
WELL...
I GUESS...

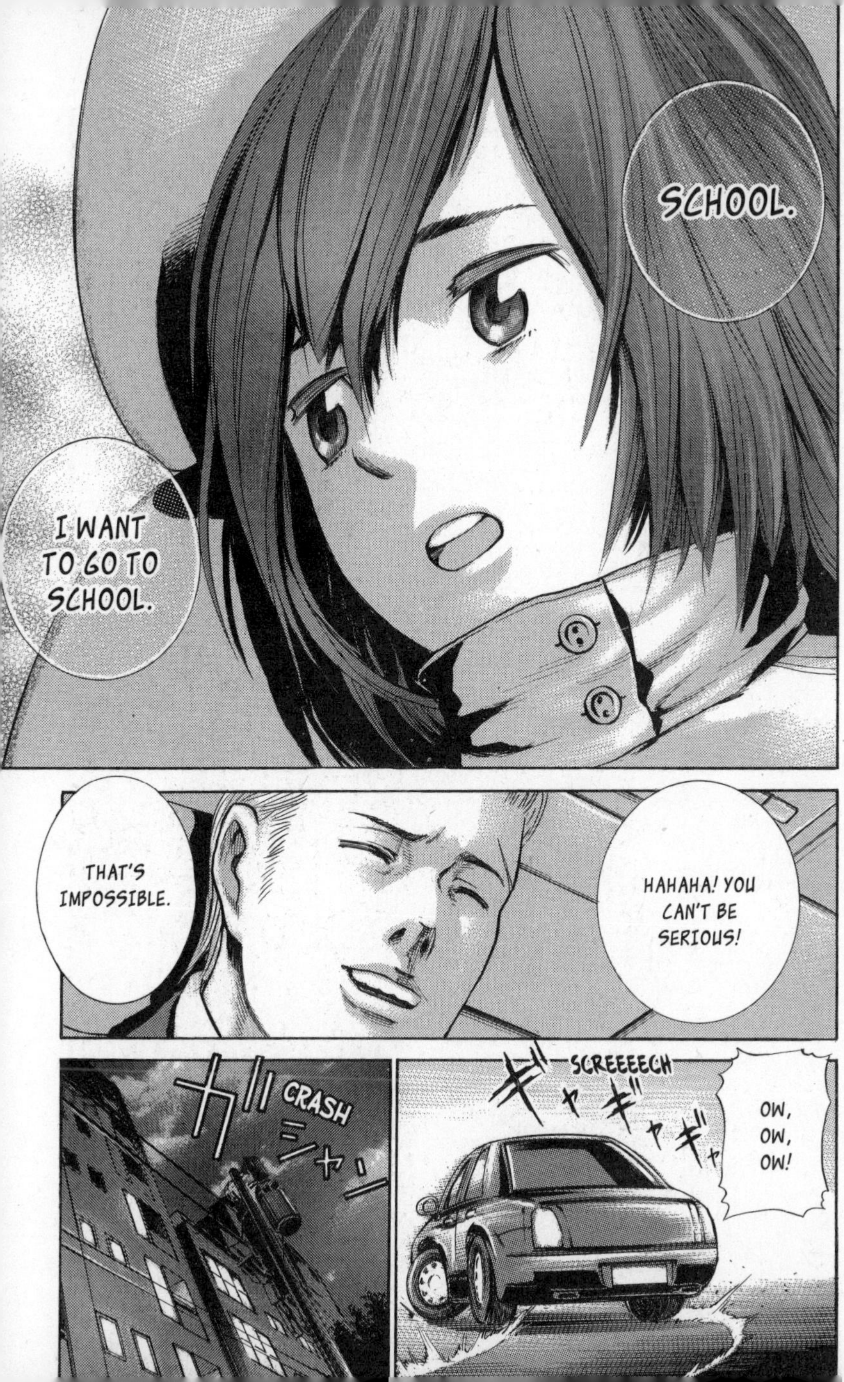
SCHOOL.
I WANT TO GO TO SCHOOL.
HAHAHA! YOU CAN'T BE SERIOUS!
THAT'S IMPOSSIBLE.
OW, OW, OW!
ギャギャギャ
SCREEEECH
ガシャーン
CRASH

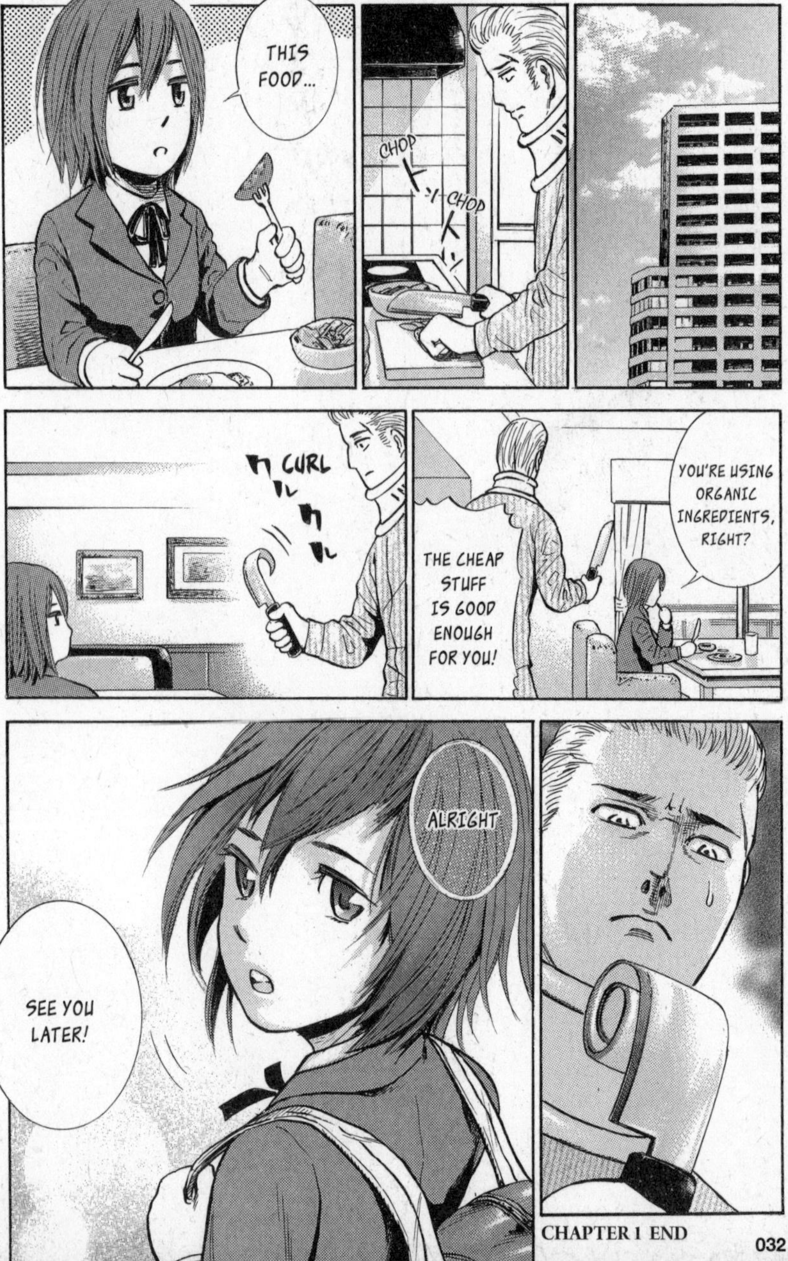
CHOP
CHOP
THIS FOOD...
YOU'RE USING ORGANIC INGREDIENTS, RIGHT?
THE CHEAP STUFF IS GOOD ENOUGH FOR YOU!
CURL
ALRIGHT
SEE YOU LATER!

CHAPTER 1 END

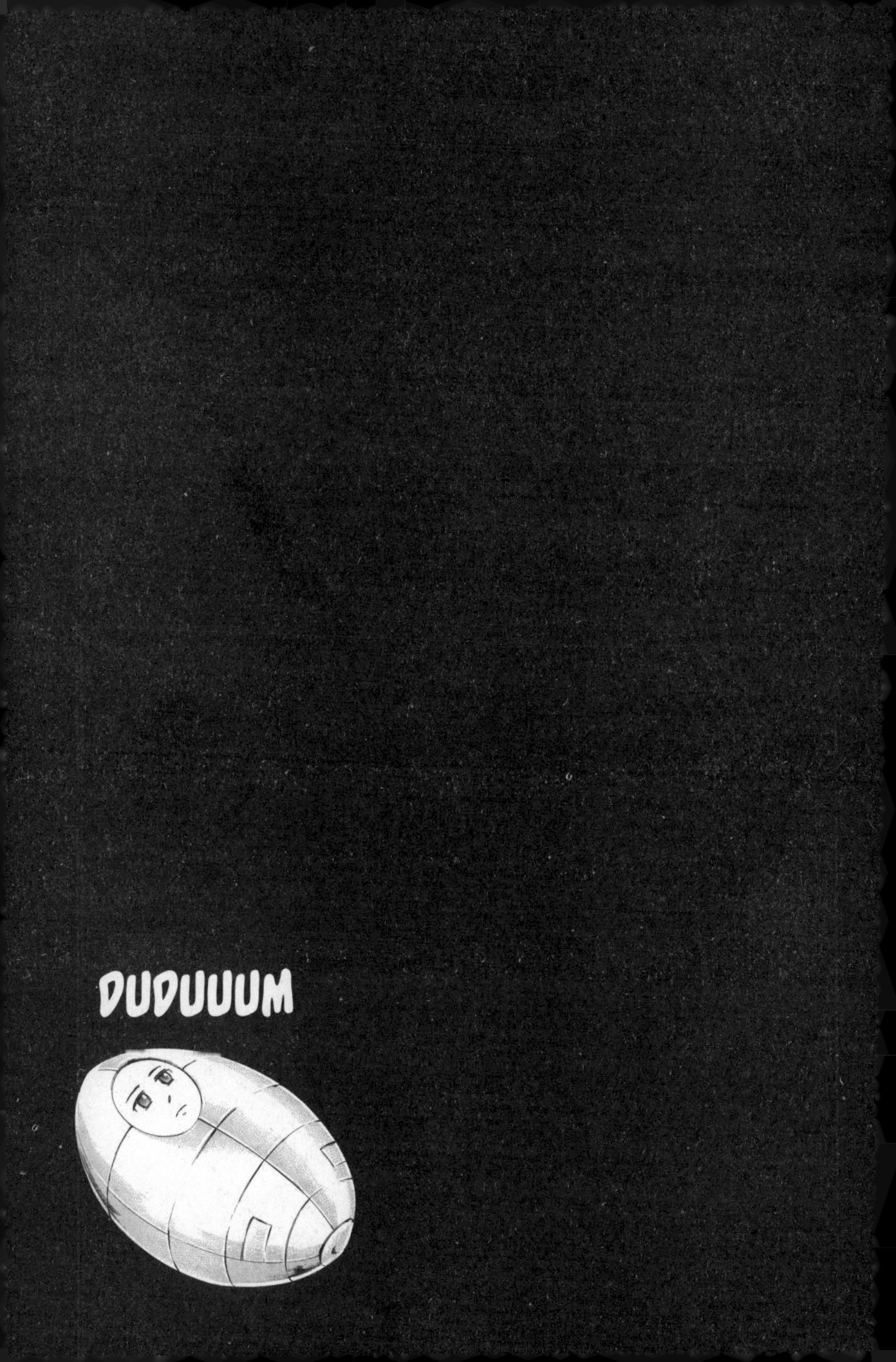
DUDUUUM

CHAPTER 2 THE ADULT WORLD

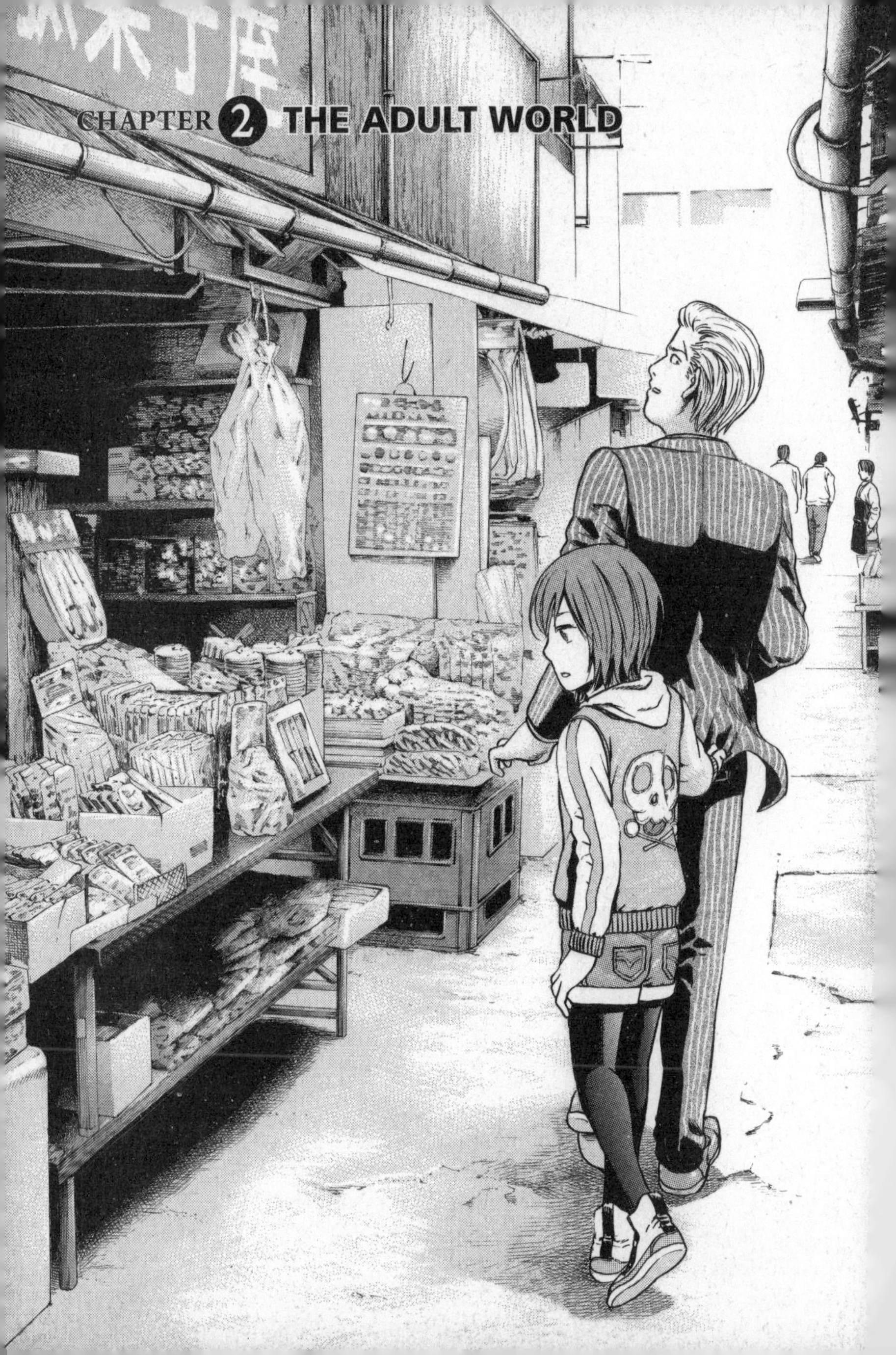

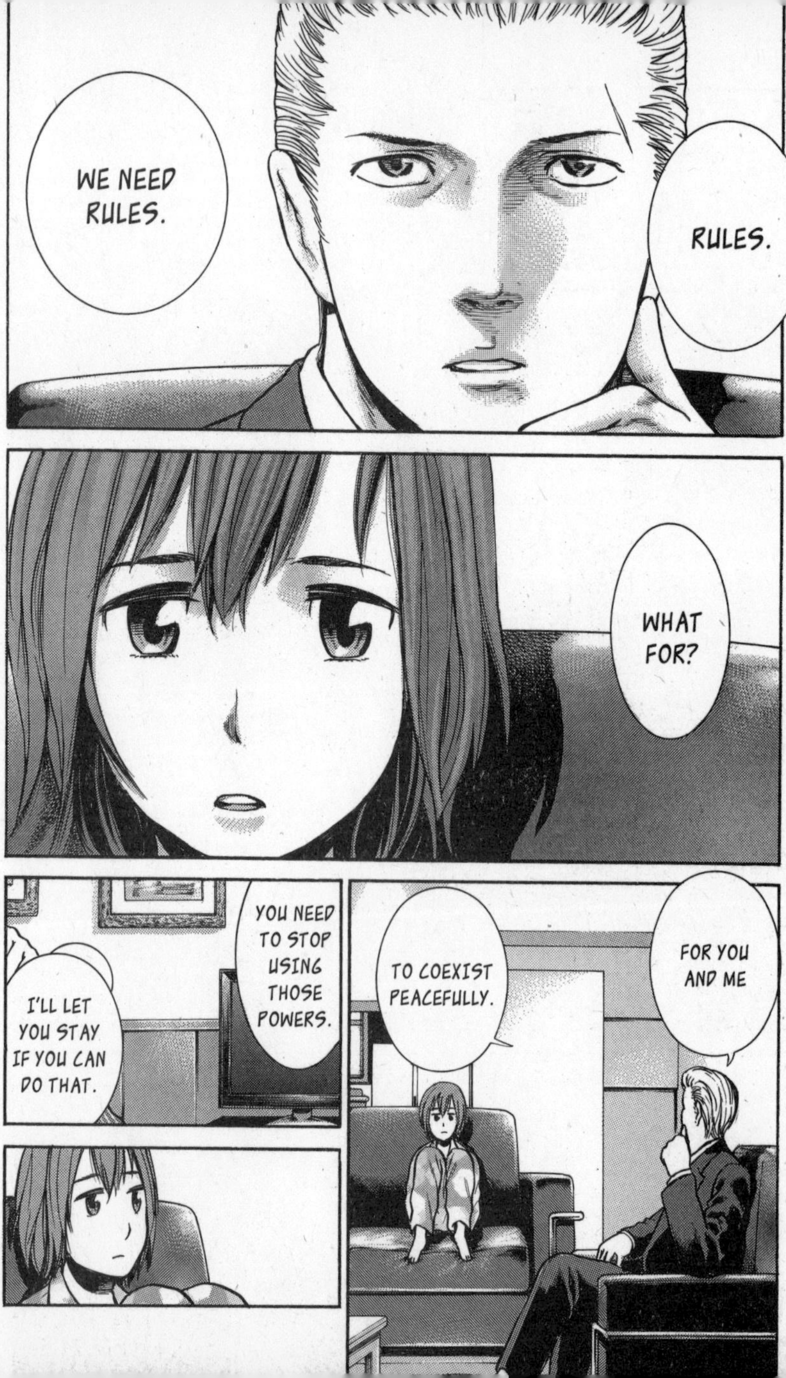
RULES.
WE NEED RULES.
WHAT FOR?
FOR YOU AND ME
TO COEXIST PEACEFULLY.
YOU NEED TO STOP USING THOSE POWERS.
I'LL LET YOU STAY IF YOU CAN DO THAT.

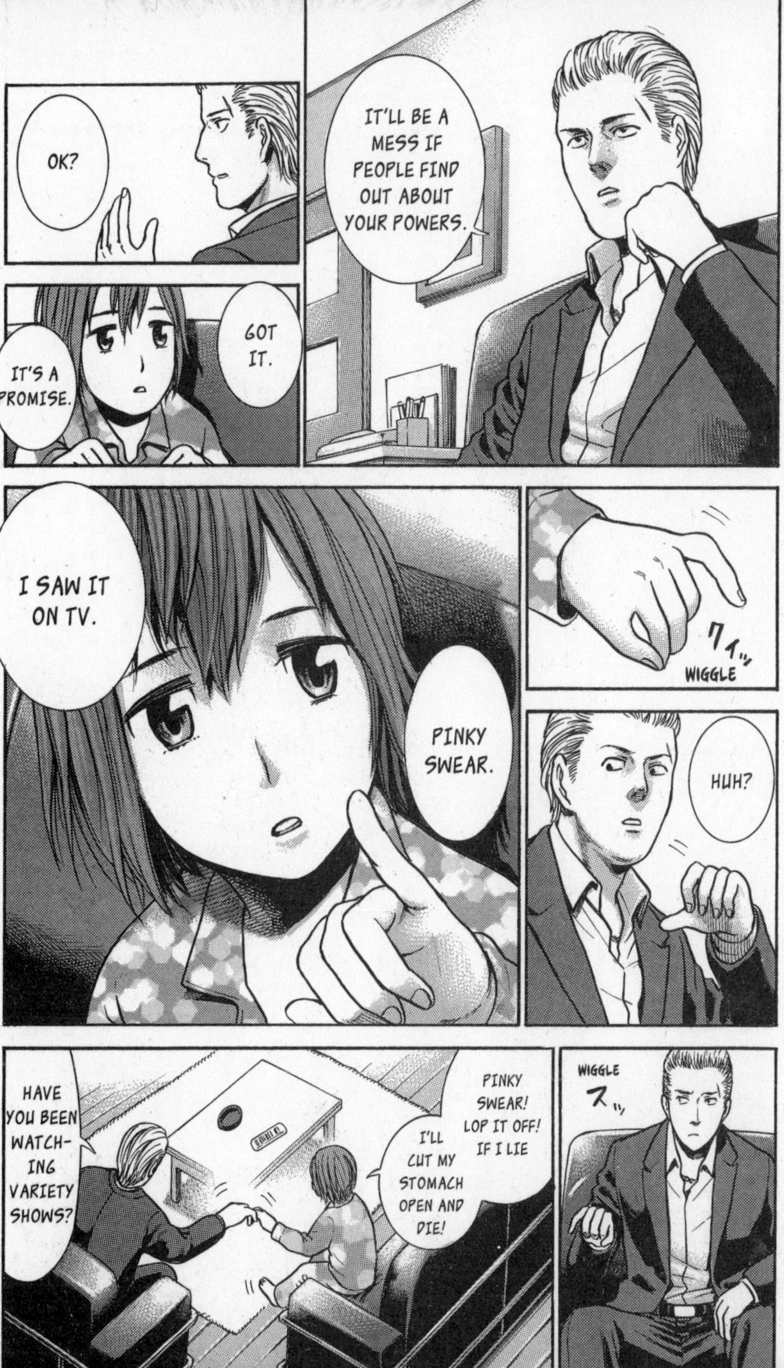
IT'LL BE A MESS IF PEOPLE FIND OUT ABOUT YOUR POWERS.
OK?
GOT IT.
IT'S A PROMISE.
クイッ
WIGGLE
HUH?
PINKY SWEAR.
I SAW IT ON TV.
WIGGLE
スッ
PINKY SWEAR! LOP IT OFF! IF I LIE
I'LL CUT MY STOMACH OPEN AND DIE!
HAVE YOU BEEN WATCHING VARIETY SHOWS?

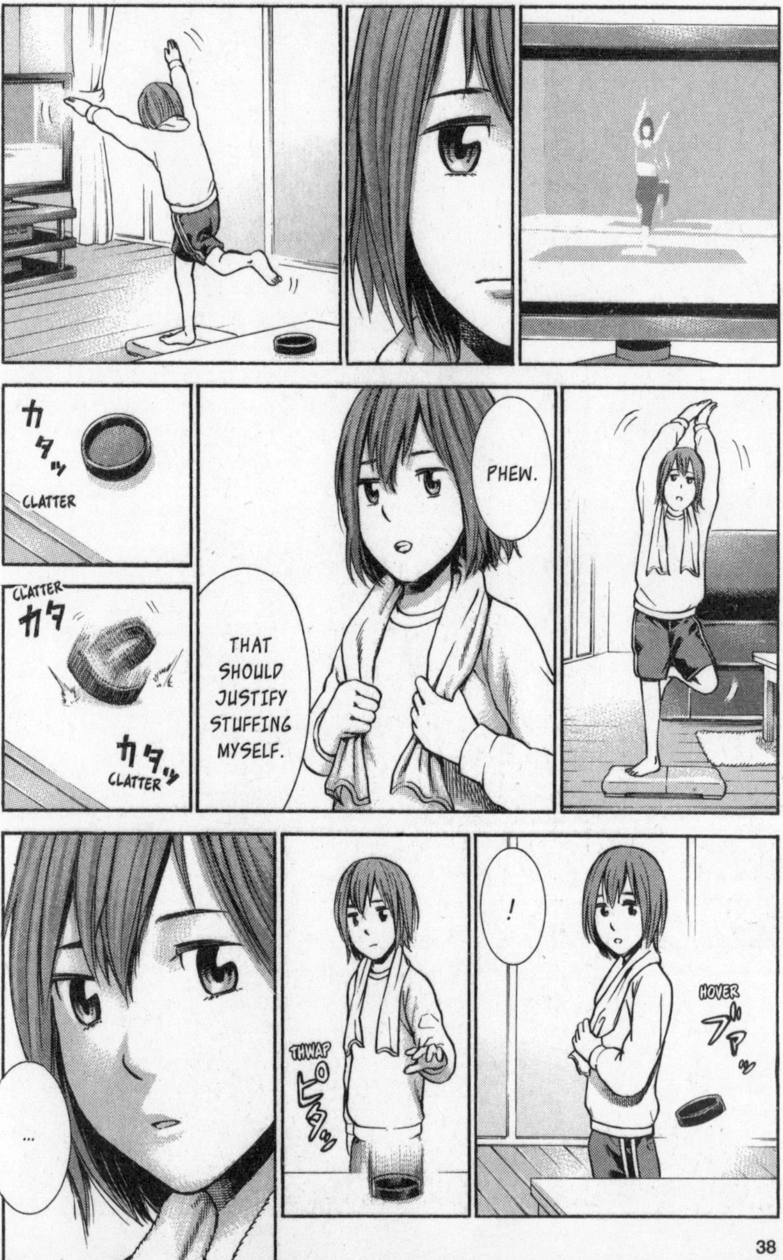
PHEW.
THAT SHOULD JUSTIFY STUFFING MYSELF.
カタッ
CLATTER
CLATTER
カタ
カタッ
CLATTER
!
HOVER
ブァッ
THWAP
ピタッ
...

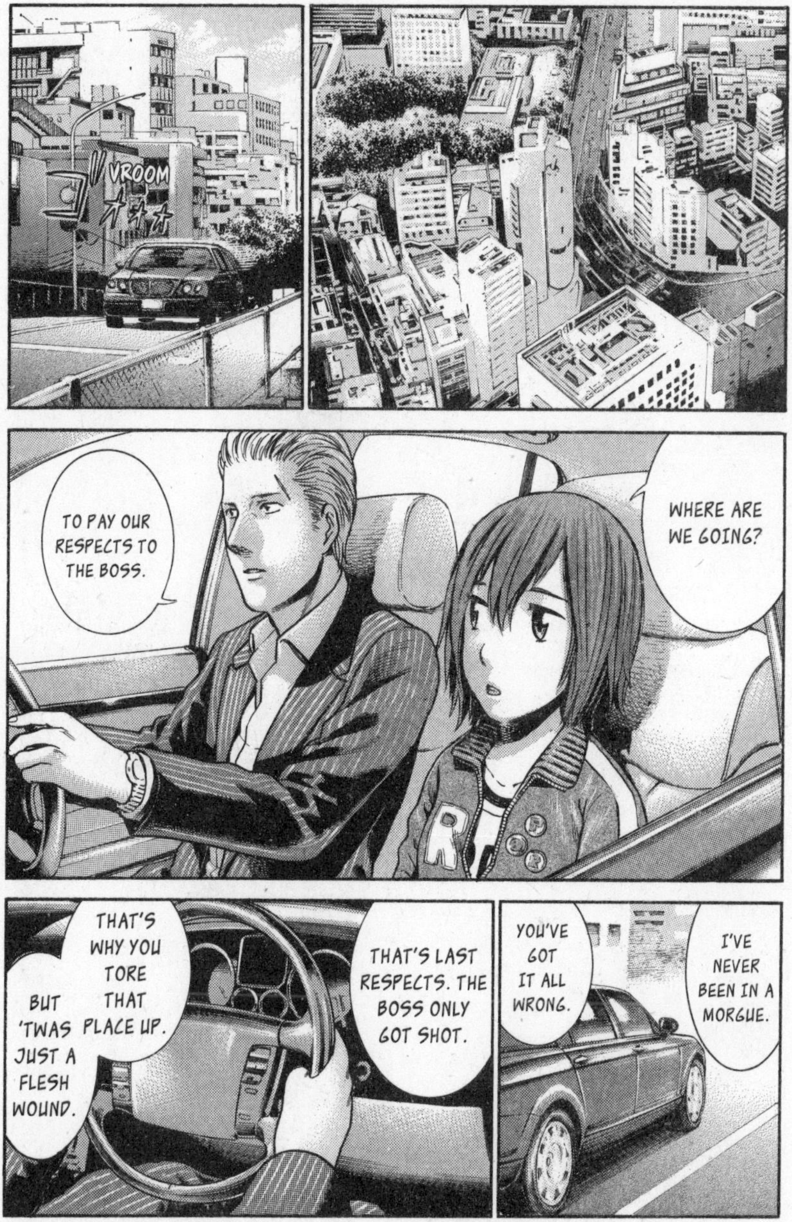
VROOM
WHERE ARE WE GOING?
TO PAY OUR RESPECTS TO THE BOSS.
I'VE NEVER BEEN IN A MORGUE.
YOU'VE GOT IT ALL WRONG.
THAT'S LAST RESPECTS. THE BOSS ONLY GOT SHOT.
THAT'S WHY YOU TORE THAT PLACE UP.
BUT 'TWAS JUST A FLESH WOUND.

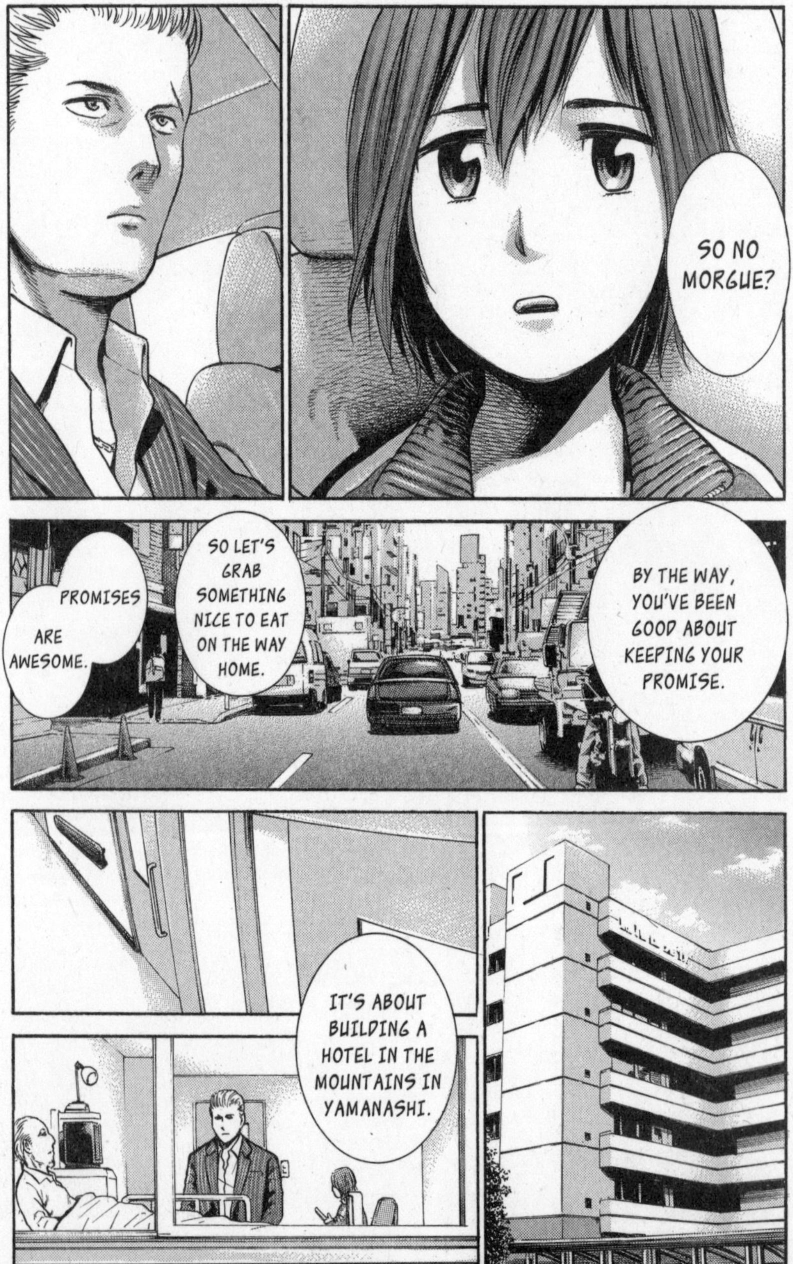
SO NO MORGUE?
BY THE WAY, YOU'VE BEEN GOOD ABOUT KEEPING YOUR PROMISE.
SO LET'S GRAB SOMETHING NICE TO EAT ON THE WAY HOME.
PROMISES ARE AWESOME.
IT'S ABOUT BUILDING A HOTEL IN THE MOUNTAINS IN YAMANASHI.

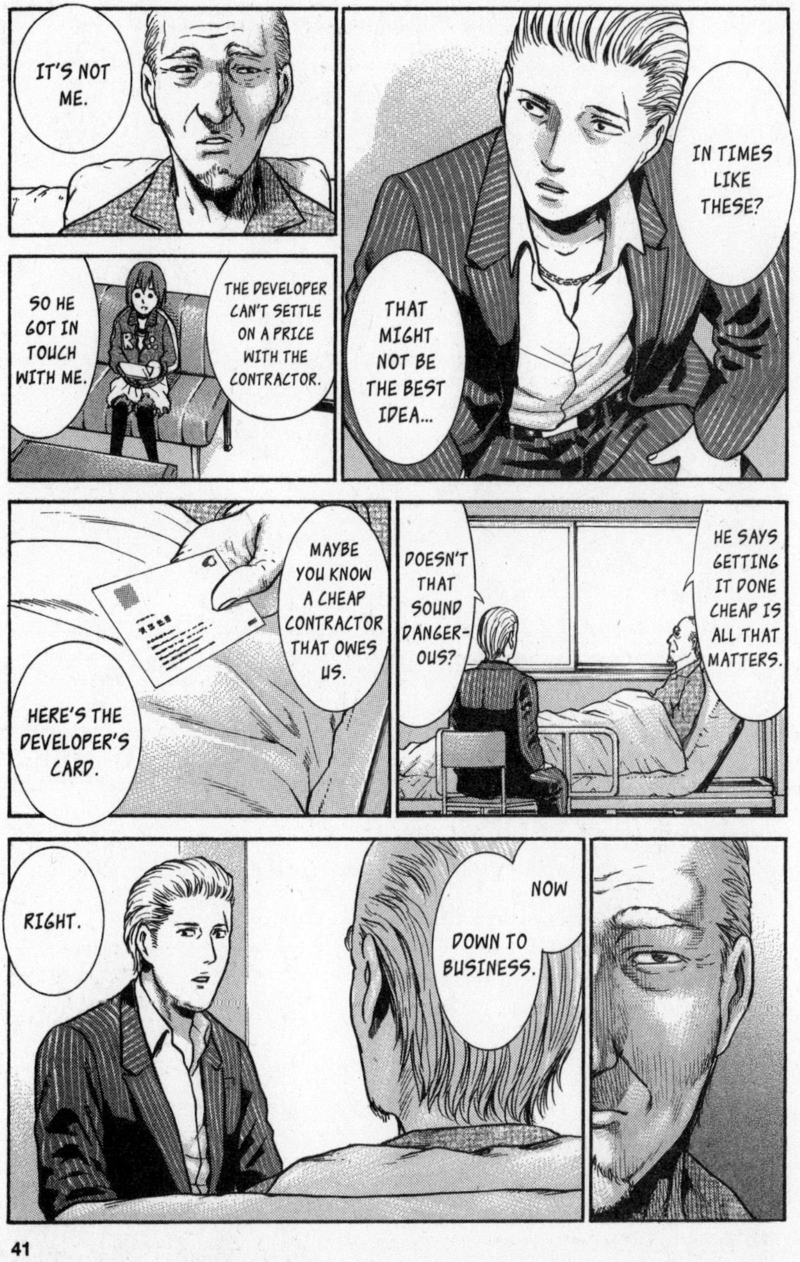
IN TIMES LIKE THESE?
THAT MIGHT NOT BE THE BEST IDEA...
IT'S NOT ME.
THE DEVELOPER CAN'T SETTLE ON A PRICE WITH THE CONTRACTOR.
SO HE GOT IN TOUCH WITH ME.
HE SAYS GETTING IT DONE CHEAP IS ALL THAT MATTERS.
DOESN'T THAT SOUND DANGER-OUS?
MAYBE YOU KNOW A CHEAP CONTRACTOR THAT OWES US.
HERE'S THE DEVELOPER'S CARD.
NOW
DOWN TO BUSINESS.
RIGHT.

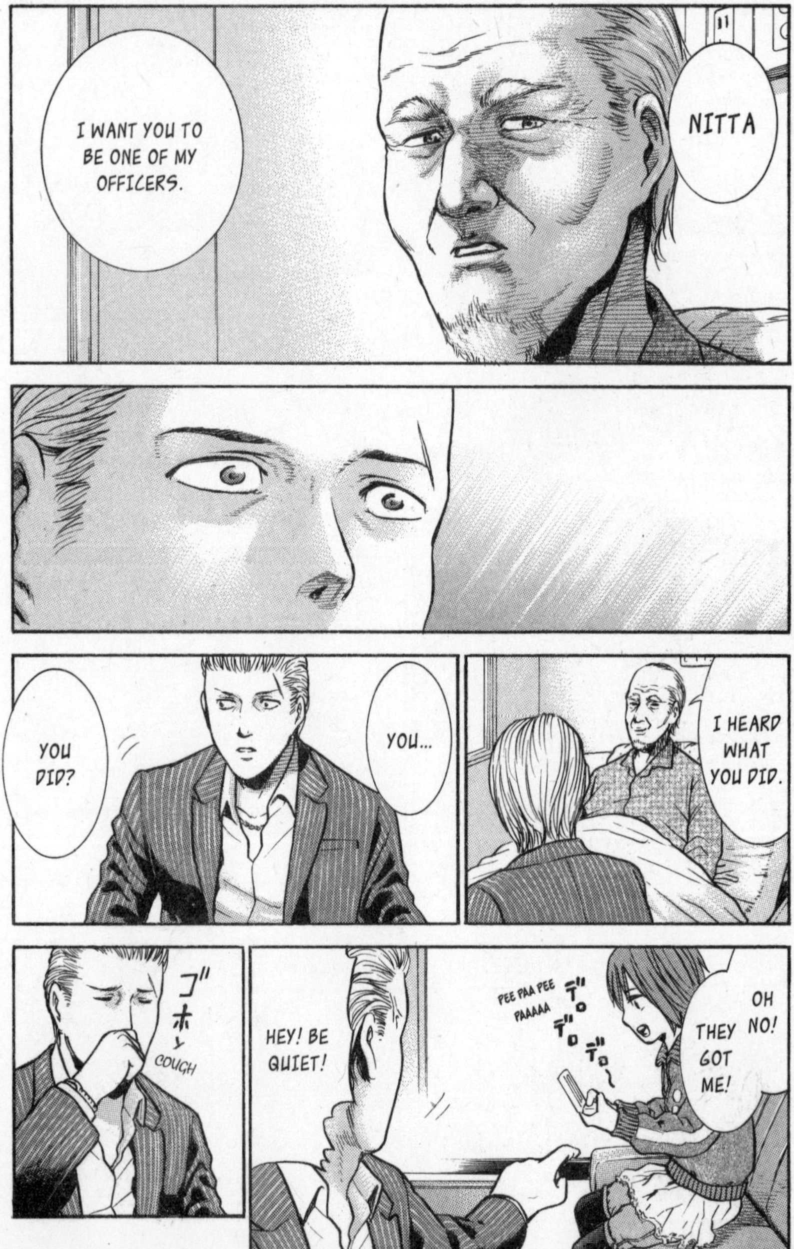
NITTA
I WANT YOU TO BE ONE OF MY OFFICERS.
I HEARD WHAT YOU DID.
YOU...
YOU DID?
OH NO!
THEY GOT ME!
PEE PAA PEE PAAAAA
HEY! BE QUIET!
ゴホッ
COUGH

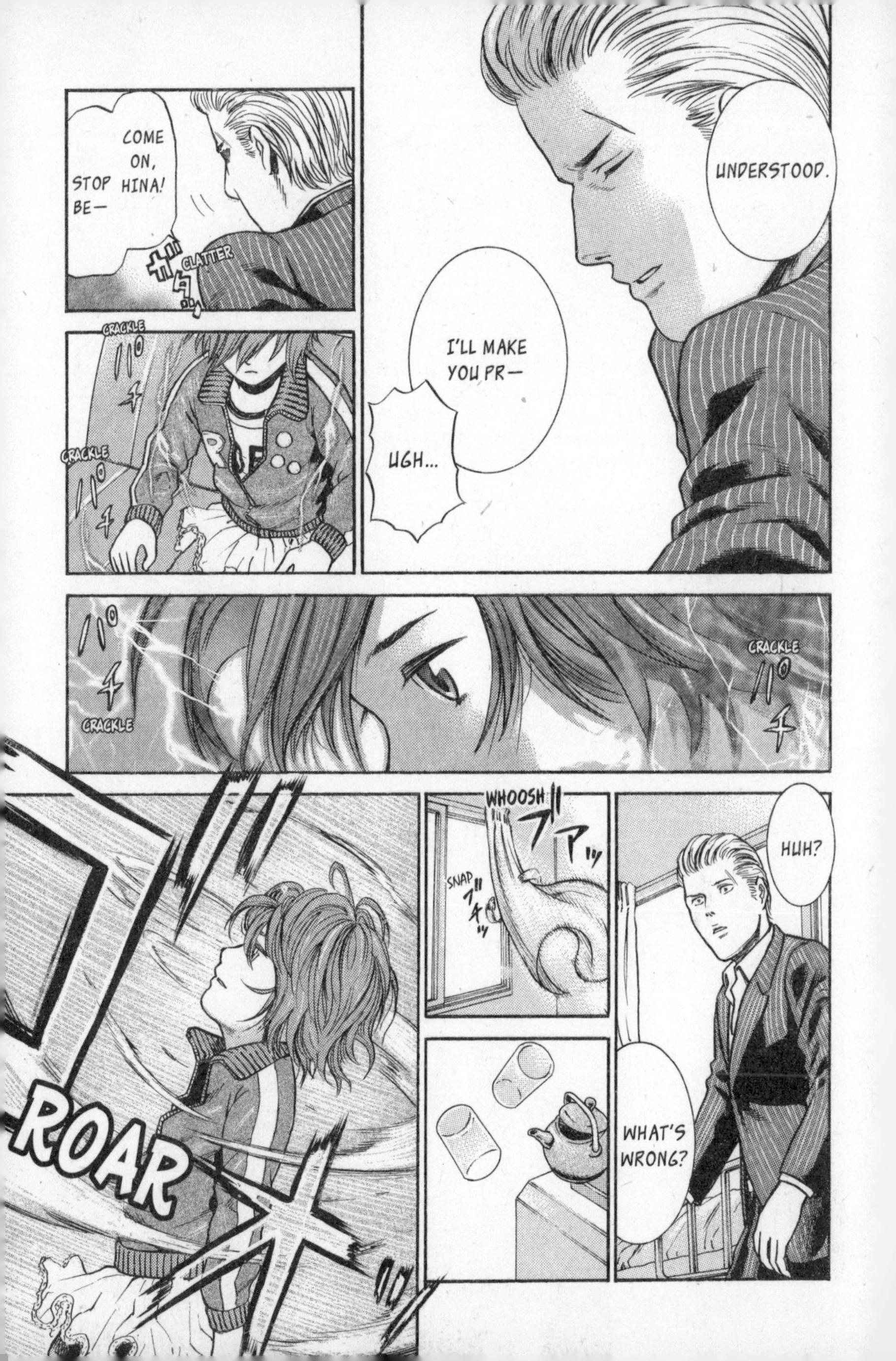
UNDERSTOOD.
I'LL MAKE YOU PR—
UGH...
COME ON, HINA! STOP BE—
CLATTER
CRACKLE
CRACKLE
CRACKLE
CRACKLE
HUH?
WHAT'S WRONG?
WHOOSH
SNAP
ROAR

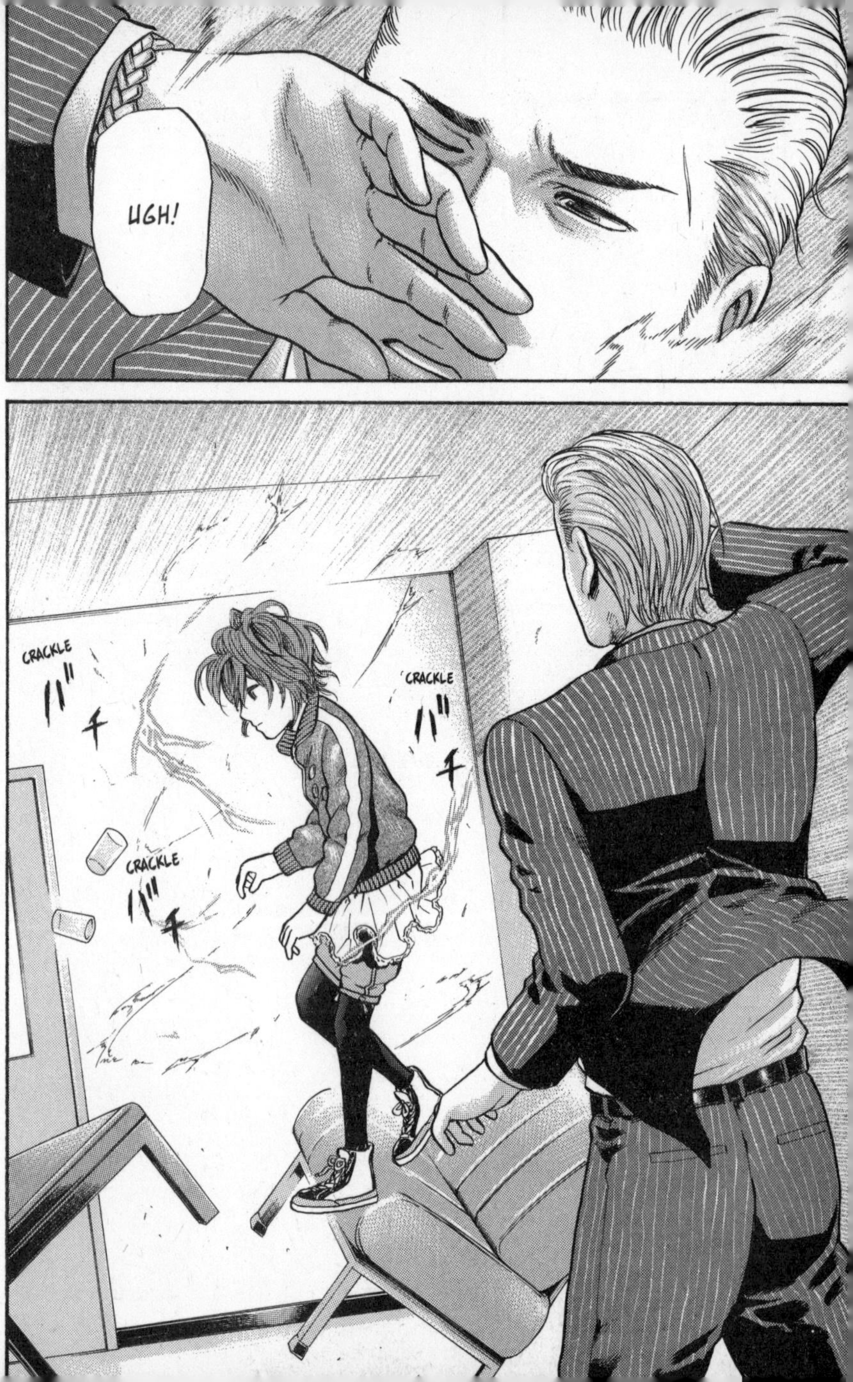
UGH!
CRACKLE
バチ
CRACKLE
バチ
CRACKLE
バチ

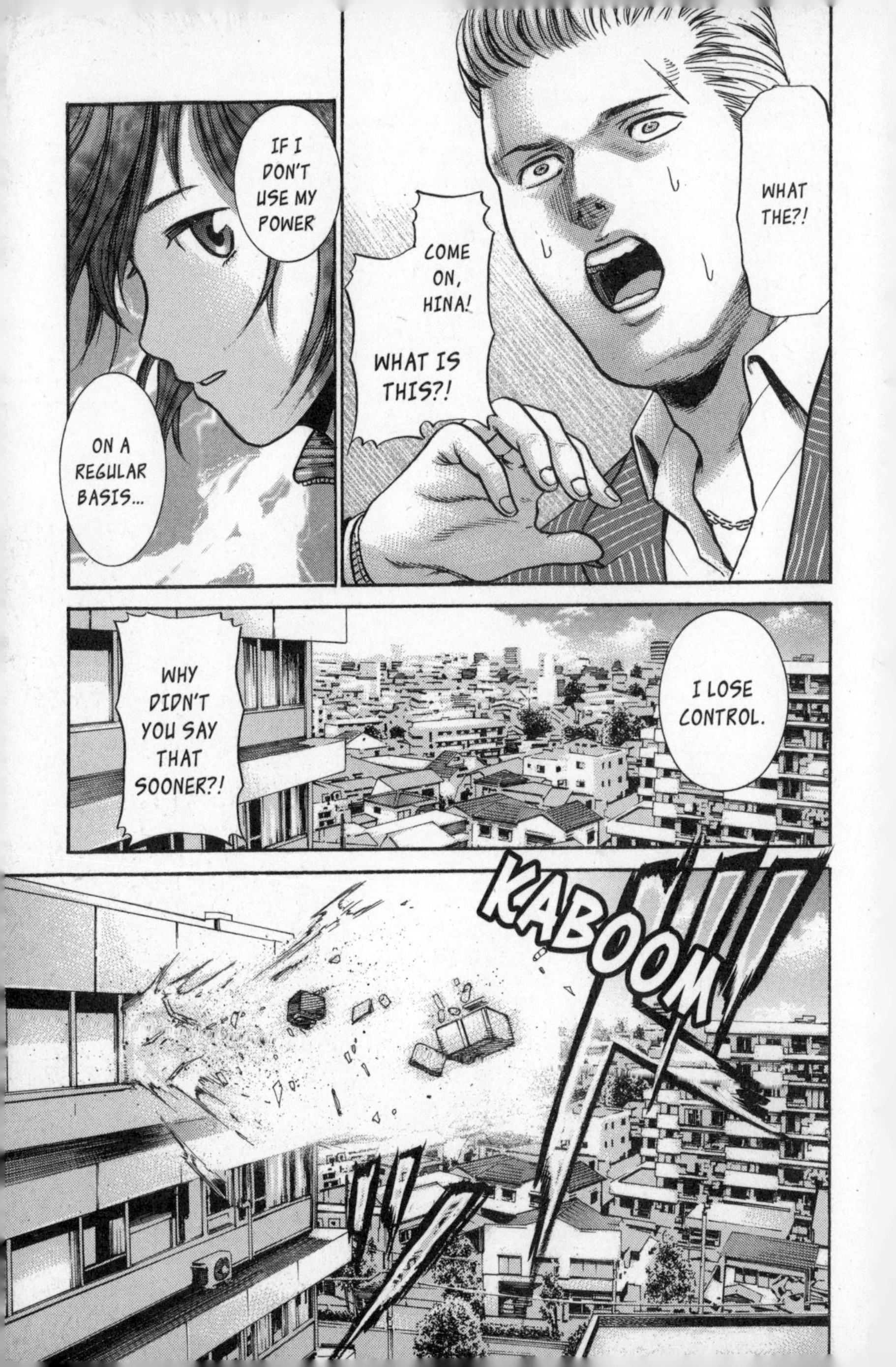
WHAT THE?!
COME ON, HINA!
WHAT IS THIS?!
IF I DON'T USE MY POWER
ON A REGULAR BASIS...
I LOSE CONTROL.
WHY DIDN'T YOU SAY THAT SOONER?!
KABOOM

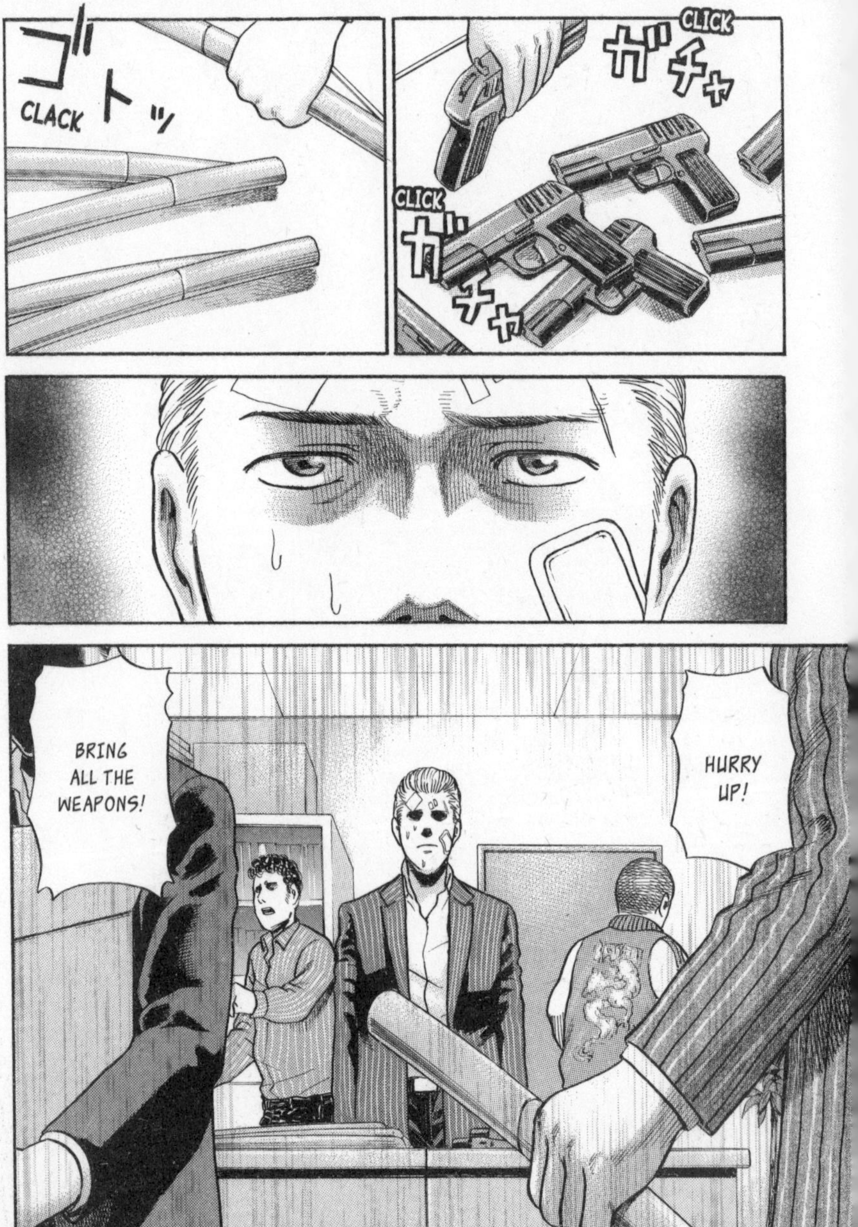

ガチャ
CLICK
ガチャ
CLICK
ゴトッ
CLACK
HURRY UP!
BRING ALL THE WEAPONS!

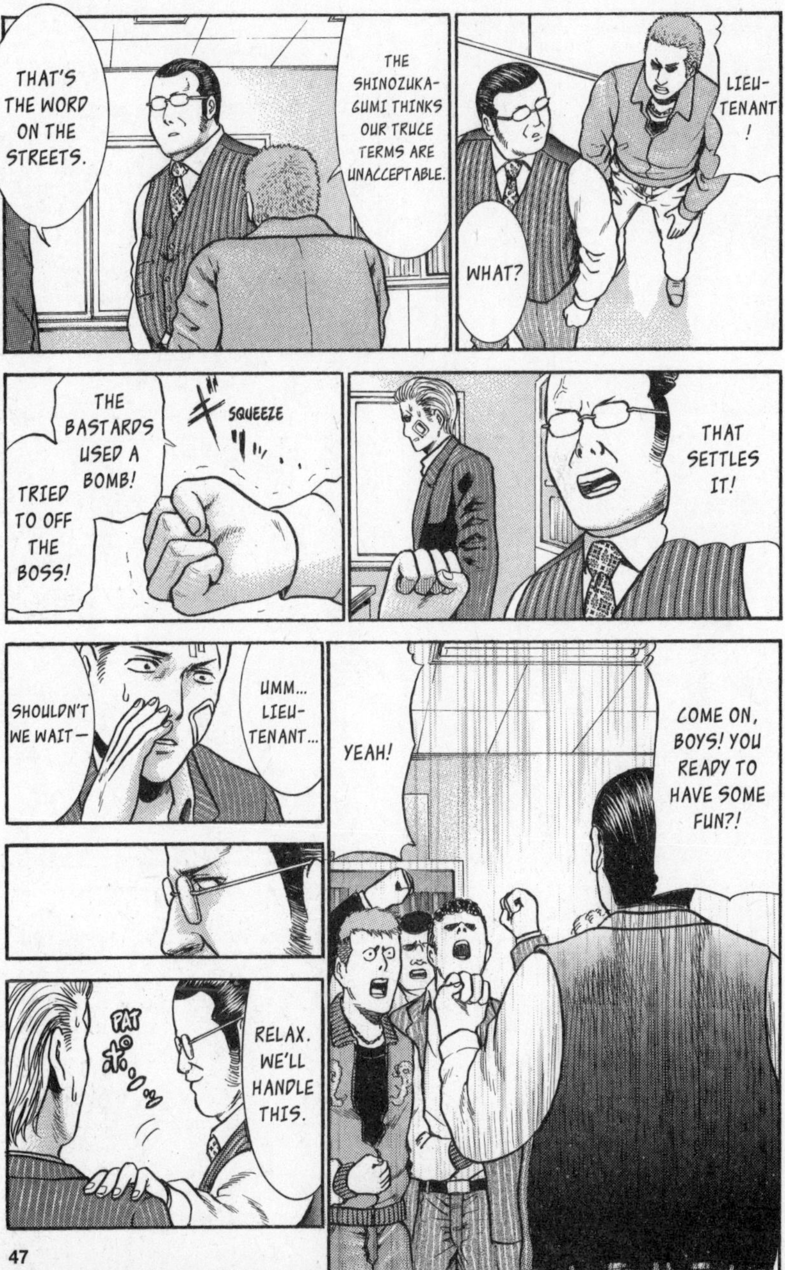
LIEU-TENANT!
WHAT?
THE SHINOZUKA-GUMI THINKS OUR TRUCE TERMS ARE UNACCEPTABLE.
THAT'S THE WORD ON THE STREETS.
THAT SETTLES IT!
THE BASTARDS USED A BOMB!
SQUEEZE
TRIED TO OFF THE BOSS!
COME ON, BOYS! YOU READY TO HAVE SOME FUN?!
YEAH!
UMM... LIEU-TENANT...
SHOULDN'T WE WAIT—
PAT
RELAX. WE'LL HANDLE THIS.

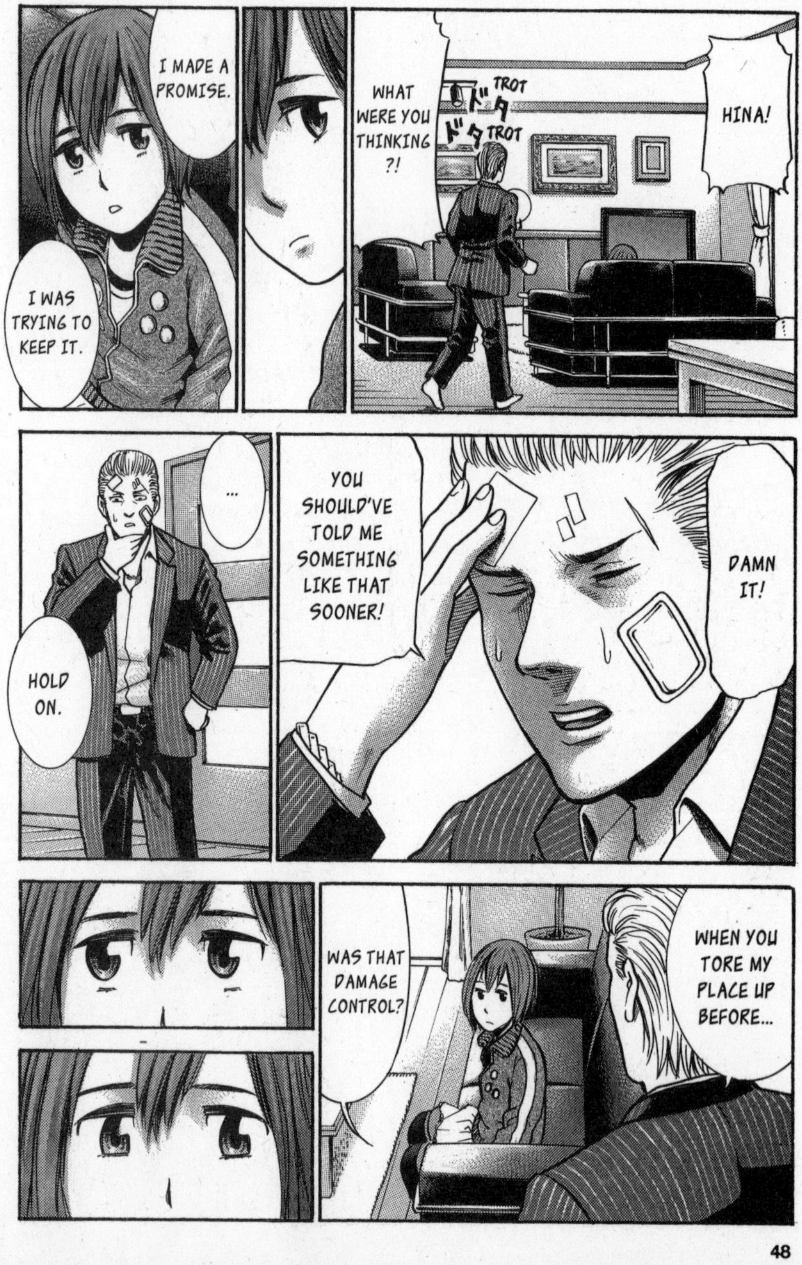
HINA!
WHAT WERE YOU THINKING ?!
ドタ TROT
ドタ TROT
I MADE A PROMISE.
I WAS TRYING TO KEEP IT.
DAMN IT!
YOU SHOULD'VE TOLD ME SOMETHING LIKE THAT SOONER!
...
HOLD ON.
WHEN YOU TORE MY PLACE UP BEFORE...
WAS THAT DAMAGE CONTROL?

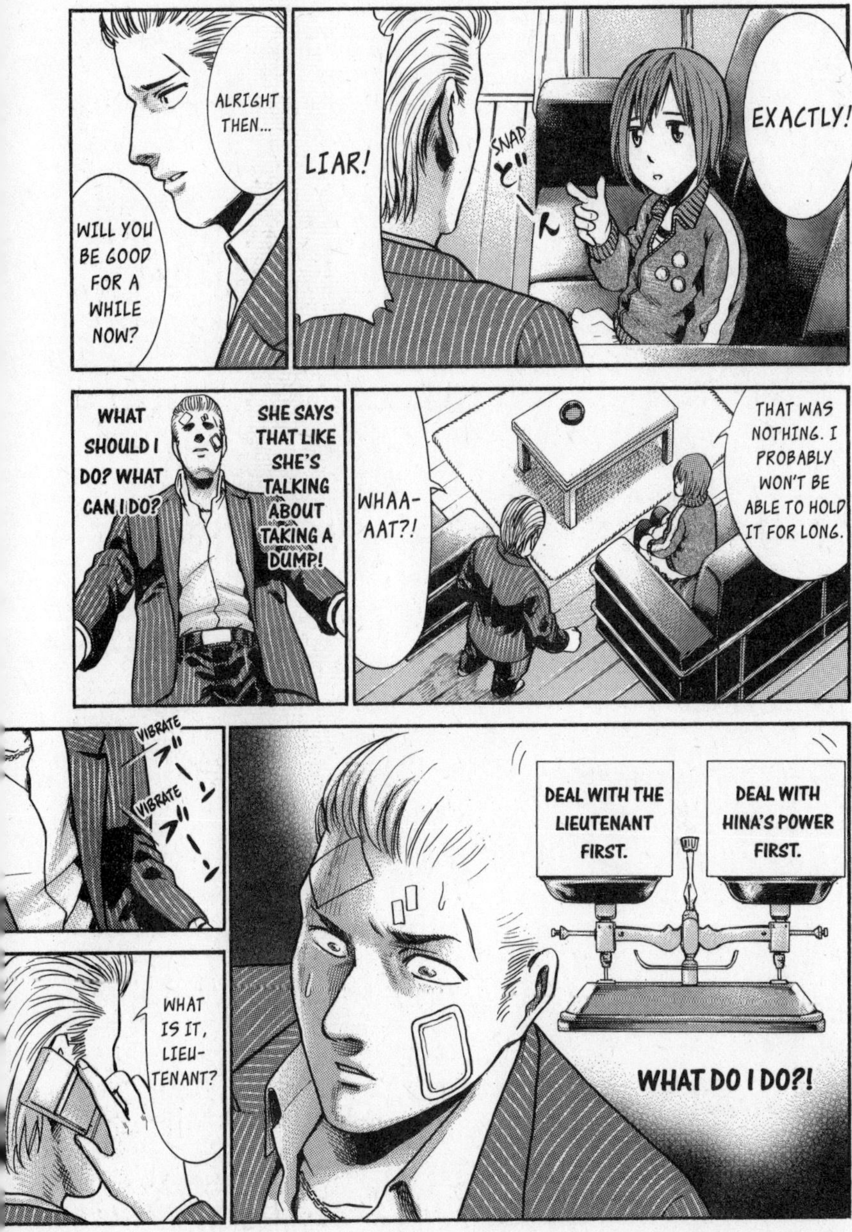
EXACTLY!
SNAP
どーん
LIAR!
ALRIGHT THEN...
WILL YOU BE GOOD FOR A WHILE NOW?
THAT WAS NOTHING. I PROBABLY WON'T BE ABLE TO HOLD IT FOR LONG.
WHAA-AAT?!
SHE SAYS THAT LIKE SHE'S TALKING ABOUT TAKING A DUMP!
WHAT SHOULD I DO? WHAT CAN I DO?
DEAL WITH HINA'S POWER FIRST.
DEAL WITH THE LIEUTENANT FIRST.
WHAT DO I DO?!
VIBRATE
VIBRATE
WHAT IS IT, LIEUTENANT?

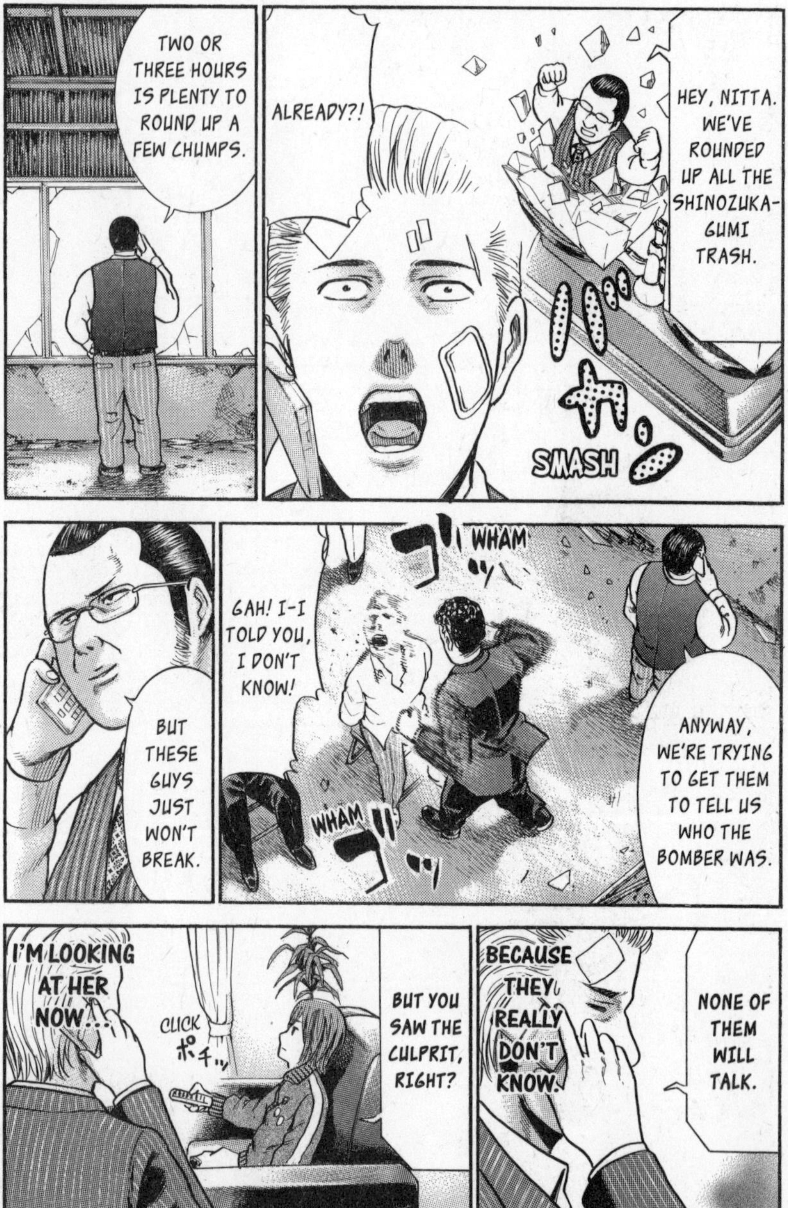
HEY, NITTA. WE'VE ROUNDED UP ALL THE SHINOZUKA-GUMI TRASH.
ALREADY?!
SMASH
TWO OR THREE HOURS IS PLENTY TO ROUND UP A FEW CHUMPS.
ANYWAY, WE'RE TRYING TO GET THEM TO TELL US WHO THE BOMBER WAS.
WHAM
GAH! I-I TOLD YOU, I DON'T KNOW!
WHAM
BUT THESE GUYS JUST WON'T BREAK.
NONE OF THEM WILL TALK.
BECAUSE THEY REALLY DON'T KNOW.
BUT YOU SAW THE CULPRIT, RIGHT?
CLICK
ポチッ
I'M LOOKING AT HER NOW...

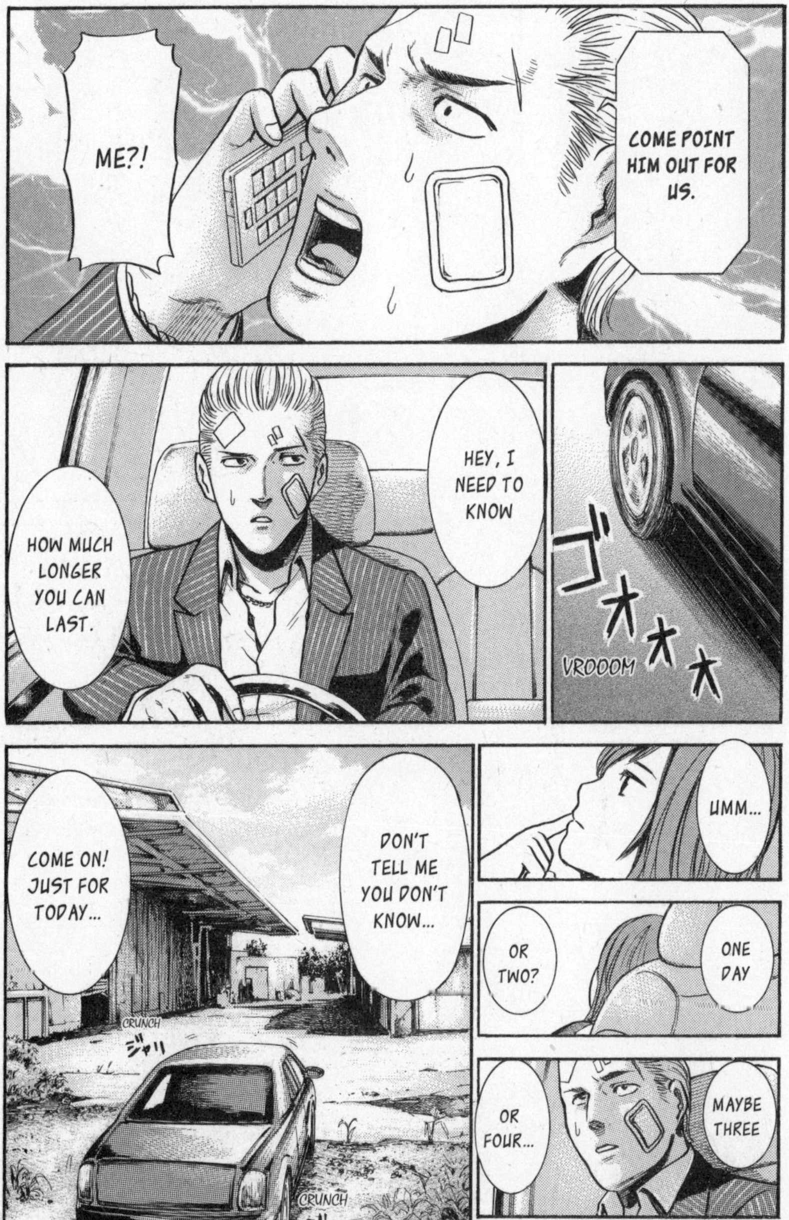
COME POINT HIM OUT FOR US.
ME?!
ゴオォォ
VROOOM
HEY, I NEED TO KNOW
HOW MUCH LONGER YOU CAN LAST.
UMM...
ONE DAY
OR TWO?
MAYBE THREE
OR FOUR...
DON'T TELL ME YOU DON'T KNOW...
COME ON! JUST FOR TODAY...
CRUNCH
ジャリ
CRUNCH
ジャリ

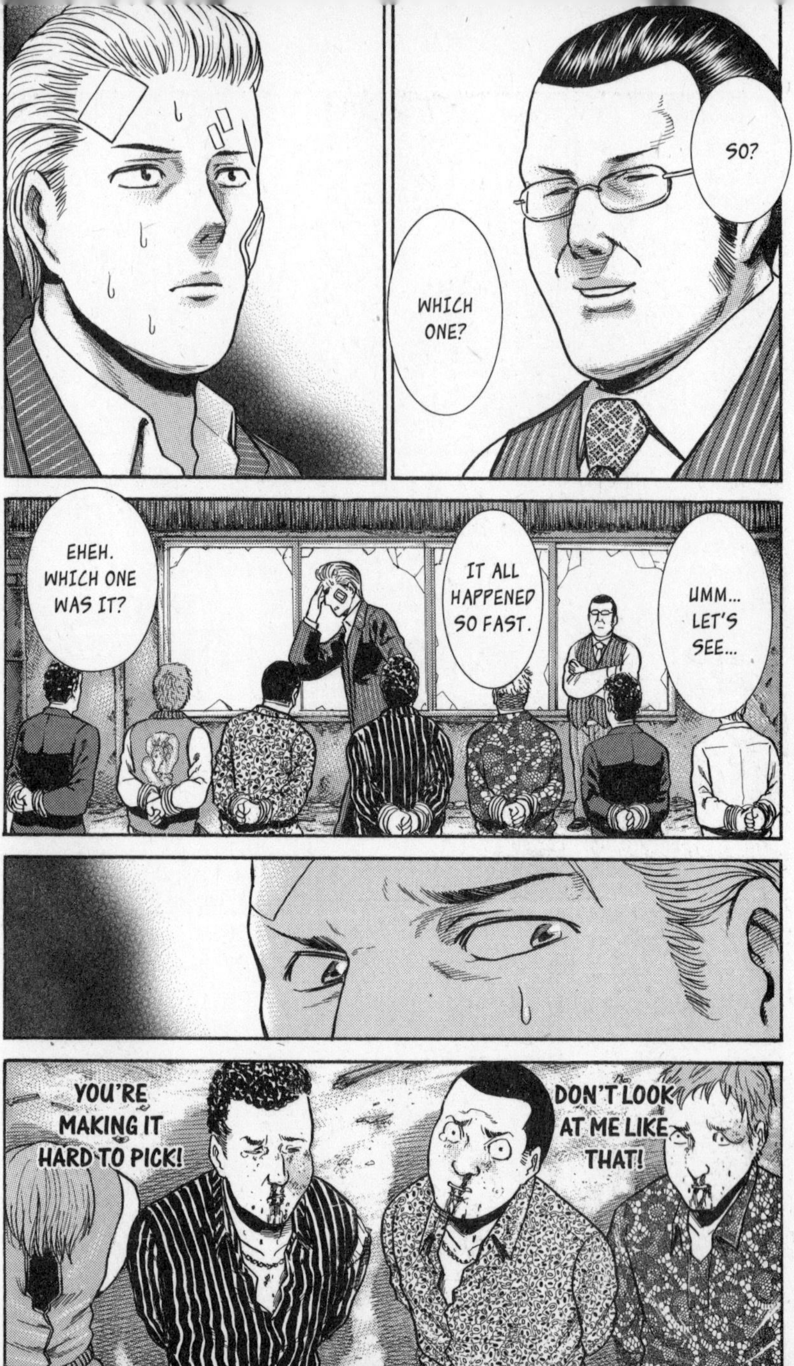
SO?
WHICH ONE?
UMM... LET'S SEE...
IT ALL HAPPENED SO FAST.
EHEH. WHICH ONE WAS IT?
DON'T LOOK AT ME LIKE THAT!
YOU'RE MAKING IT HARD TO PICK!

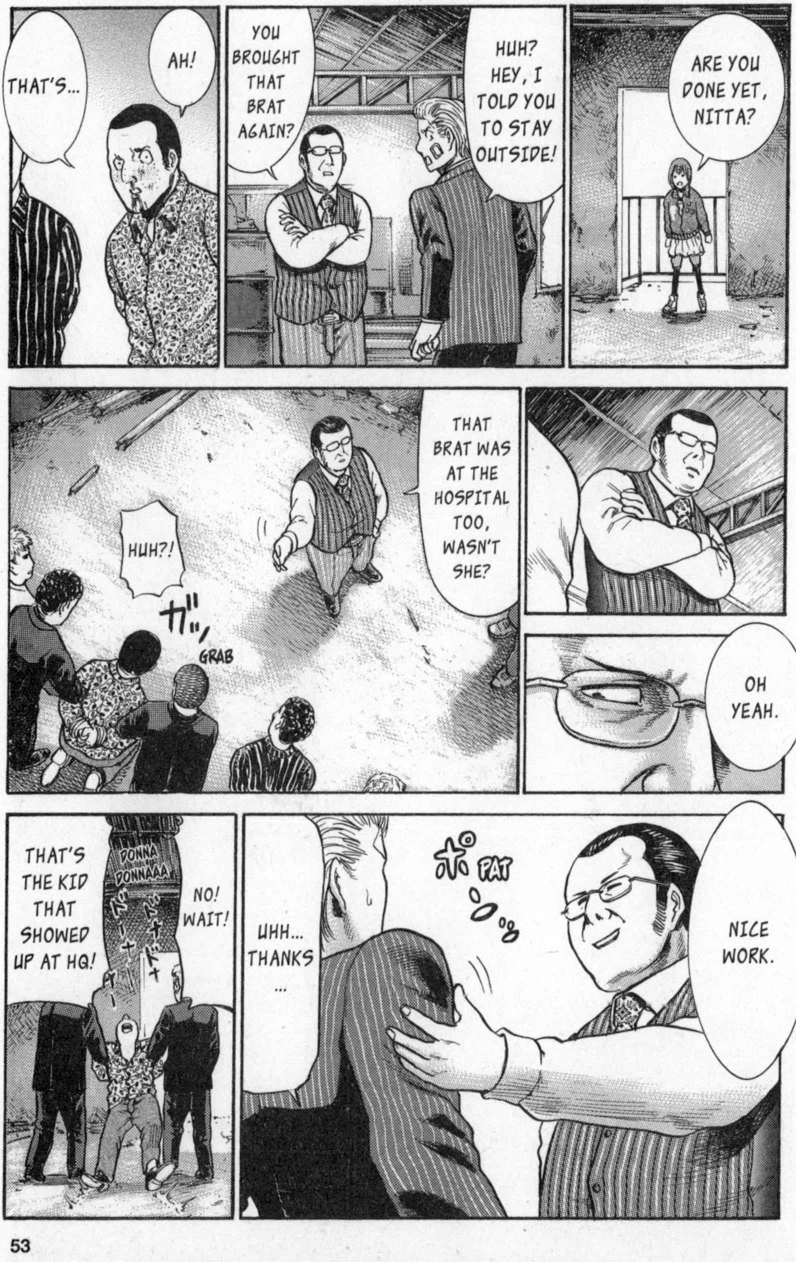
ARE YOU DONE YET, NITTA?
HUH? HEY, I TOLD YOU TO STAY OUTSIDE!
YOU BROUGHT THAT BRAT AGAIN?
AH!
THAT'S...
OH YEAH.
THAT BRAT WAS AT THE HOSPITAL TOO, WASN'T SHE?
HUH?!
ガッ
GRAB
NICE WORK.
PAT
UHH... THANKS ...
NO! WAIT!
THAT'S THE KID THAT SHOWED UP AT HQ!
DONNA DONNAAA

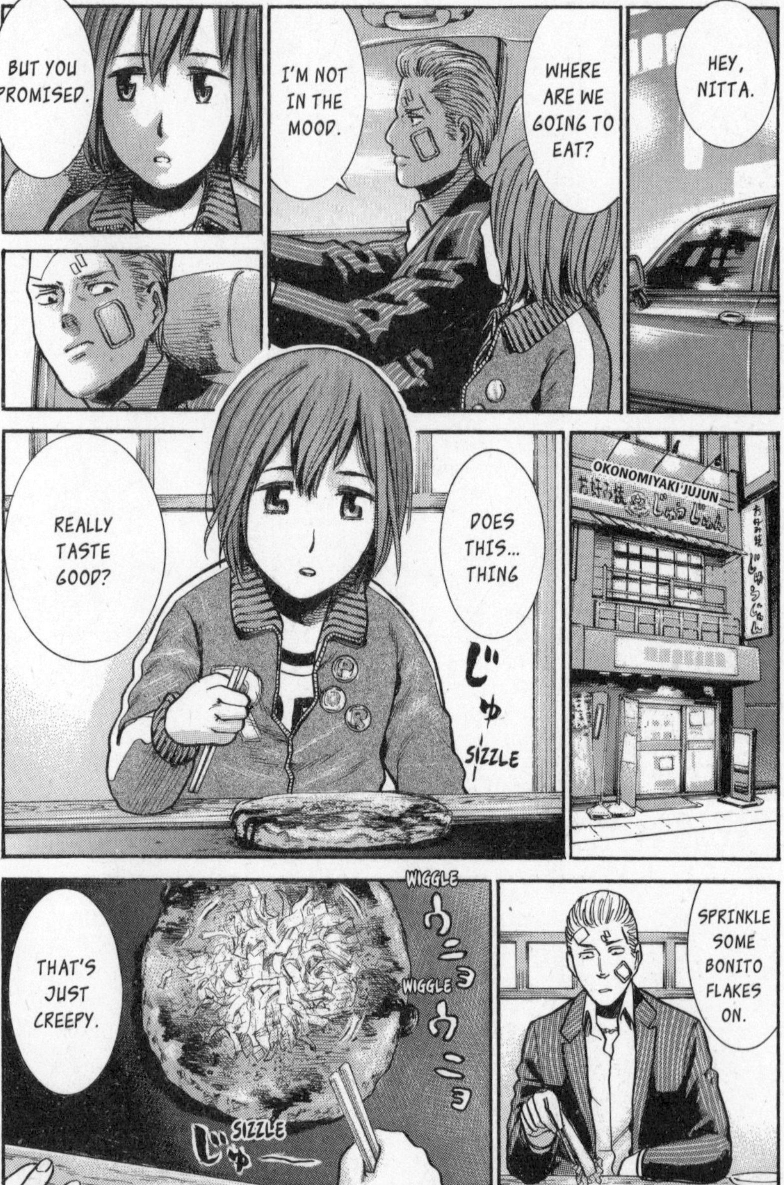
HEY, NITTA.
WHERE ARE WE GOING TO EAT?
I'M NOT IN THE MOOD.
BUT YOU PROMISED.
OKONOMIYAKI JUJUN
DOES THIS... THING
REALLY TASTE GOOD?
じゅ
SIZZLE
SPRINKLE SOME BONITO FLAKES ON.
WIGGLE
ウニョ
WIGGLE
ウニョ
THAT'S JUST CREEPY.
SIZZLE
じゅー

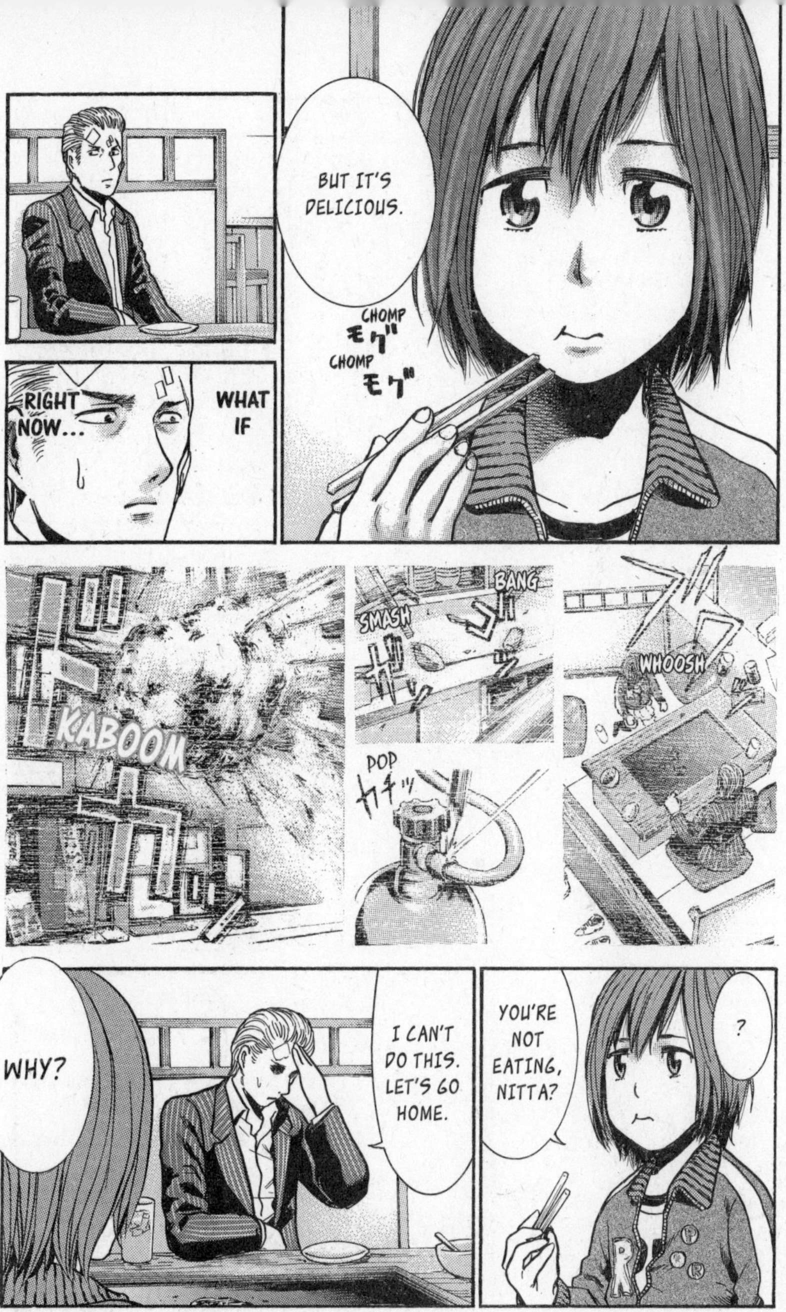
BUT IT'S DELICIOUS.
CHOMP
モグ
CHOMP
モグ
WHAT IF
RIGHT NOW...
WHOOSH
BANG
SMASH
POP
カチッ
KABOOM
?
YOU'RE NOT EATING, NITTA?
I CAN'T DO THIS. LET'S GO HOME.
WHY?

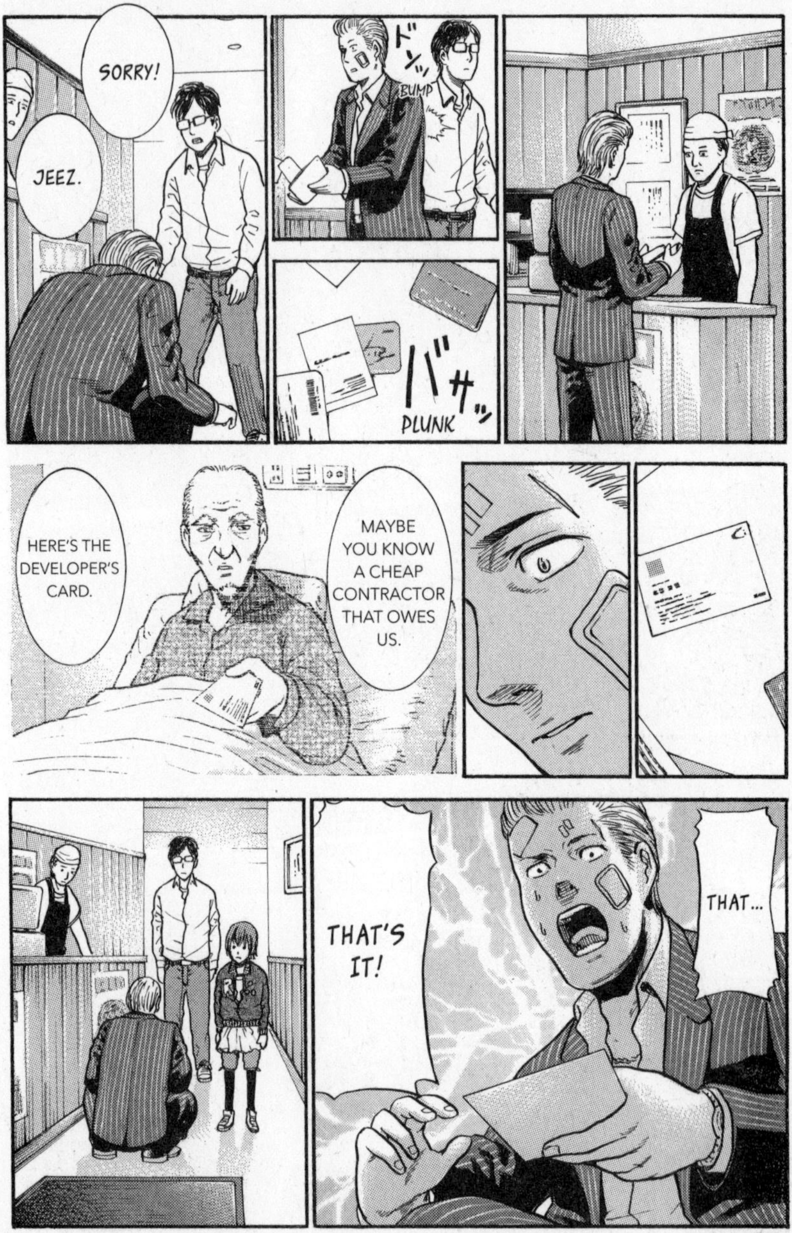
ドンッ
BUMP
バサッ
PLUNK
SORRY!
JEEZ.
MAYBE YOU KNOW A CHEAP CONTRACTOR THAT OWES US.
HERE'S THE DEVELOPER'S CARD.
THAT...
THAT'S IT!

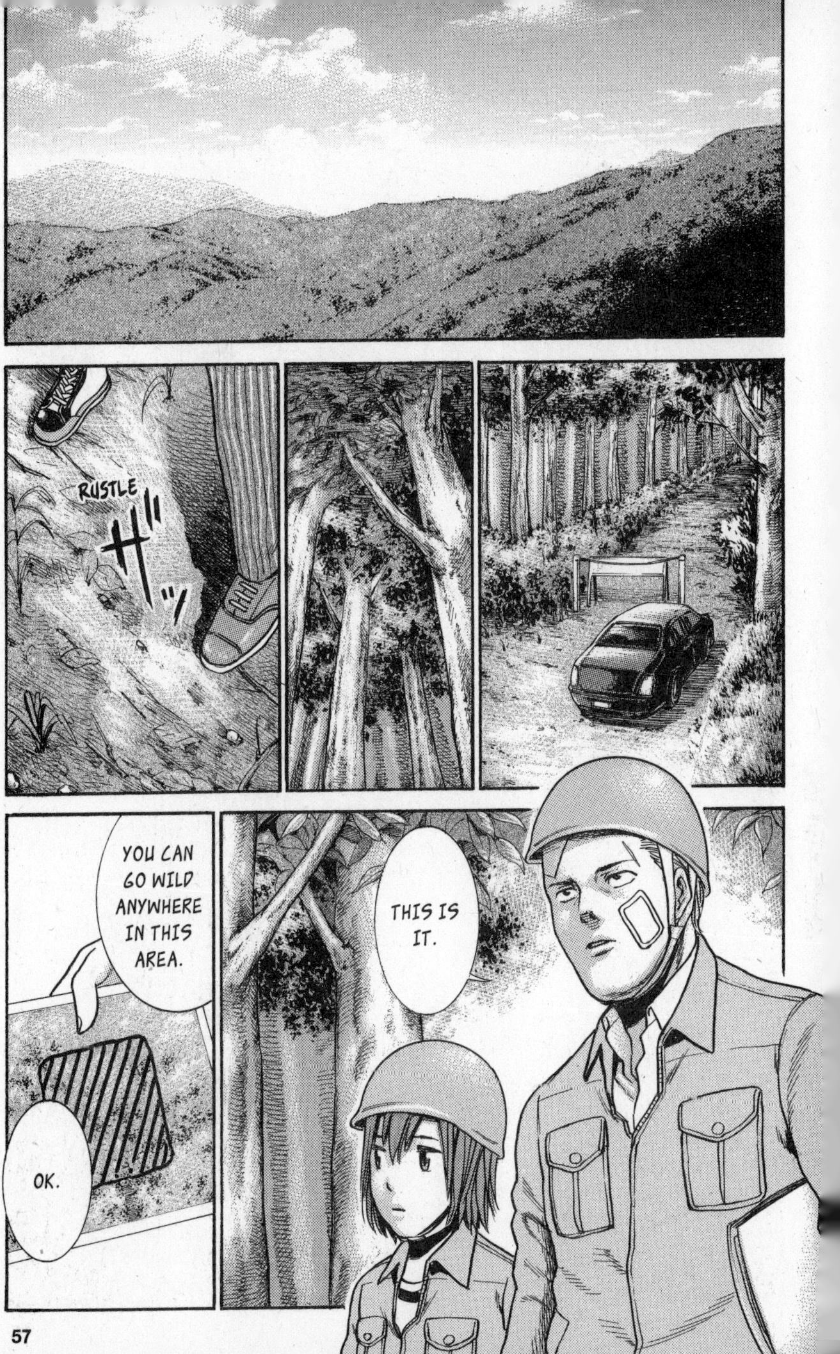
RUSTLE
ザッ
THIS IS IT.
YOU CAN GO WILD ANYWHERE IN THIS AREA.
OK.

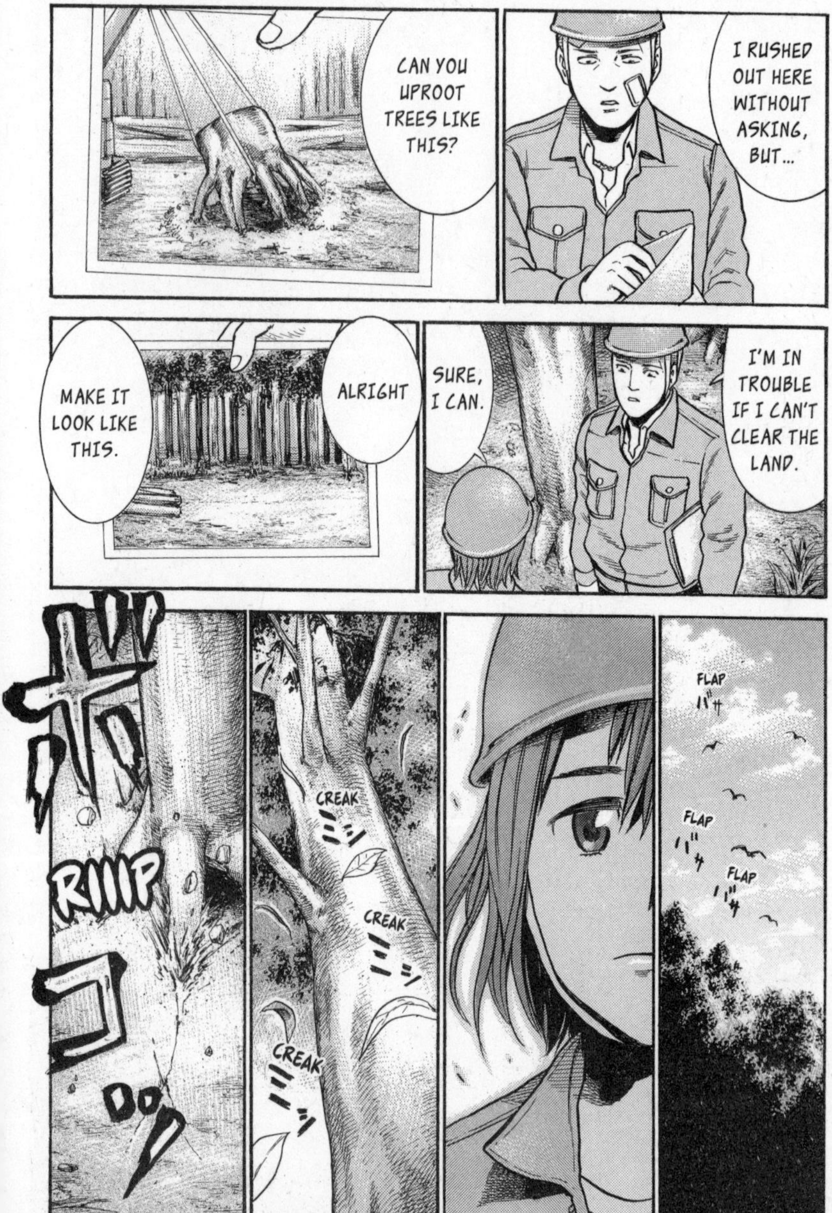
I RUSHED OUT HERE WITHOUT ASKING, BUT...
CAN YOU UPROOT TREES LIKE THIS?
I'M IN TROUBLE IF I CAN'T CLEAR THE LAND.
SURE, I CAN.
ALRIGHT
MAKE IT LOOK LIKE THIS.
FLAP
FLAP
FLAP
CREAK
CREAK
CREAK
RIIIP

TAP
コツ

TAP
コツ

IN...

INCREDI-
BLE!

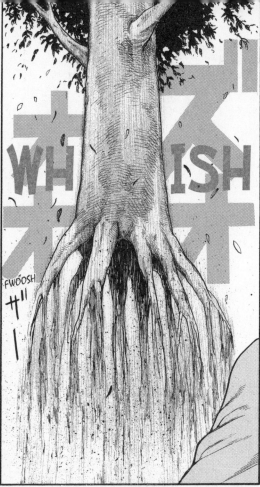

WH ISH

FWOOSH
ザ―

THUD

CRACK
バキ

CRACK
バキ

バキ

CRACK

THUD

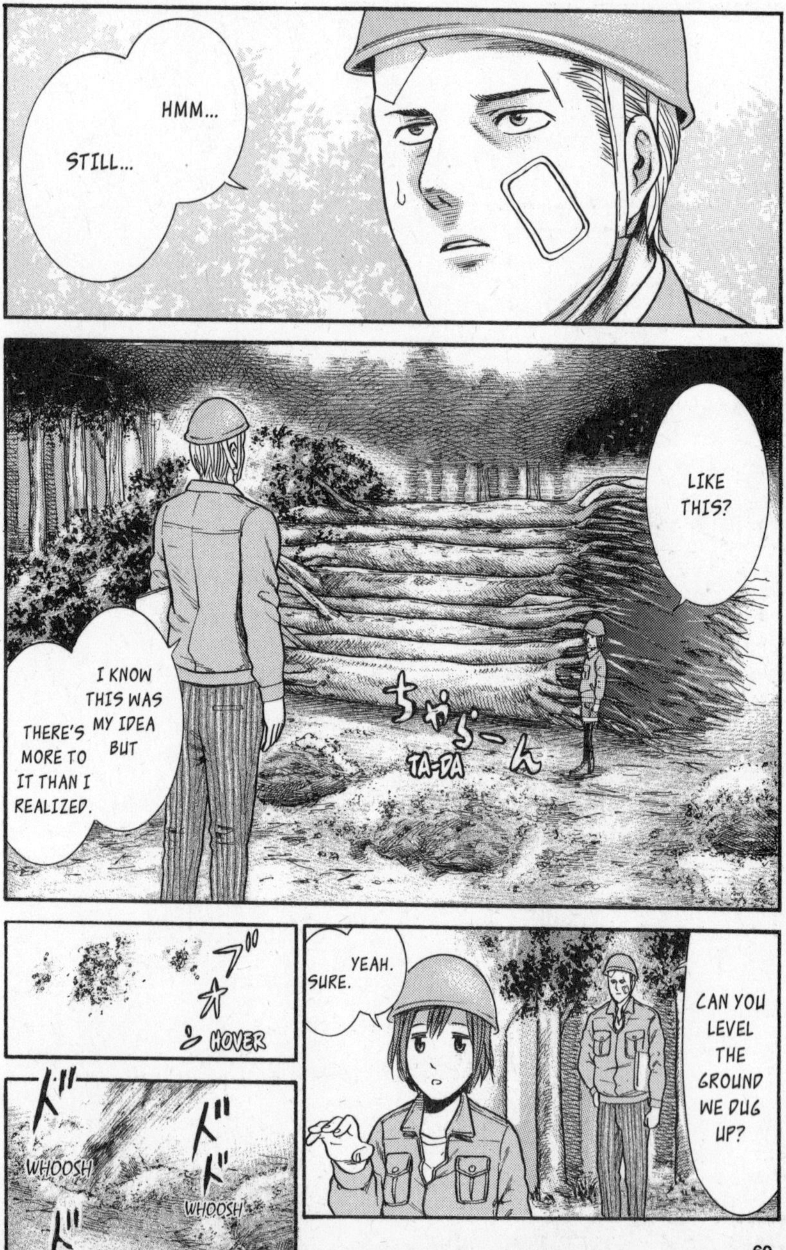
HMM...
STILL...
LIKE THIS?
TA-DA
I KNOW THIS WAS MY IDEA BUT
THERE'S MORE TO IT THAN I REALIZED.
CAN YOU LEVEL THE GROUND WE DUG UP?
YEAH. SURE.
HOVER
WHOOSH
WHOOSH

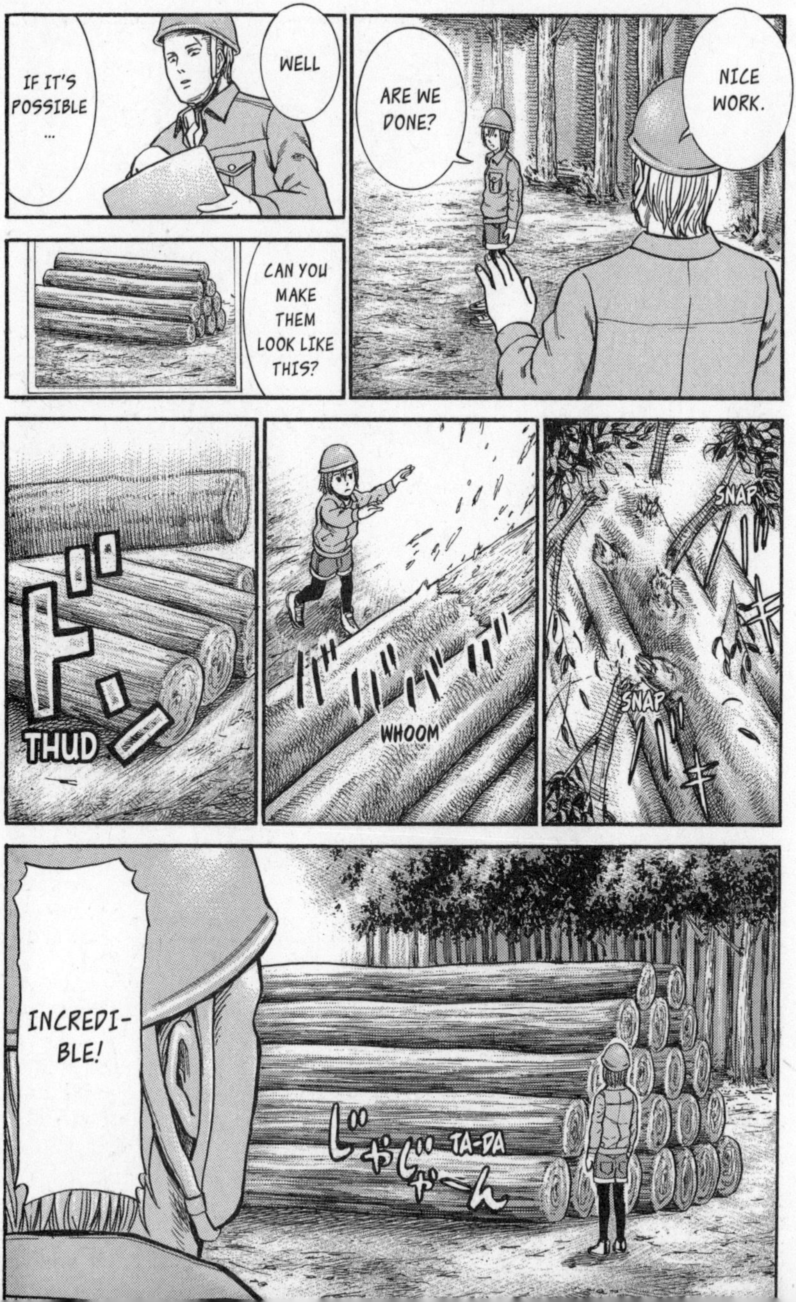
NICE WORK.
ARE WE DONE?
WELL
IF IT'S POSSIBLE ...
CAN YOU MAKE THEM LOOK LIKE THIS?
SNAP
SNAP
WHOOM
THUD
じゃじゃーん
TA-DA
INCREDI-BLE!

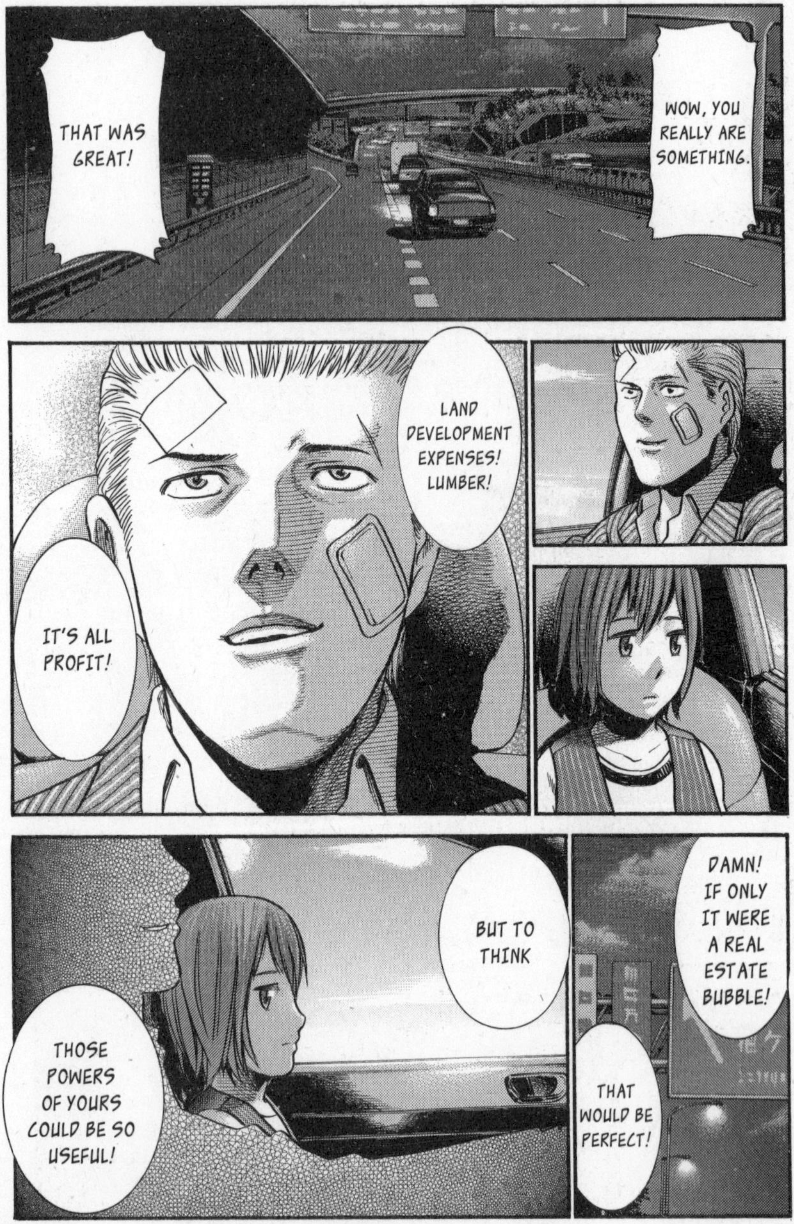
WOW, YOU REALLY ARE SOMETHING.
THAT WAS GREAT!
LAND DEVELOPMENT EXPENSES! LUMBER!
IT'S ALL PROFIT!
DAMN! IF ONLY IT WERE A REAL ESTATE BUBBLE!
THAT WOULD BE PERFECT!
BUT TO THINK
THOSE POWERS OF YOURS COULD BE SO USEFUL!

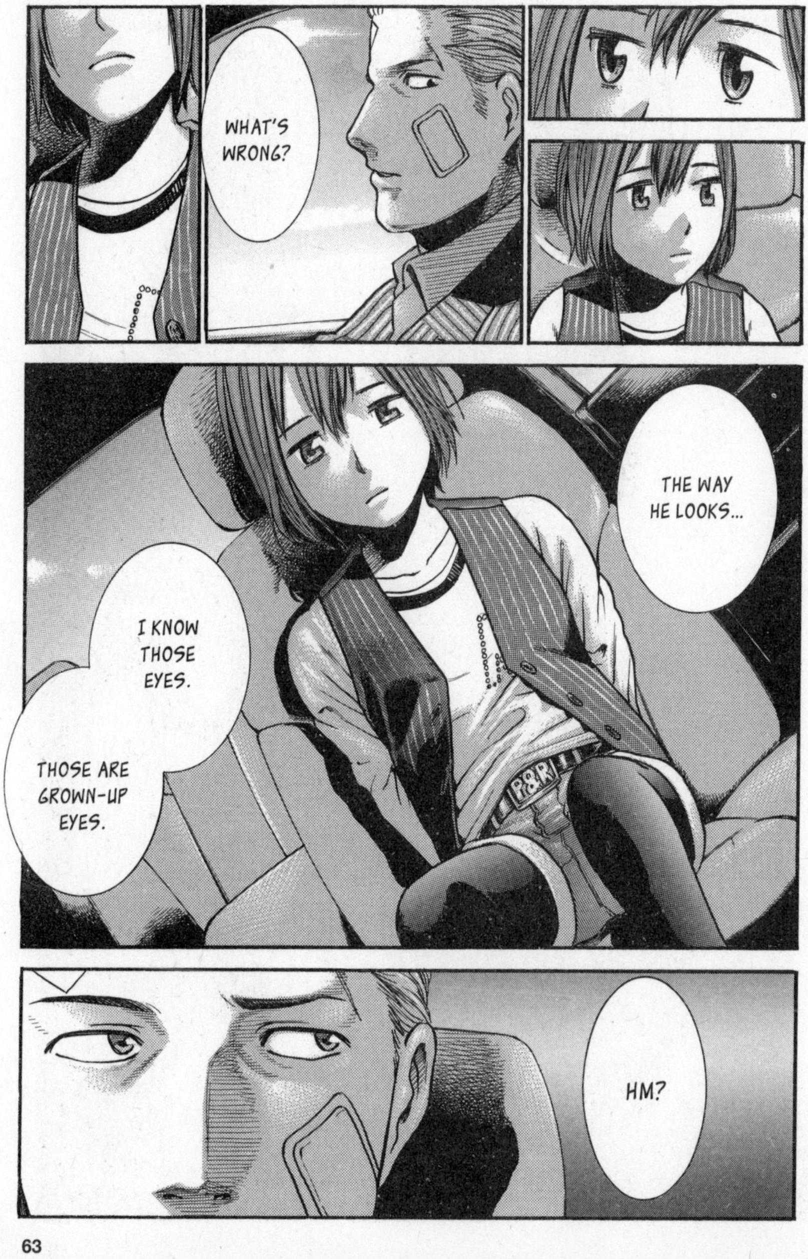
WHAT'S WRONG?
THE WAY HE LOOKS...
I KNOW THOSE EYES.
THOSE ARE GROWN-UP EYES.
HM?

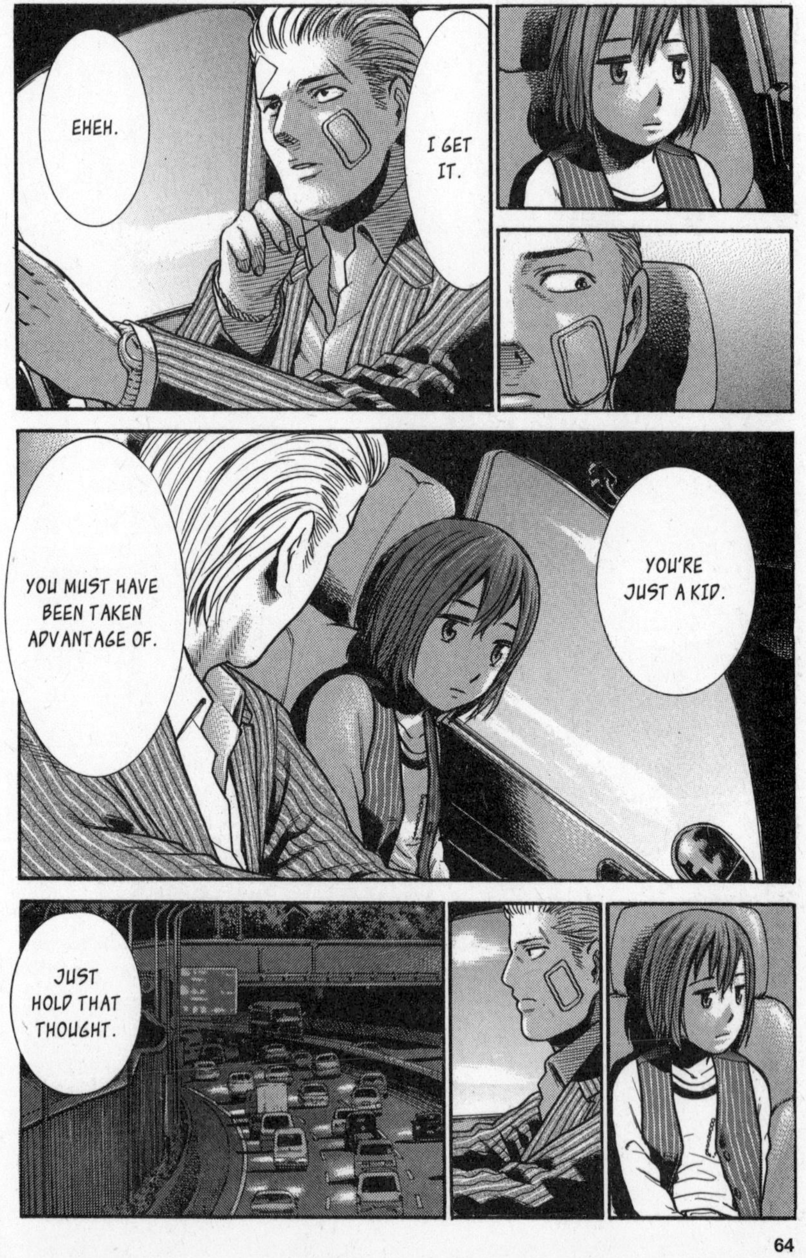
I GET IT.
EHEH.
YOU'RE JUST A KID.
YOU MUST HAVE BEEN TAKEN ADVANTAGE OF.
JUST HOLD THAT THOUGHT.

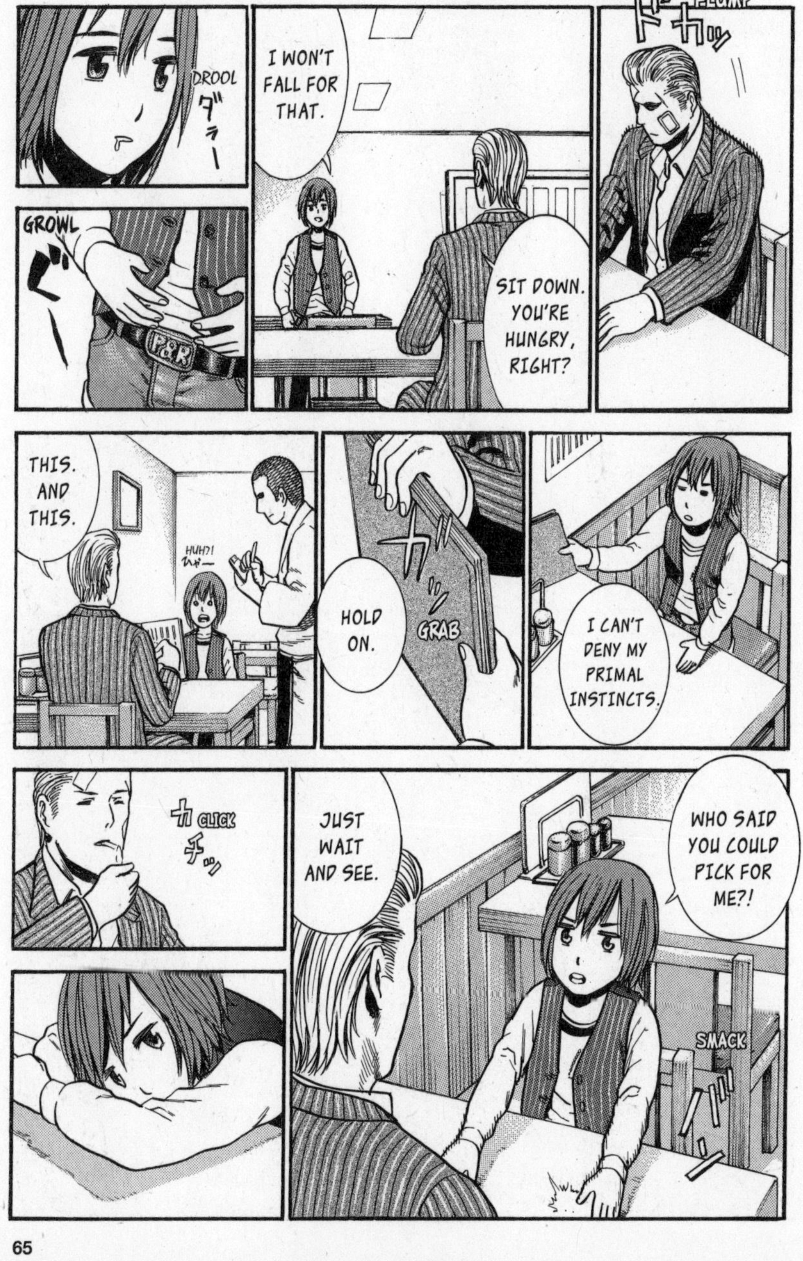
ドカッ
FLUMP
I WON'T FALL FOR THAT.
SIT DOWN. YOU'RE HUNGRY, RIGHT?
DROOL
ダラー
GROWL
I CAN'T DENY MY PRIMAL INSTINCTS.
ガッ
GRAB
HOLD ON.
THIS. AND THIS.
HUH?!
WHO SAID YOU COULD PICK FOR ME?!
SMACK
JUST WAIT AND SEE.
カチッ
CLICK

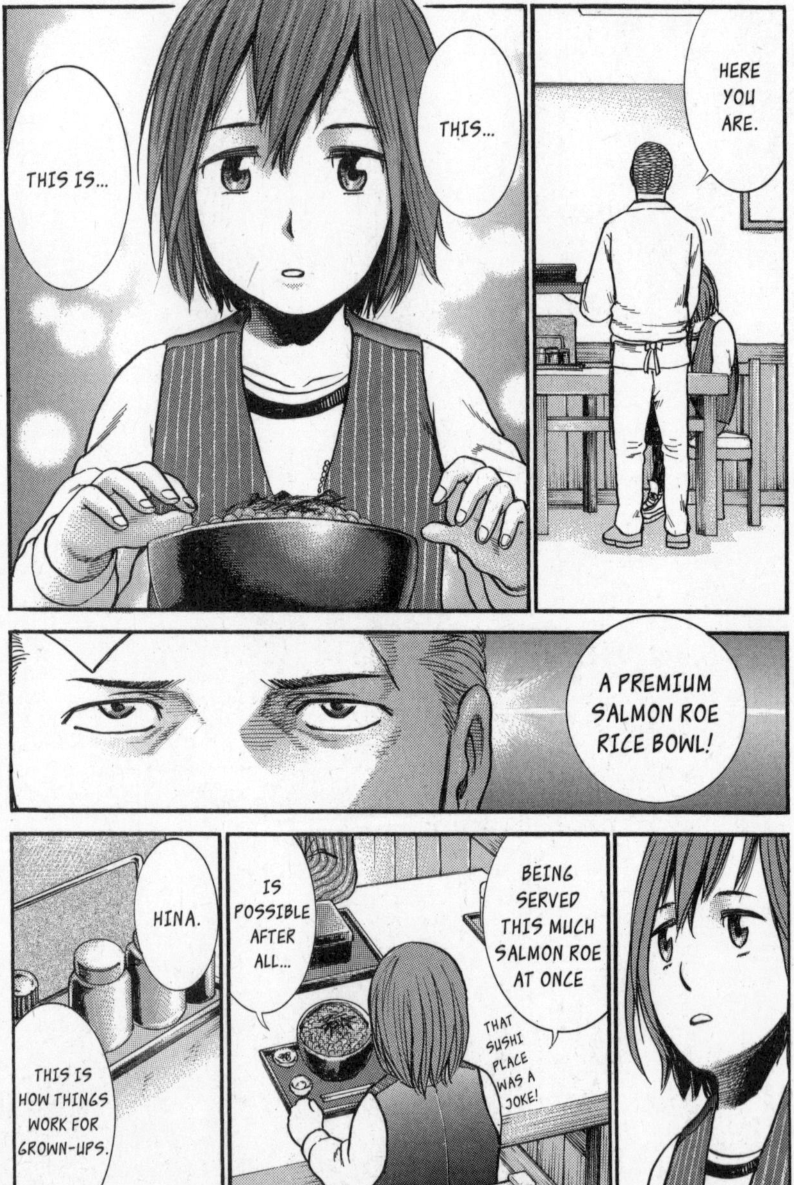
HERE YOU ARE.
THIS...
THIS IS...
A PREMIUM SALMON ROE RICE BOWL!
BEING SERVED THIS MUCH SALMON ROE AT ONCE
IS POSSIBLE AFTER ALL...
THAT SUSHI PLACE WAS A JOKE!
HINA.
THIS IS HOW THINGS WORK FOR GROWN-UPS.

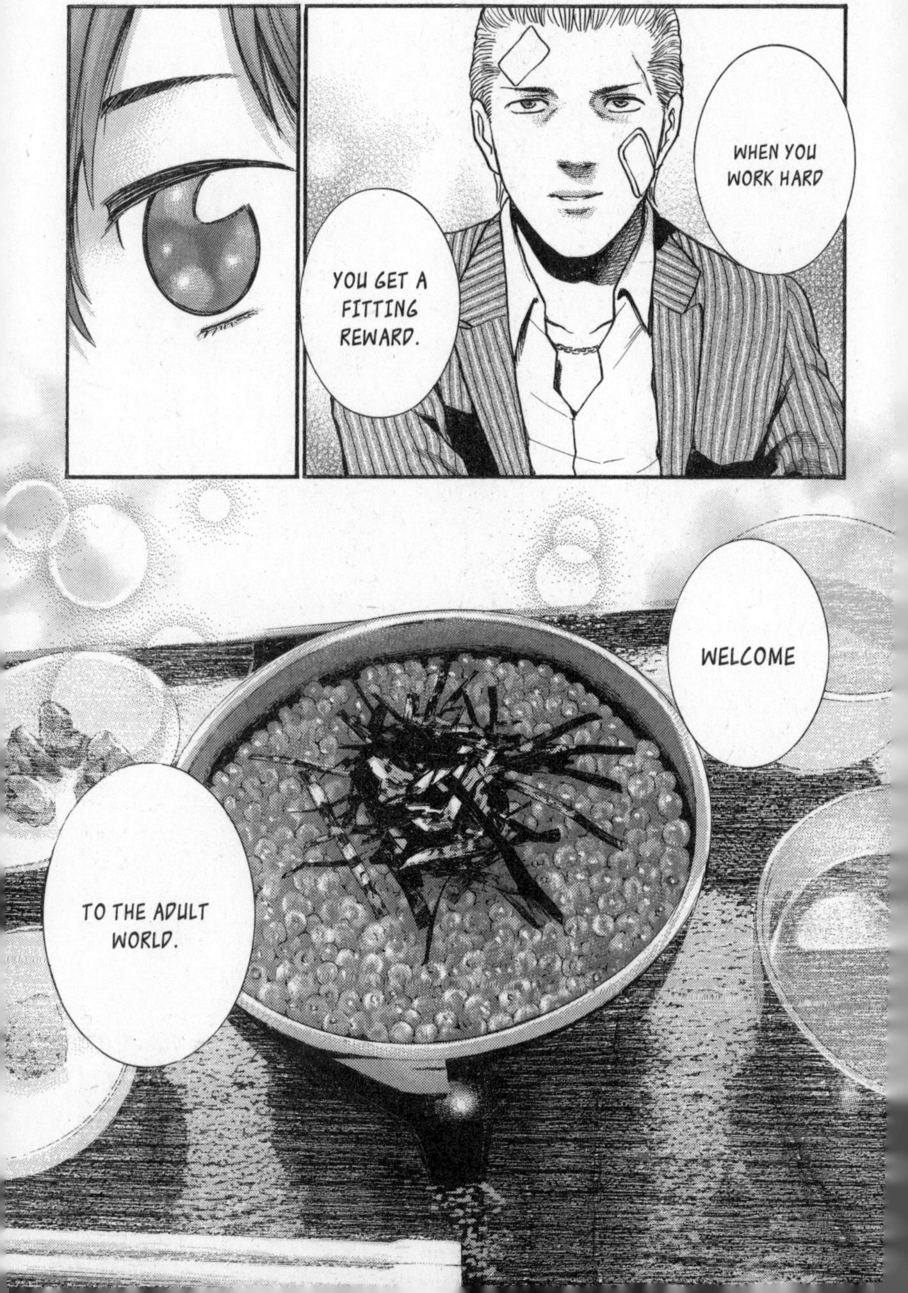
WHEN YOU WORK HARD
YOU GET A FITTING REWARD.
WELCOME
TO THE ADULT WORLD.

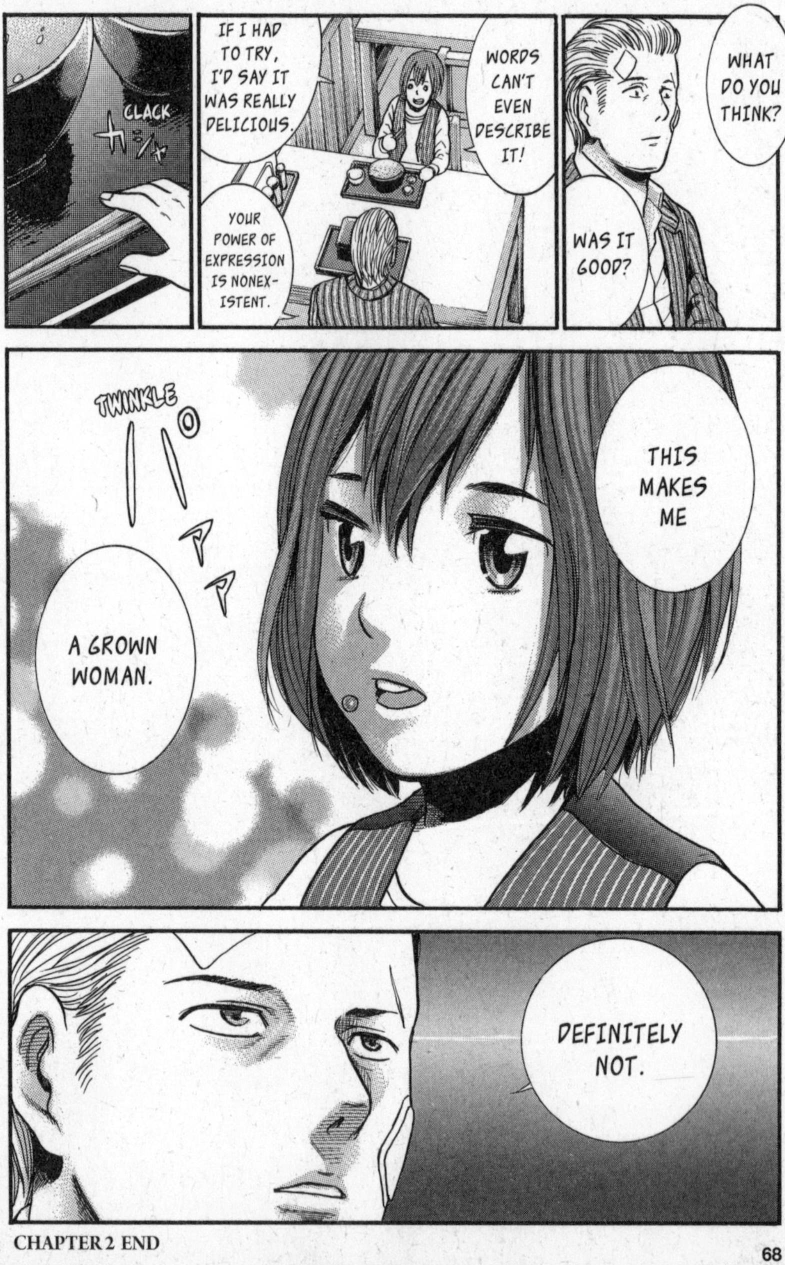
WHAT DO YOU THINK?
WAS IT GOOD?
WORDS CAN'T EVEN DESCRIBE IT!
IF I HAD TO TRY, I'D SAY IT WAS REALLY DELICIOUS.
YOUR POWER OF EXPRESSION IS NONEX-ISTENT.
CLACK
THIS MAKES ME
A GROWN WOMAN.
TWINKLE
DEFINITELY NOT.

CHAPTER 2 END

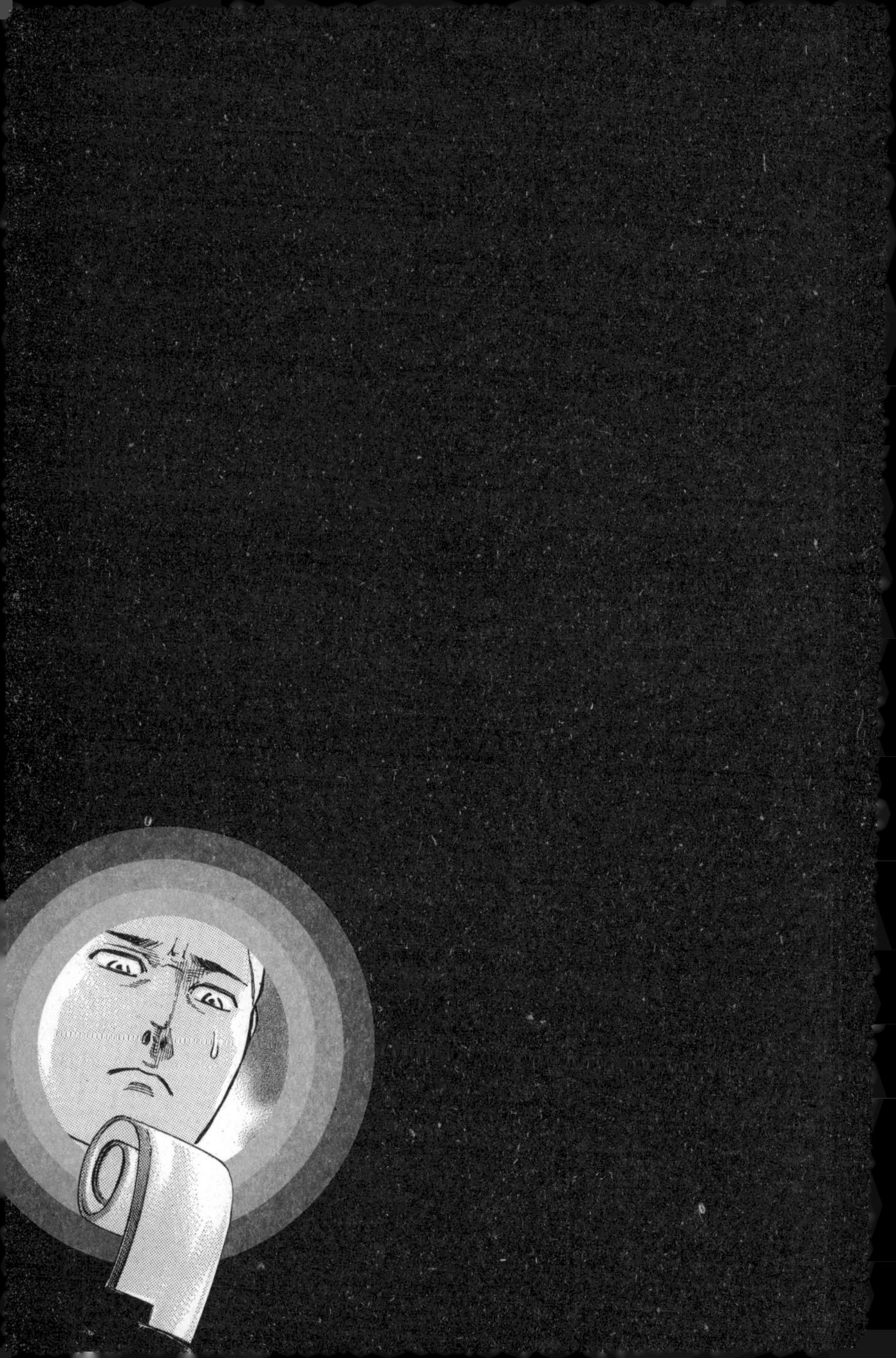

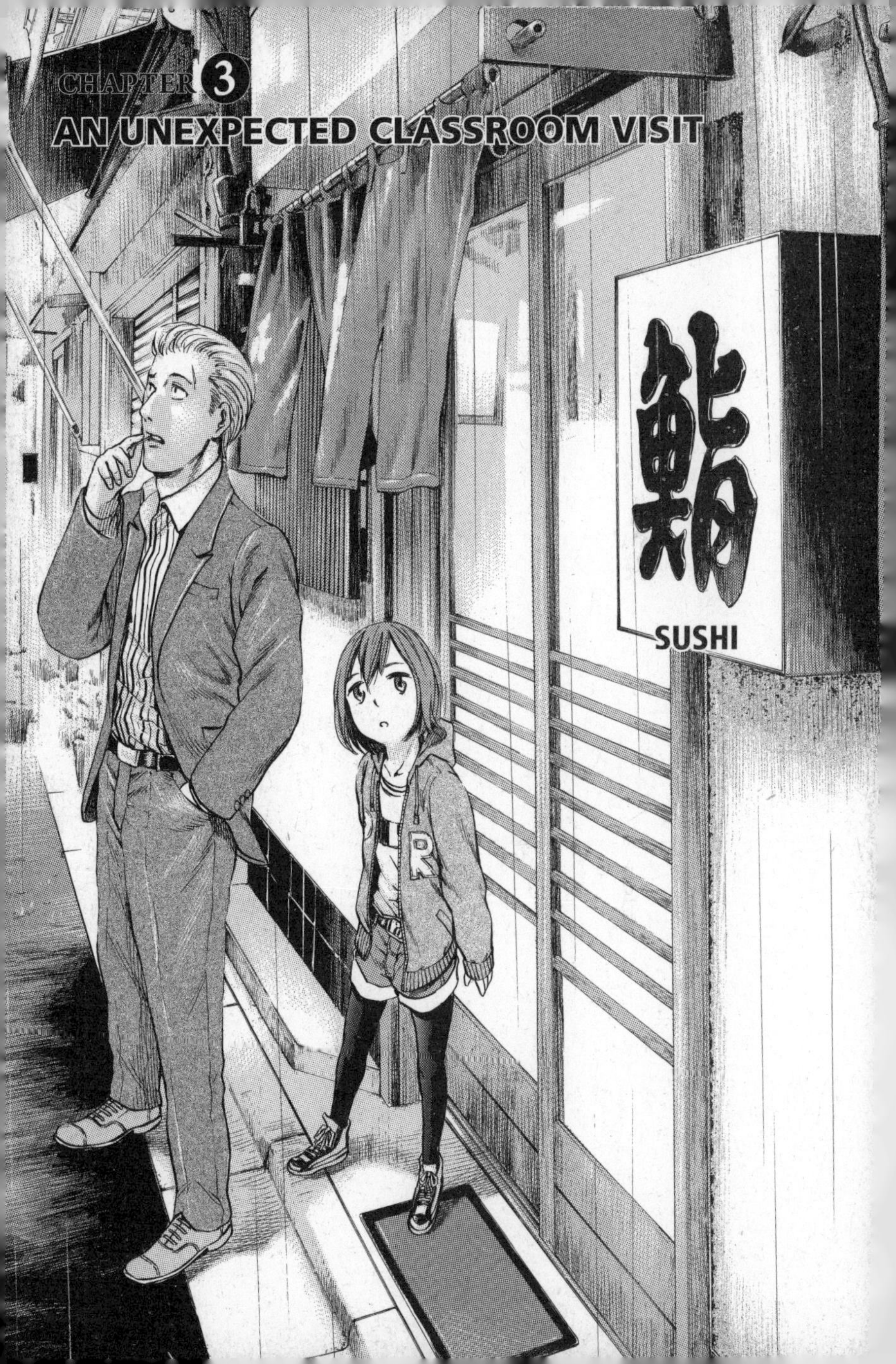
CHAPTER 3
AN UNEXPECTED CLASSROOM VISIT
鮨
SUSHI

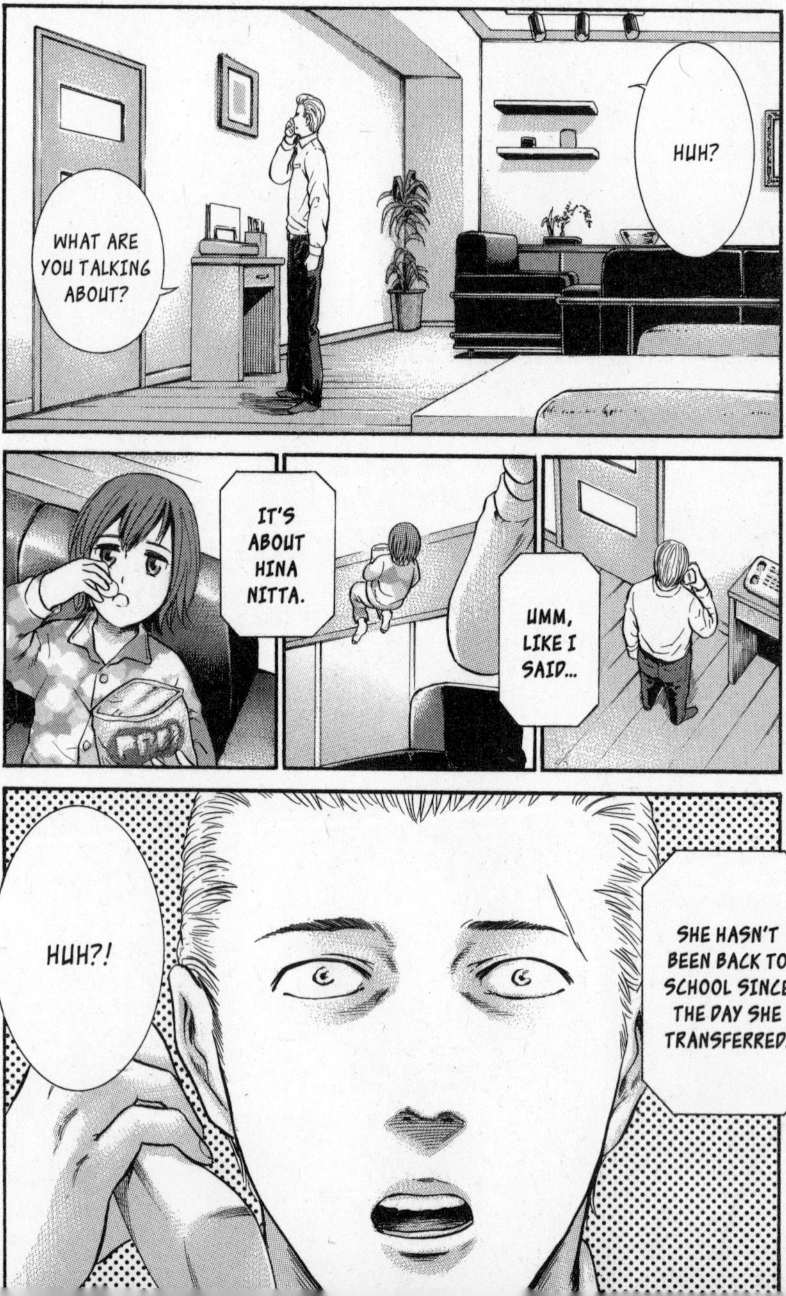
HUH?
WHAT ARE YOU TALKING ABOUT?
UMM, LIKE I SAID...
IT'S ABOUT HINA NITTA.
SHE HASN'T BEEN BACK TO SCHOOL SINCE THE DAY SHE TRANSFERRED.
HUH?!

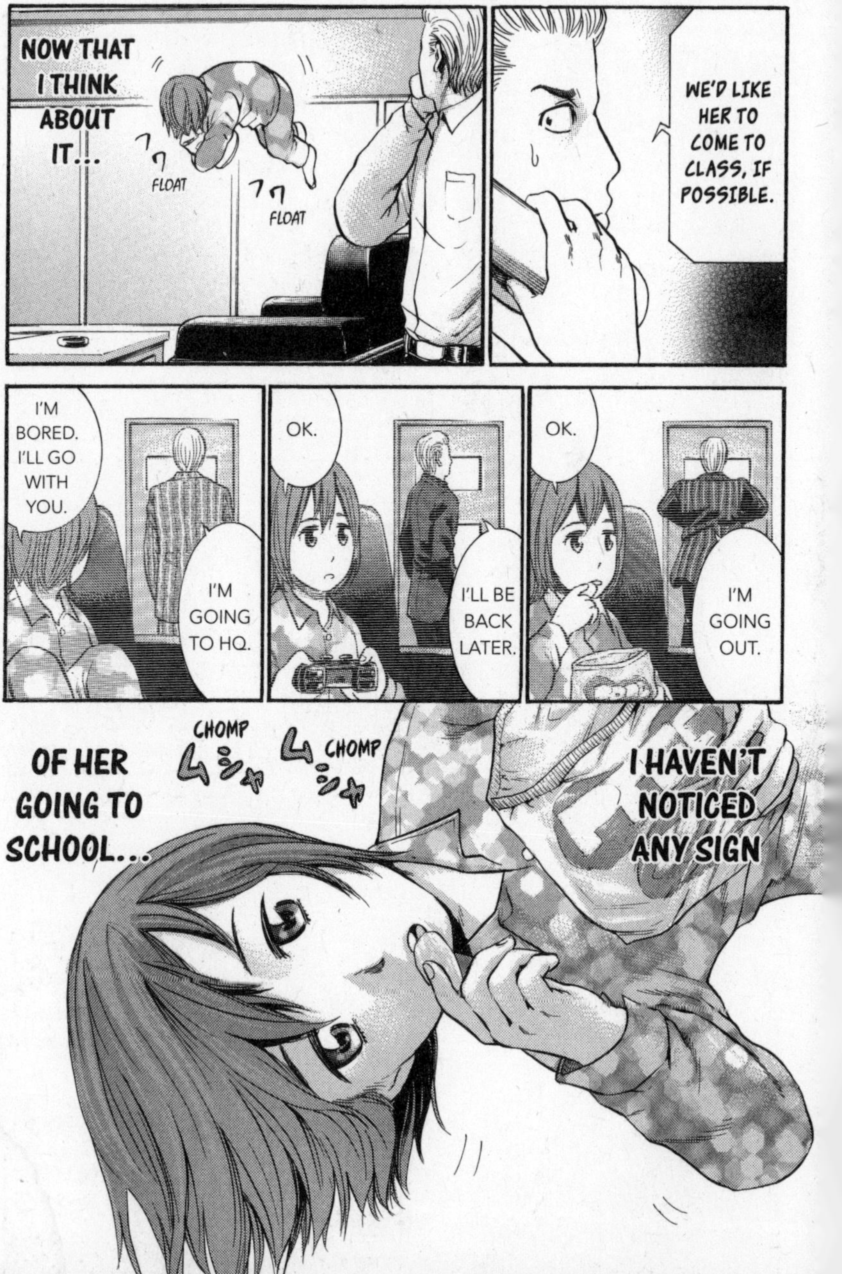

WE'D LIKE HER TO COME TO CLASS, IF POSSIBLE.
NOW THAT I THINK ABOUT IT...
FLOAT
FLOAT
I'M GOING OUT.
OK.
I'LL BE BACK LATER.
OK.
I'M GOING TO HQ.
I'M BORED. I'LL GO WITH YOU.
I HAVEN'T NOTICED ANY SIGN
CHOMP
CHOMP
OF HER GOING TO SCHOOL...

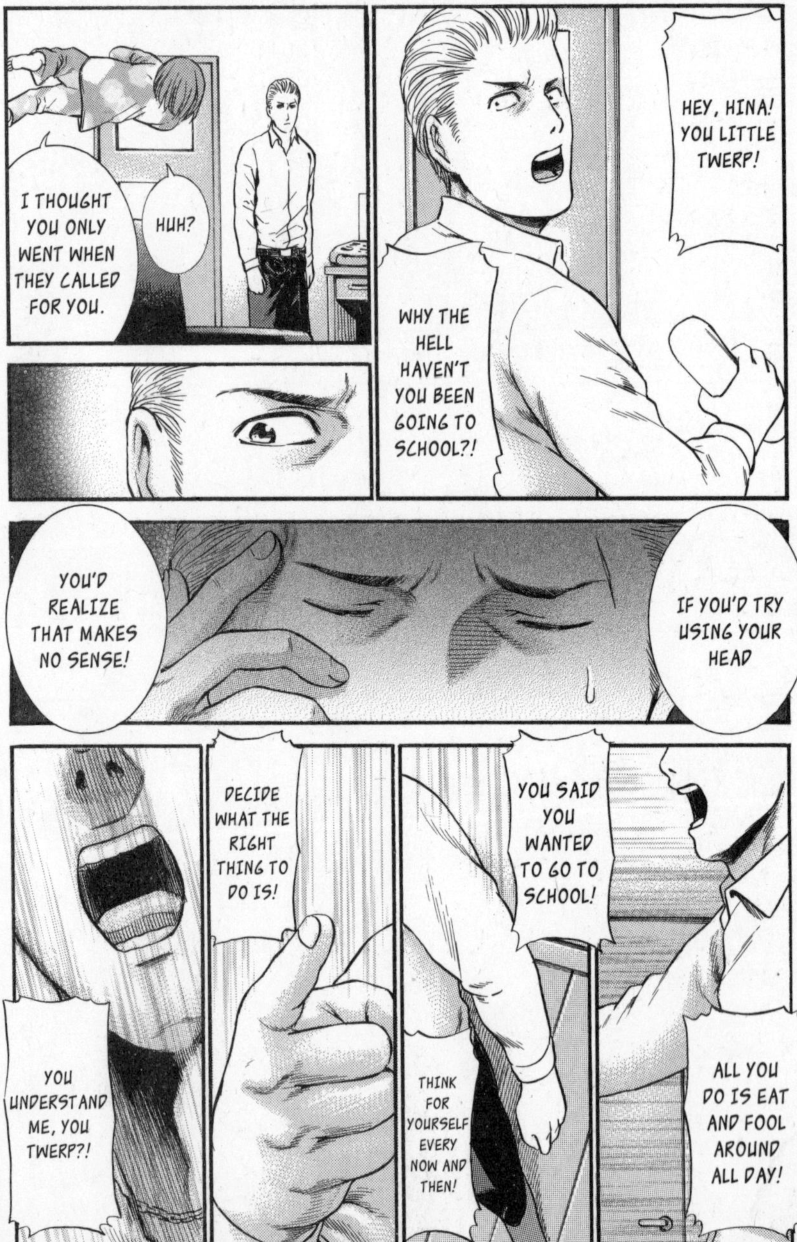
HEY, HINA! YOU LITTLE TWERP!
WHY THE HELL HAVEN'T YOU BEEN GOING TO SCHOOL?!
HUH?
I THOUGHT YOU ONLY WENT WHEN THEY CALLED FOR YOU.
IF YOU'D TRY USING YOUR HEAD
YOU'D REALIZE THAT MAKES NO SENSE!
YOU SAID YOU WANTED TO GO TO SCHOOL!
ALL YOU DO IS EAT AND FOOL AROUND ALL DAY!
THINK FOR YOURSELF EVERY NOW AND THEN!
DECIDE WHAT THE RIGHT THING TO DO IS!
YOU UNDERSTAND ME, YOU TWERP?!

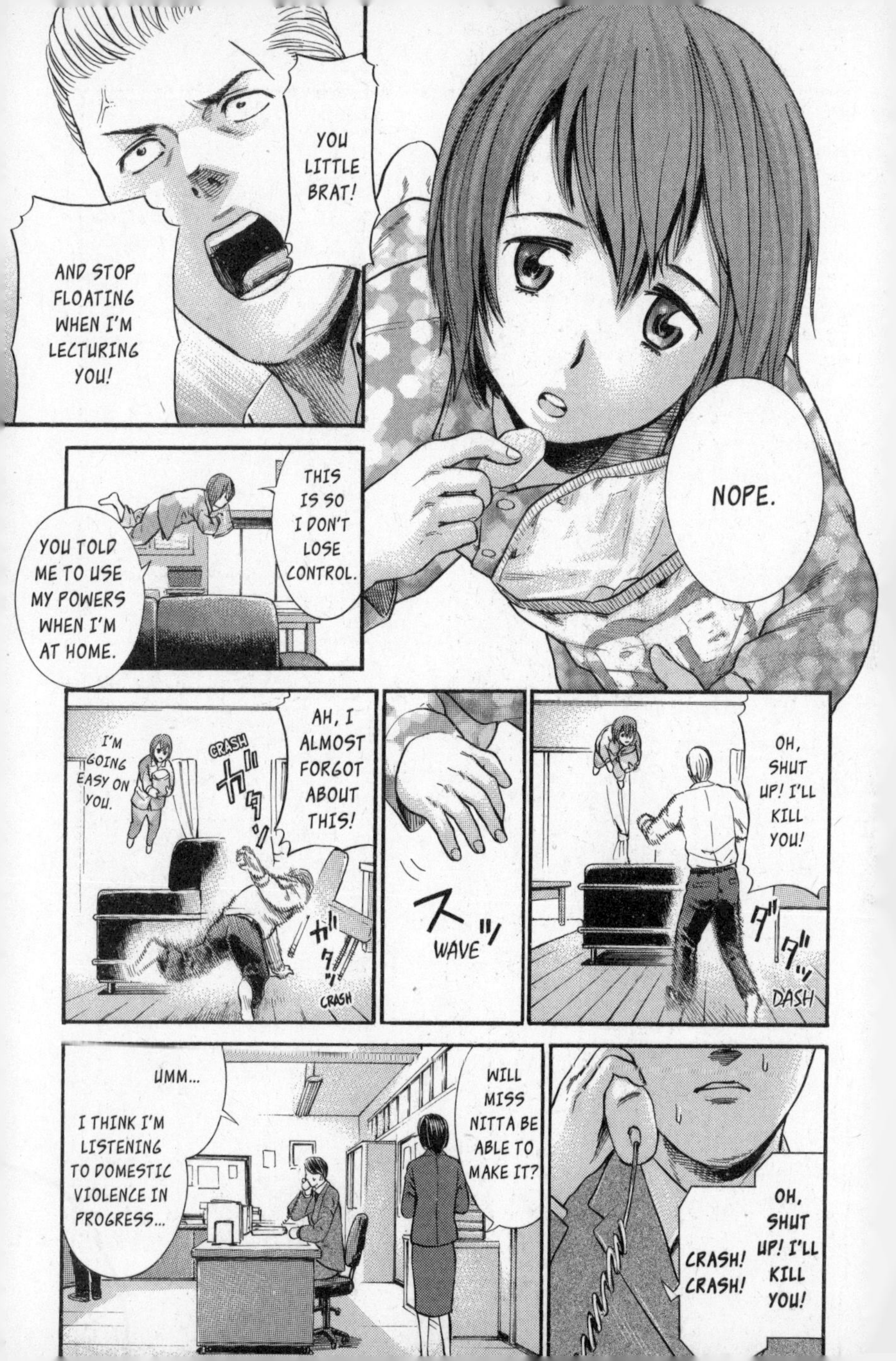
NOPE.
YOU LITTLE BRAT!
AND STOP FLOATING WHEN I'M LECTURING YOU!
THIS IS SO I DON'T LOSE CONTROL.
YOU TOLD ME TO USE MY POWERS WHEN I'M AT HOME.
OH, SHUT UP! I'LL KILL YOU!
ダダッ
DASH
スッ
WAVE
AH, I ALMOST FORGOT ABOUT THIS!
ガタッ
CRASH
I'M GOING EASY ON YOU.
ガタッ
CRASH
OH, SHUT UP! I'LL KILL YOU!
CRASH! CRASH!
WILL MISS NITTA BE ABLE TO MAKE IT?
UMM...
I THINK I'M LISTENING TO DOMESTIC VIOLENCE IN PROGRESS...

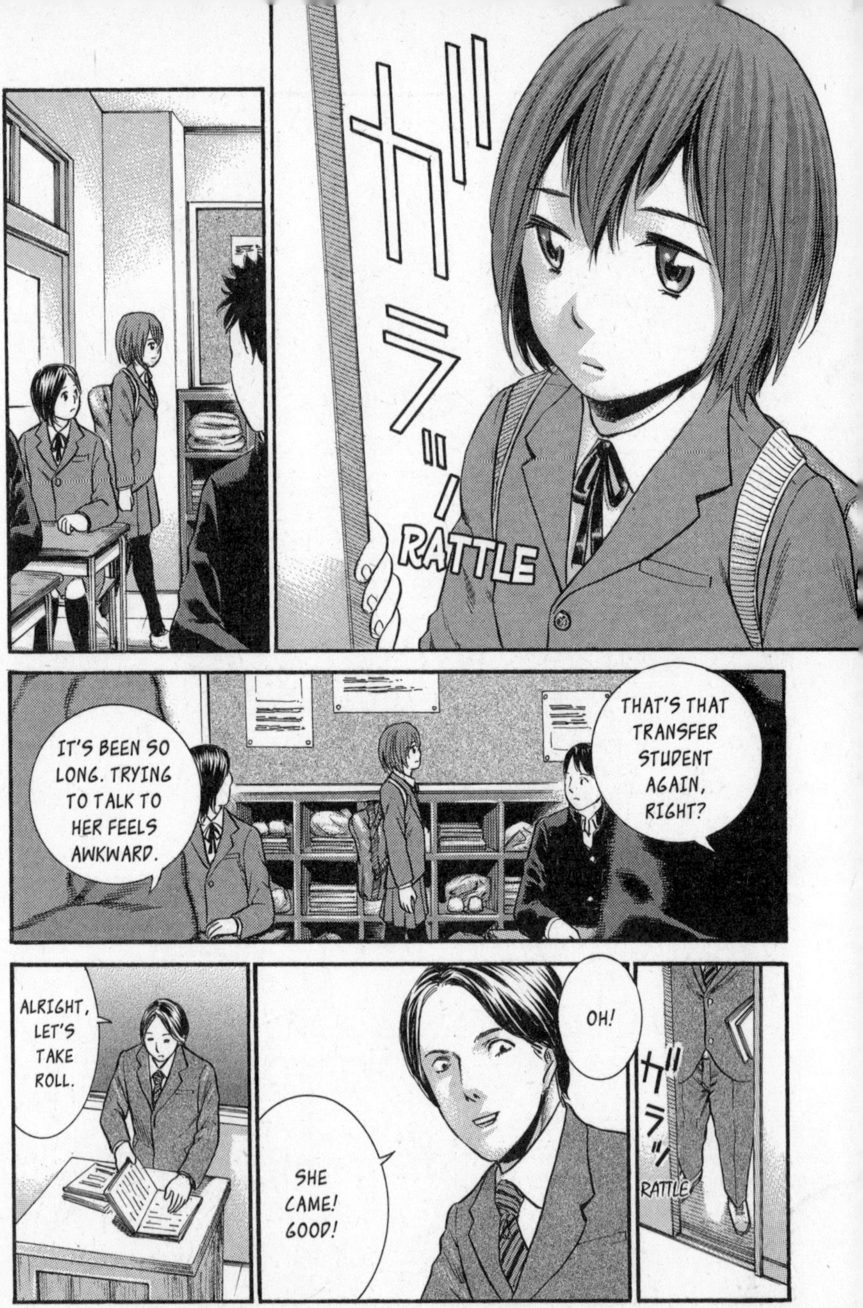
ガラッ
RATTLE
THAT'S THAT TRANSFER STUDENT AGAIN, RIGHT?
IT'S BEEN SO LONG. TRYING TO TALK TO HER FEELS AWKWARD.
ガラッ
RATTLE
OH!
SHE CAME! GOOD!
ALRIGHT, LET'S TAKE ROLL.

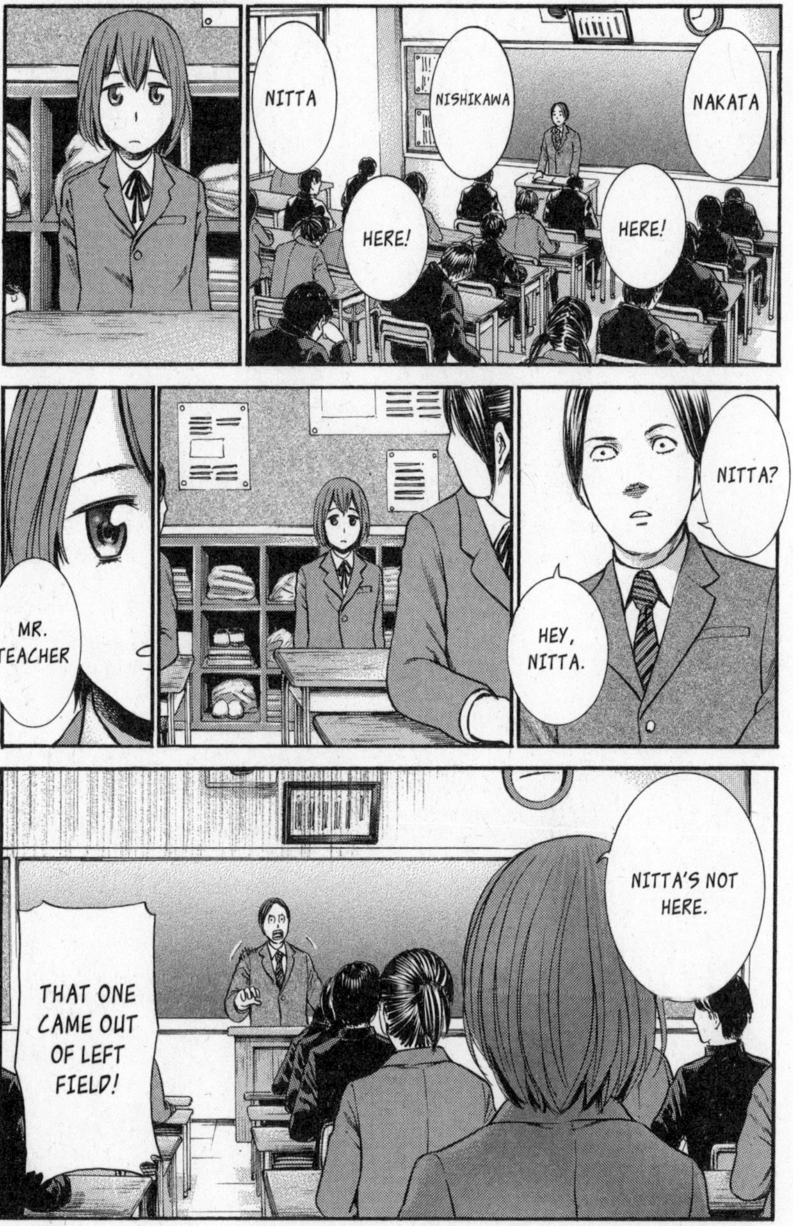
NAKATA
HERE!
NISHIKAWA
HERE!
NITTA
NITTA?
HEY, NITTA.
MR. TEACHER
NITTA'S NOT HERE.
THAT ONE CAME OUT OF LEFT FIELD!

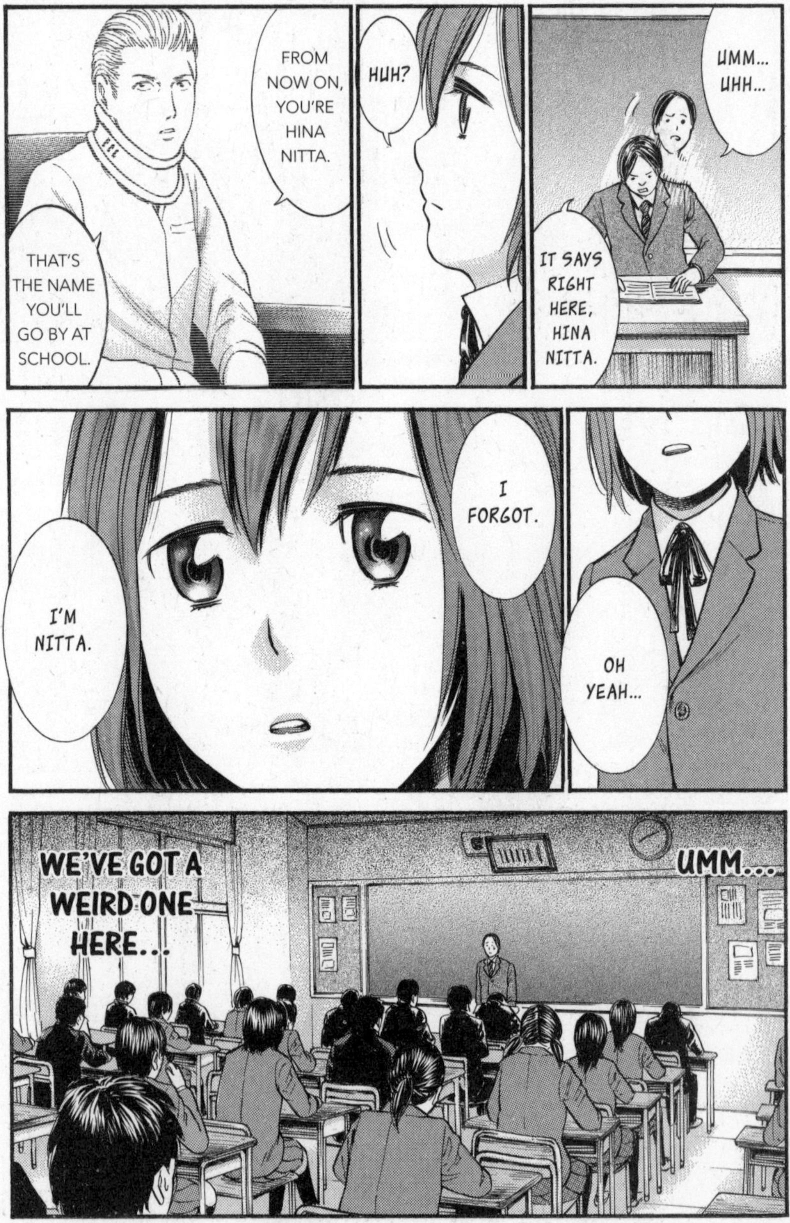
UMM... UHH...
IT SAYS RIGHT HERE, HINA NITTA.
HUH?
FROM NOW ON, YOU'RE HINA NITTA.
THAT'S THE NAME YOU'LL GO BY AT SCHOOL.
OH YEAH...
I FORGOT.
I'M NITTA.
UMM...
WE'VE GOT A WEIRD ONE HERE...

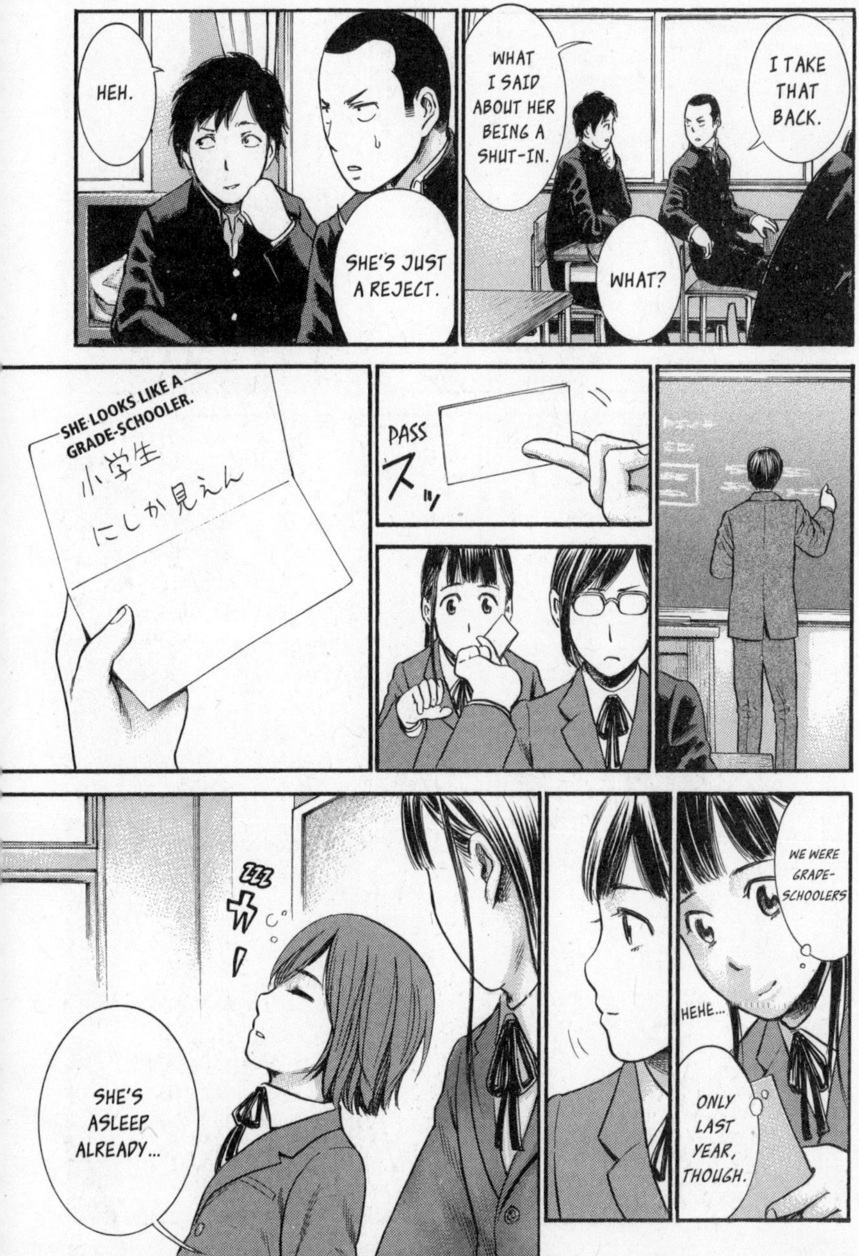

I TAKE THAT BACK.
WHAT I SAID ABOUT HER BEING A SHUT-IN.
WHAT?
HEH.
SHE'S JUST A REJECT.
PASS
スッ
SHE LOOKS LIKE A GRADE-SCHOOLER.
小学生にしか見えん
WE WERE GRADE-SCHOOLERS
HEHE...
ONLY LAST YEAR, THOUGH.
ZZZ
SHE'S ASLEEP ALREADY...

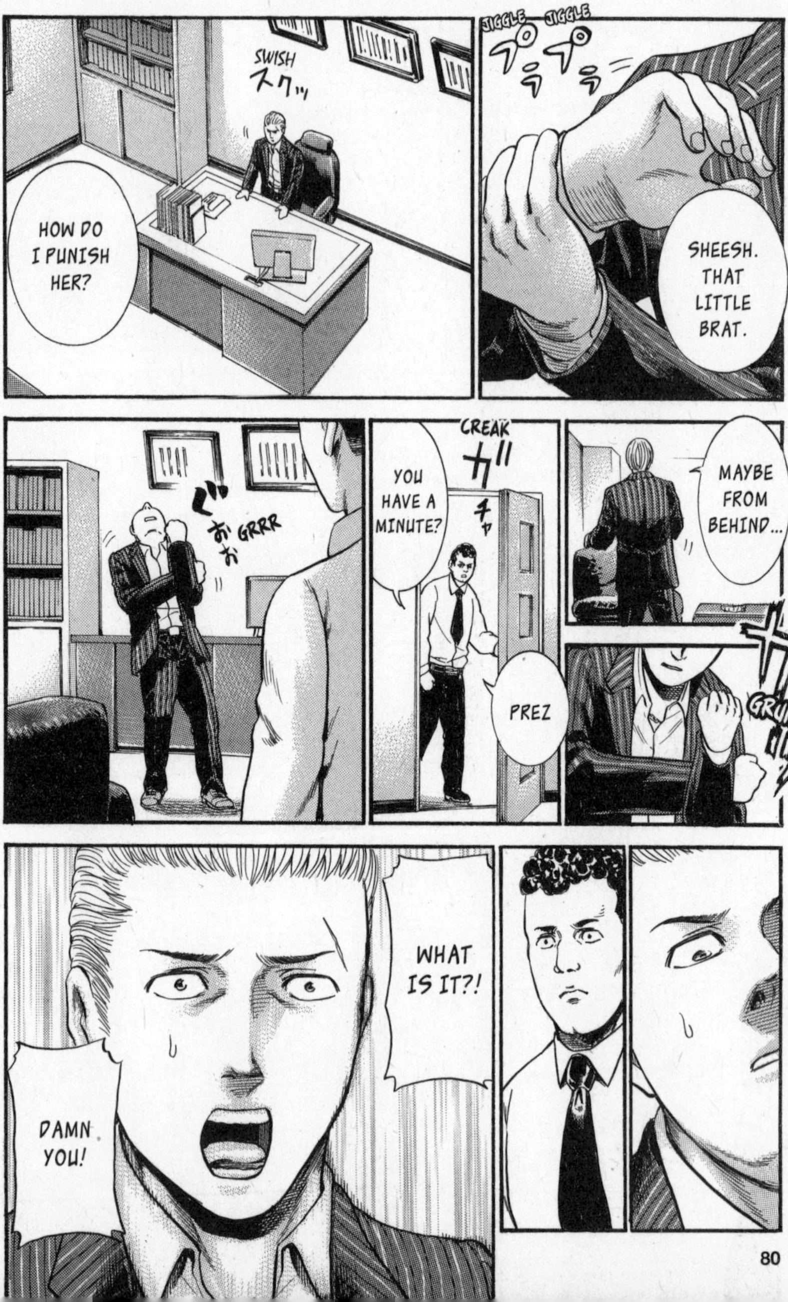
JIGGLE JIGGLE
プラプラ
SHEESH. THAT LITTLE BRAT.
SWISH
スクッ
HOW DO I PUNISH HER?
MAYBE FROM BEHIND...
ガバッ
GRUNT
CREAK
ガチャ
YOU HAVE A MINUTE?
PREZ
ぐおお
GRRR
WHAT IS IT?!
DAMN YOU!

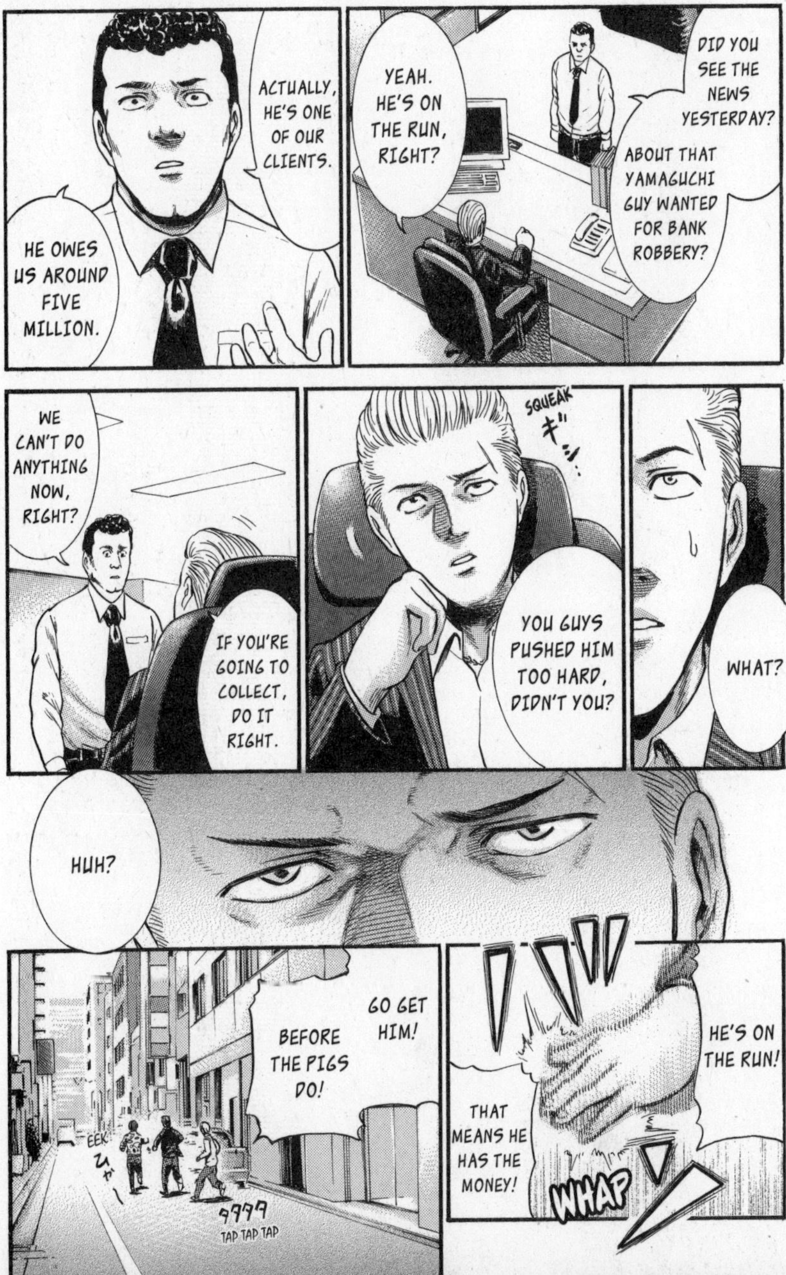
DID YOU SEE THE NEWS YESTERDAY?
ABOUT THAT YAMAGUCHI GUY WANTED FOR BANK ROBBERY?
YEAH. HE'S ON THE RUN, RIGHT?
ACTUALLY, HE'S ONE OF OUR CLIENTS.
HE OWES US AROUND FIVE MILLION.
WHAT?
SQUEAK
ギシ…
YOU GUYS PUSHED HIM TOO HARD, DIDN'T YOU?
WE CAN'T DO ANYTHING NOW, RIGHT?
IF YOU'RE GOING TO COLLECT, DO IT RIGHT.
HUH?
HE'S ON THE RUN!
THAT MEANS HE HAS THE MONEY!
WHAP
GO GET HIM!
BEFORE THE PIGS DO!
EEK
ひっ
タタタ
TAP TAP TAP

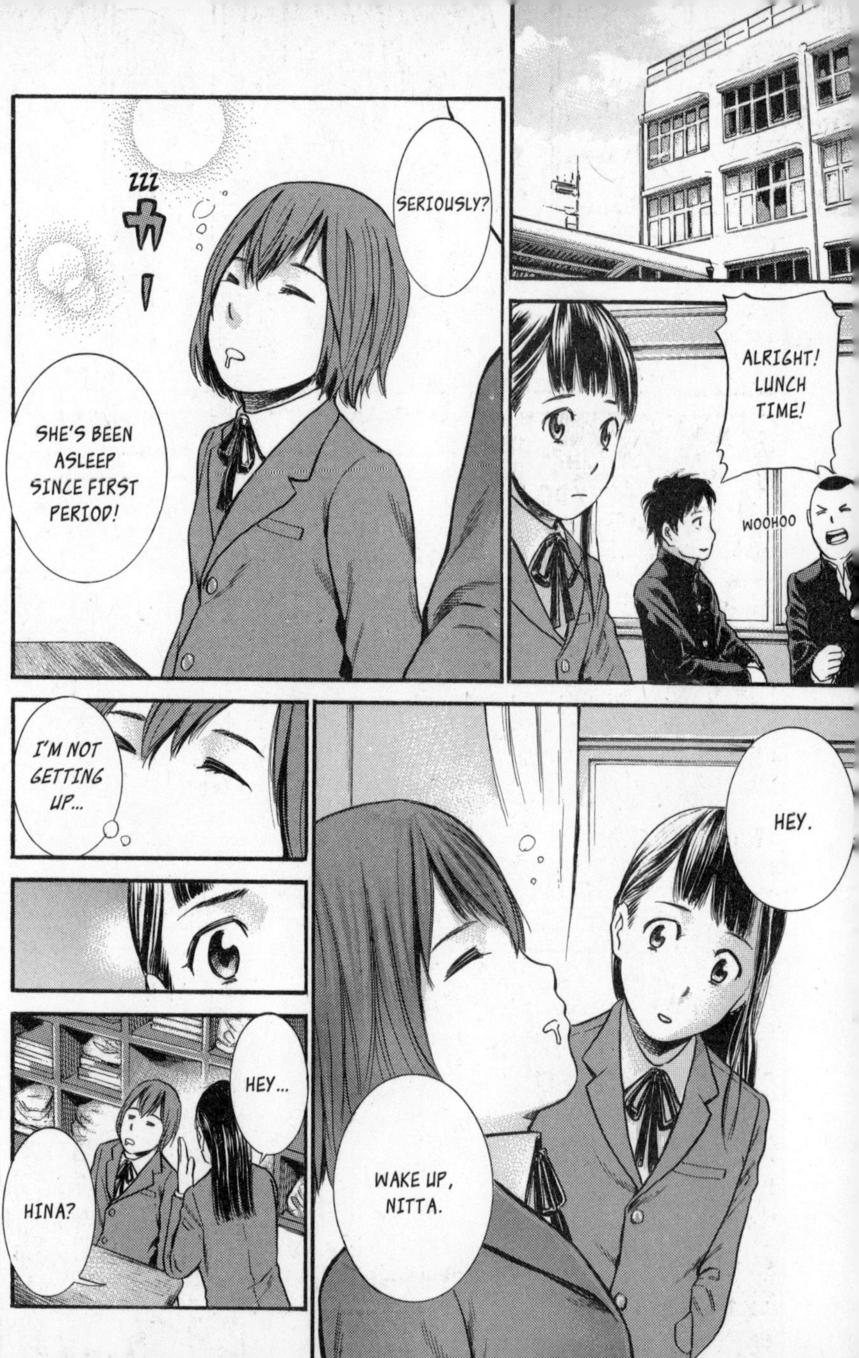
ALRIGHT! LUNCH TIME!
WOOHOO
SERIOUSLY?
ZZZ
SHE'S BEEN ASLEEP SINCE FIRST PERIOD!
HEY.
WAKE UP, NITTA.
I'M NOT GETTING UP...
HEY...
HINA?

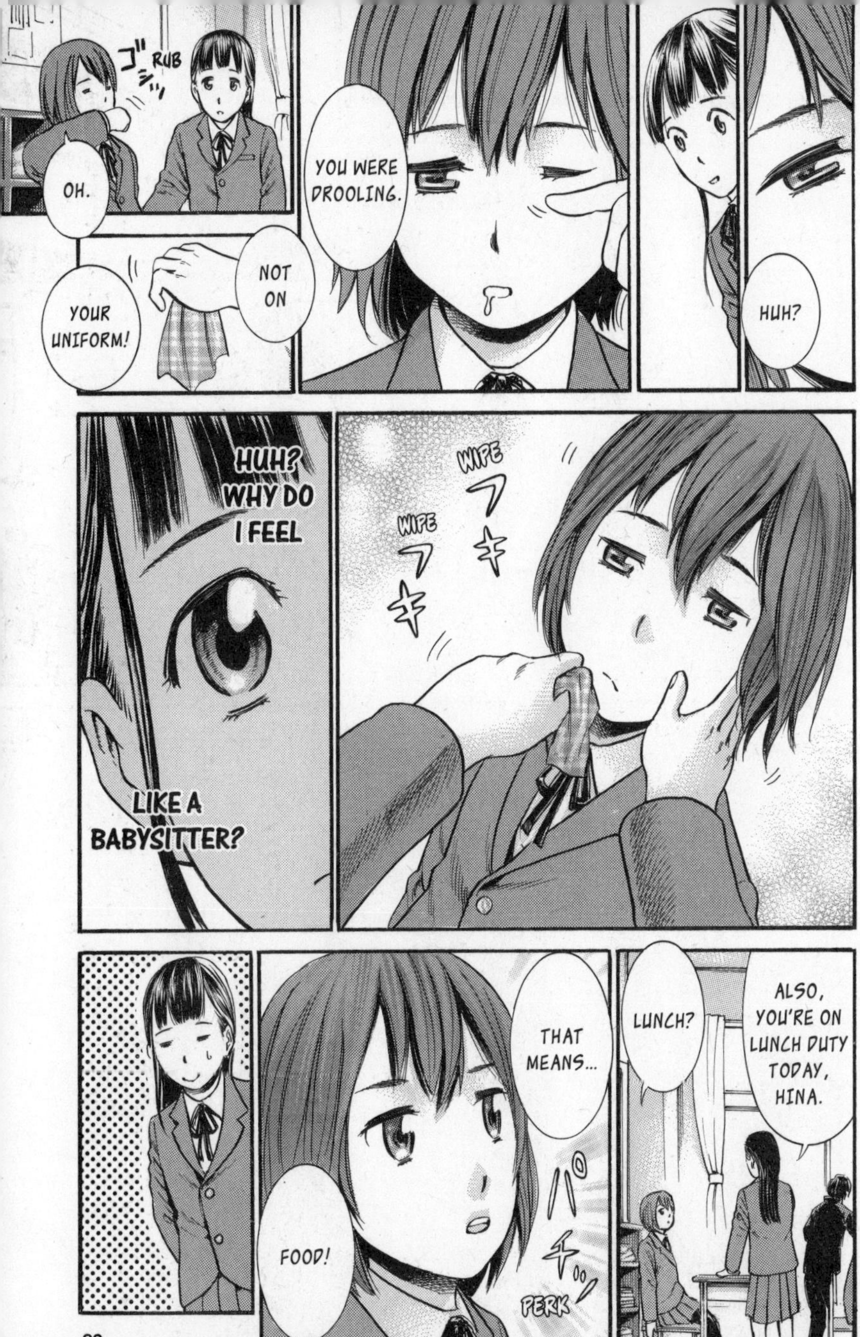
HUH?
YOU WERE DROOLING.
RUB
OH.
NOT ON
YOUR UNIFORM!
WIPE
WIPE
HUH? WHY DO I FEEL
LIKE A BABYSITTER?
ALSO, YOU'RE ON LUNCH DUTY TODAY, HINA.
LUNCH?
THAT MEANS...
FOOD!
PERK

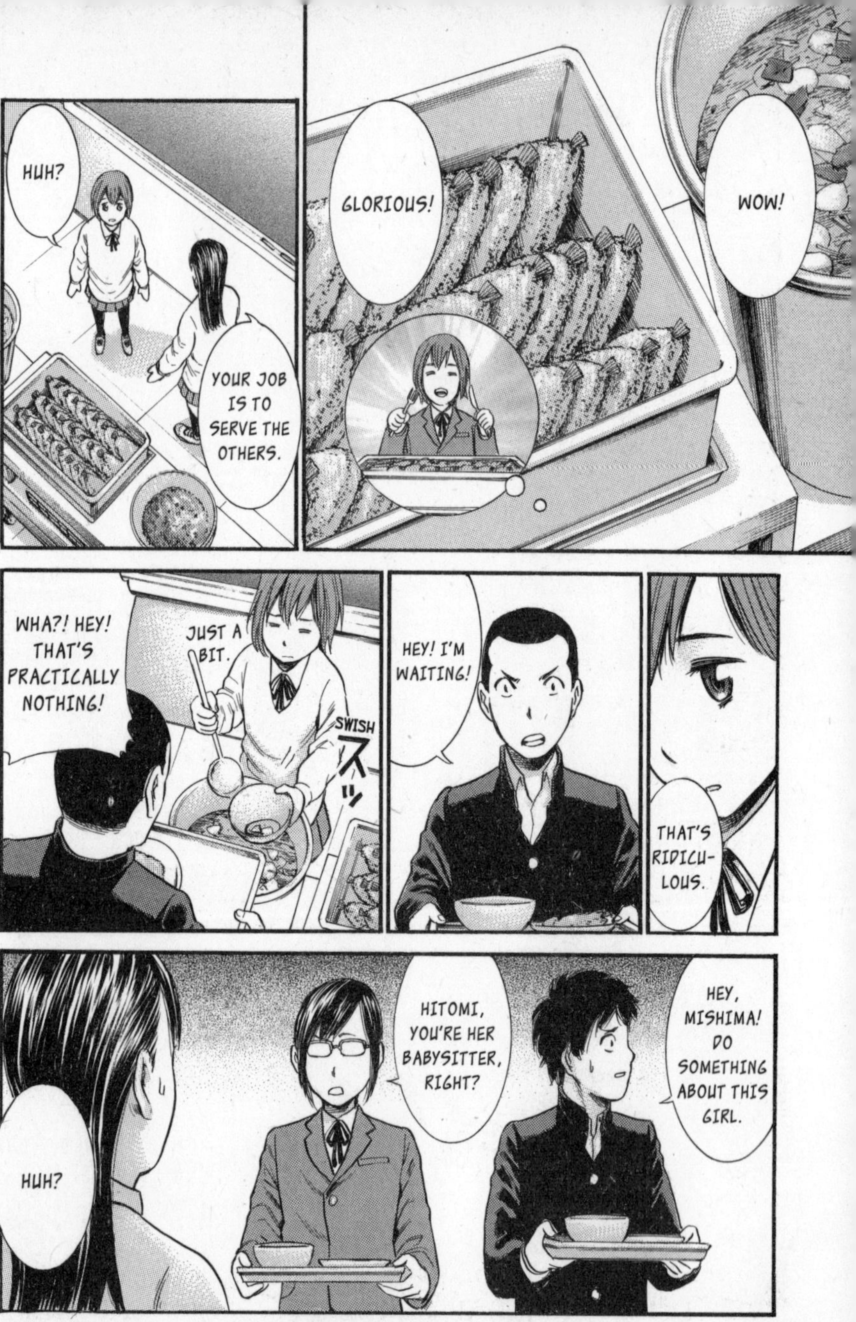
WOW!
GLORIOUS!
HUH?
YOUR JOB IS TO SERVE THE OTHERS.
THAT'S RIDICULOUS.
HEY! I'M WAITING!
JUST A BIT.
SWISH
WHA?! HEY! THAT'S PRACTICALLY NOTHING!
HEY, MISHIMA! DO SOMETHING ABOUT THIS GIRL.
HITOMI, YOU'RE HER BABYSITTER, RIGHT?
HUH?

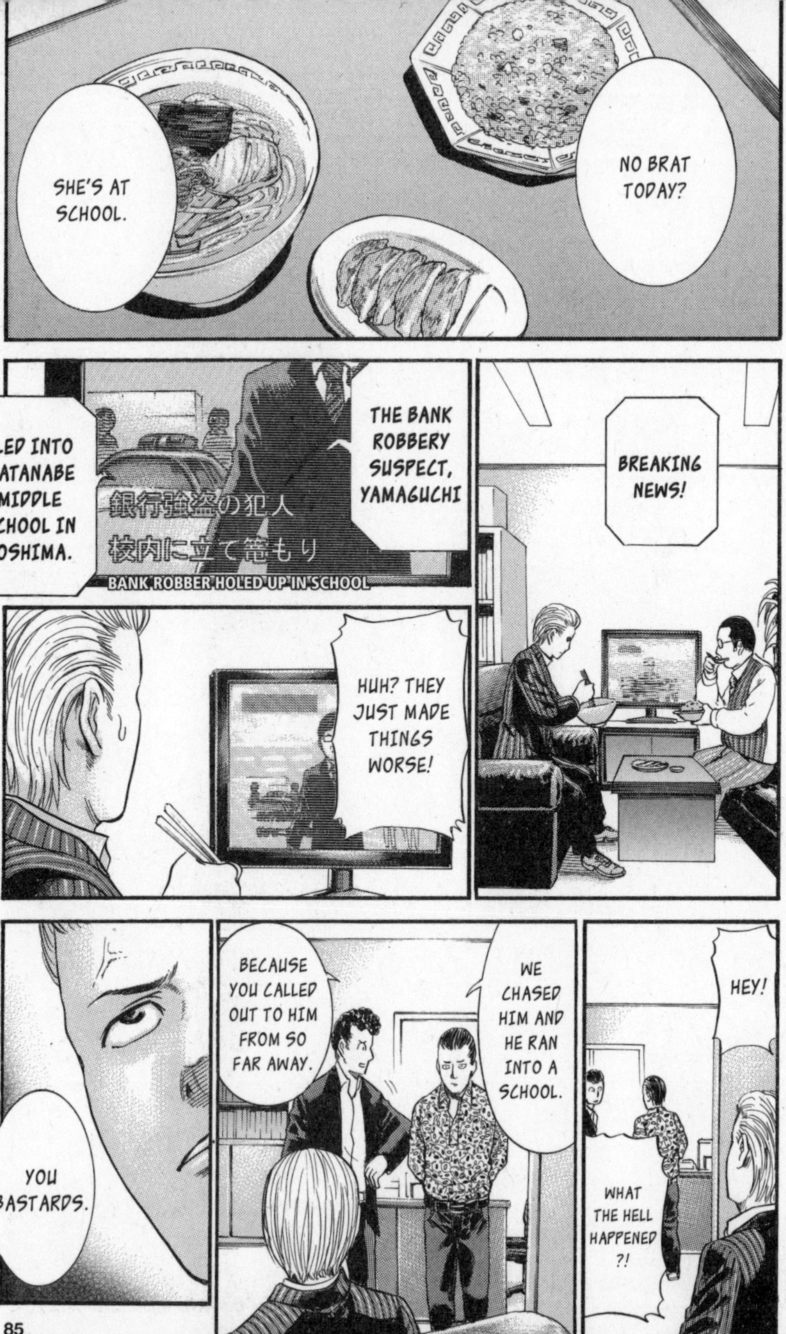
NO BRAT TODAY?
SHE'S AT SCHOOL.
BREAKING NEWS!
THE BANK ROBBERY SUSPECT, YAMAGUCHI
FLED INTO WATANABE MIDDLE SCHOOL IN TOSHIMA.
銀行強盗の犯人
校内に立て篭もり
BANK ROBBER HOLED UP IN SCHOOL
HUH? THEY JUST MADE THINGS WORSE!
HEY!
WHAT THE HELL HAPPENED?!
WE CHASED HIM AND HE RAN INTO A SCHOOL.
BECAUSE YOU CALLED OUT TO HIM FROM SO FAR AWAY.
YOU BASTARDS.

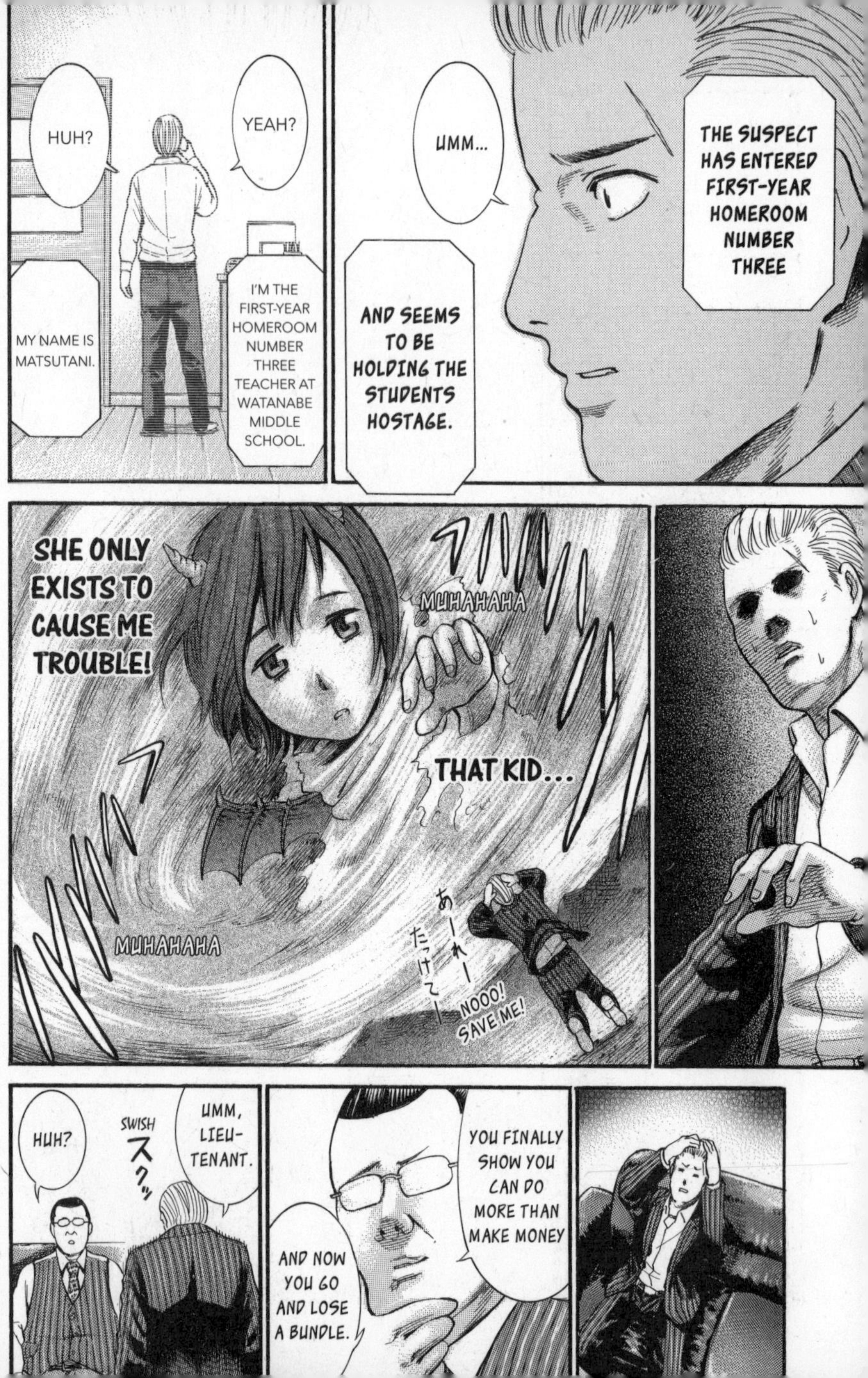
THE SUSPECT HAS ENTERED FIRST-YEAR HOMEROOM NUMBER THREE
UMM...
AND SEEMS TO BE HOLDING THE STUDENTS HOSTAGE.
YEAH?
HUH?
I'M THE FIRST-YEAR HOMEROOM NUMBER THREE TEACHER AT WATANABE MIDDLE SCHOOL.
MY NAME IS MATSUTANI.
THAT KID...
SHE ONLY EXISTS TO CAUSE ME TROUBLE!
MUHAHAHA
あーれー
たっけてー
NOOO! SAVE ME!
MUHAHAHA
YOU FINALLY SHOW YOU CAN DO MORE THAN MAKE MONEY
AND NOW YOU GO AND LOSE A BUNDLE.
UMM, LIEU-TENANT.
SWISH
スクッ
HUH?

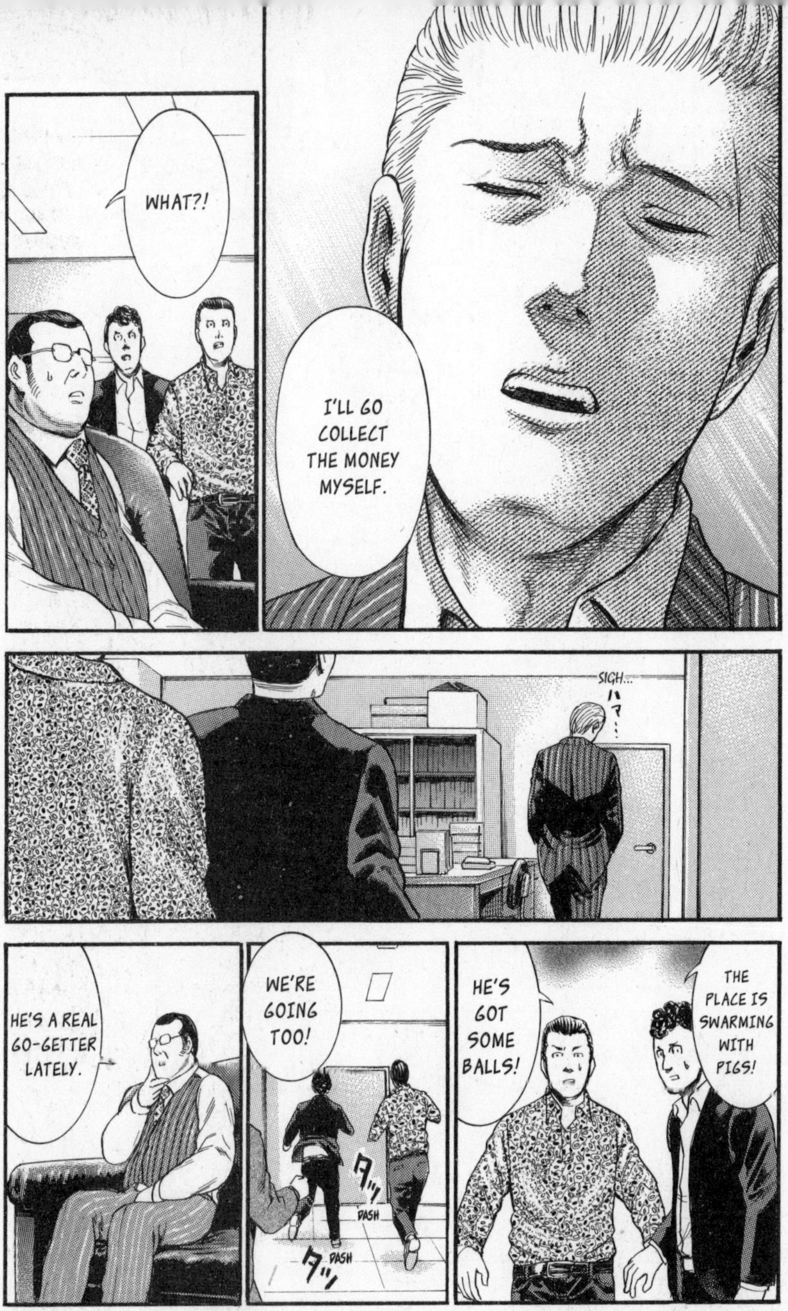
I'LL GO COLLECT THE MONEY MYSELF.
WHAT?!
SIGH...
ハァ…
THE PLACE IS SWARMING WITH PIGS!
HE'S GOT SOME BALLS!
WE'RE GOING TOO!
タッ
DASH
タッ
DASH
HE'S A REAL GO-GETTER LATELY.

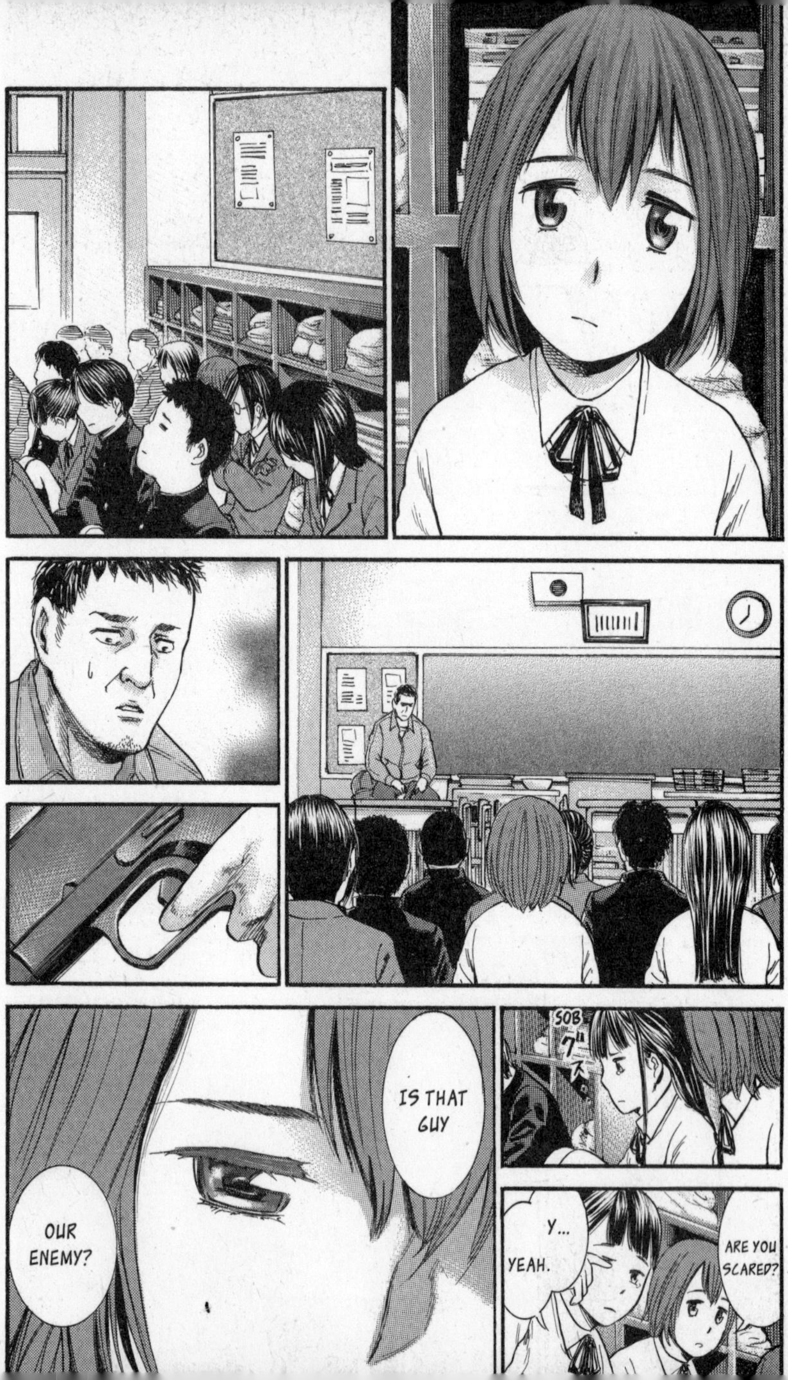
SOB
グス
ARE YOU SCARED?
Y... YEAH.
IS THAT GUY
OUR ENEMY?

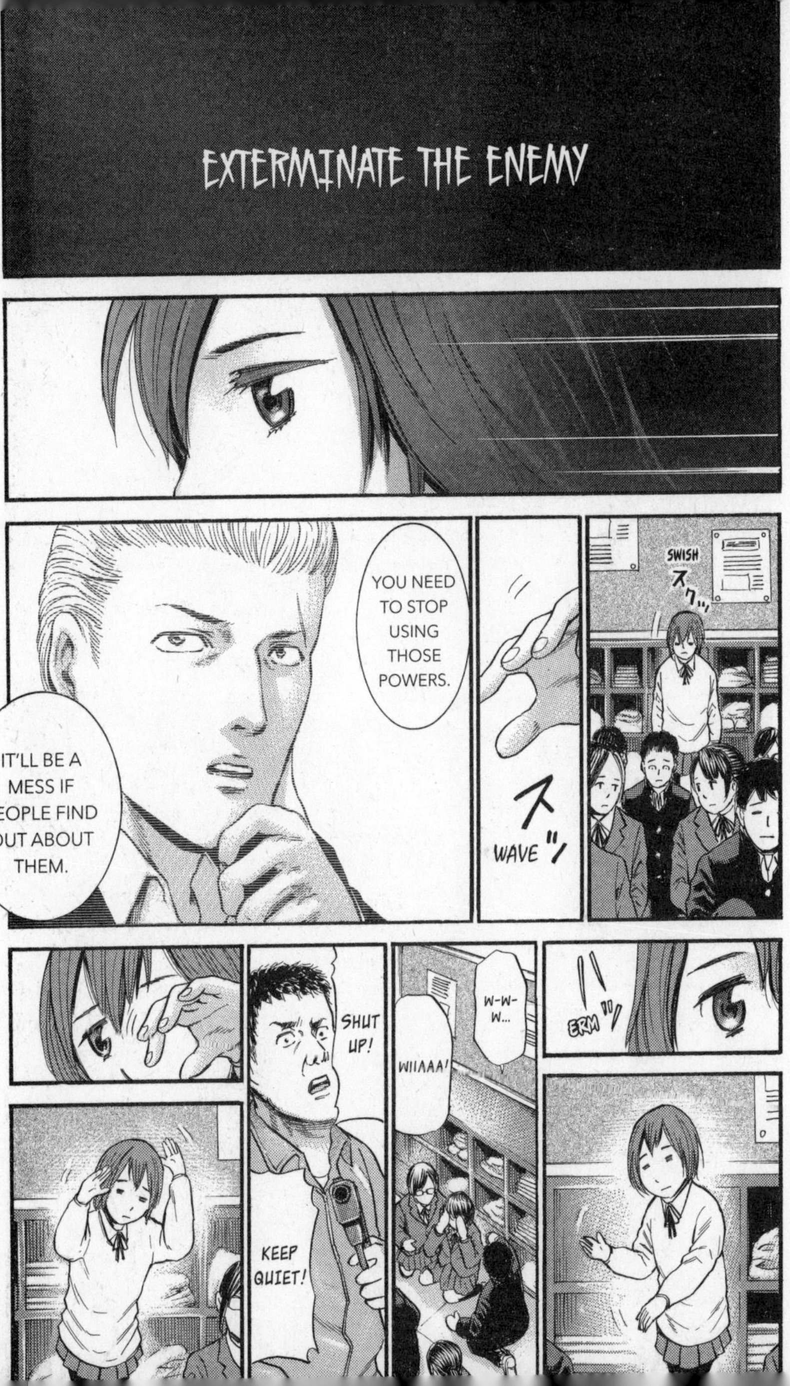
EXTERMINATE THE ENEMY
SWISH
スクッ
スッ
WAVE
YOU NEED TO STOP USING THOSE POWERS.
IT'LL BE A MESS IF PEOPLE FIND OUT ABOUT THEM.
ハッ
ERM
W-W-W...
WIIAAA!
SHUT UP!
KEEP QUIET!

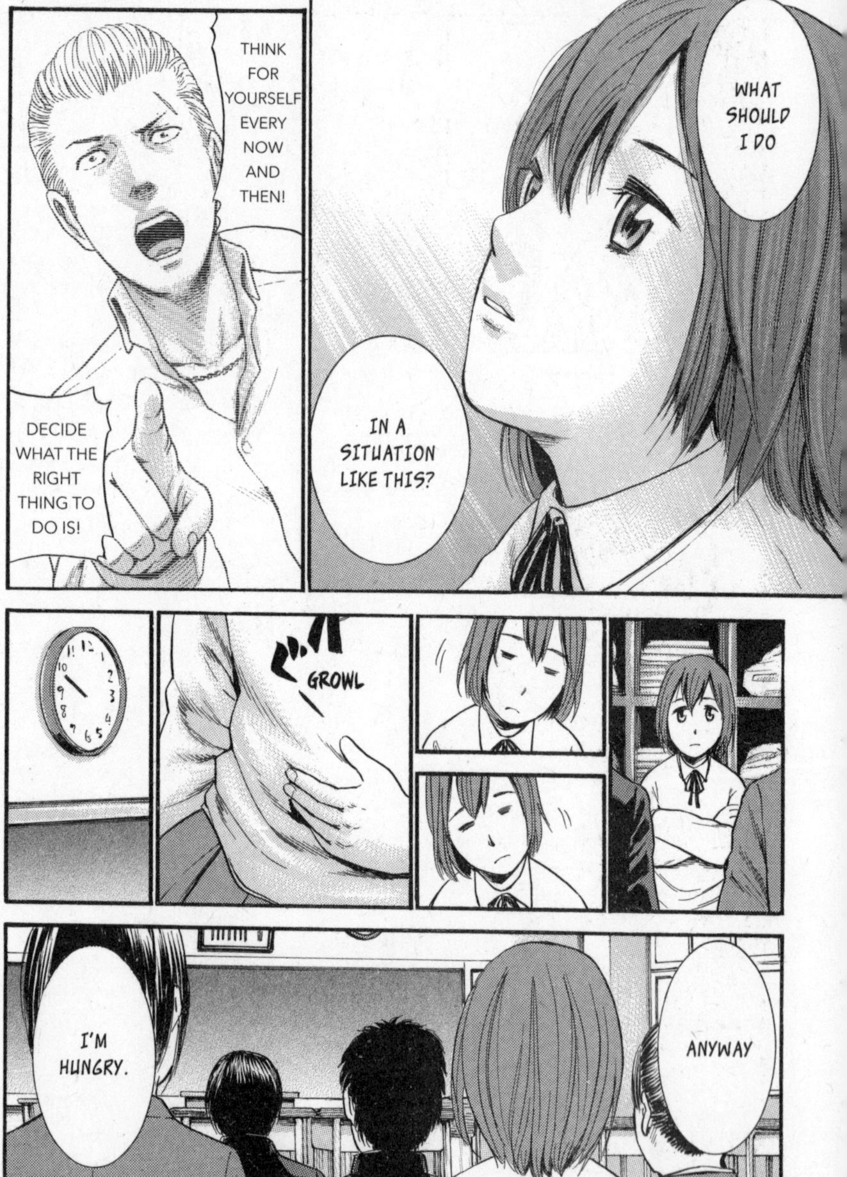
WHAT SHOULD I DO
IN A SITUATION LIKE THIS?
THINK FOR YOURSELF EVERY NOW AND THEN!
DECIDE WHAT THE RIGHT THING TO DO IS!
GROWL
ANYWAY
I'M HUNGRY.

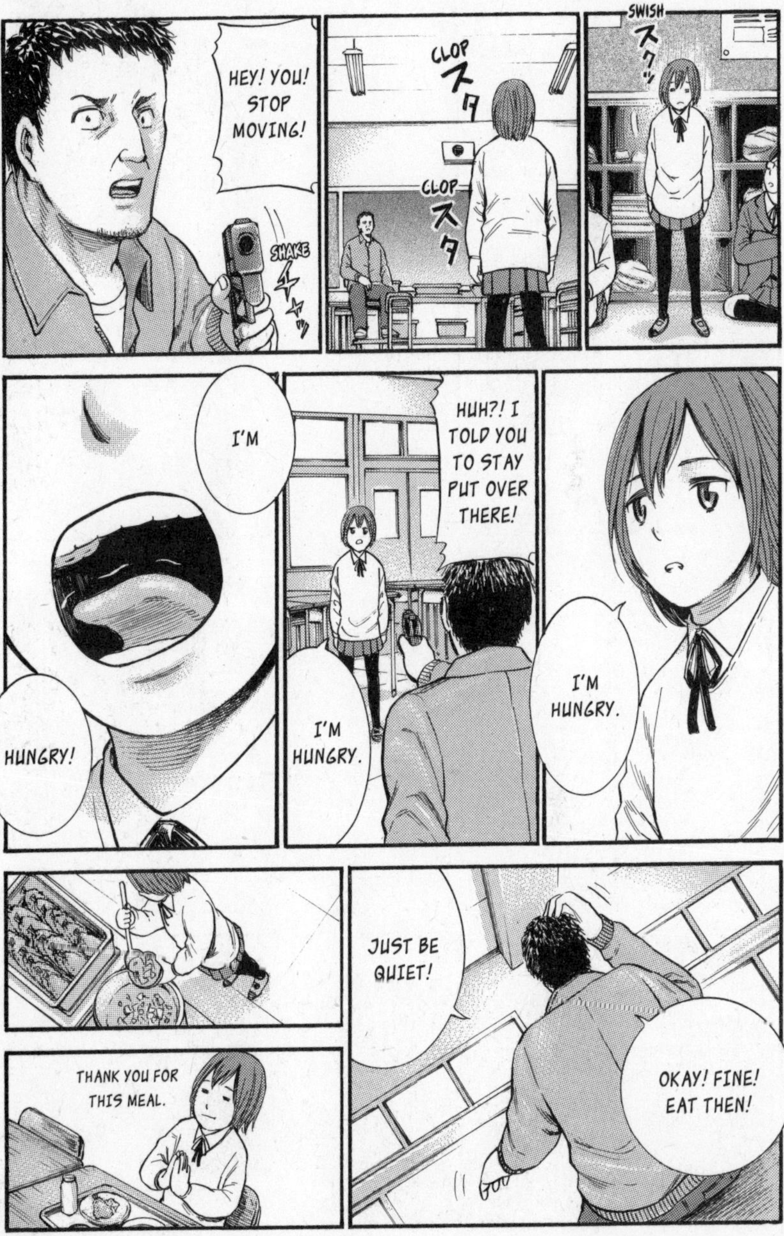
SWISH
スクッ
CLOP
スタ
CLOP
スタ
HEY! YOU! STOP MOVING!
SHAKE
I'M HUNGRY.
HUH?! I TOLD YOU TO STAY PUT OVER THERE!
I'M HUNGRY.
I'M
HUNGRY!
JUST BE QUIET!
OKAY! FINE! EAT THEN!
THANK YOU FOR THIS MEAL.

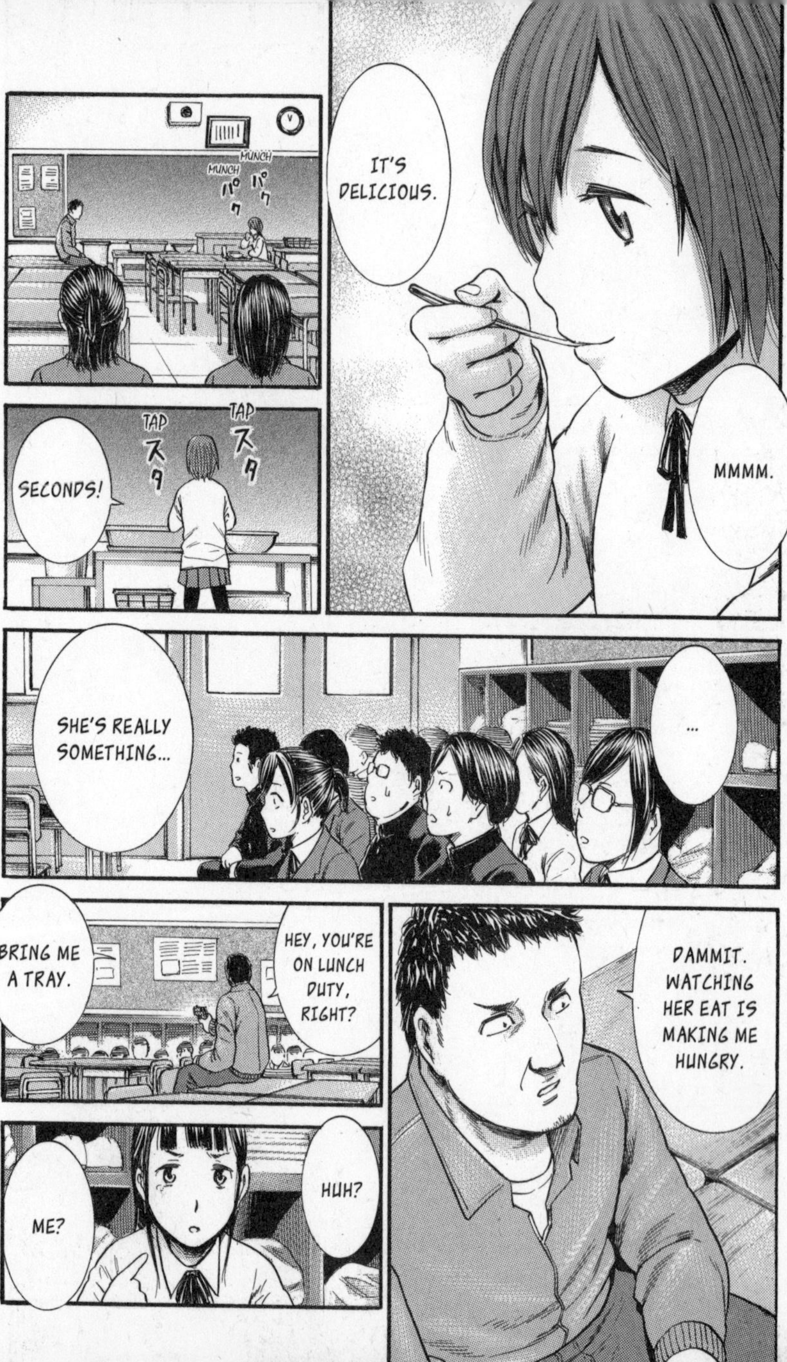
IT'S DELICIOUS.
MMMM.
MUNCH パク
MUNCH パク
TAP スタ
TAP スタ
SECONDS!
...
SHE'S REALLY SOMETHING...
DAMMIT. WATCHING HER EAT IS MAKING ME HUNGRY.
HEY, YOU'RE ON LUNCH DUTY, RIGHT?
BRING ME A TRAY.
HUH?
ME?

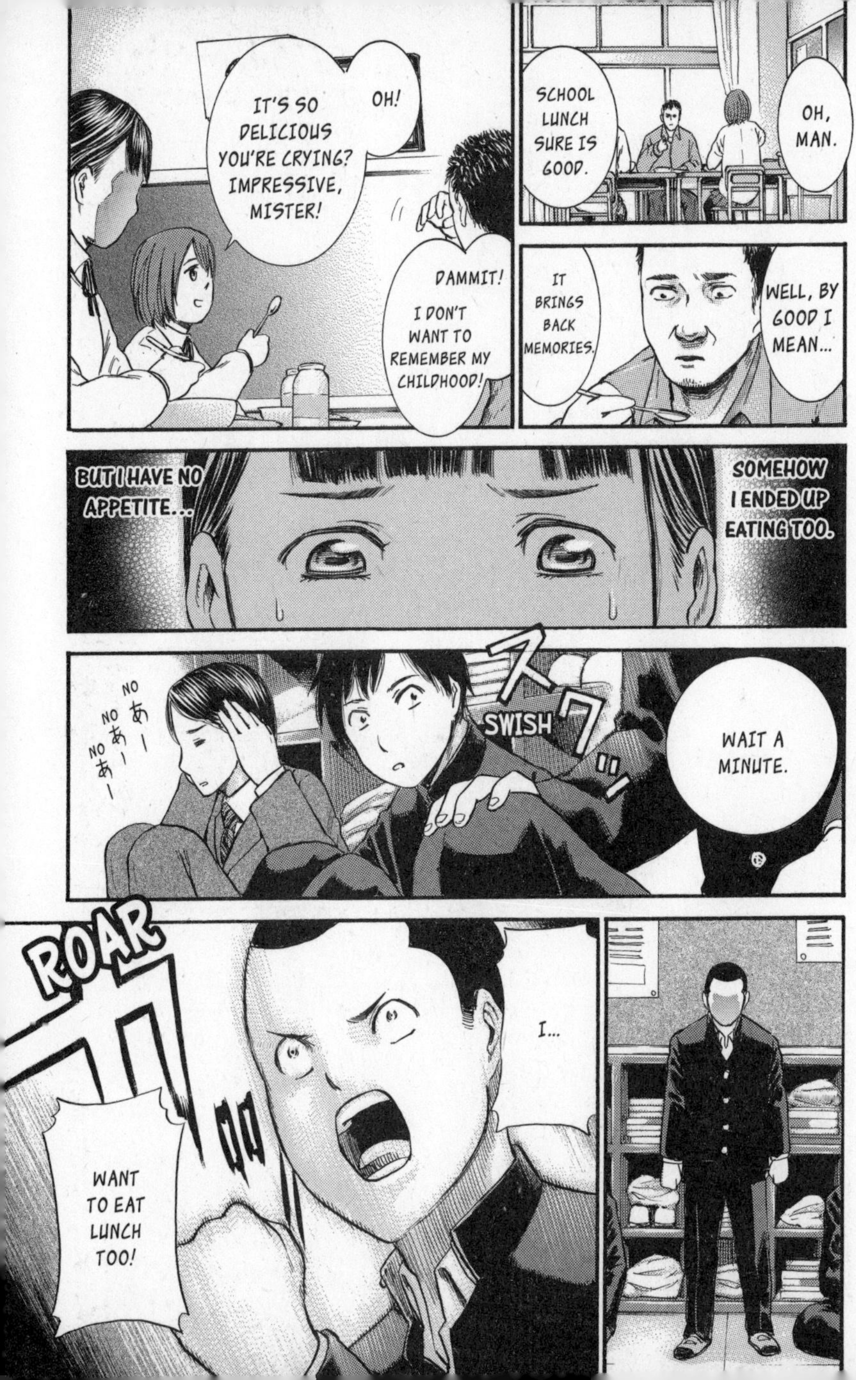
OH, MAN.
SCHOOL LUNCH SURE IS GOOD.
WELL, BY GOOD I MEAN...
IT BRINGS BACK MEMORIES.
OH!
IT'S SO DELICIOUS YOU'RE CRYING? IMPRESSIVE, MISTER!
DAMMIT!
I DON'T WANT TO REMEMBER MY CHILDHOOD!
SOMEHOW I ENDED UP EATING TOO.
BUT I HAVE NO APPETITE...
WAIT A MINUTE.
SWISH
NO あー
NO あー
NO あー
I...
WANT TO EAT LUNCH TOO!
ROAR

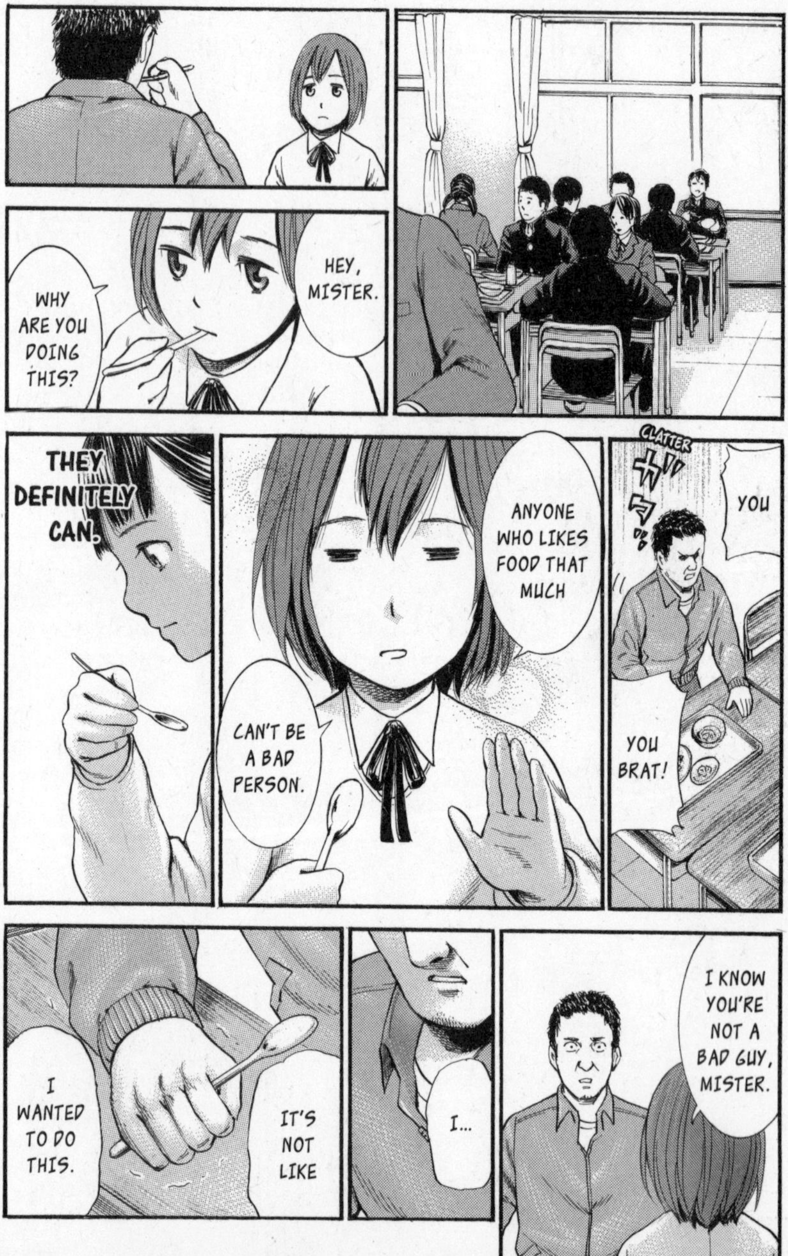
HEY, MISTER.
WHY ARE YOU DOING THIS?
CLATTER
YOU
YOU BRAT!
ANYONE WHO LIKES FOOD THAT MUCH
CAN'T BE A BAD PERSON.
THEY DEFINITELY CAN.
I KNOW YOU'RE NOT A BAD GUY, MISTER.
I...
IT'S NOT LIKE
I WANTED TO DO THIS.

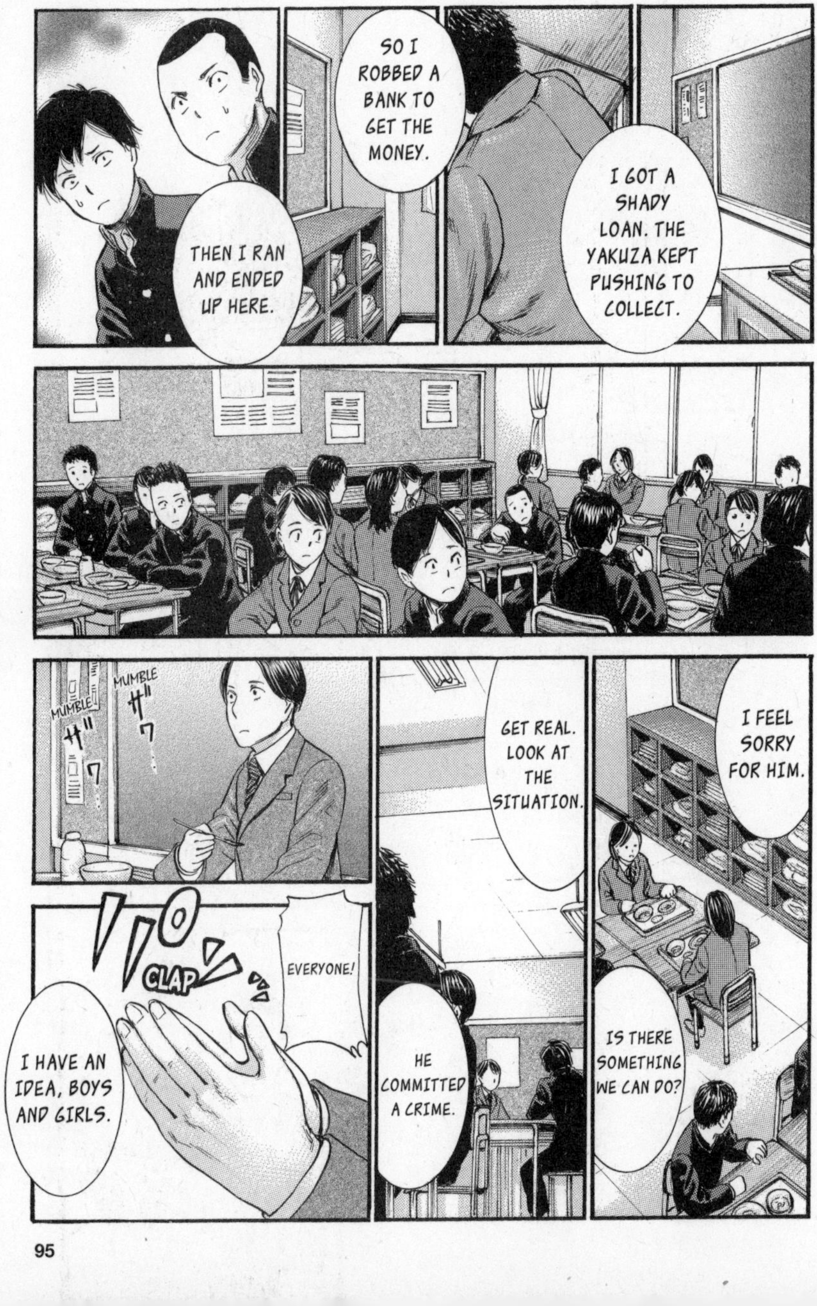
I GOT A SHADY LOAN. THE YAKUZA KEPT PUSHING TO COLLECT.
SO I ROBBED A BANK TO GET THE MONEY.
THEN I RAN AND ENDED UP HERE.
I FEEL SORRY FOR HIM.
IS THERE SOMETHING WE CAN DO?
GET REAL. LOOK AT THE SITUATION.
HE COMMITTED A CRIME.
MUMBLE
ザワ
MUMBLE
ザワ
CLAP
EVERYONE!
I HAVE AN IDEA, BOYS AND GIRLS.

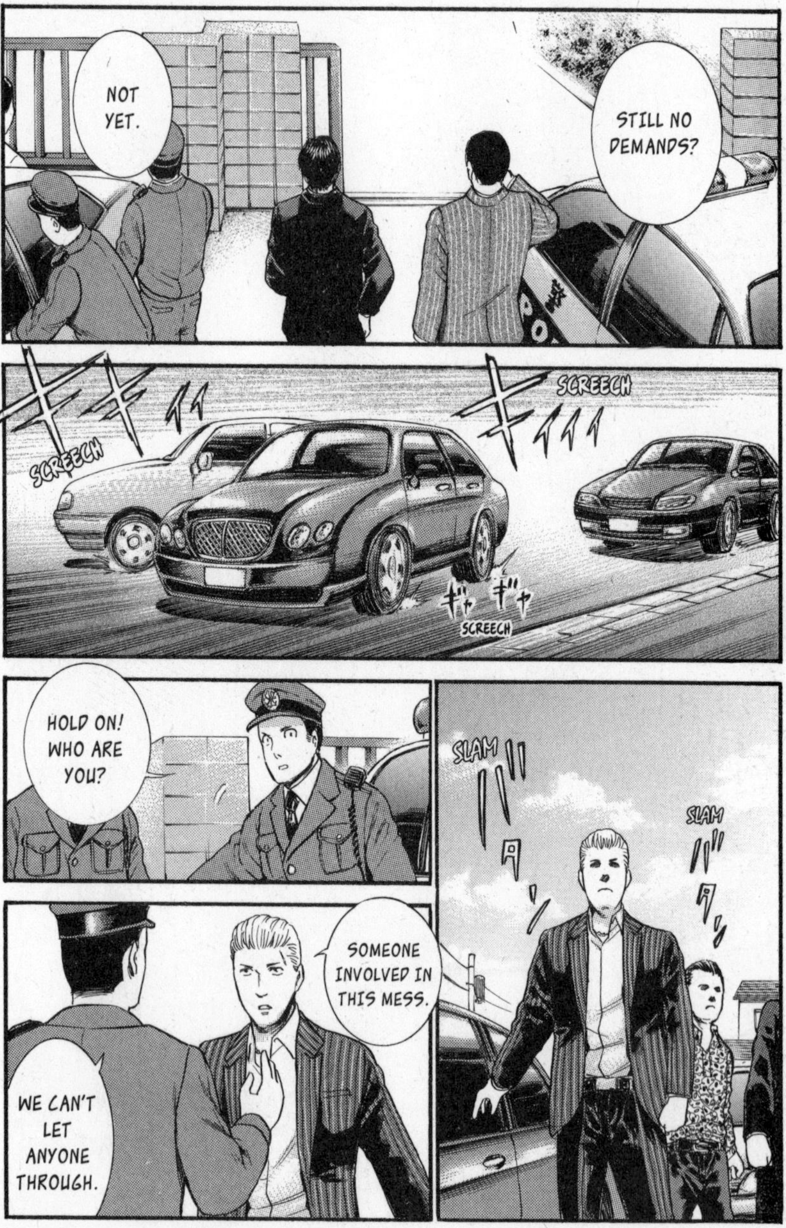
STILL NO DEMANDS?
NOT YET.
SCREECH
SCREECH
SCREECH
SLAM
SLAM
HOLD ON! WHO ARE YOU?
SOMEONE INVOLVED IN THIS MESS.
WE CAN'T LET ANYONE THROUGH.

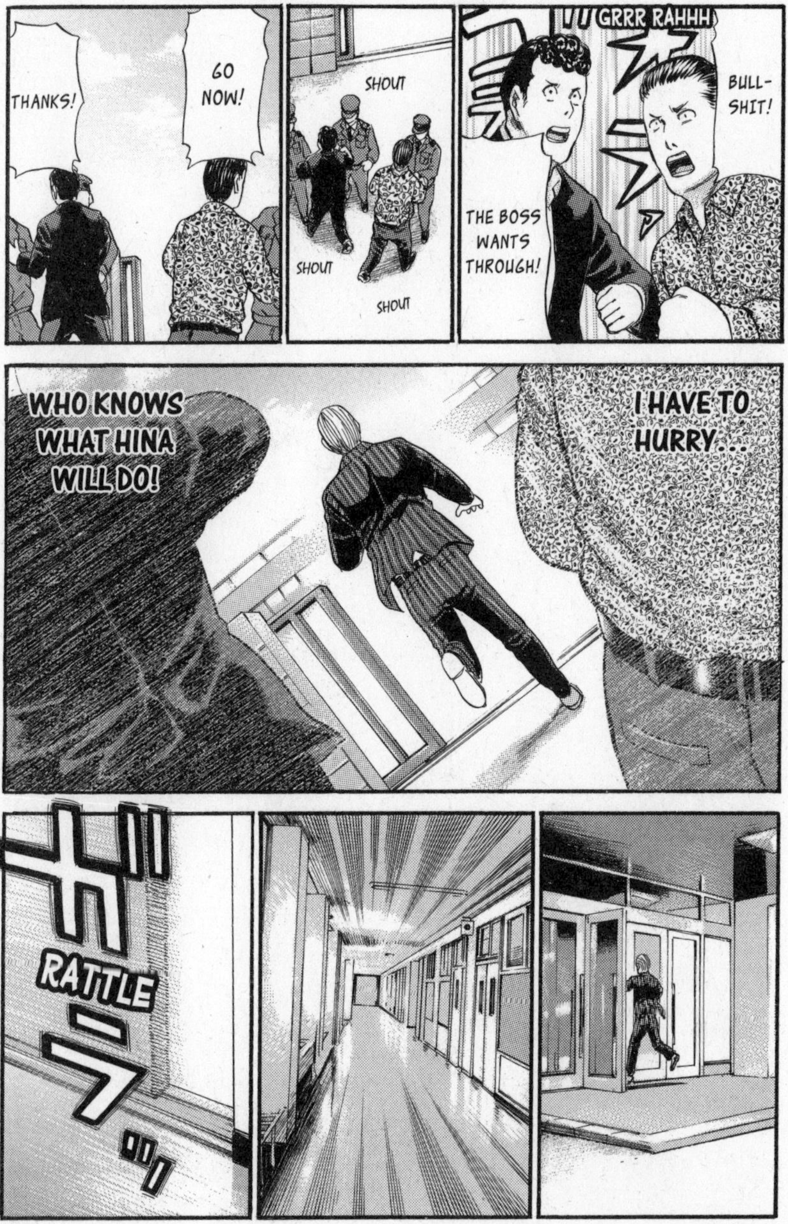
GRRR RAHHH
BULL-SHIT!
THE BOSS WANTS THROUGH!
SHOUT
SHOUT
SHOUT
GO NOW!
THANKS!
I HAVE TO HURRY...
WHO KNOWS WHAT HINA WILL DO!
RATTLE

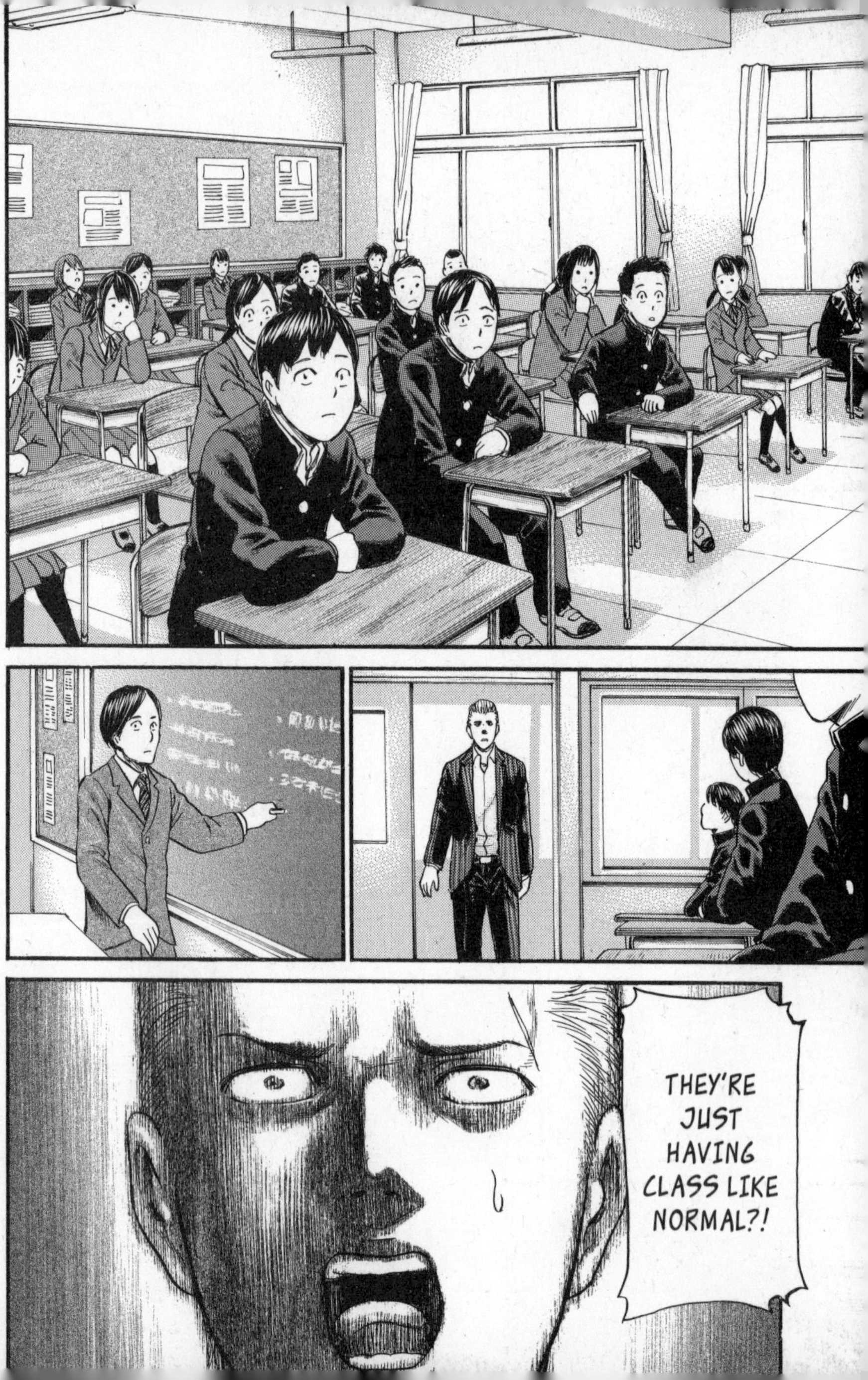
THEY'RE JUST HAVING CLASS LIKE NORMAL?!

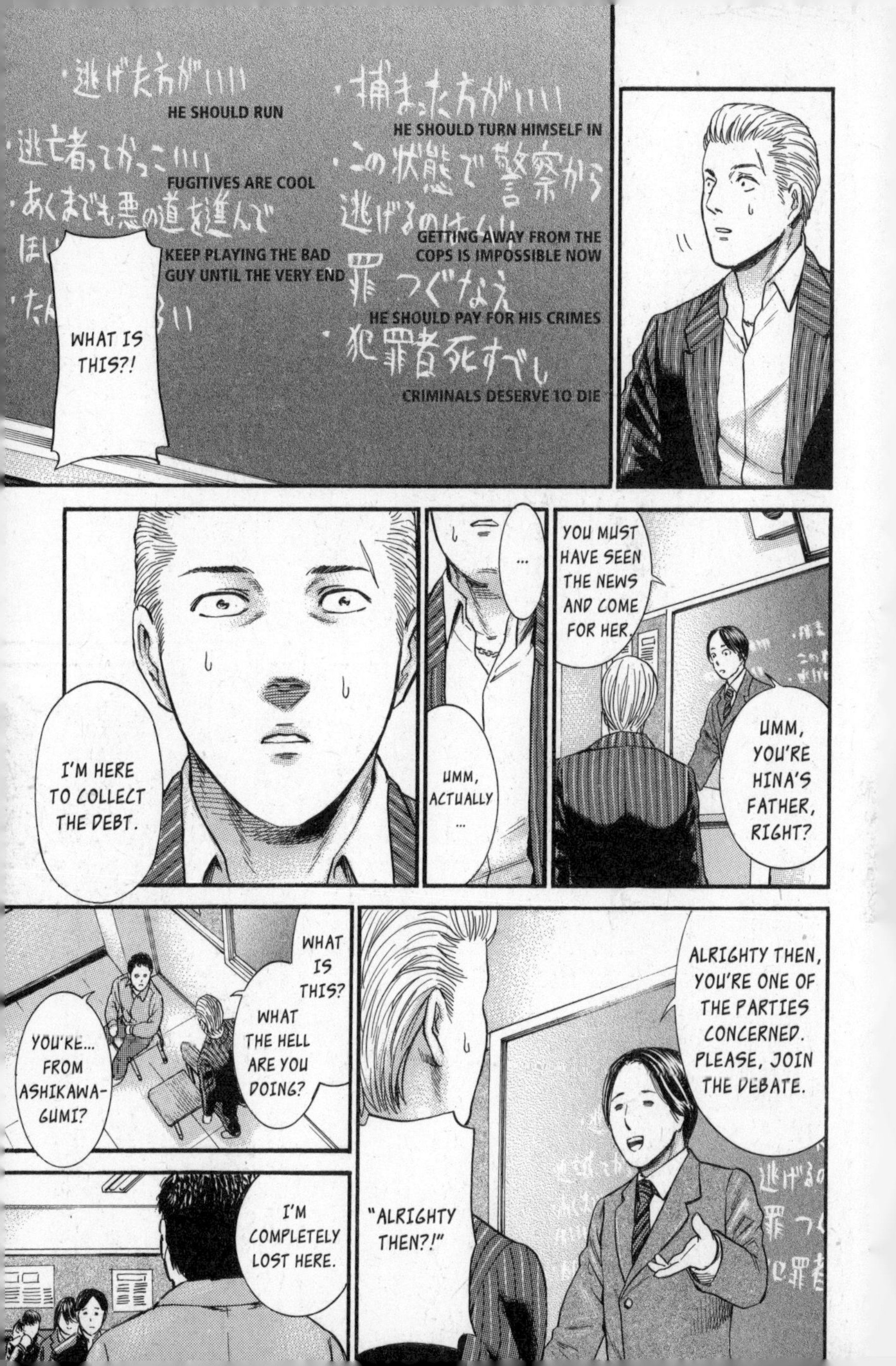
・捕まった方がいい
HE SHOULD TURN HIMSELF IN
・この状態で警察から逃げるのは無理
GETTING AWAY FROM THE COPS IS IMPOSSIBLE NOW
・罪つぐなえ
HE SHOULD PAY FOR HIS CRIMES
・犯罪者死すべし
CRIMINALS DESERVE TO DIE
・逃げた方がいい
HE SHOULD RUN
・逃亡者ってかっこいい
FUGITIVES ARE COOL
・あくまでも悪の道を進んで
KEEP PLAYING THE BAD GUY UNTIL THE VERY END
WHAT IS THIS?!
YOU MUST HAVE SEEN THE NEWS AND COME FOR HER.
UMM, YOU'RE HINA'S FATHER, RIGHT?
...
UMM, ACTUALLY ...
I'M HERE TO COLLECT THE DEBT.
ALRIGHTY THEN, YOU'RE ONE OF THE PARTIES CONCERNED. PLEASE, JOIN THE DEBATE.
"ALRIGHTY THEN?!"
WHAT IS THIS?
WHAT THE HELL ARE YOU DOING?
YOU'RE... FROM ASHIKAWA-GUMI?
I'M COMPLETELY LOST HERE.

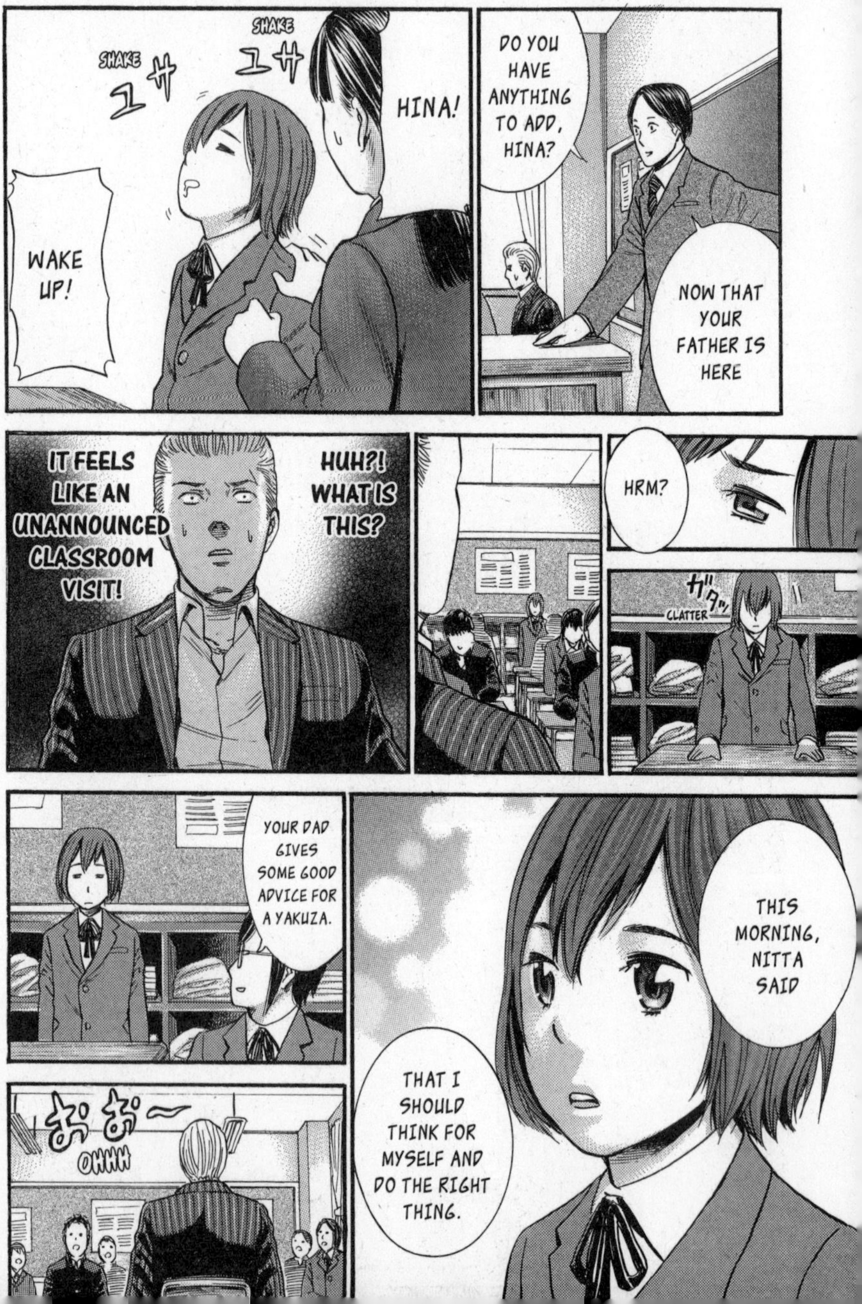
DO YOU HAVE ANYTHING TO ADD, HINA?
NOW THAT YOUR FATHER IS HERE
ユサ
SHAKE
ユサ
SHAKE
HINA!
WAKE UP!
HRM?
ガタッ
CLATTER
HUH?! WHAT IS THIS?
IT FEELS LIKE AN UNANNOUNCED CLASSROOM VISIT!
THIS MORNING, NITTA SAID
THAT I SHOULD THINK FOR MYSELF AND DO THE RIGHT THING.
YOUR DAD GIVES SOME GOOD ADVICE FOR A YAKUZA.
おぉ～
OHHH

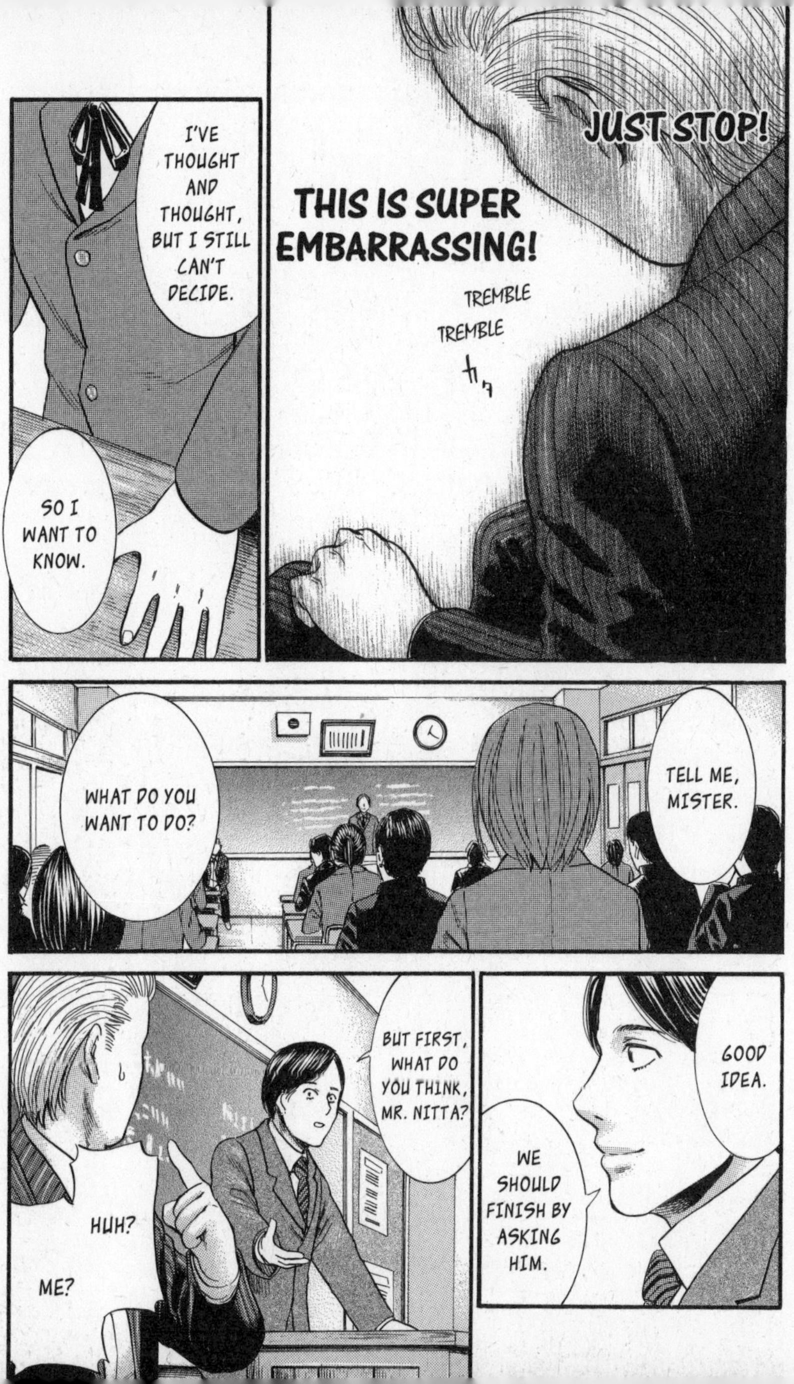
JUST STOP!
THIS IS SUPER EMBARRASSING!
TREMBLE
TREMBLE
I'VE THOUGHT AND THOUGHT, BUT I STILL CAN'T DECIDE.
SO I WANT TO KNOW.
TELL ME, MISTER.
WHAT DO YOU WANT TO DO?
GOOD IDEA.
WE SHOULD FINISH BY ASKING HIM.
BUT FIRST, WHAT DO YOU THINK, MR. NITTA?
HUH?
ME?

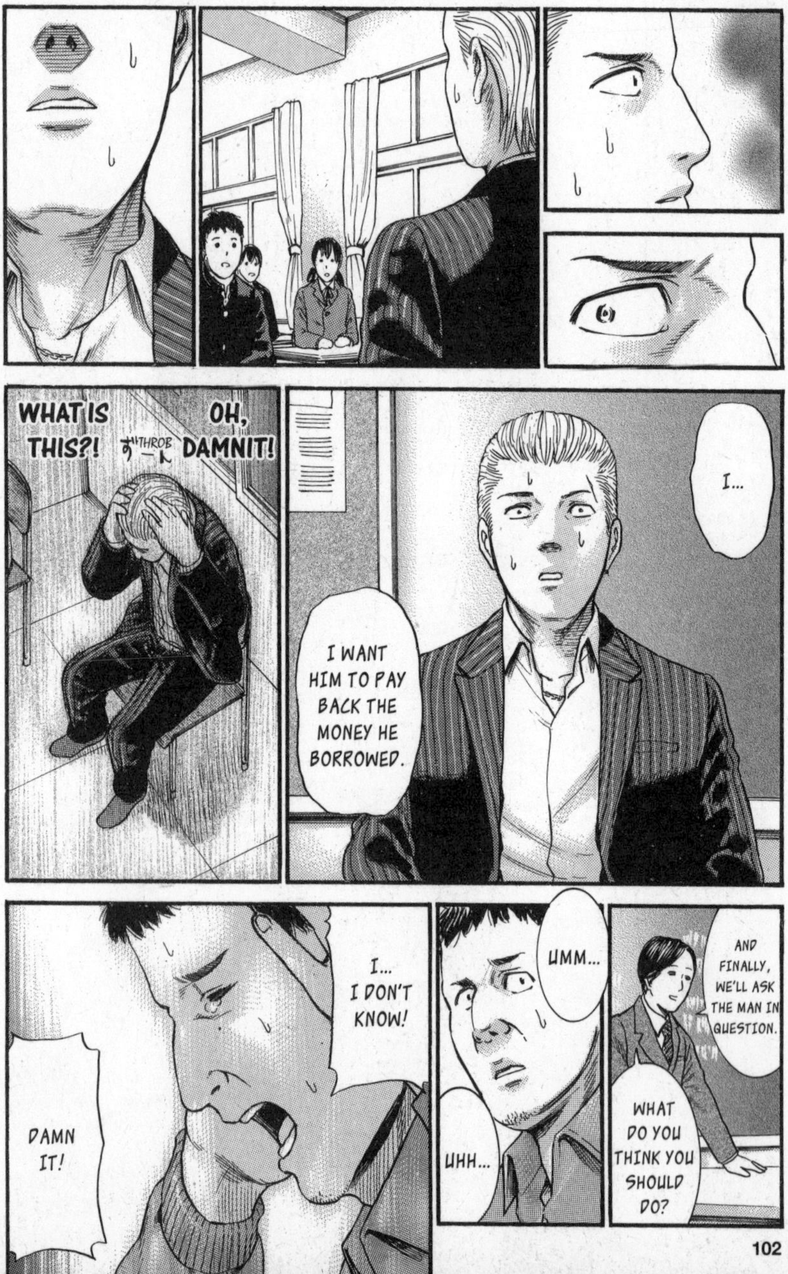
I...
I WANT HIM TO PAY BACK THE MONEY HE BORROWED.
OH, DAMNIT!
ずーん THROB
WHAT IS THIS?!
AND FINALLY, WE'LL ASK THE MAN IN QUESTION.
WHAT DO YOU THINK YOU SHOULD DO?
UMM...
UHH...
I... I DON'T KNOW!
DAMN IT!

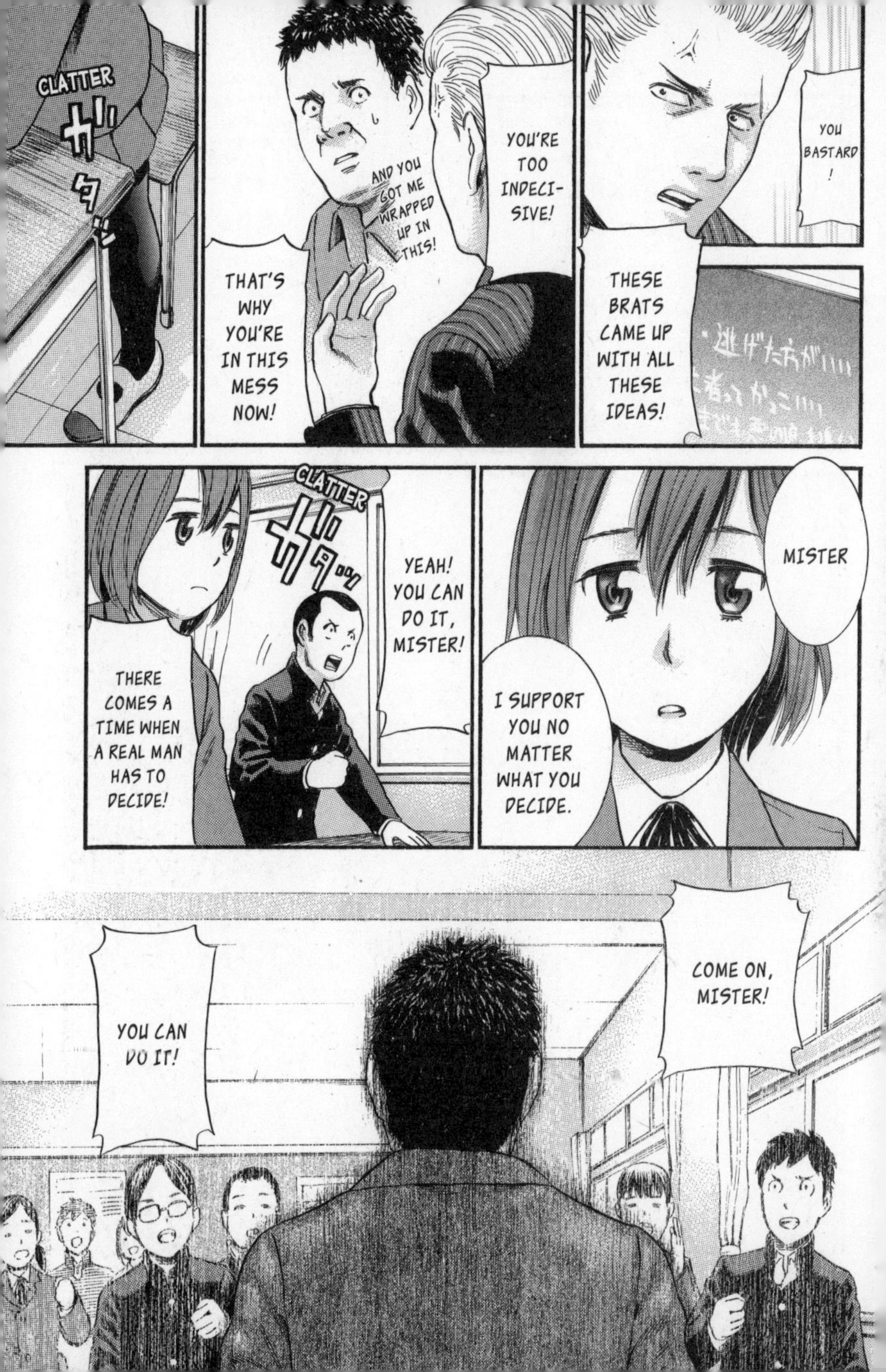
YOU BASTARD!
THESE BRATS CAME UP WITH ALL THESE IDEAS!
YOU'RE TOO INDECISIVE!
AND YOU GOT ME WRAPPED UP IN THIS!
THAT'S WHY YOU'RE IN THIS MESS NOW!
CLATTER
MISTER
I SUPPORT YOU NO MATTER WHAT YOU DECIDE.
CLATTER
YEAH! YOU CAN DO IT, MISTER!
THERE COMES A TIME WHEN A REAL MAN HAS TO DECIDE!
COME ON, MISTER!
YOU CAN DO IT!

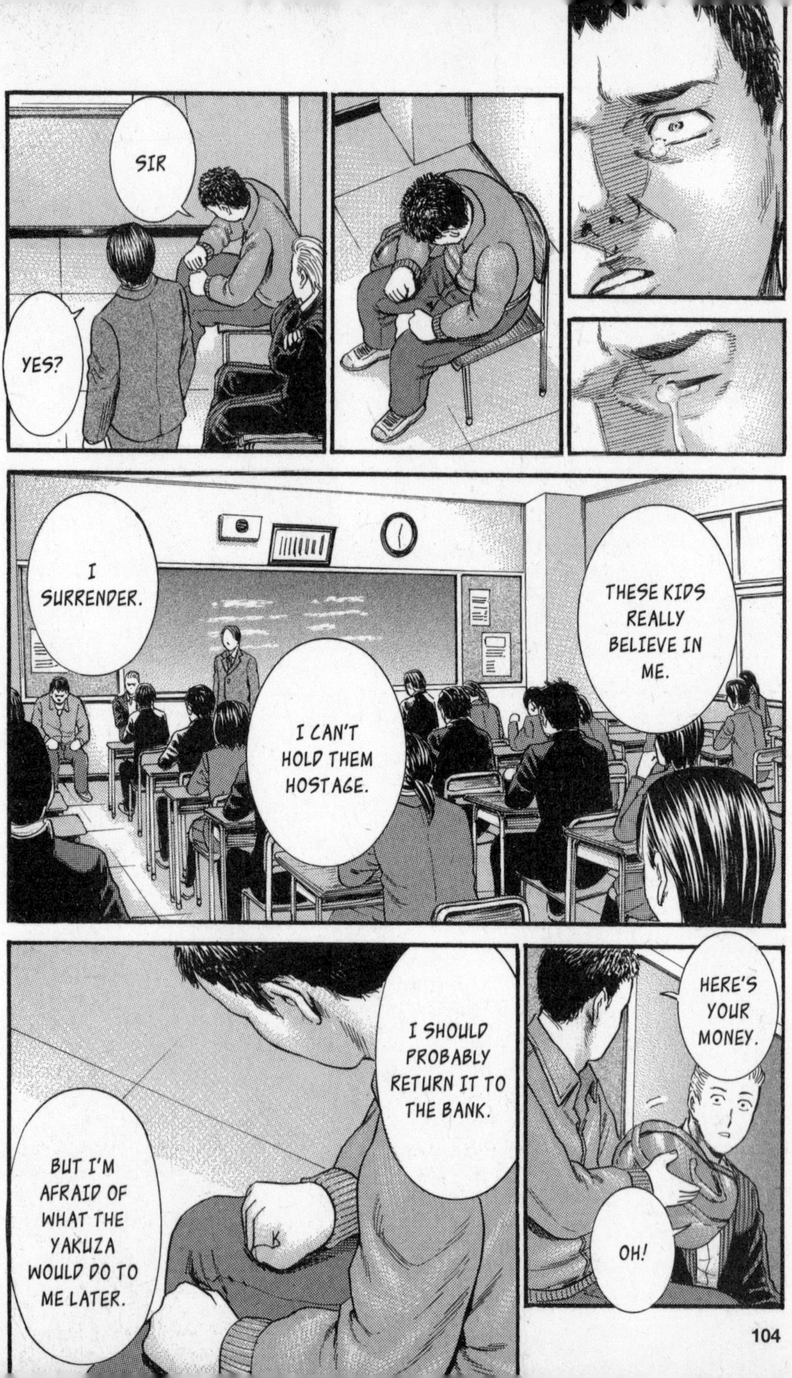
SIR
YES?
THESE KIDS REALLY BELIEVE IN ME.
I CAN'T HOLD THEM HOSTAGE.
I SURRENDER.
HERE'S YOUR MONEY.
OH!
I SHOULD PROBABLY RETURN IT TO THE BANK.
BUT I'M AFRAID OF WHAT THE YAKUZA WOULD DO TO ME LATER.

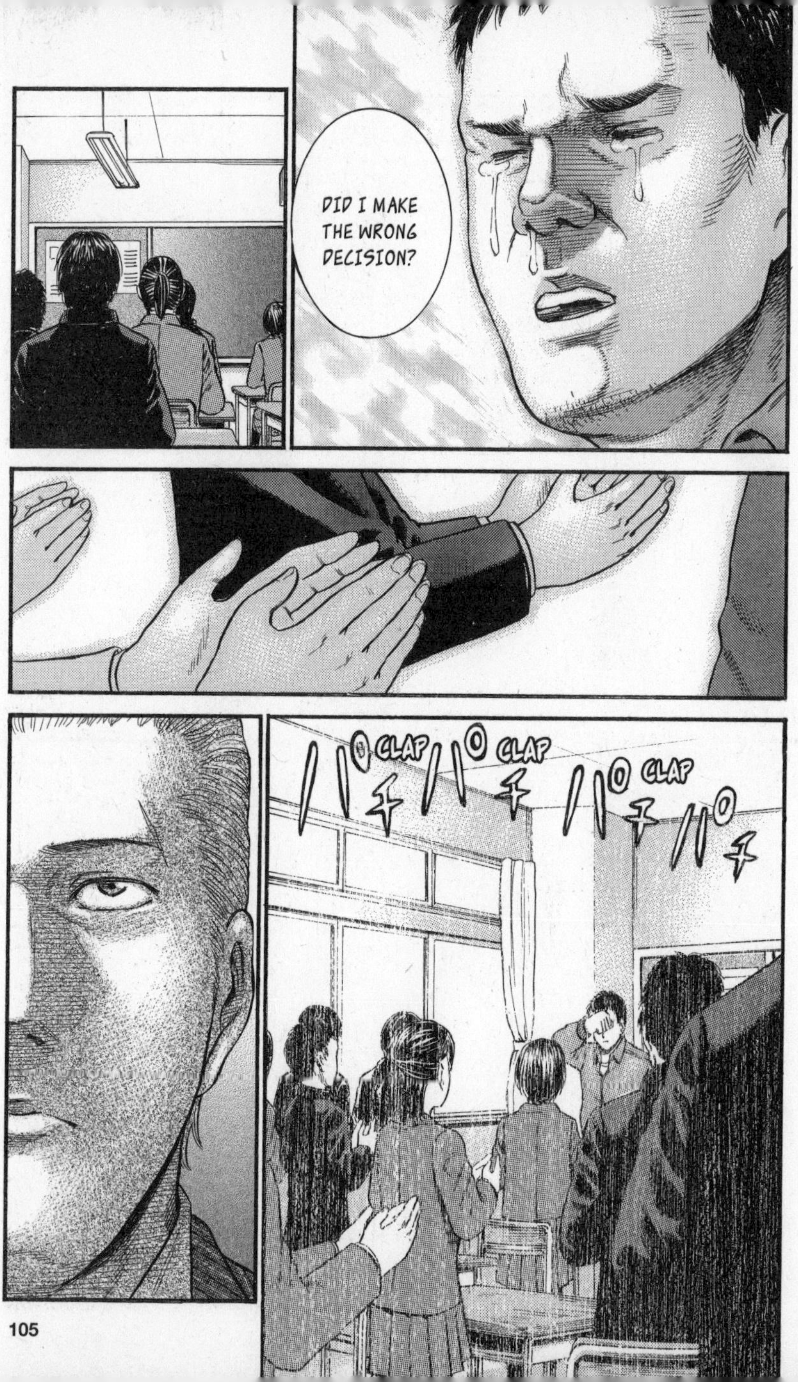
DID I MAKE THE WRONG DECISION?
パチ
CLAP
パチ
CLAP
パチ
CLAP
パチ

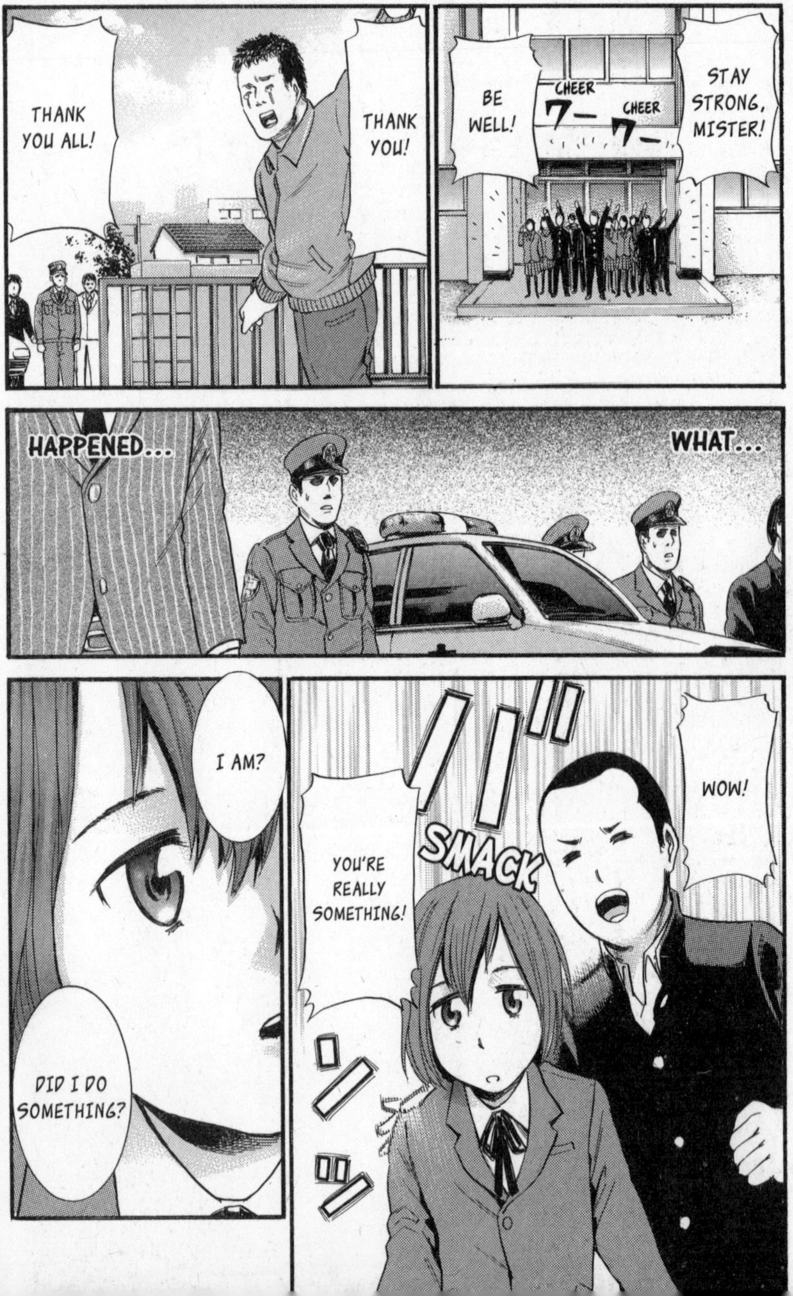
STAY STRONG, MISTER!
CHEER
CHEER
BE WELL!
THANK YOU!
THANK YOU ALL!
WHAT...
HAPPENED...
WOW!
SMACK
YOU'RE REALLY SOMETHING!
I AM?
DID I DO SOMETHING?

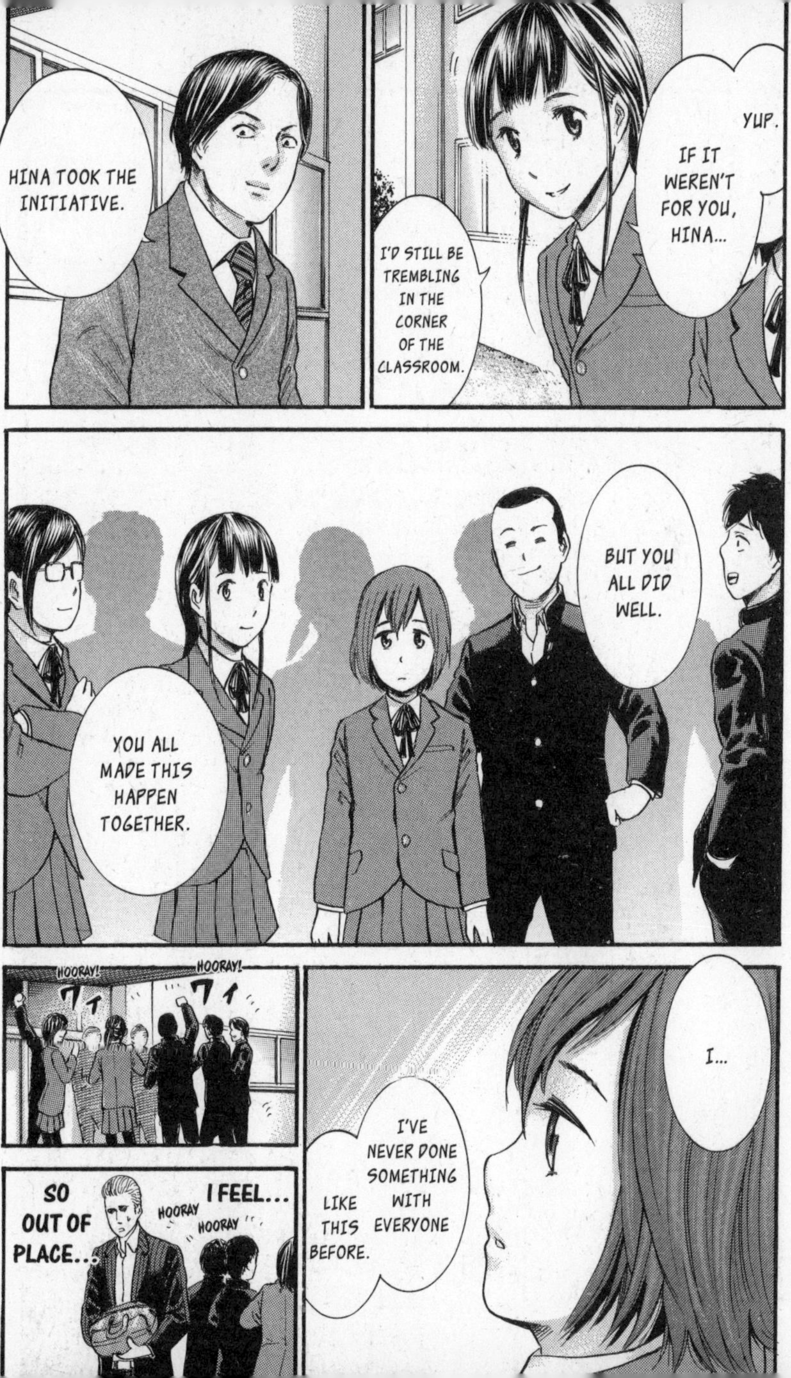
YUP.
IF IT WEREN'T FOR YOU, HINA...
I'D STILL BE TREMBLING IN THE CORNER OF THE CLASSROOM.
HINA TOOK THE INITIATIVE.
BUT YOU ALL DID WELL.
YOU ALL MADE THIS HAPPEN TOGETHER.
I...
I'VE NEVER DONE SOMETHING WITH EVERYONE LIKE THIS BEFORE.
HOORAY!
ワイ
HOORAY!
ワイ
I FEEL...
SO OUT OF PLACE...
HOORAY
HOORAY

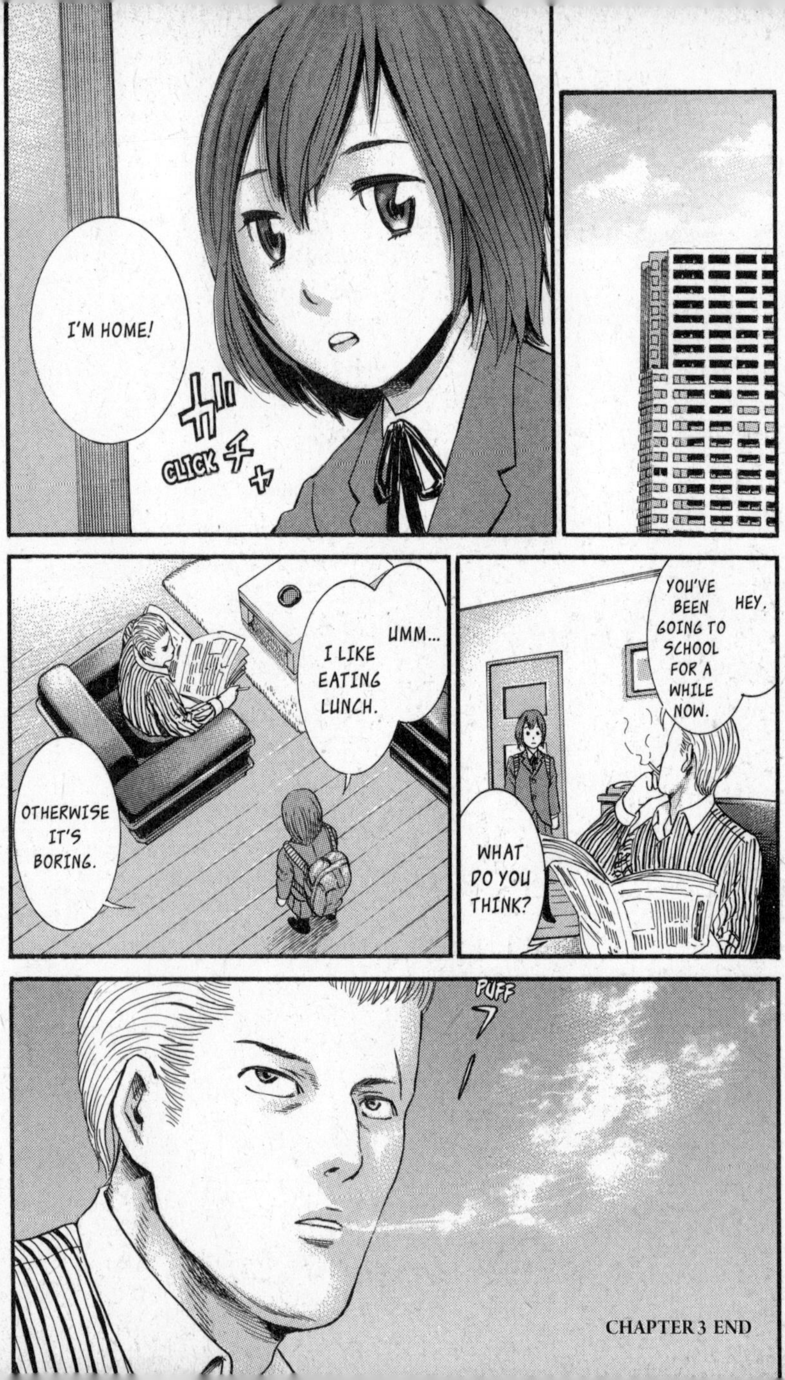
I'M HOME!
CLICK
HEY.
YOU'VE BEEN GOING TO SCHOOL FOR A WHILE NOW.
WHAT DO YOU THINK?
UMM...
I LIKE EATING LUNCH.
OTHERWISE IT'S BORING.
PUFF

CHAPTER 3 END

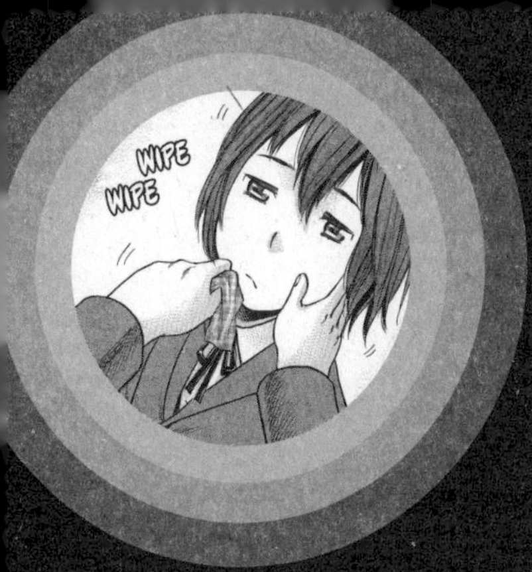
WIPE
WIPE

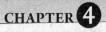

IN A SATURDAY NIGHT FEVER MOOD TONIGHT!

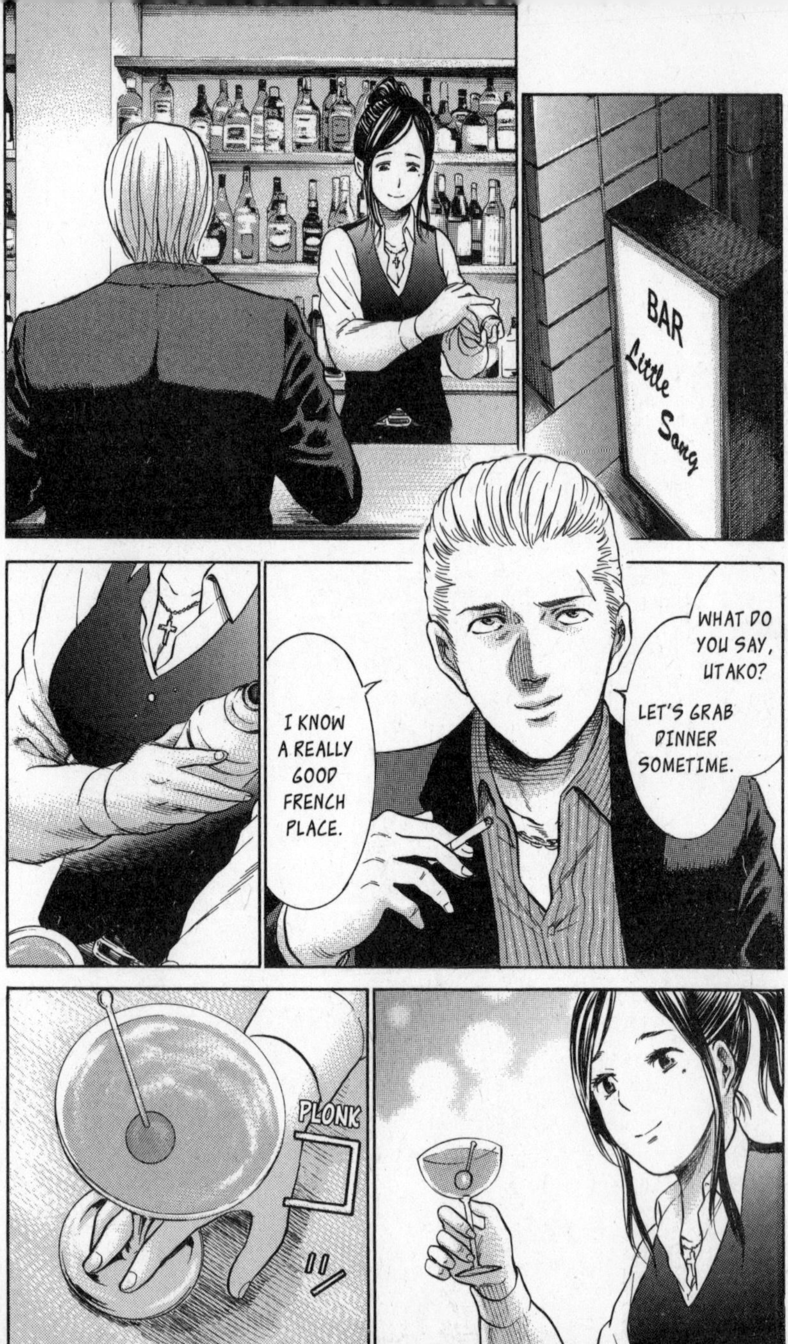
BAR
Little Song
WHAT DO YOU SAY, UTAKO?
LET'S GRAB DINNER SOMETIME.
I KNOW A REALLY GOOD FRENCH PLACE.
PLONK

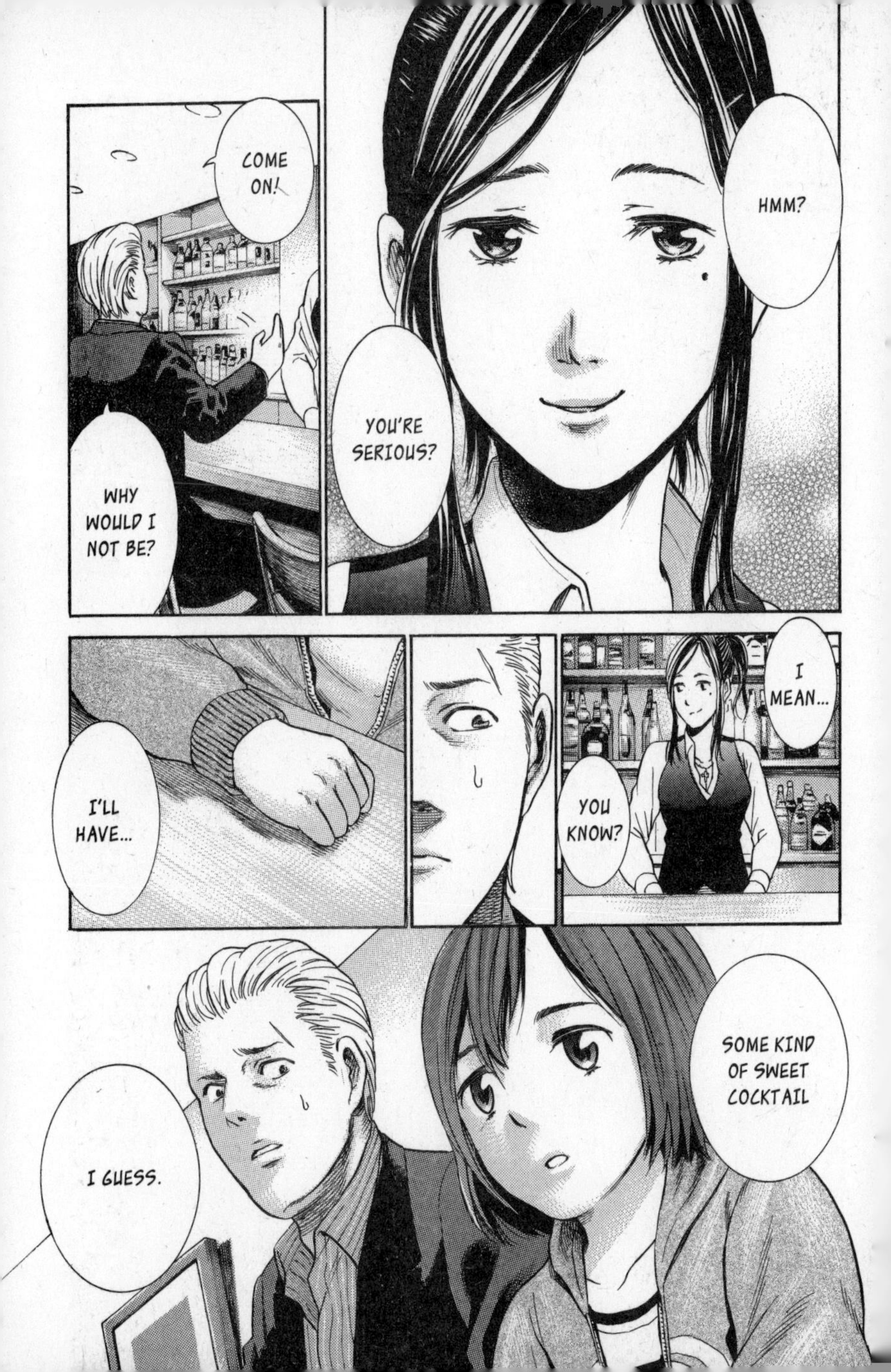
HMM?
YOU'RE SERIOUS?
COME ON!
WHY WOULD I NOT BE?
I MEAN...
YOU KNOW?
I'LL HAVE...
SOME KIND OF SWEET COCKTAIL
I GUESS.

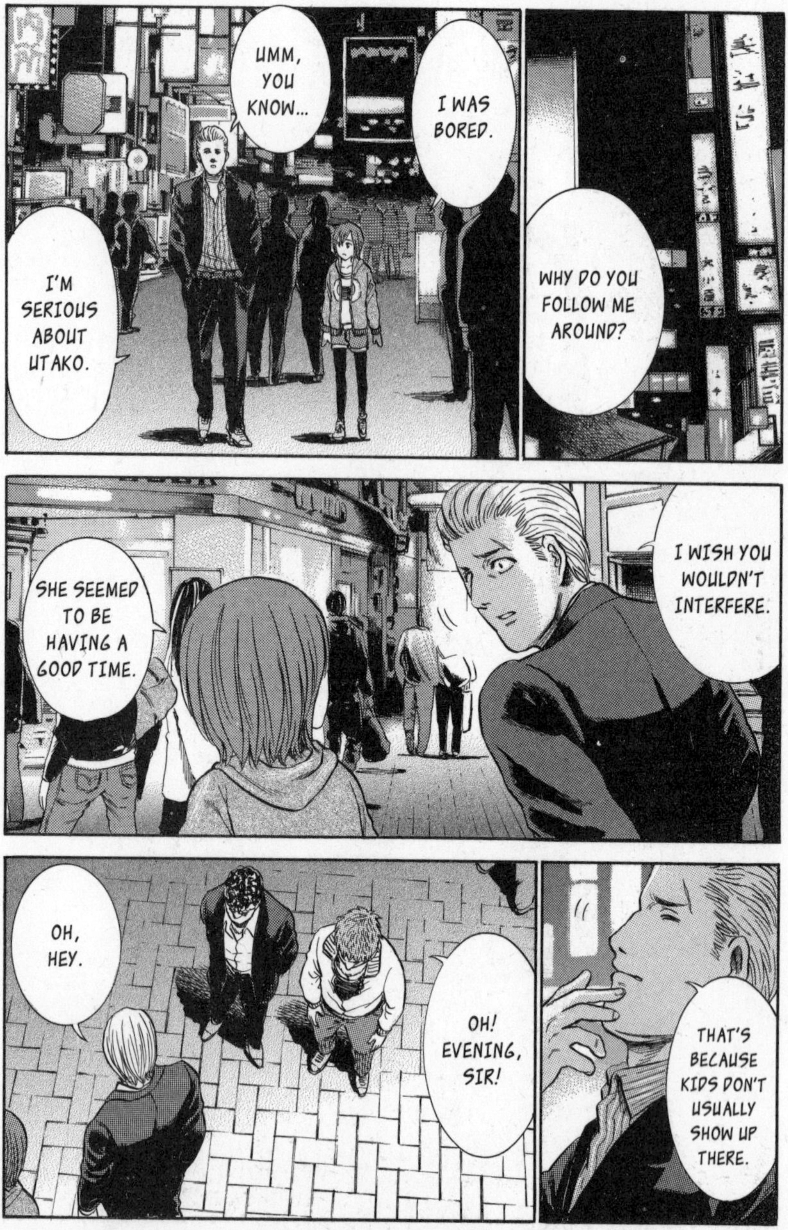
WHY DO YOU FOLLOW ME AROUND?
UMM, YOU KNOW...
I WAS BORED.
I'M SERIOUS ABOUT UTAKO.
I WISH YOU WOULDN'T INTERFERE.
SHE SEEMED TO BE HAVING A GOOD TIME.
THAT'S BECAUSE KIDS DON'T USUALLY SHOW UP THERE.
OH! EVENING, SIR!
OH, HEY.

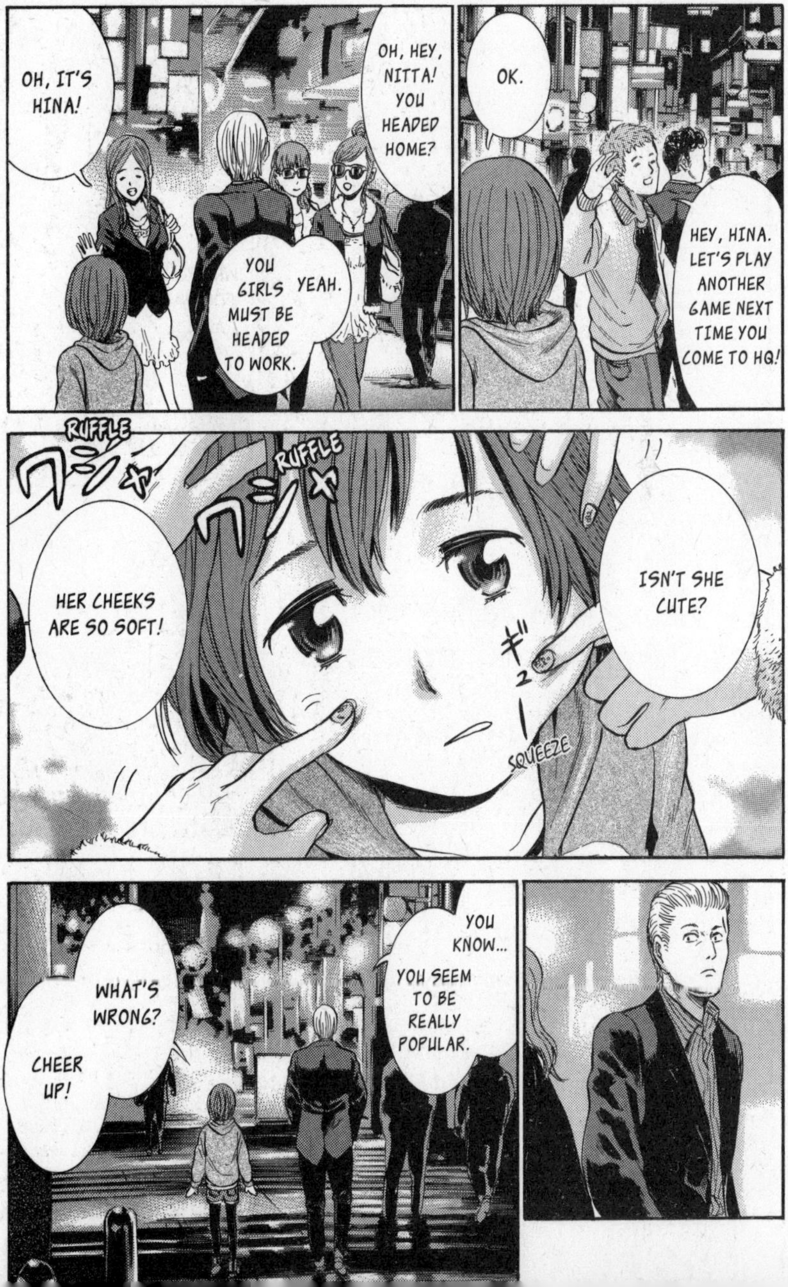
OK.
HEY, HINA. LET'S PLAY ANOTHER GAME NEXT TIME YOU COME TO HQ!
OH, HEY, NITTA! YOU HEADED HOME?
OH, IT'S HINA!
YEAH.
YOU GIRLS MUST BE HEADED TO WORK.
ISN'T SHE CUTE?
SQUEEZE
RUFFLE
RUFFLE
HER CHEEKS ARE SO SOFT!
YOU KNOW... YOU SEEM TO BE REALLY POPULAR.
WHAT'S WRONG? CHEER UP!

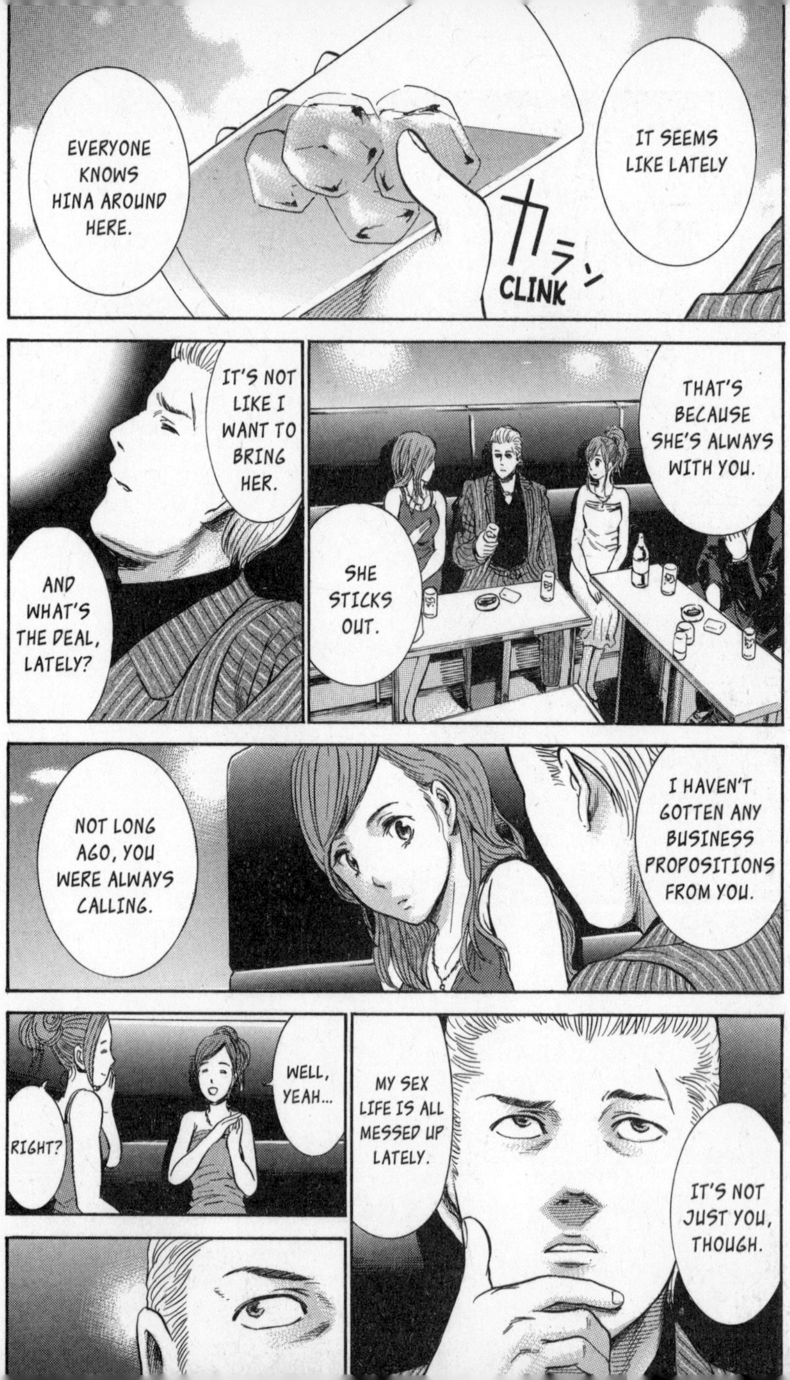
IT SEEMS LIKE LATELY
カラン
CLINK
EVERYONE KNOWS HINA AROUND HERE.
THAT'S BECAUSE SHE'S ALWAYS WITH YOU.
SHE STICKS OUT.
IT'S NOT LIKE I WANT TO BRING HER.
AND WHAT'S THE DEAL, LATELY?
I HAVEN'T GOTTEN ANY BUSINESS PROPOSITIONS FROM YOU.
NOT LONG AGO, YOU WERE ALWAYS CALLING.
MY SEX LIFE IS ALL MESSED UP LATELY.
IT'S NOT JUST YOU, THOUGH.
WELL, YEAH...
RIGHT?

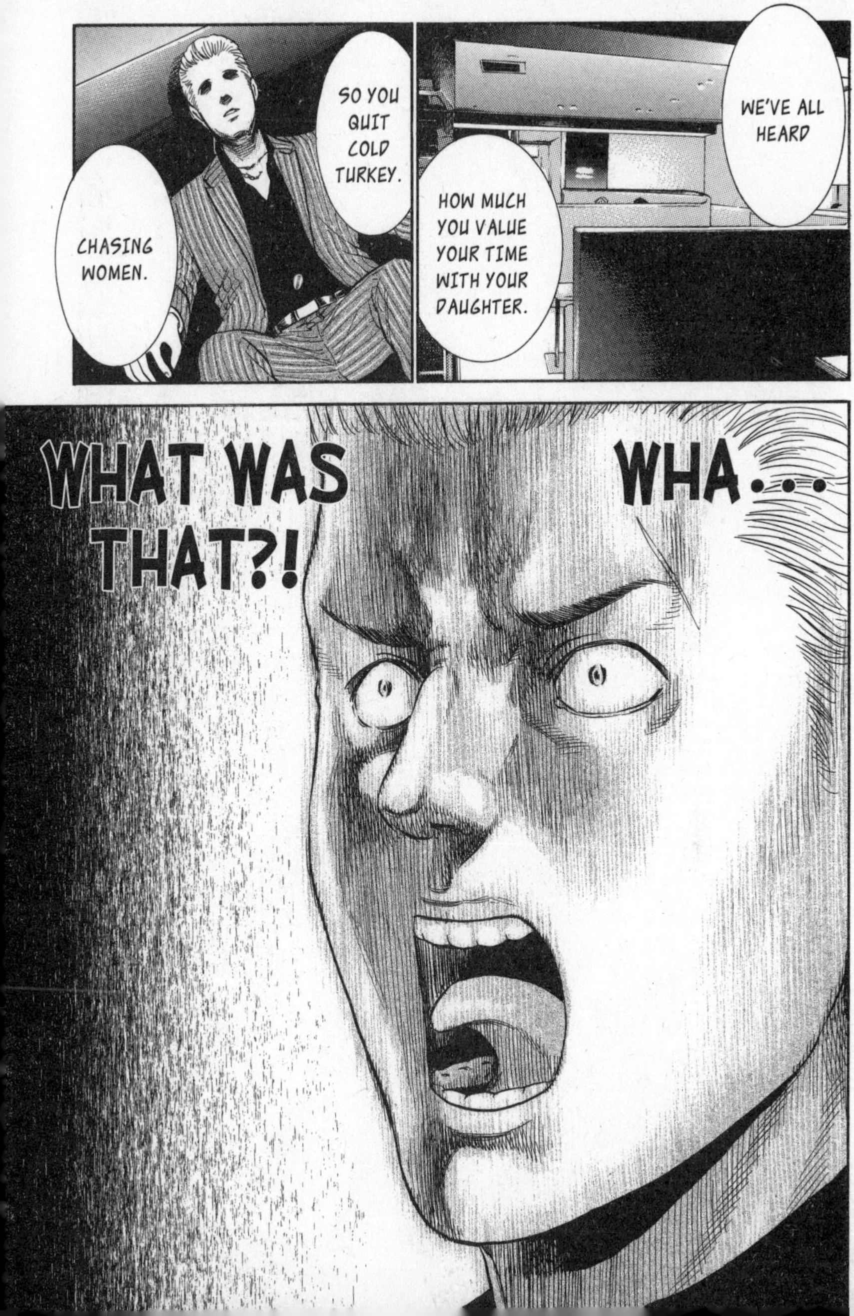
WE'VE ALL HEARD
HOW MUCH YOU VALUE YOUR TIME WITH YOUR DAUGHTER.
SO YOU QUIT COLD TURKEY.
CHASING WOMEN.
WHA...
WHAT WAS THAT?!

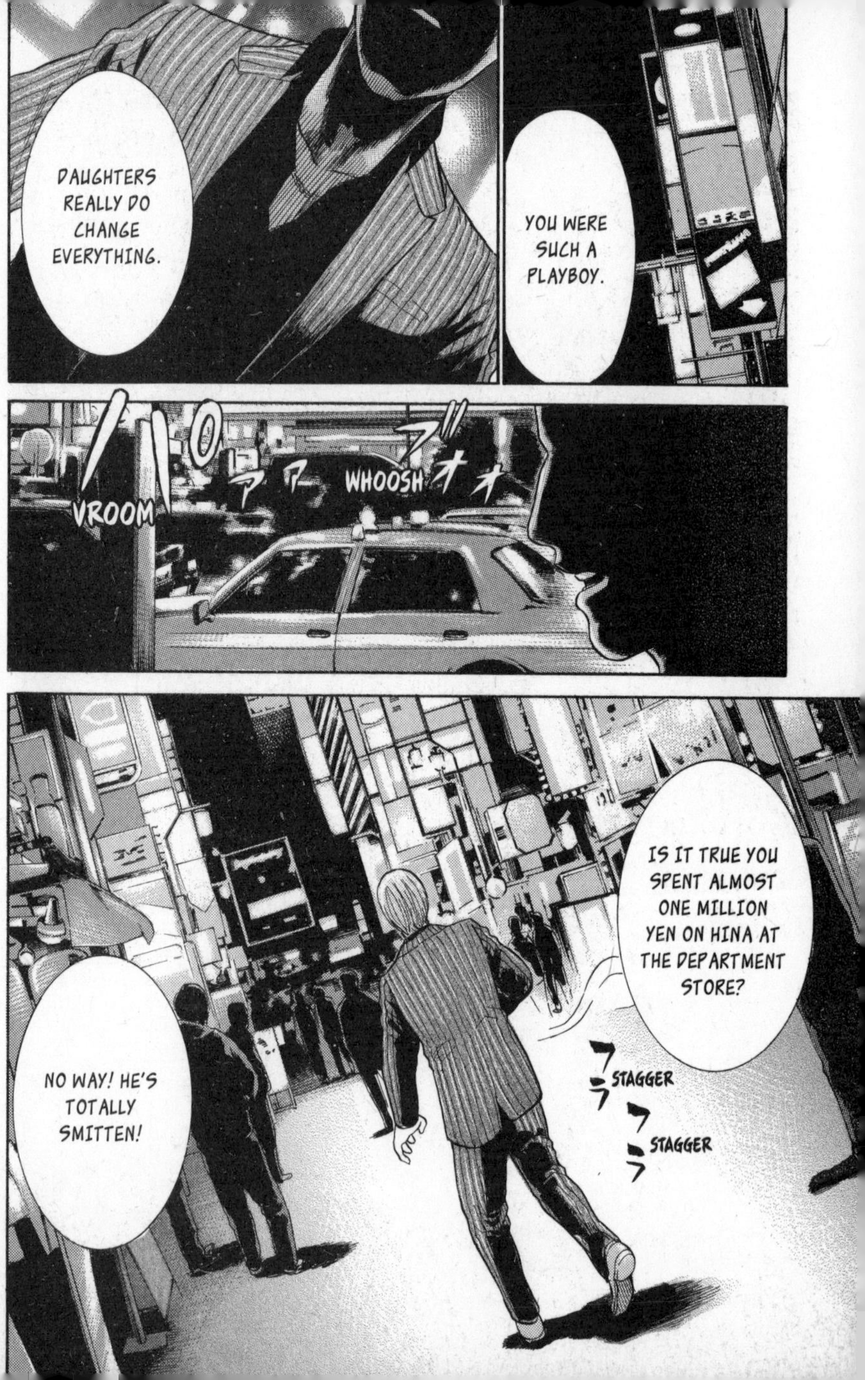
YOU WERE SUCH A PLAYBOY.
DAUGHTERS REALLY DO CHANGE EVERYTHING.
WHOOSH
VROOM
IS IT TRUE YOU SPENT ALMOST ONE MILLION YEN ON HINA AT THE DEPARTMENT STORE?
STAGGER
STAGGER
NO WAY! HE'S TOTALLY SMITTEN!

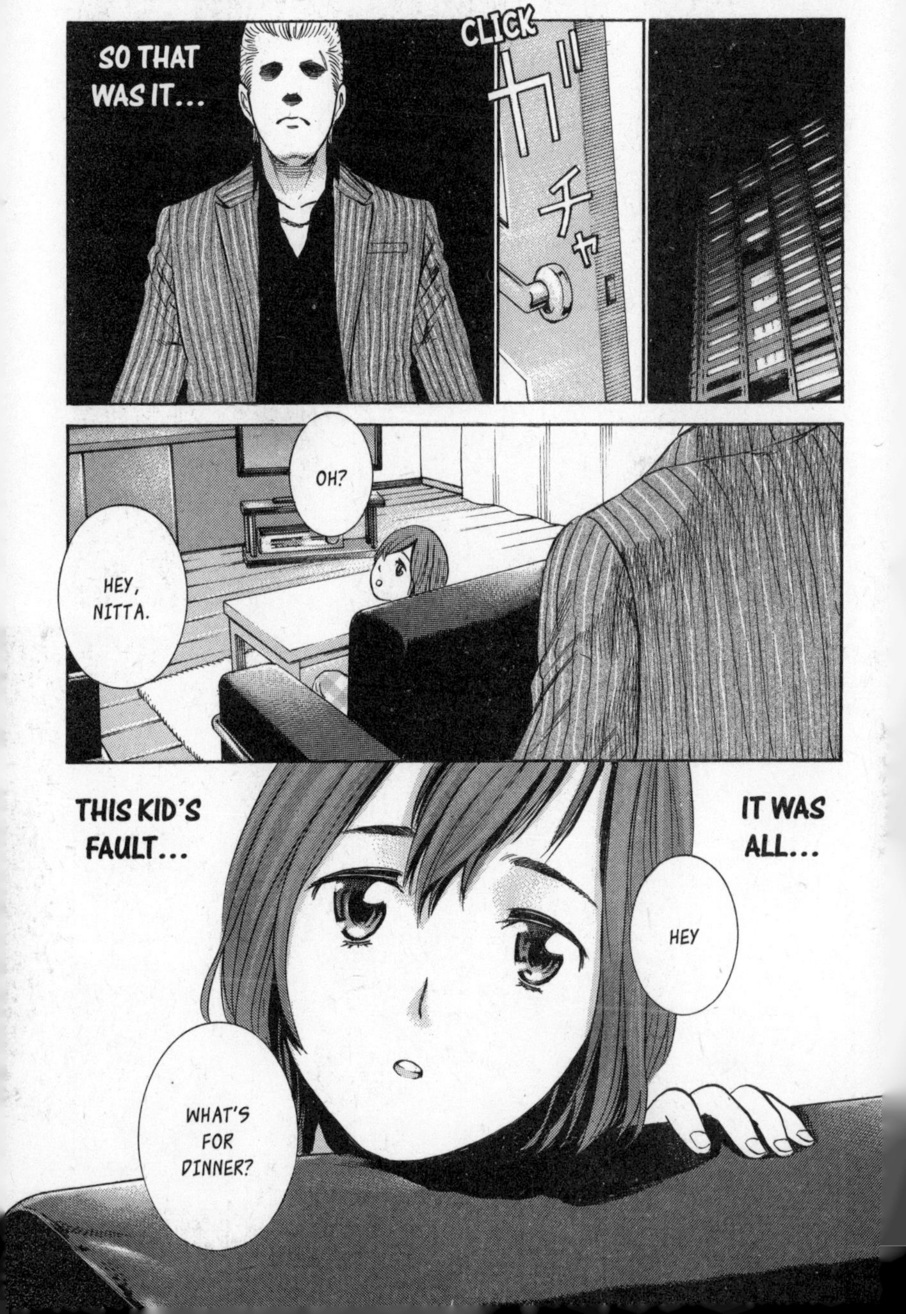
ガチャ
CLICK
SO THAT WAS IT...
OH?
HEY, NITTA.
IT WAS ALL...
THIS KID'S FAULT...
HEY
WHAT'S FOR DINNER?

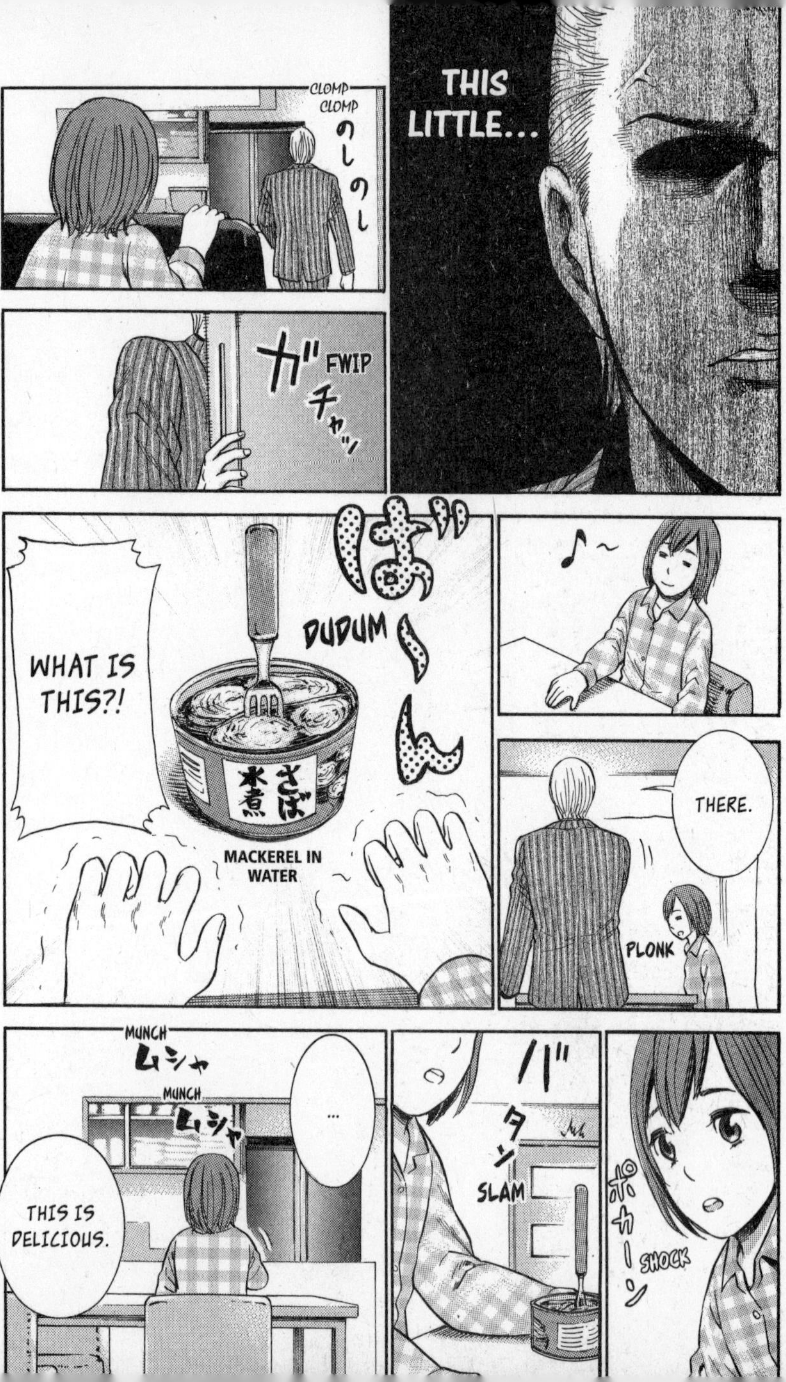

THIS LITTLE...
CLOMP CLOMP
のしのし
ガチャッ
FWIP
♪~
THERE.
PLONK
ばぁん
DUDUM
WHAT IS THIS?!
さば水煮
MACKEREL IN WATER
ポカーン
SHOCK
バタン
SLAM
...
MUNCH
ムシャ
MUNCH
ムシャ
THIS IS DELICIOUS.

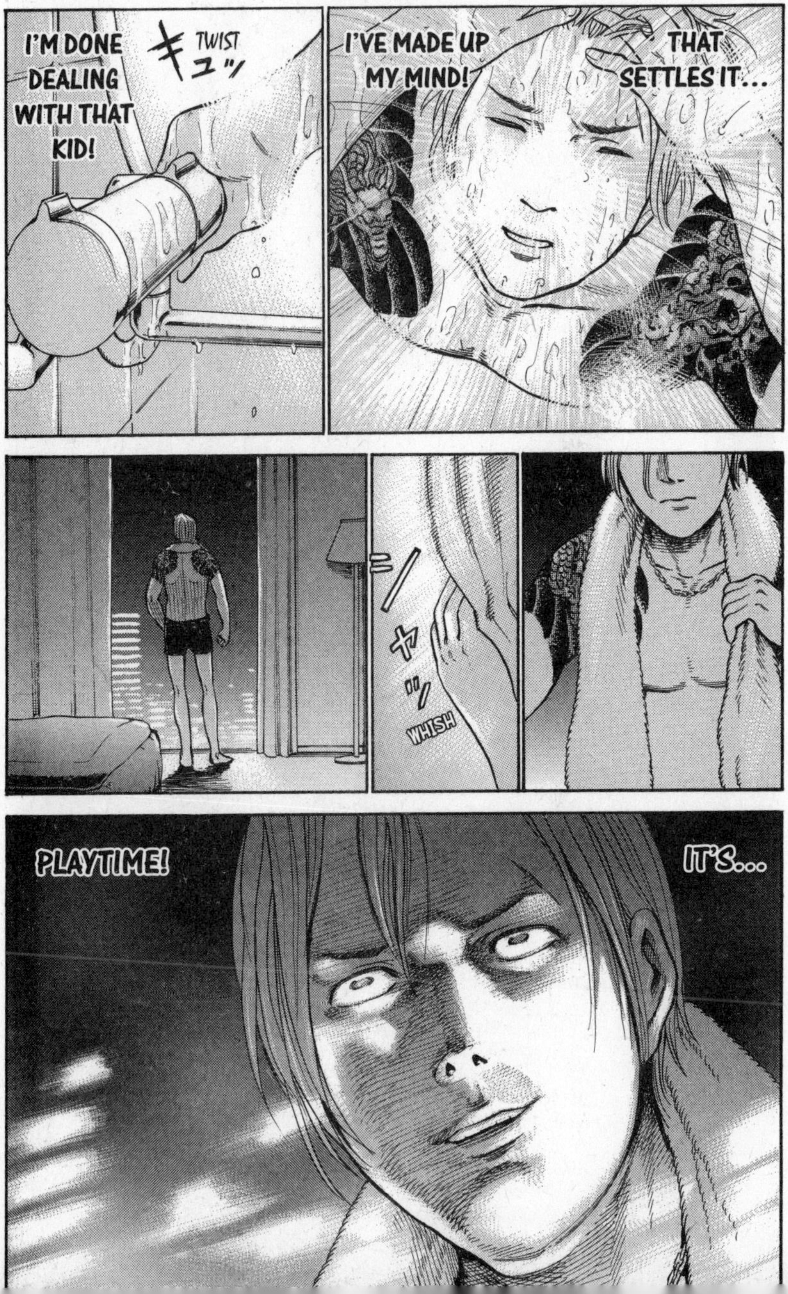
THAT SETTLES IT...
I'VE MADE UP MY MIND!
キュッ TWIST
I'M DONE DEALING WITH THAT KID!
WHISH
IT'S...
PLAYTIME!

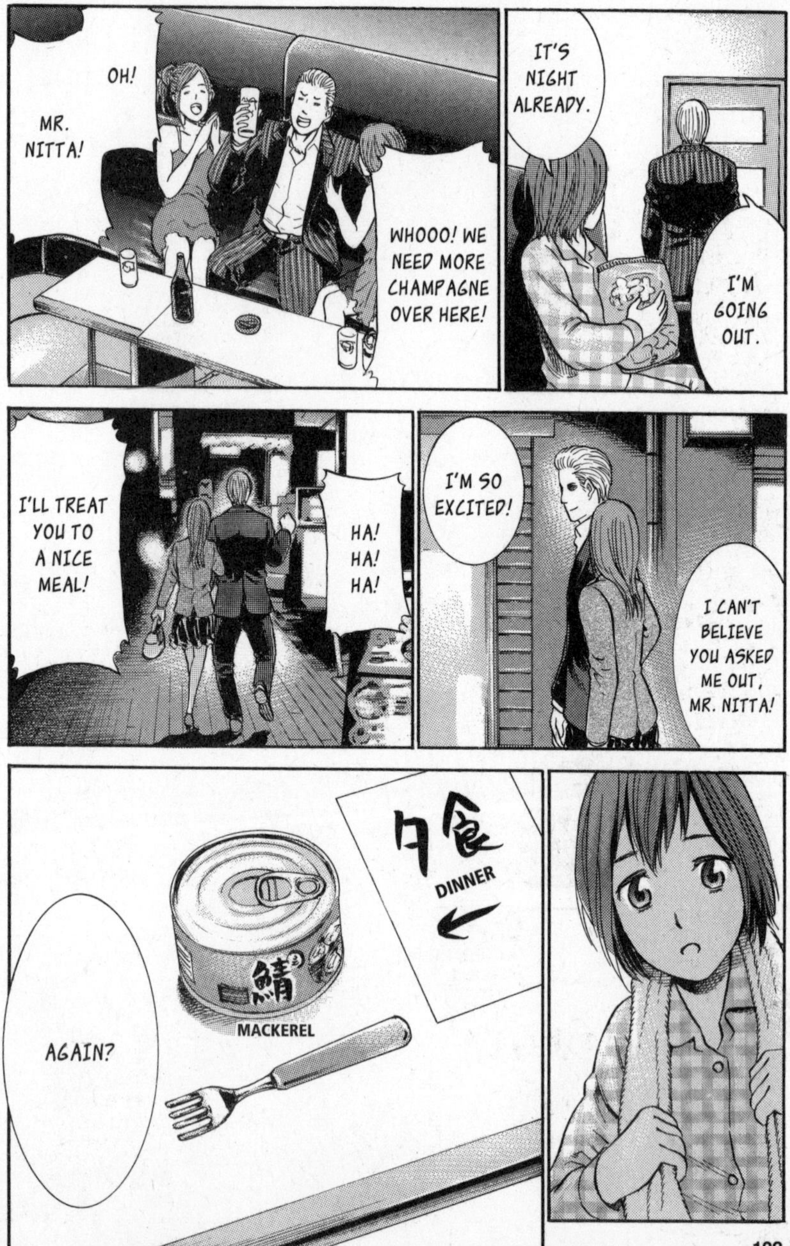
IT'S NIGHT ALREADY.
I'M GOING OUT.
OH!
MR. NITTA!
WHOOO! WE NEED MORE CHAMPAGNE OVER HERE!
I'M SO EXCITED!
I CAN'T BELIEVE YOU ASKED ME OUT, MR. NITTA!
HA! HA! HA!
I'LL TREAT YOU TO A NICE MEAL!
夕食
DINNER
鯖
MACKEREL
AGAIN?

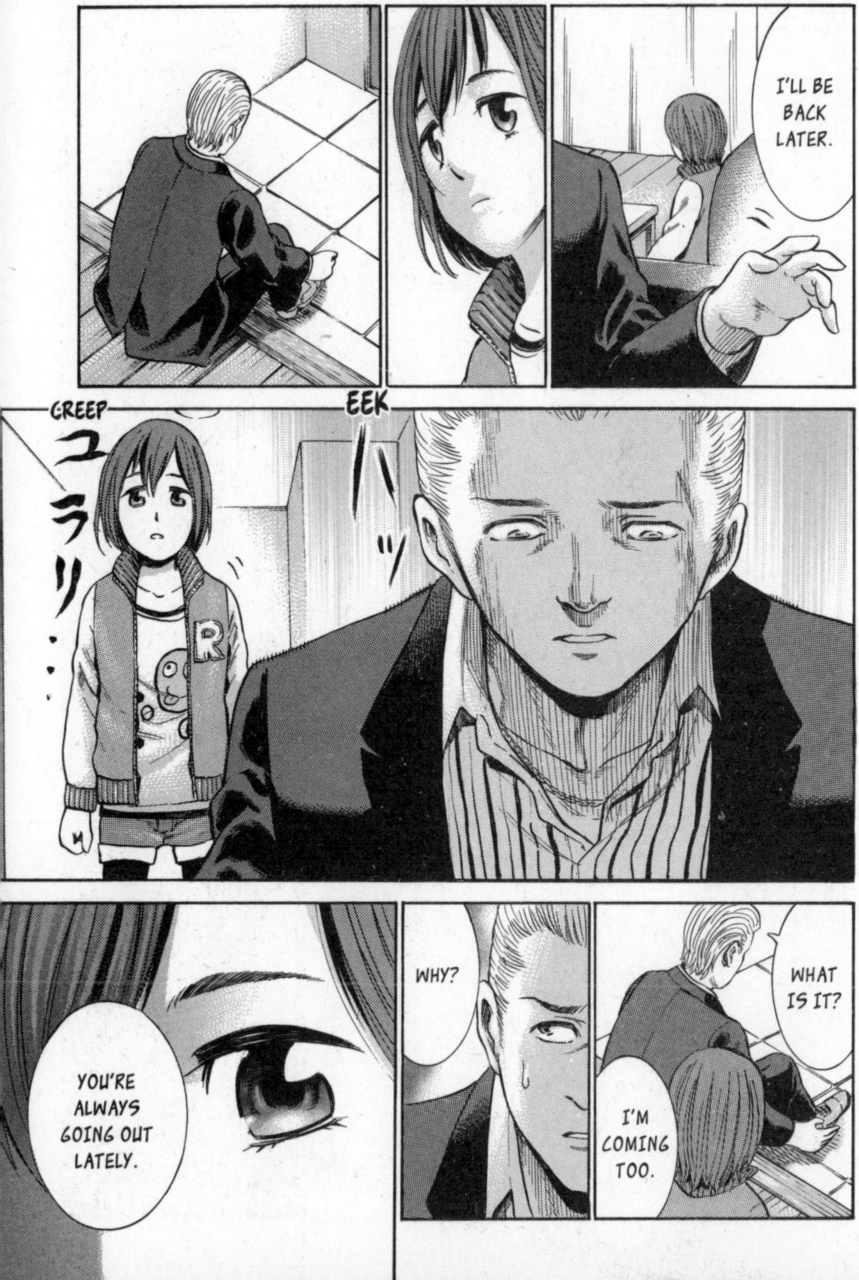
I'LL BE BACK LATER.
EEK
ハッ
CREEP
ユラリ…
WHAT IS IT?
I'M COMING TOO.
WHY?
YOU'RE ALWAYS GOING OUT LATELY.

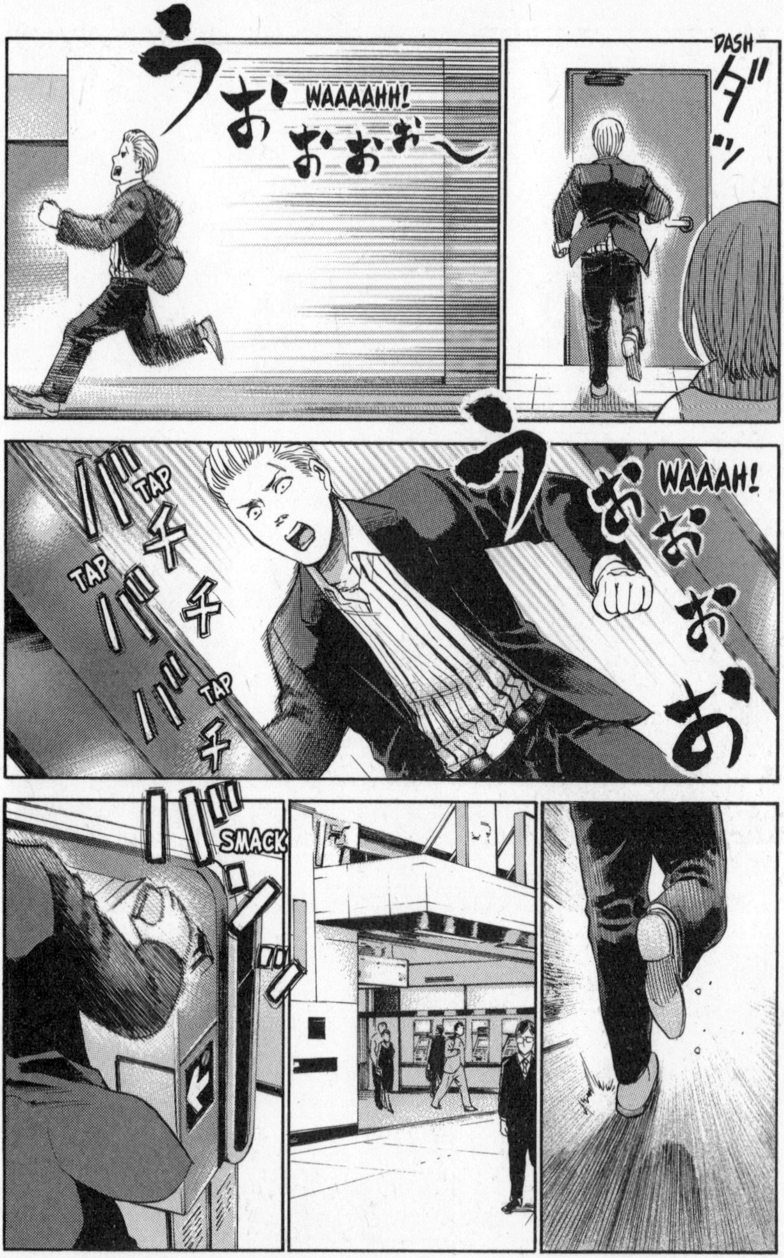
DASH
ダッ
うおおおお〜
WAAAAHH!
うおおおおお
WAAAH!
バチ
TAP
バチ
TAP
バチ
TAP
バーン
SMACK

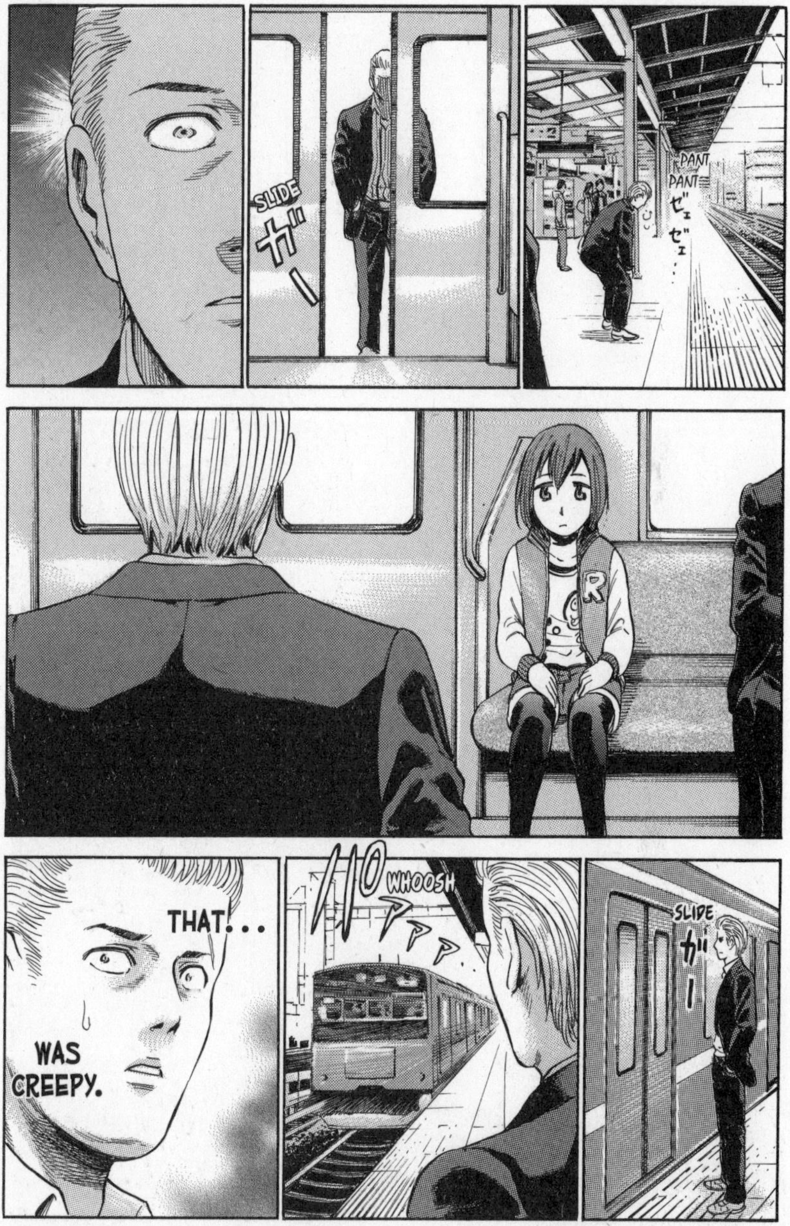
PANT PANT
ゼェ ゼェ . . .
SLIDE
ガー
SLIDE
ガー
WHOOSH
THAT. . .
WAS CREEPY.

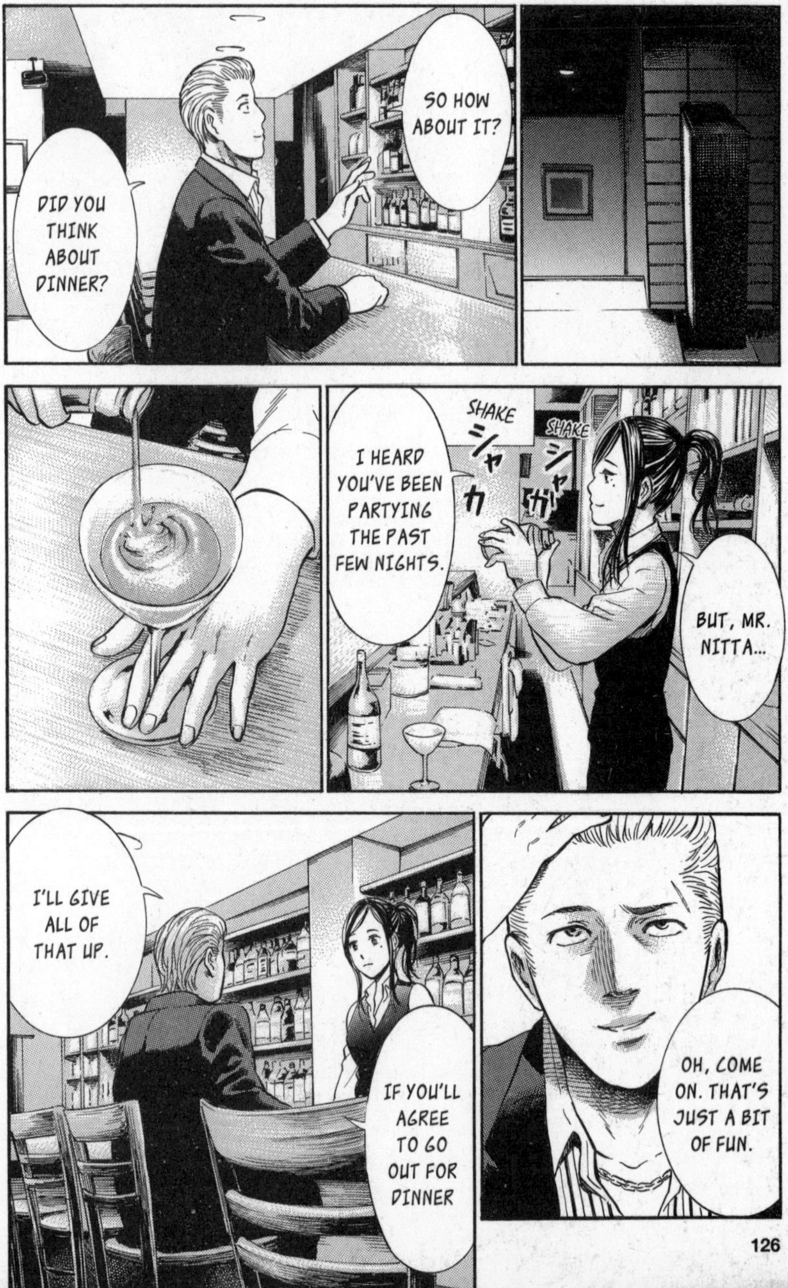
SO HOW ABOUT IT?
DID YOU THINK ABOUT DINNER?
SHAKE
シャカ
SHAKE
シャカ
BUT, MR. NITTA...
I HEARD YOU'VE BEEN PARTYING THE PAST FEW NIGHTS.
OH, COME ON. THAT'S JUST A BIT OF FUN.
I'LL GIVE ALL OF THAT UP.
IF YOU'LL AGREE TO GO OUT FOR DINNER

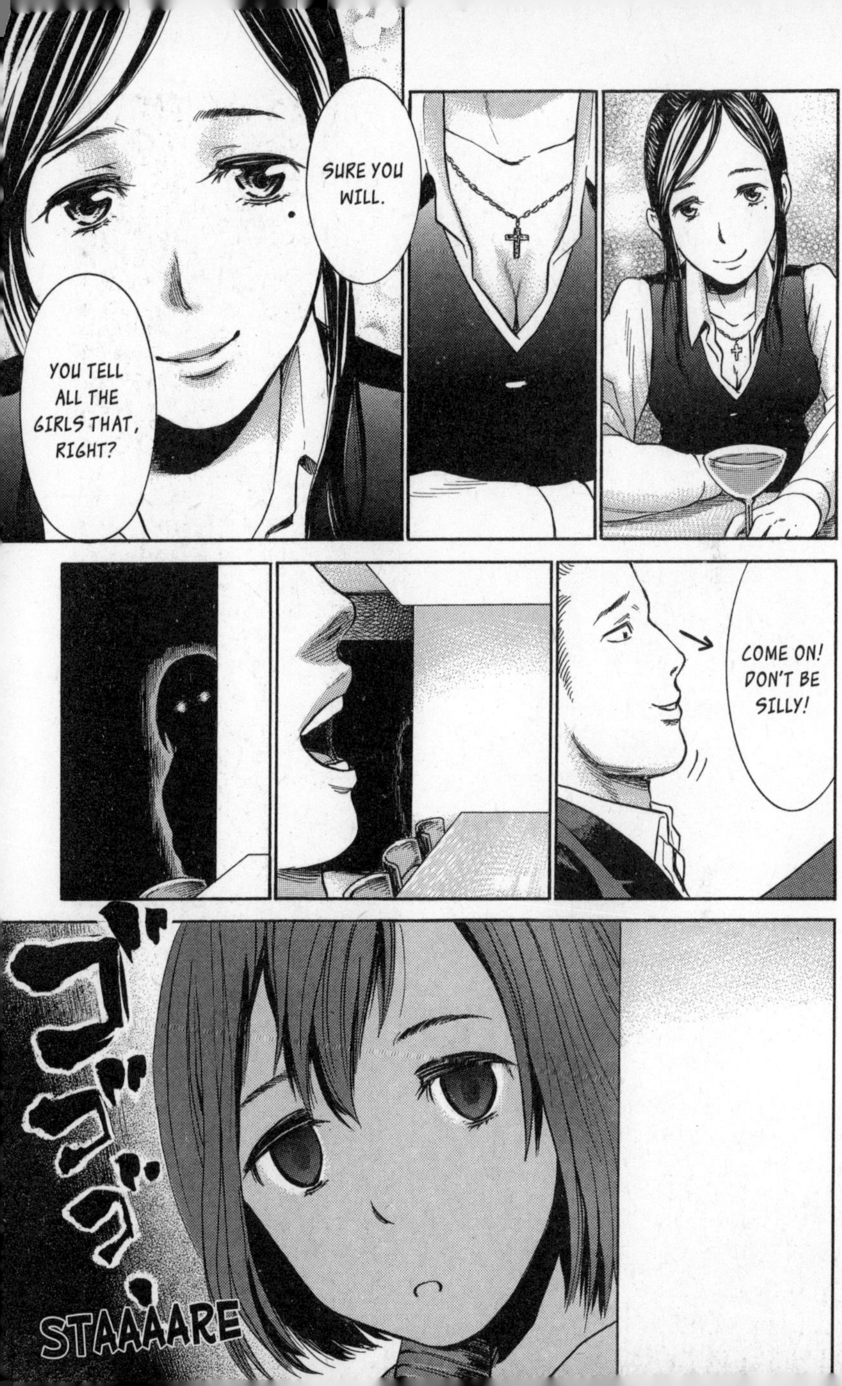
SURE YOU WILL.
YOU TELL ALL THE GIRLS THAT, RIGHT?
COME ON! DON'T BE SILLY!
STAAAARE

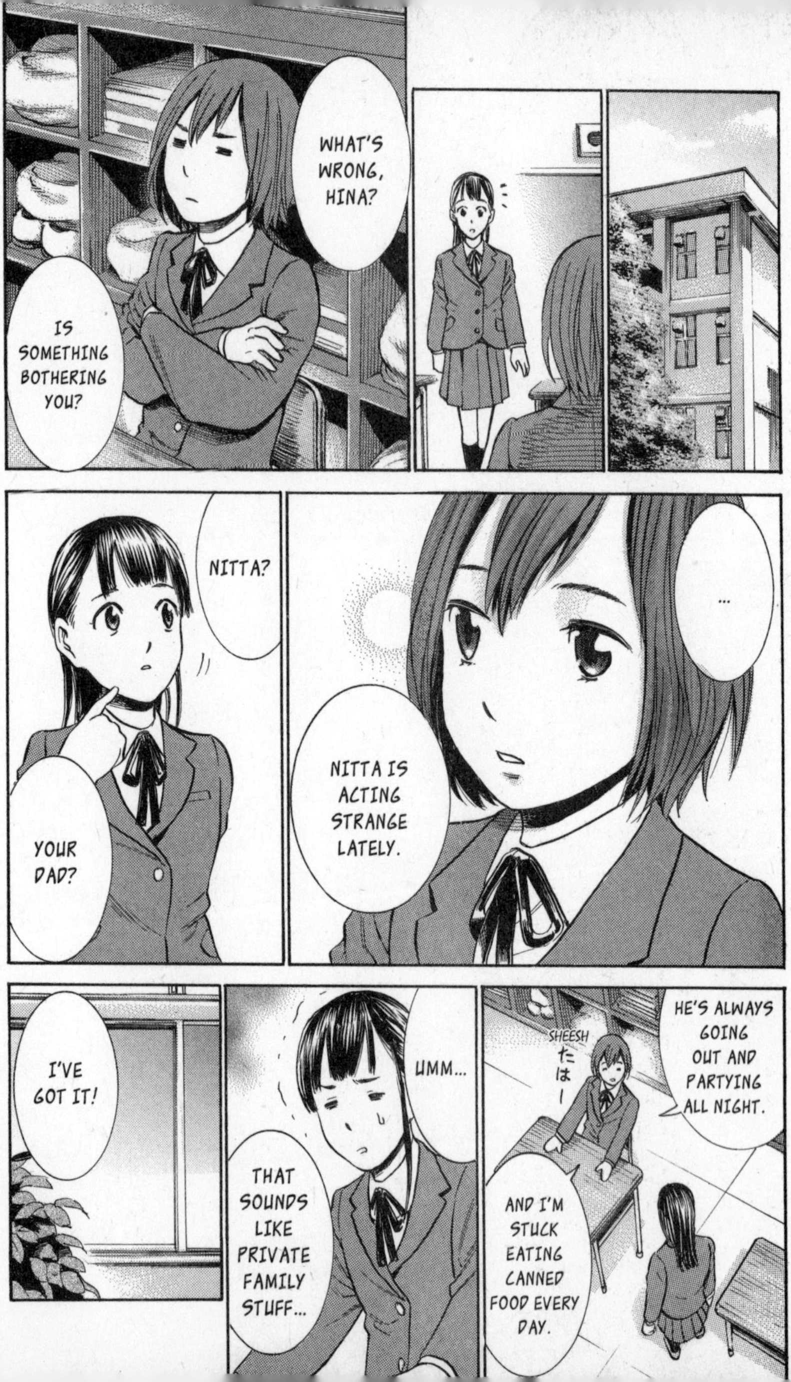
WHAT'S WRONG, HINA?
IS SOMETHING BOTHERING YOU?
...
NITTA IS ACTING STRANGE LATELY.
NITTA?
YOUR DAD?
HE'S ALWAYS GOING OUT AND PARTYING ALL NIGHT.
SHEESH
たはー
AND I'M STUCK EATING CANNED FOOD EVERY DAY.
UMM...
THAT SOUNDS LIKE PRIVATE FAMILY STUFF...
I'VE GOT IT!

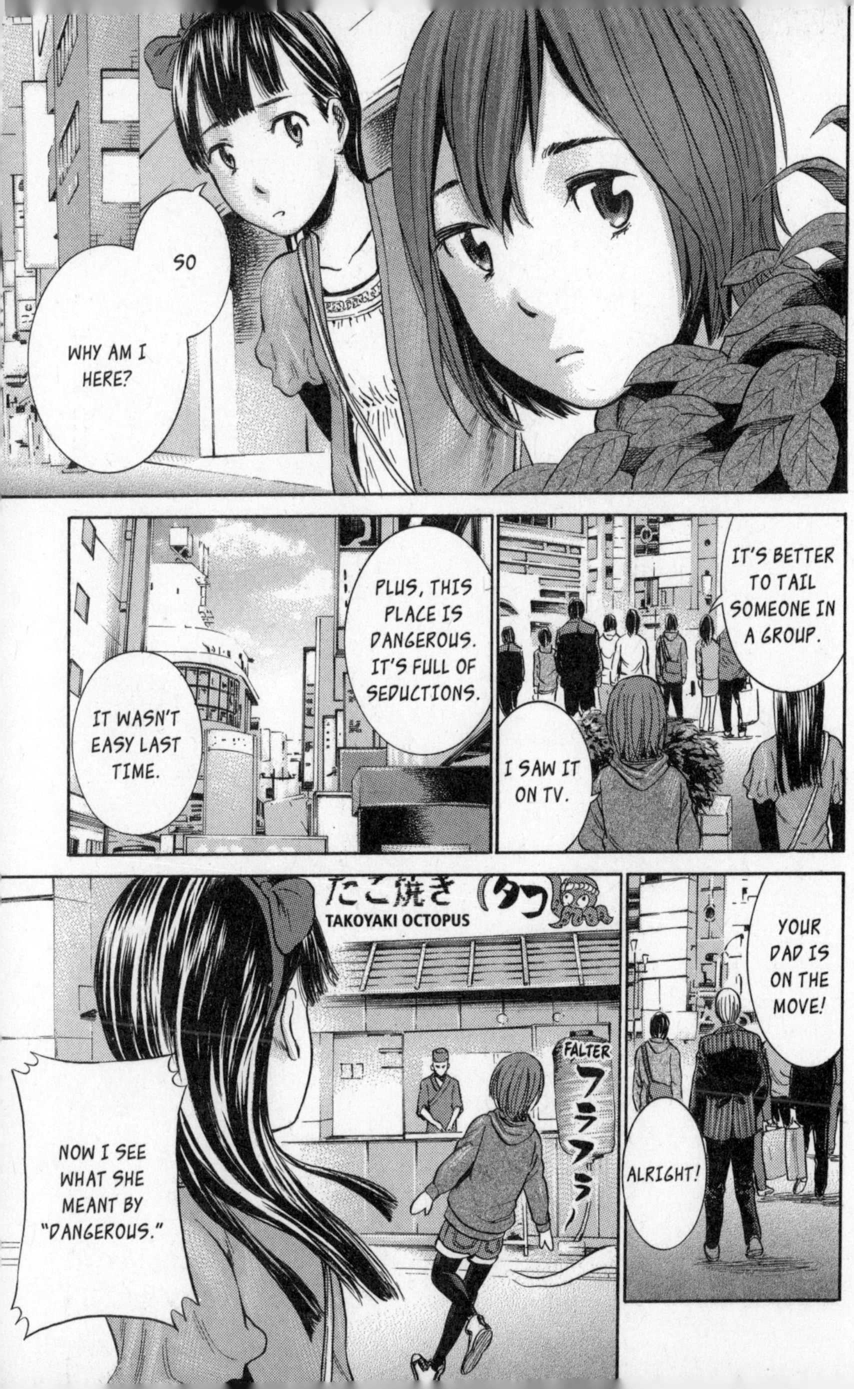
SO
WHY AM I HERE?
IT'S BETTER TO TAIL SOMEONE IN A GROUP.
I SAW IT ON TV.
PLUS, THIS PLACE IS DANGEROUS. IT'S FULL OF SEDUCTIONS.
IT WASN'T EASY LAST TIME.
YOUR DAD IS ON THE MOVE!
ALRIGHT!
たこ焼き
TAKOYAKI OCTOPUS
FALTER
フラフラ
NOW I SEE WHAT SHE MEANT BY "DANGEROUS."

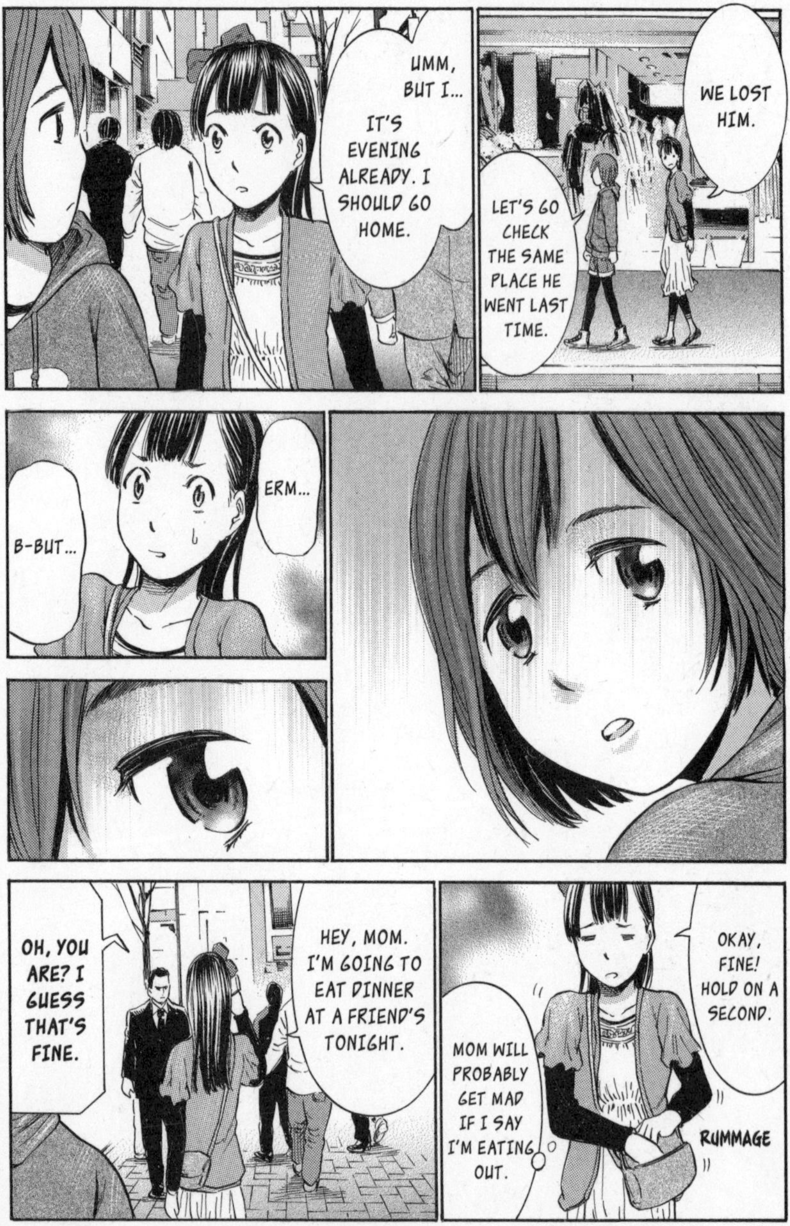
WE LOST HIM.
LET'S GO CHECK THE SAME PLACE HE WENT LAST TIME.
UMM, BUT I...
IT'S EVENING ALREADY. I SHOULD GO HOME.
ERM...
B-BUT...
OKAY, FINE! HOLD ON A SECOND.
RUMMAGE
MOM WILL PROBABLY GET MAD IF I SAY I'M EATING OUT.
HEY, MOM. I'M GOING TO EAT DINNER AT A FRIEND'S TONIGHT.
OH, YOU ARE? I GUESS THAT'S FINE.

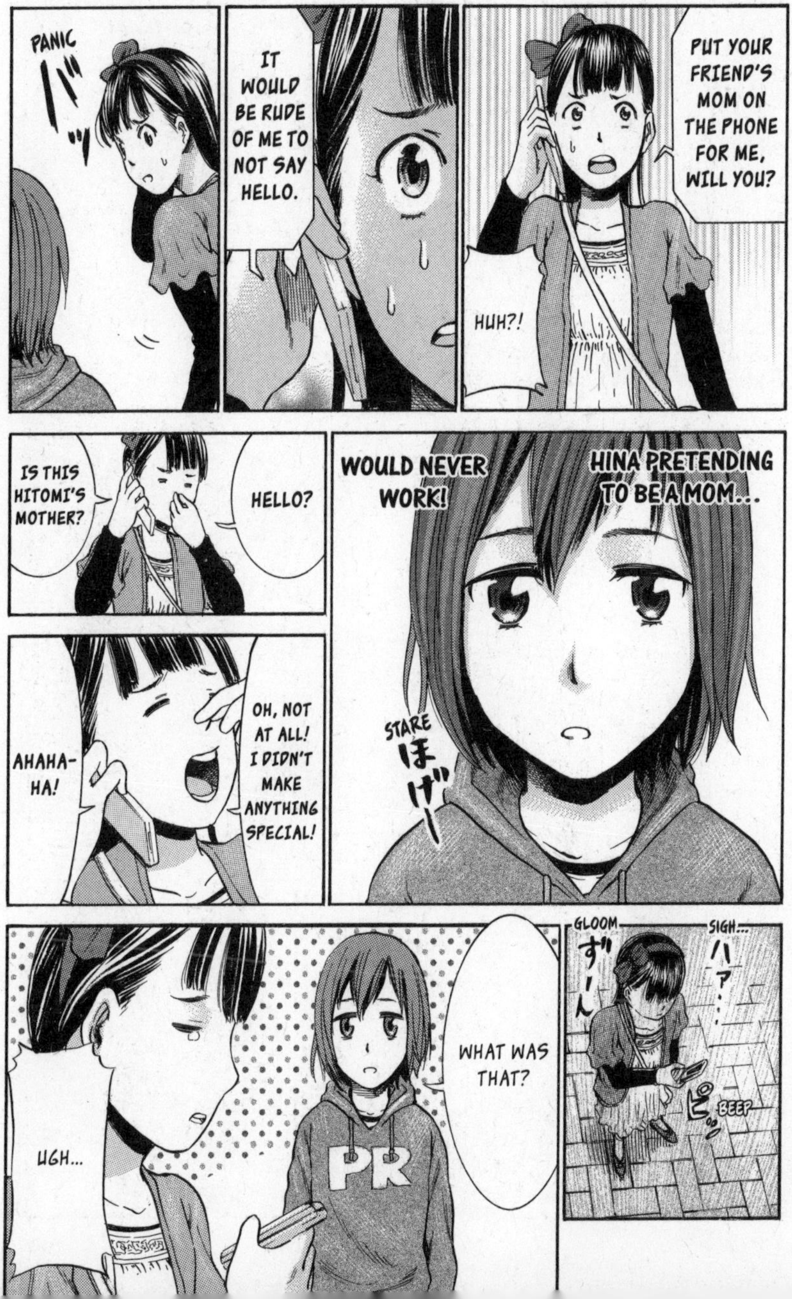
PUT YOUR FRIEND'S MOM ON THE PHONE FOR ME, WILL YOU?
HUH?!
IT WOULD BE RUDE OF ME TO NOT SAY HELLO.
PANIC
バッ
HINA PRETENDING TO BE A MOM...
WOULD NEVER WORK!
STARE
ほげー
HELLO?
IS THIS HITOMI'S MOTHER?
OH, NOT AT ALL! I DIDN'T MAKE ANYTHING SPECIAL!
AHAHA-HA!
SIGH...
ハァ・・・
GLOOM
ずーん
ピッ
BEEP
WHAT WAS THAT?
UGH...

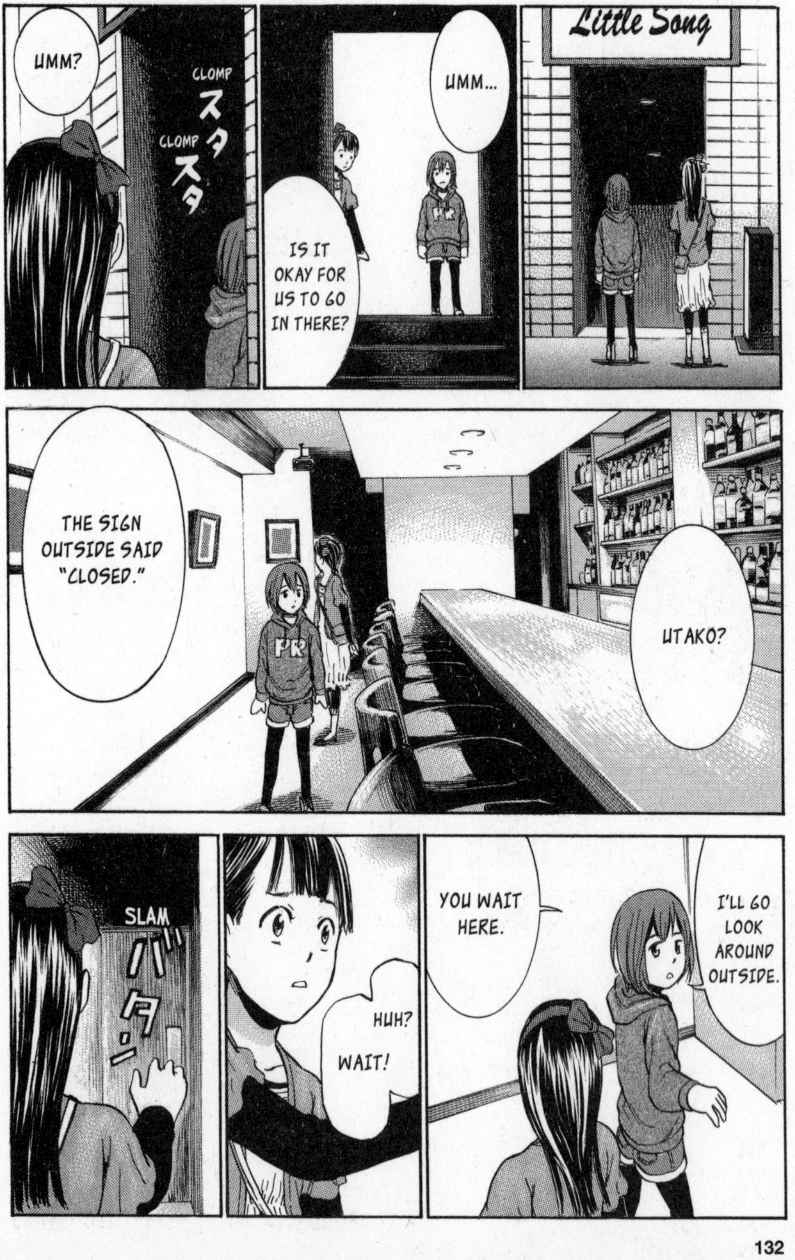
Little Song
UMM...
IS IT OKAY FOR US TO GO IN THERE?
UMM?
CLOMP スタ
CLOMP スタ
UTAKO?
THE SIGN OUTSIDE SAID "CLOSED."
I'LL GO LOOK AROUND OUTSIDE.
YOU WAIT HERE.
HUH?
WAIT!
SLAM
バタン

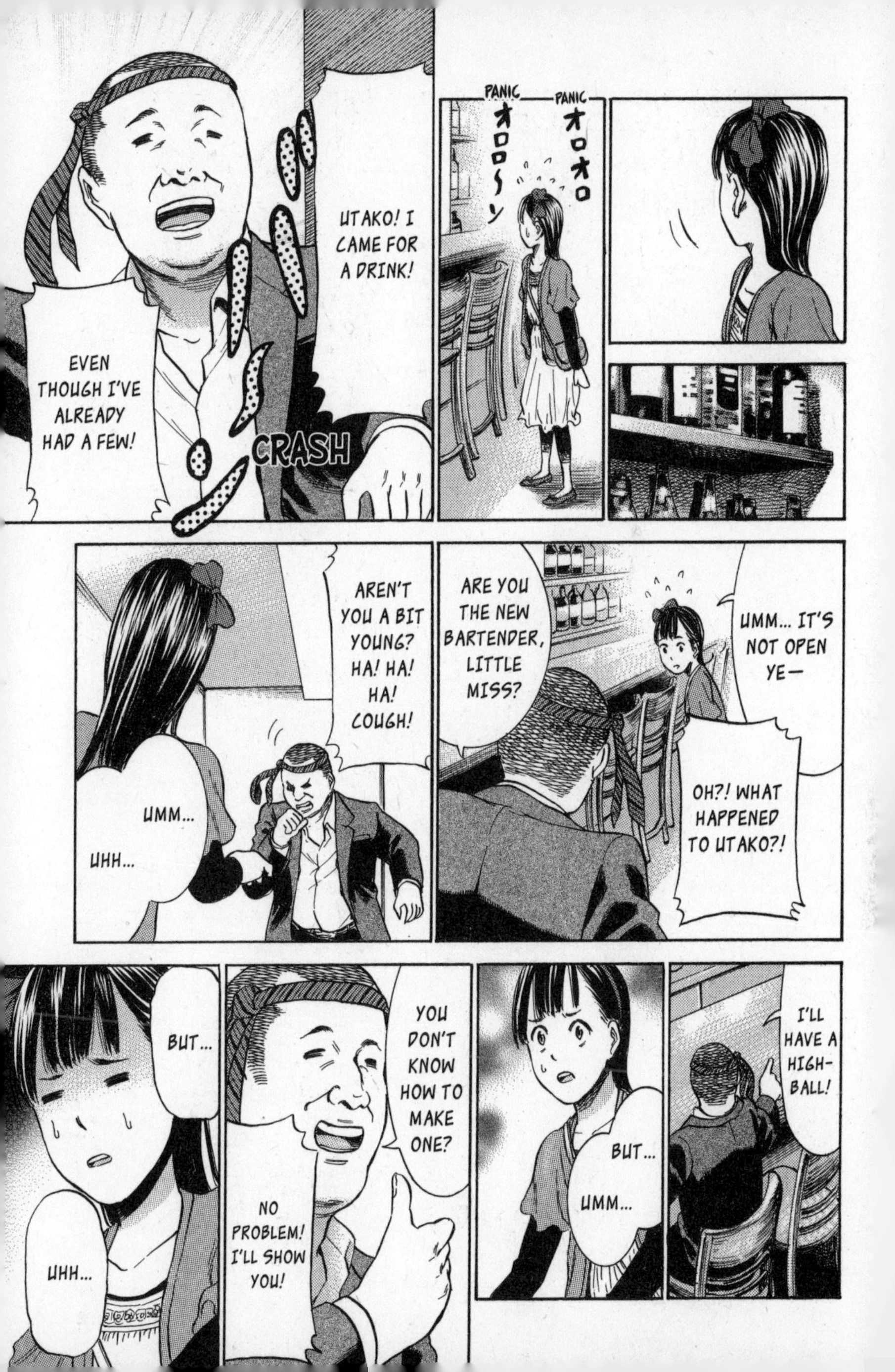
PANIC
オロオロ
PANIC
オロロ〜ン
UTAKO! I CAME FOR A DRINK!
EVEN THOUGH I'VE ALREADY HAD A FEW!
CRASH
UMM... IT'S NOT OPEN YE—
OH?! WHAT HAPPENED TO UTAKO?!
ARE YOU THE NEW BARTENDER, LITTLE MISS?
AREN'T YOU A BIT YOUNG? HA! HA! HA! COUGH!
UMM...
UHH...
I'LL HAVE A HIGH-BALL!
BUT...
UMM...
YOU DON'T KNOW HOW TO MAKE ONE?
NO PROBLEM! I'LL SHOW YOU!
BUT...
UHH...

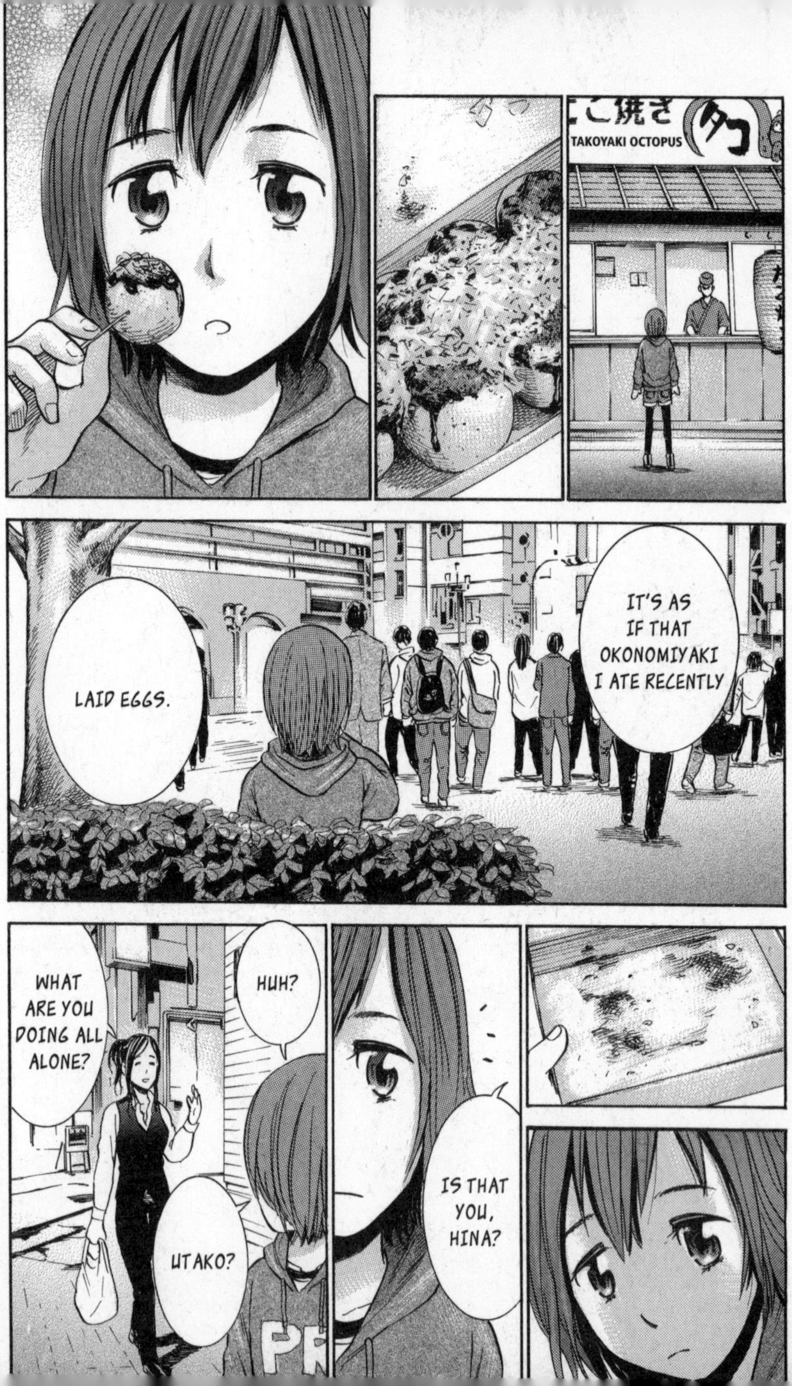
TAKOYAKI OCTOPUS
IT'S AS IF THAT OKONOMIYAKI I ATE RECENTLY
LAID EGGS.
IS THAT YOU, HINA?
HUH?
WHAT ARE YOU DOING ALL ALONE?
UTAKO?

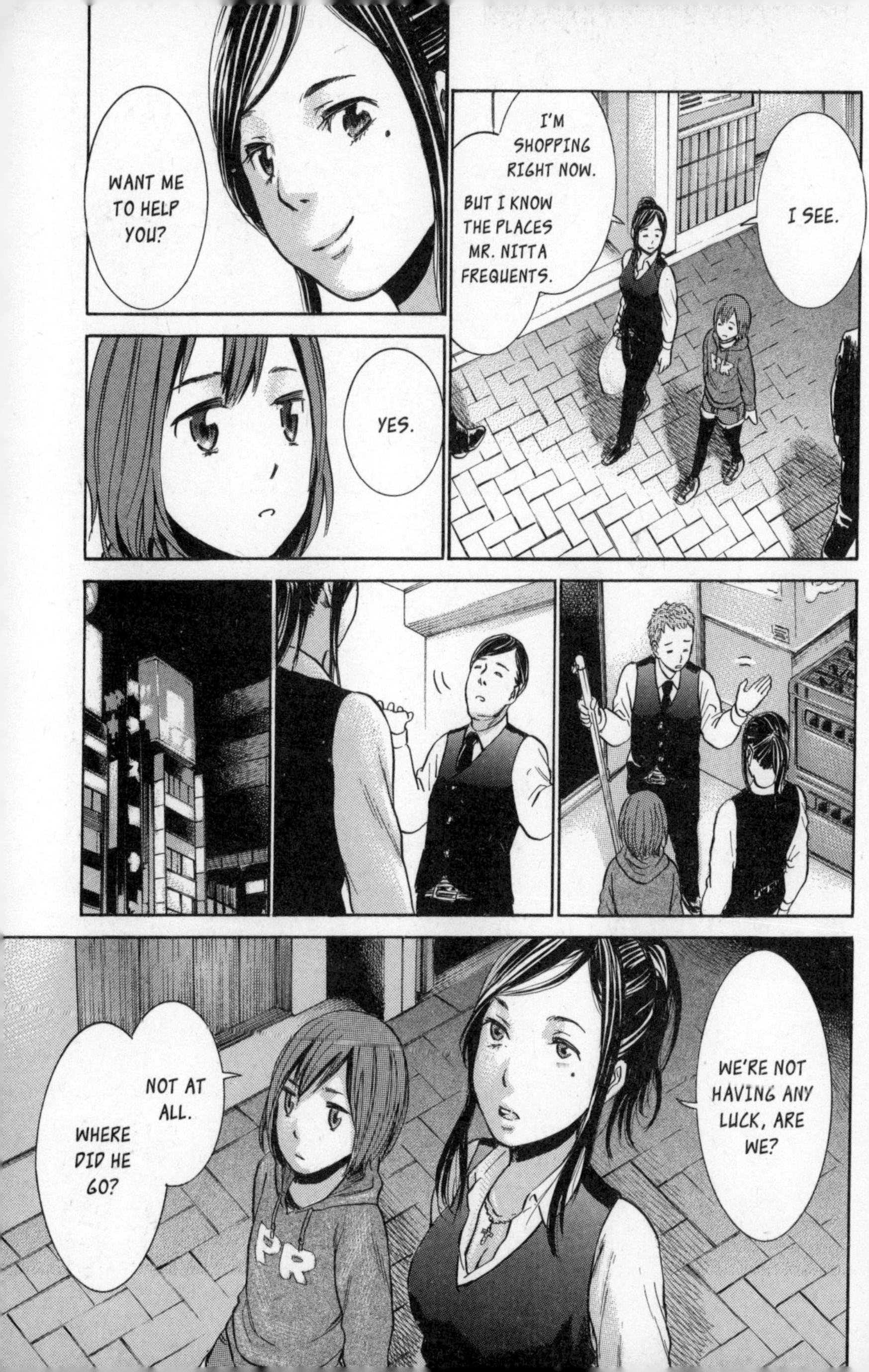
I SEE.
I'M SHOPPING RIGHT NOW.
BUT I KNOW THE PLACES MR. NITTA FREQUENTS.
WANT ME TO HELP YOU?
YES.
WE'RE NOT HAVING ANY LUCK, ARE WE?
NOT AT ALL.
WHERE DID HE GO?

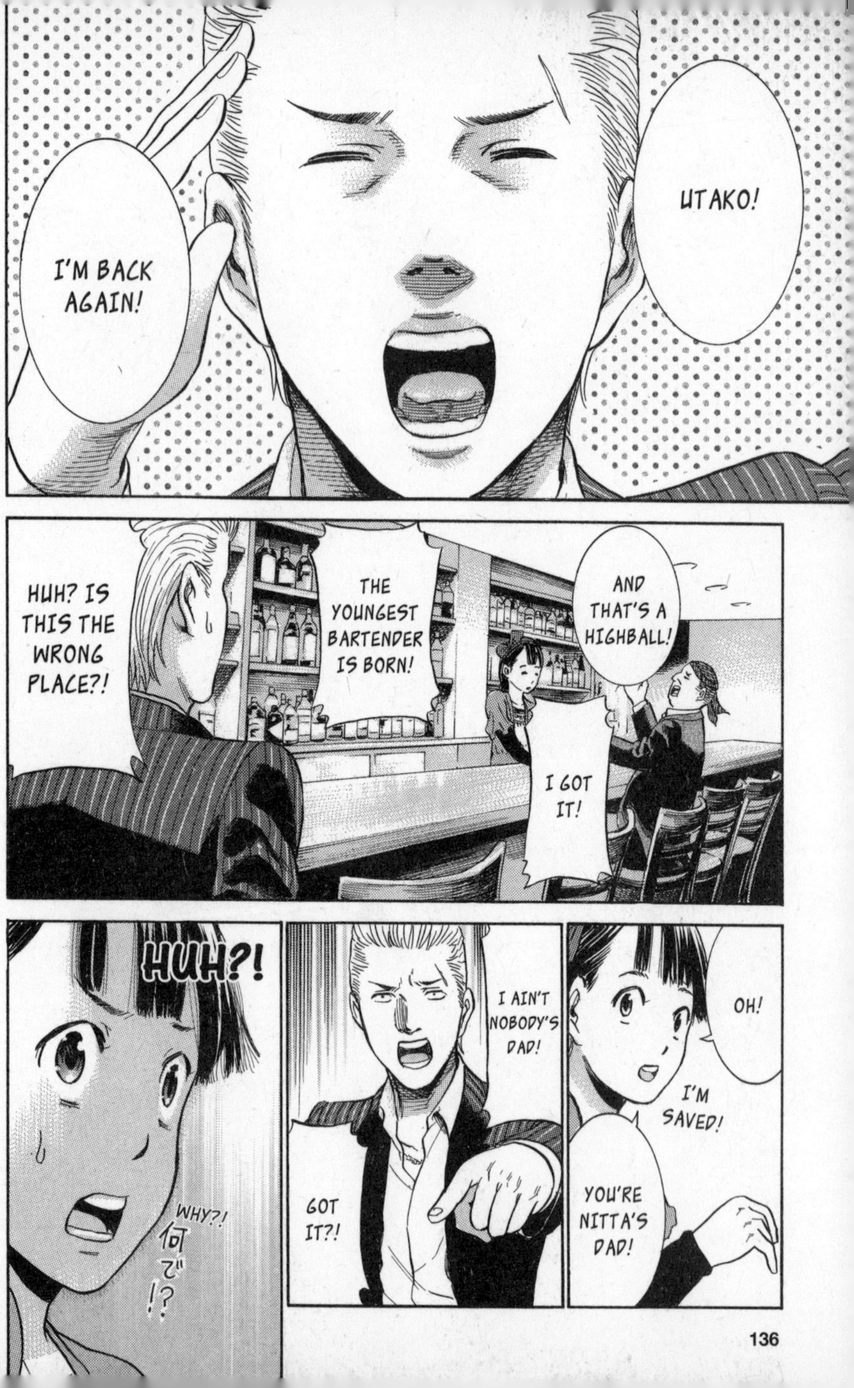
UTAKO!
I'M BACK AGAIN!
AND THAT'S A HIGHBALL!
THE YOUNGEST BARTENDER IS BORN!
I GOT IT!
HUH? IS THIS THE WRONG PLACE?!
OH!
I'M SAVED!
YOU'RE NITTA'S DAD!
I AIN'T NOBODY'S DAD!
GOT IT?!
HUH?!
WHY?!
何で!?

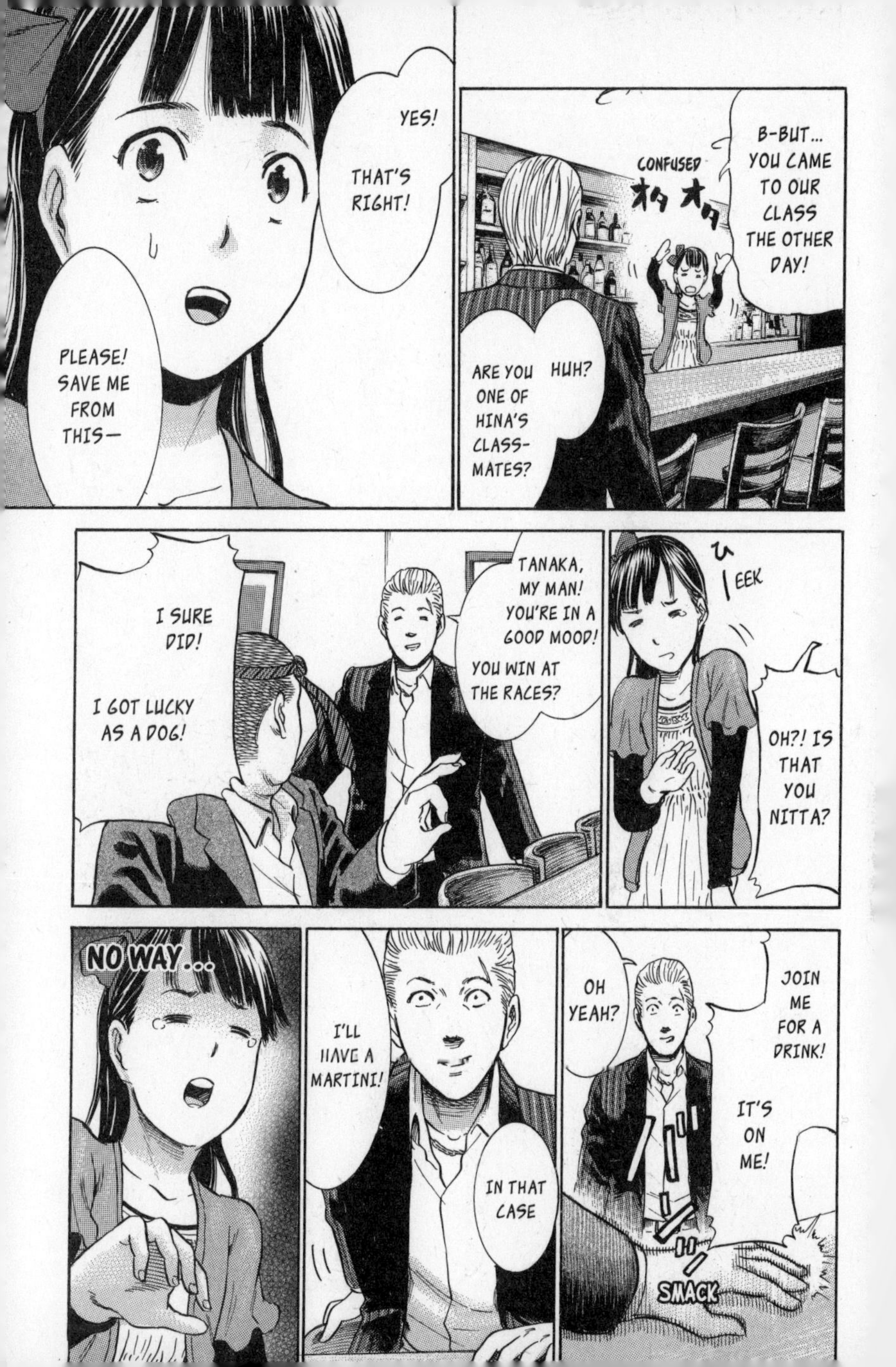
B-BUT... YOU CAME TO OUR CLASS THE OTHER DAY!
CONFUSED
オタ オタ
HUH?
ARE YOU ONE OF HINA'S CLASS-MATES?
YES! THAT'S RIGHT!
PLEASE! SAVE ME FROM THIS—
ひ
EEK
OH?! IS THAT YOU NITTA?
TANAKA, MY MAN! YOU'RE IN A GOOD MOOD! YOU WIN AT THE RACES?
I SURE DID! I GOT LUCKY AS A DOG!
JOIN ME FOR A DRINK!
OH YEAH?
IT'S ON ME!
SMACK
IN THAT CASE
I'LL HAVE A MARTINI!
NO WAY...

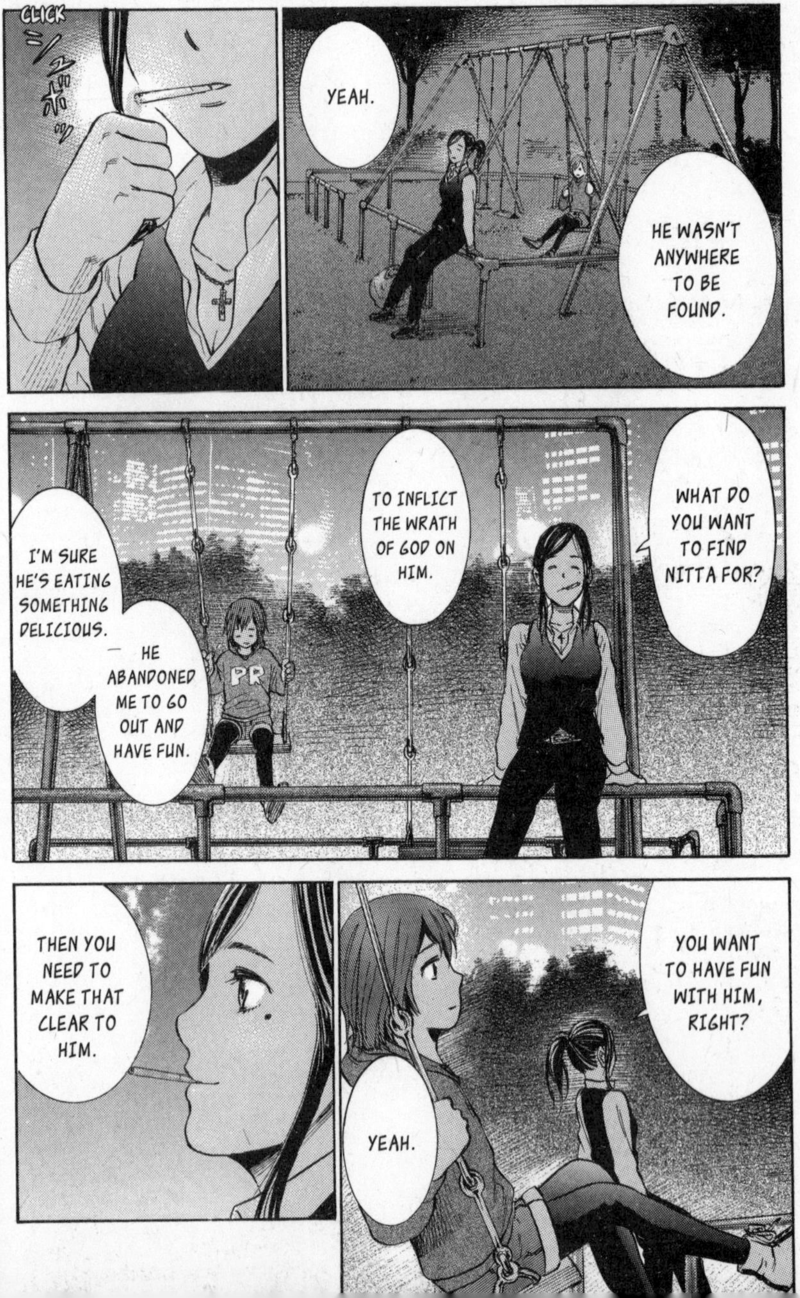
HE WASN'T ANYWHERE TO BE FOUND.
YEAH.
CLICK
WHAT DO YOU WANT TO FIND NITTA FOR?
TO INFLICT THE WRATH OF GOD ON HIM.
I'M SURE HE'S EATING SOMETHING DELICIOUS.
— HE ABANDONED ME TO GO OUT AND HAVE FUN.
YOU WANT TO HAVE FUN WITH HIM, RIGHT?
YEAH.
THEN YOU NEED TO MAKE THAT CLEAR TO HIM.

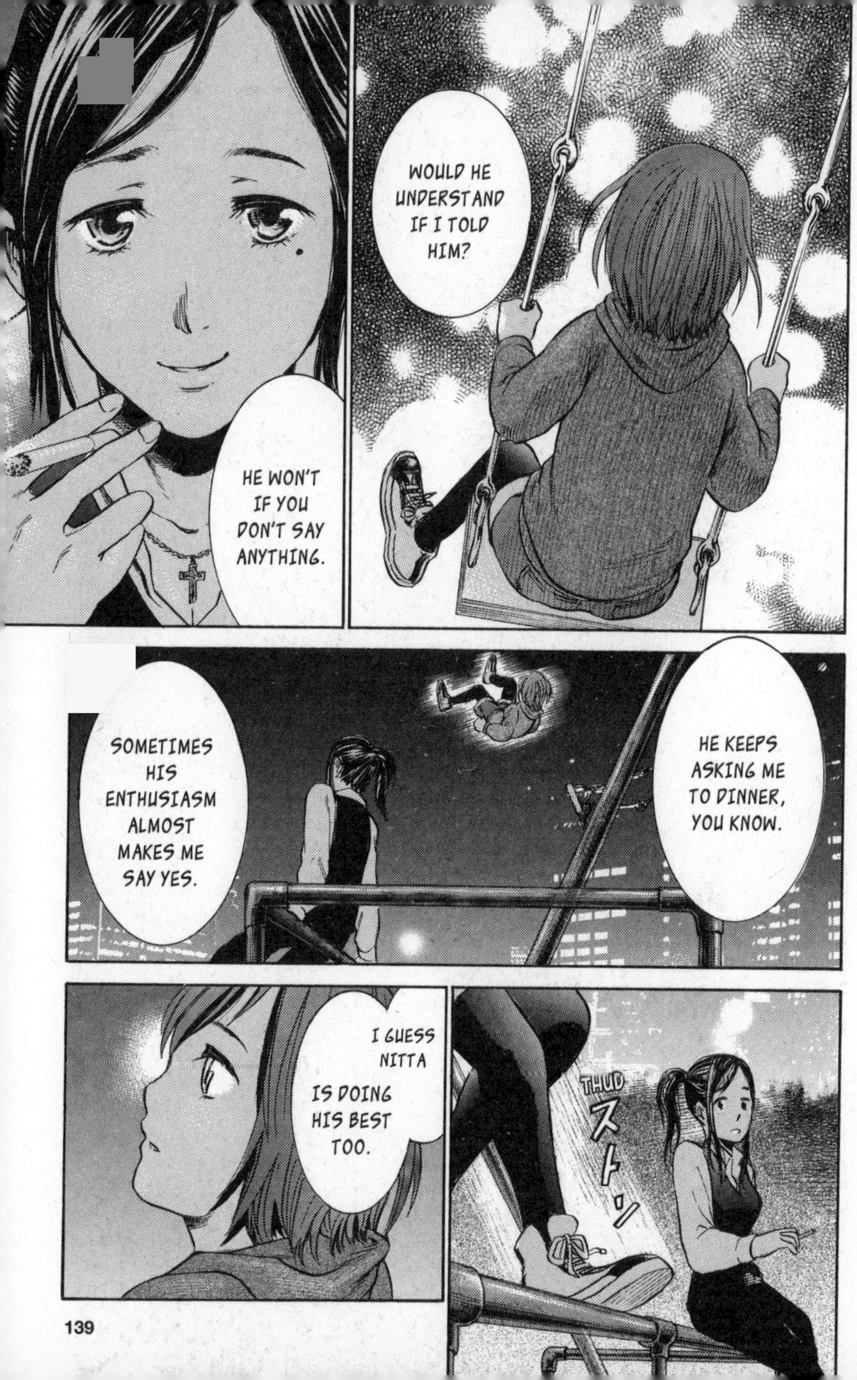
WOULD HE UNDERSTAND IF I TOLD HIM?
HE WON'T IF YOU DON'T SAY ANYTHING.
HE KEEPS ASKING ME TO DINNER, YOU KNOW.
SOMETIMES HIS ENTHUSIASM ALMOST MAKES ME SAY YES.
THUD
ストン
I GUESS NITTA
IS DOING HIS BEST TOO.

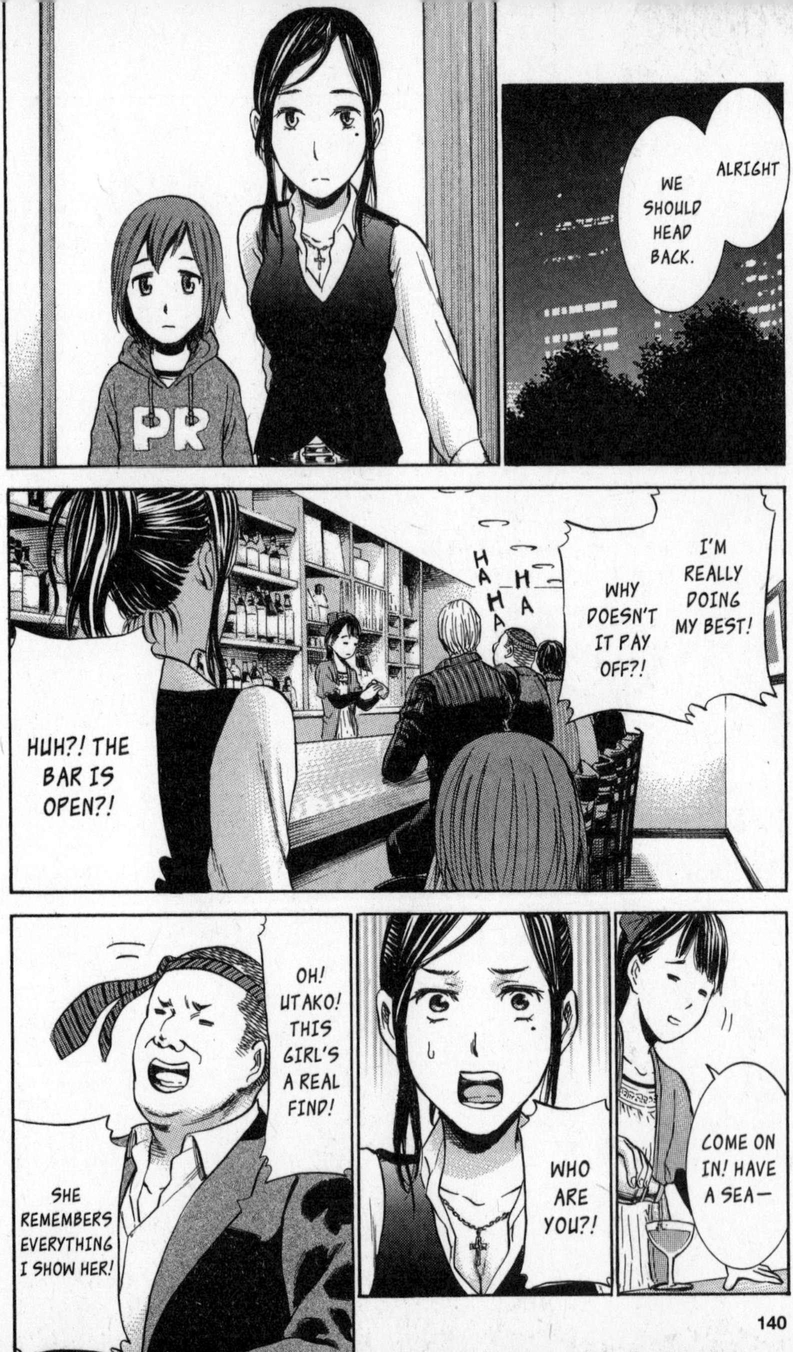
ALRIGHT
WE SHOULD HEAD BACK.
I'M REALLY DOING MY BEST!
WHY DOESN'T IT PAY OFF?!
HAHAHA
HA
HUH?! THE BAR IS OPEN?!
COME ON IN! HAVE A SEA—
WHO ARE YOU?!
OH! UTAKO! THIS GIRL'S A REAL FIND!
SHE REMEMBERS EVERYTHING I SHOW HER!

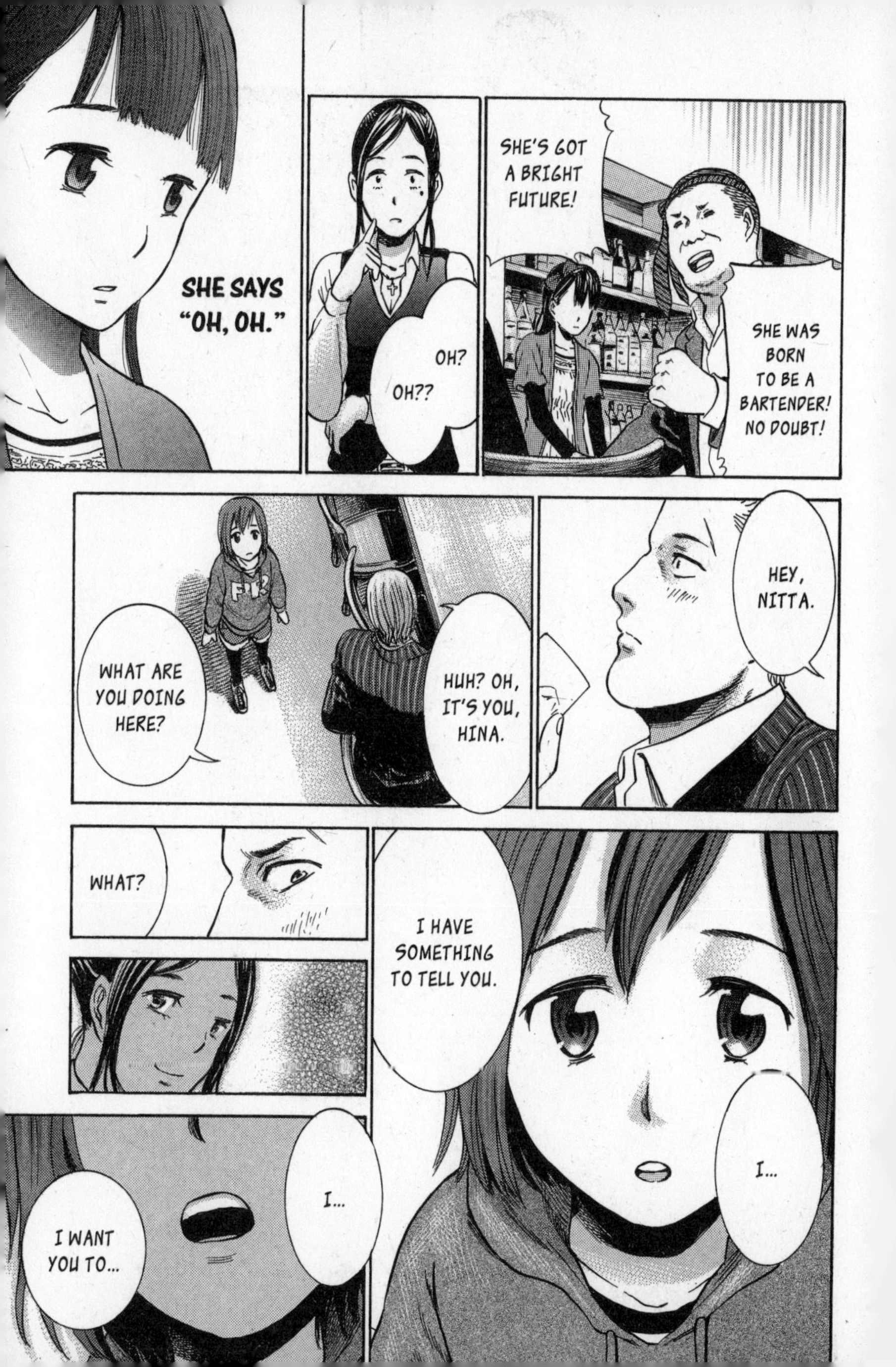
SHE'S GOT A BRIGHT FUTURE!
SHE WAS BORN TO BE A BARTENDER! NO DOUBT!
OH? OH??
SHE SAYS "OH, OH."
HEY, NITTA.
HUH? OH, IT'S YOU, HINA.
WHAT ARE YOU DOING HERE?
I HAVE SOMETHING TO TELL YOU.
I...
WHAT?
I...
I WANT YOU TO...

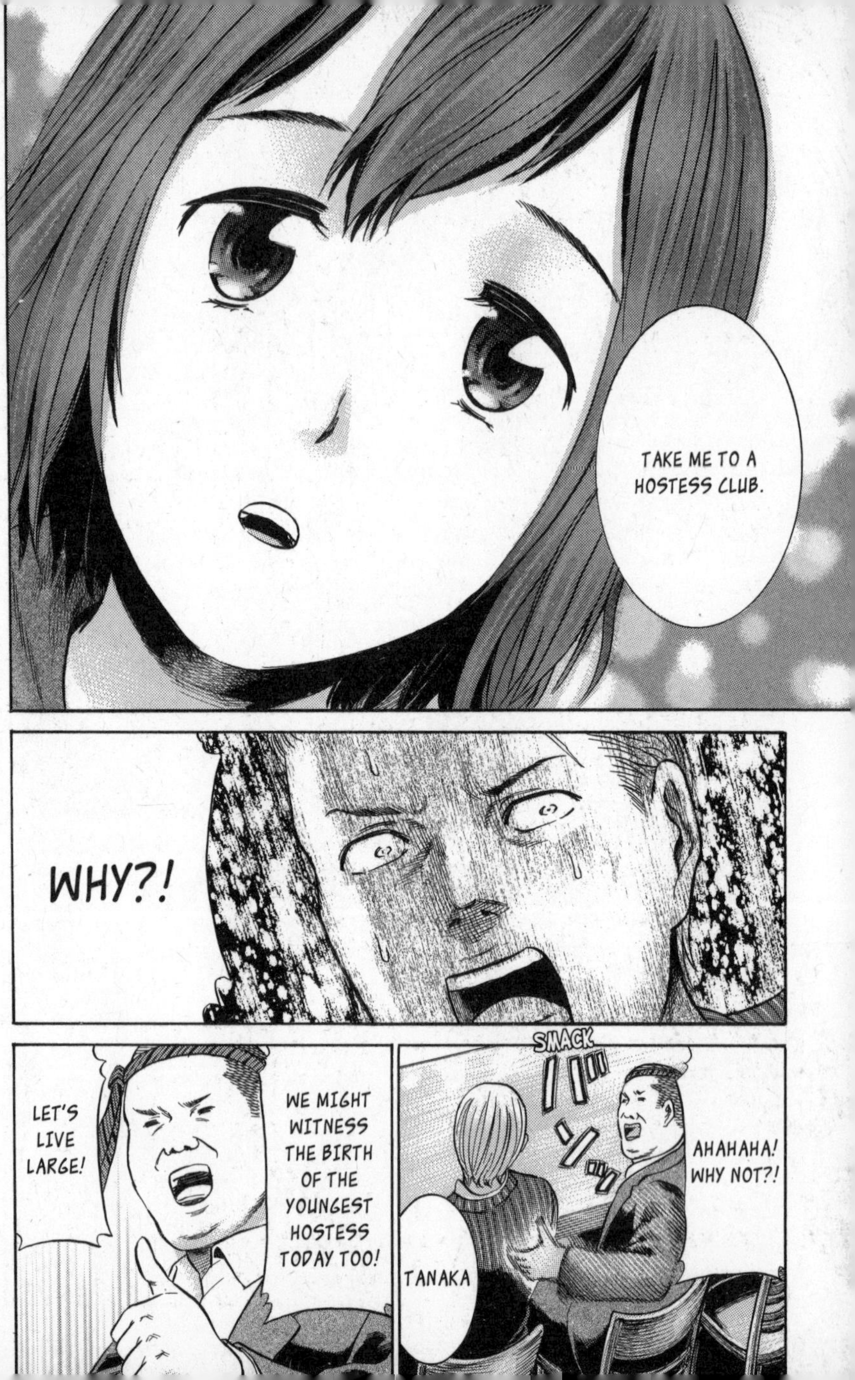
TAKE ME TO A HOSTESS CLUB.
WHY?!
SMACK
AHAHAHA! WHY NOT?!
TANAKA
WE MIGHT WITNESS THE BIRTH OF THE YOUNGEST HOSTESS TODAY TOO!
LET'S LIVE LARGE!

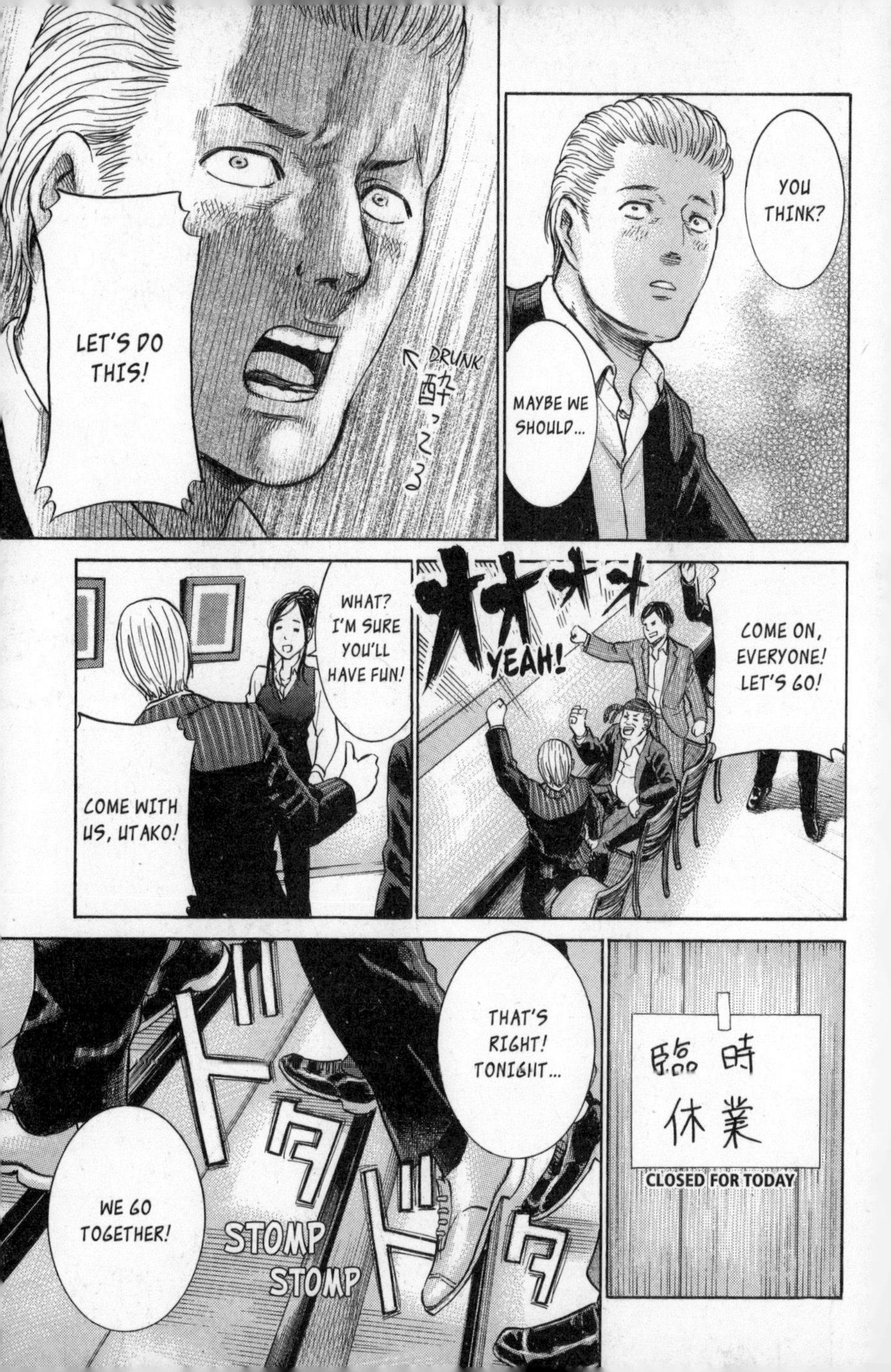
YOU THINK?
MAYBE WE SHOULD...
LET'S DO THIS!
DRUNK
酔ってる
YEAH!
COME ON, EVERYONE! LET'S GO!
WHAT? I'M SURE YOU'LL HAVE FUN!
COME WITH US, UTAKO!
臨時休業
CLOSED FOR TODAY
THAT'S RIGHT! TONIGHT...
WE GO TOGETHER!
STOMP
STOMP

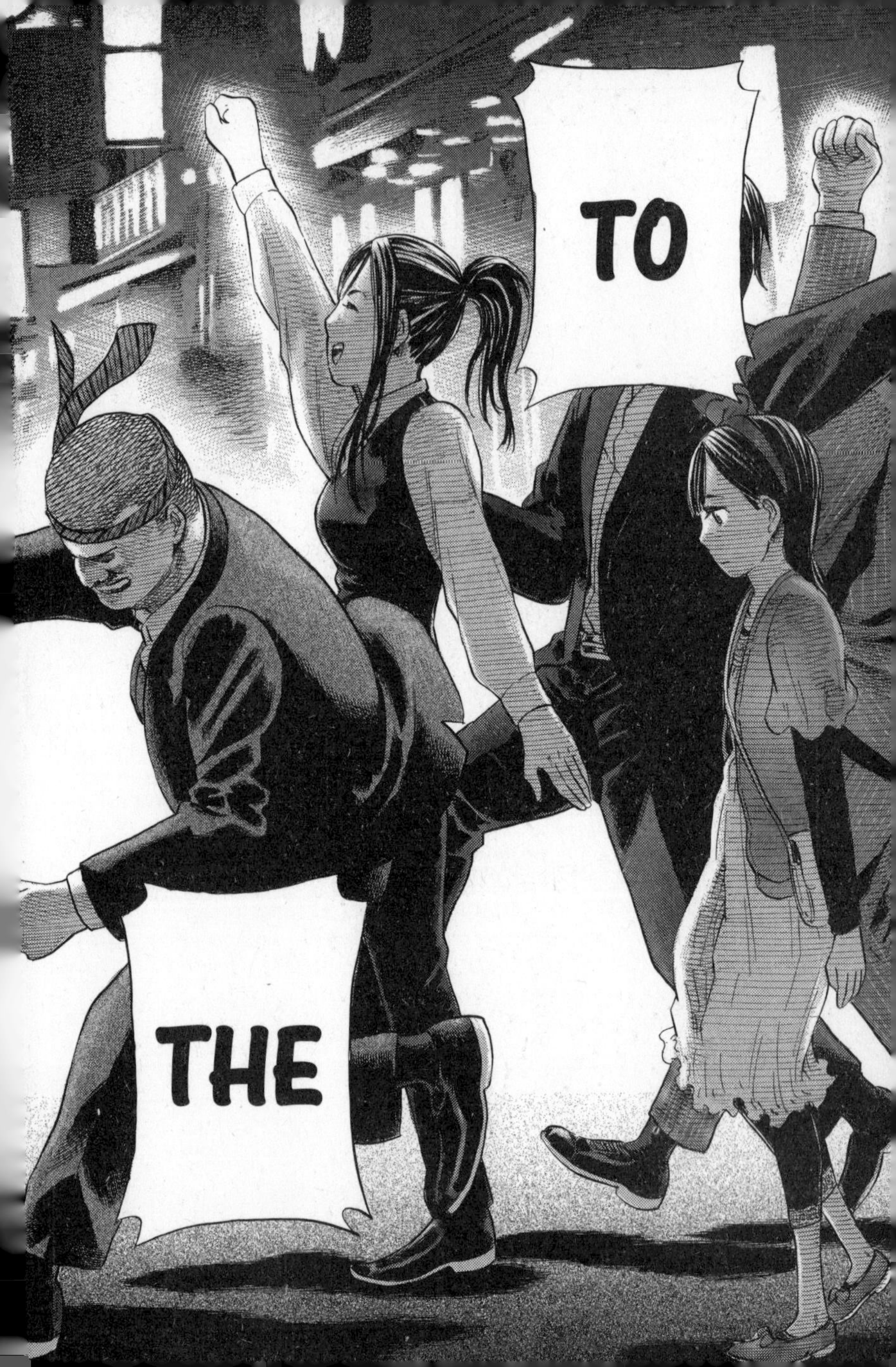
TO
THE

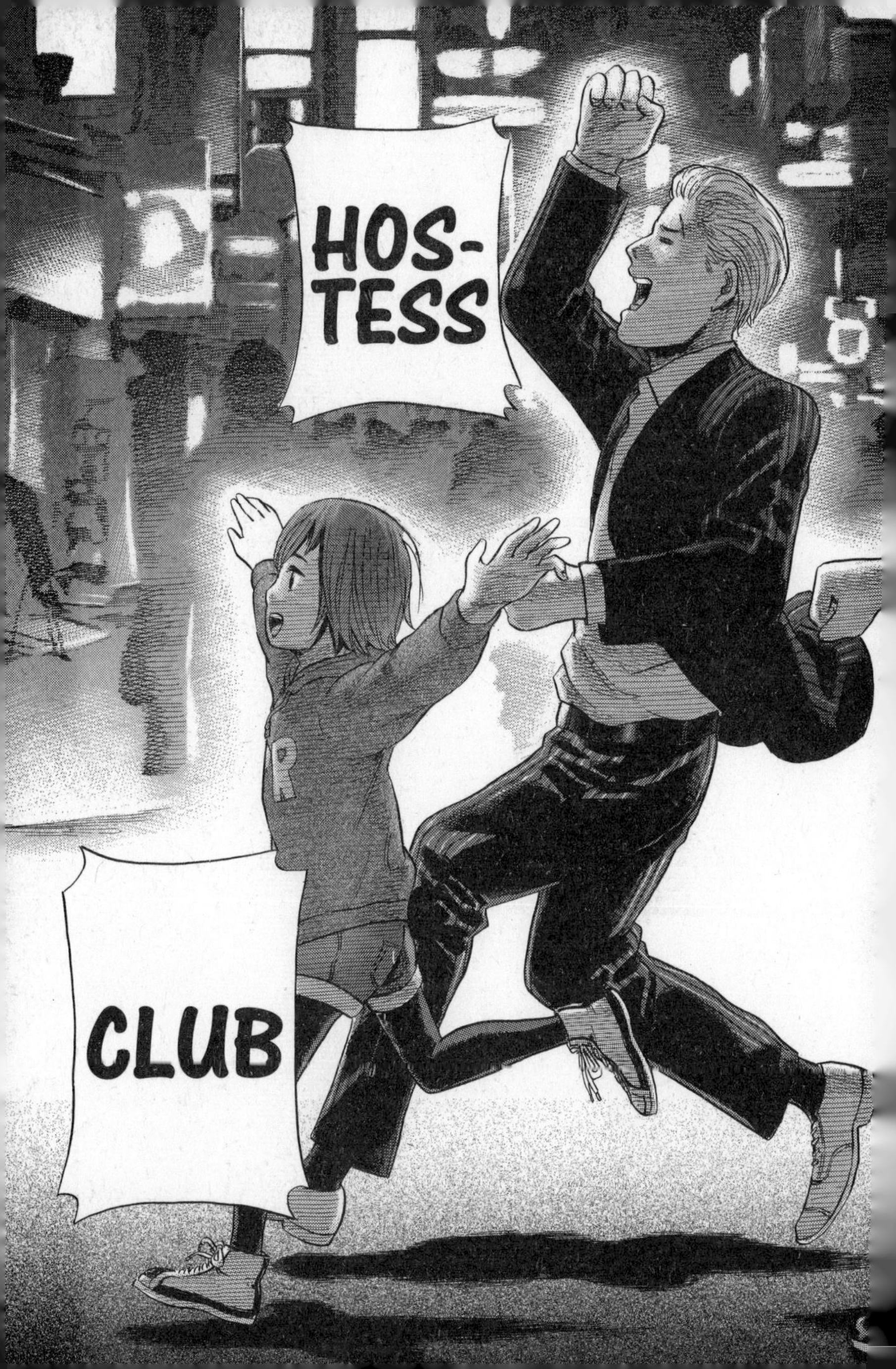
HOS-
TESS
CLUB

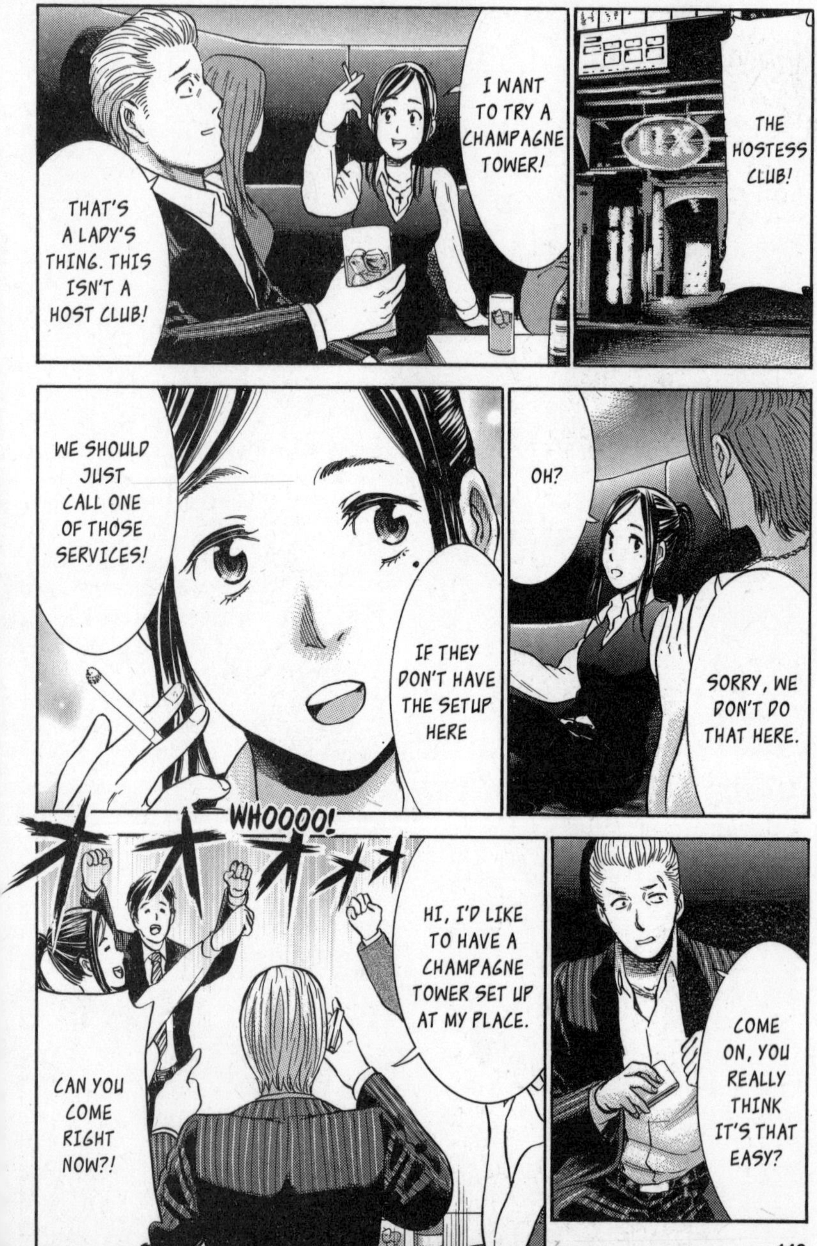
THE HOSTESS CLUB!
I WANT TO TRY A CHAMPAGNE TOWER!
THAT'S A LADY'S THING. THIS ISN'T A HOST CLUB!
OH?
SORRY, WE DON'T DO THAT HERE.
IF THEY DON'T HAVE THE SETUP HERE
WE SHOULD JUST CALL ONE OF THOSE SERVICES!
COME ON, YOU REALLY THINK IT'S THAT EASY?
WHOOOO!
HI, I'D LIKE TO HAVE A CHAMPAGNE TOWER SET UP AT MY PLACE.
CAN YOU COME RIGHT NOW?!

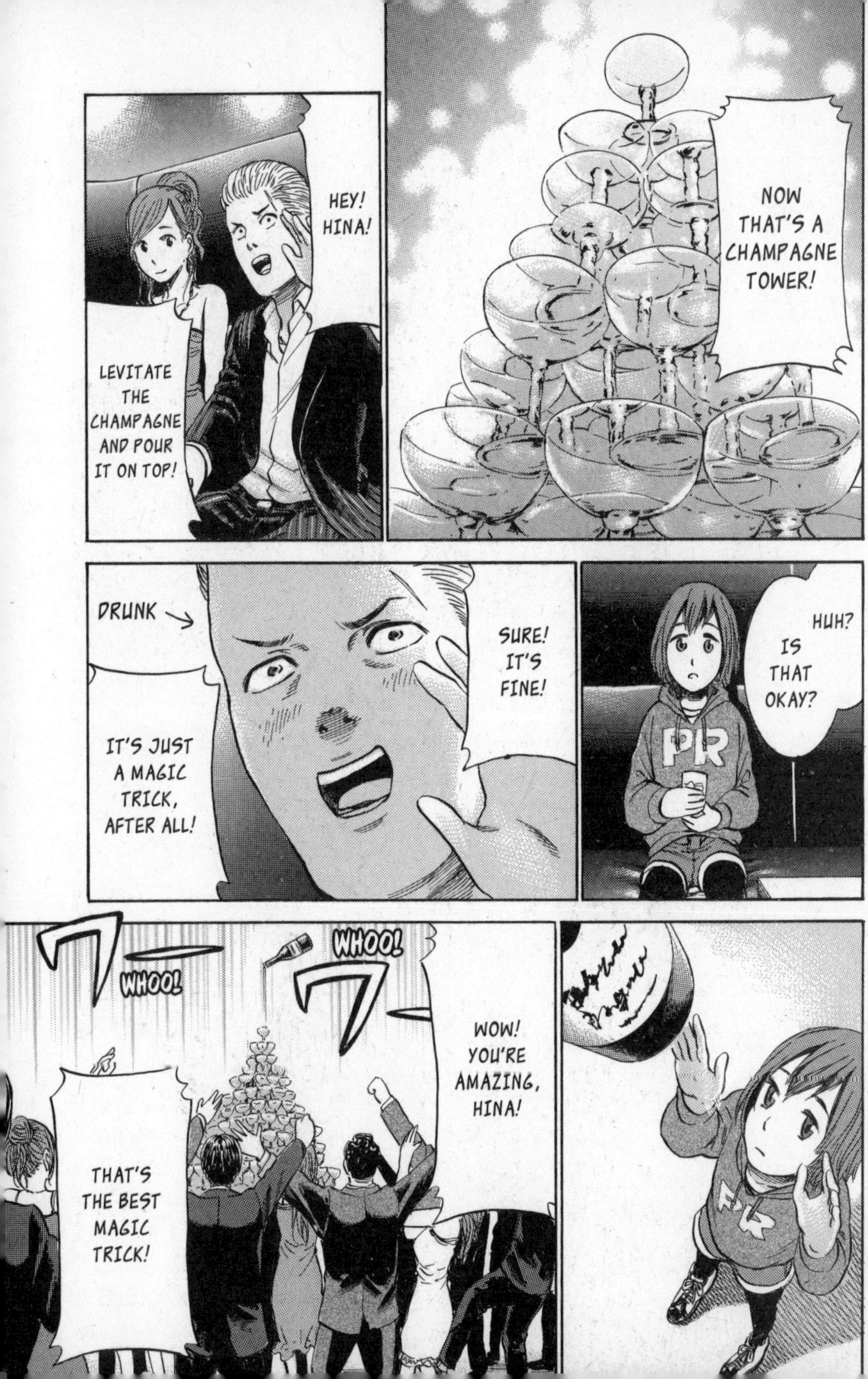
NOW THAT'S A CHAMPAGNE TOWER!
HEY! HINA!
LEVITATE THE CHAMPAGNE AND POUR IT ON TOP!
HUH? IS THAT OKAY?
SURE! IT'S FINE!
DRUNK
IT'S JUST A MAGIC TRICK, AFTER ALL!
WHOO!
WOW! YOU'RE AMAZING, HINA!
WHOO!
THAT'S THE BEST MAGIC TRICK!

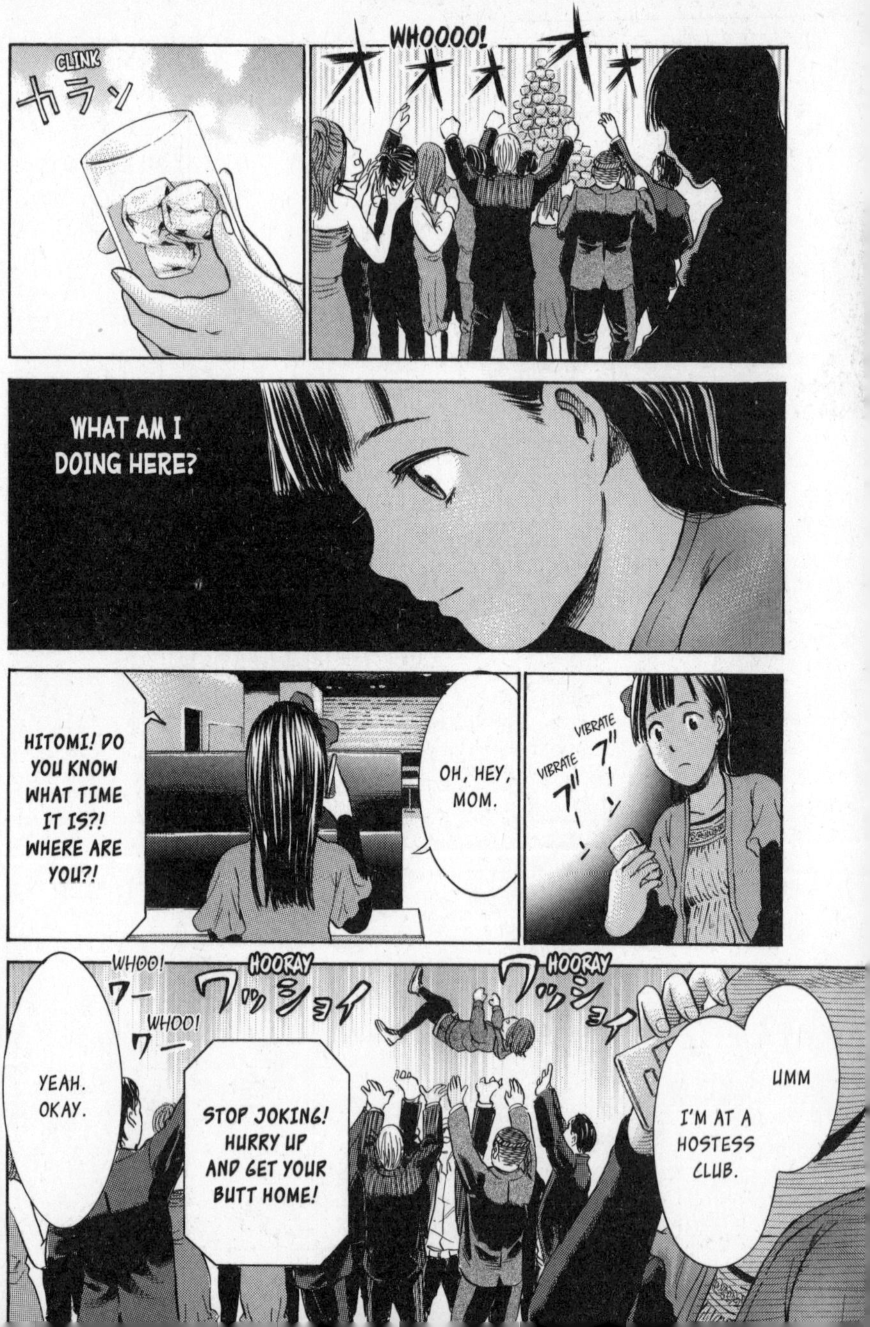
WHOOOOO!
オオオオオ
CLINK
カランッ
WHAT AM I DOING HERE?
VIBRATE
ブーン
VIBRATE
ブーン
OH, HEY, MOM.
HITOMI! DO YOU KNOW WHAT TIME IT IS?! WHERE ARE YOU?!
HOORAY
ワッショイ
UMM
I'M AT A HOSTESS CLUB.
HOORAY
ワッショイ
WHOO!
ワー
WHOO!
ワー
STOP JOKING! HURRY UP AND GET YOUR BUTT HOME!
YEAH. OKAY.

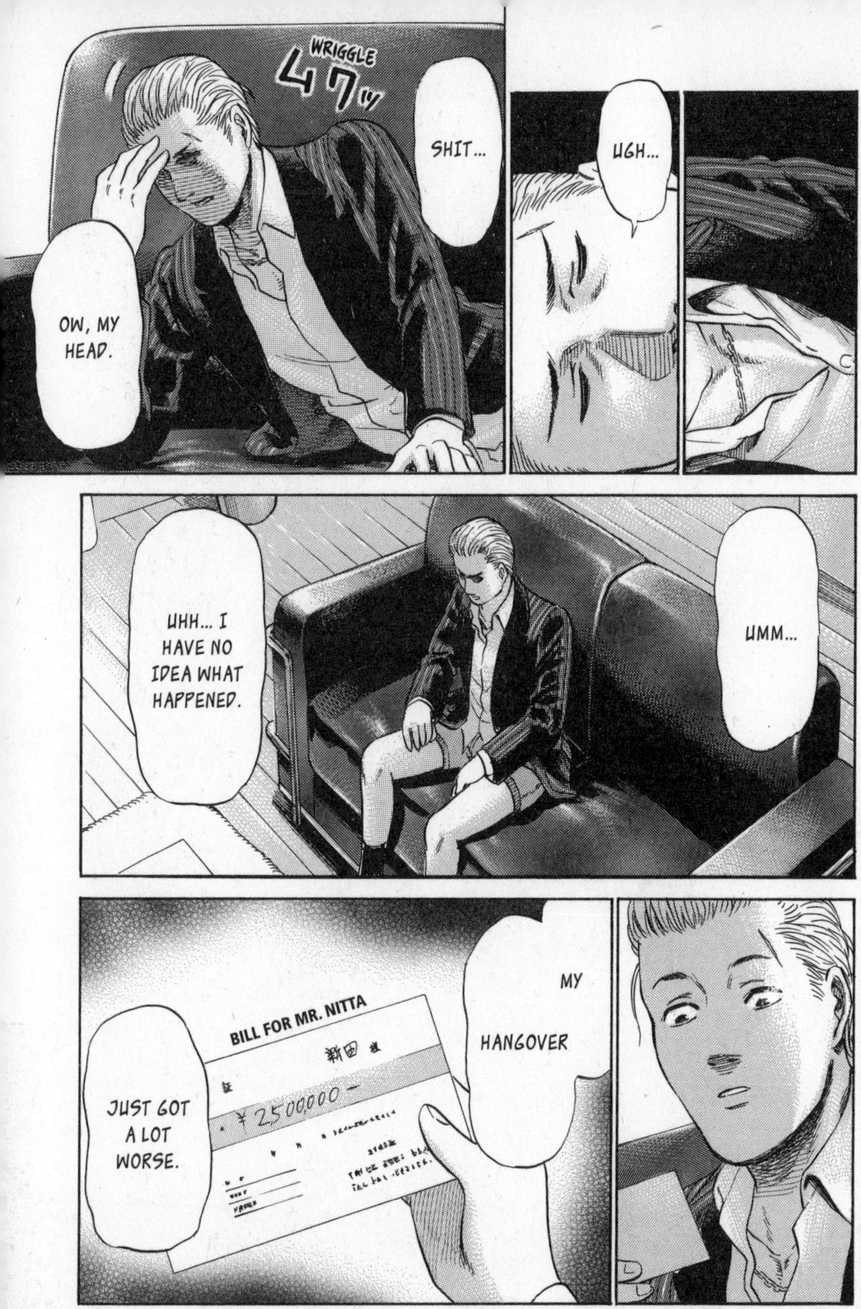
UGH...
WRIGGLE
ムクッ
SHIT...
OW, MY HEAD.
UMM...
UHH... I HAVE NO IDEA WHAT HAPPENED.
MY
HANGOVER
BILL FOR MR. NITTA
新田 様
¥2,500,000ー
JUST GOT A LOT WORSE.

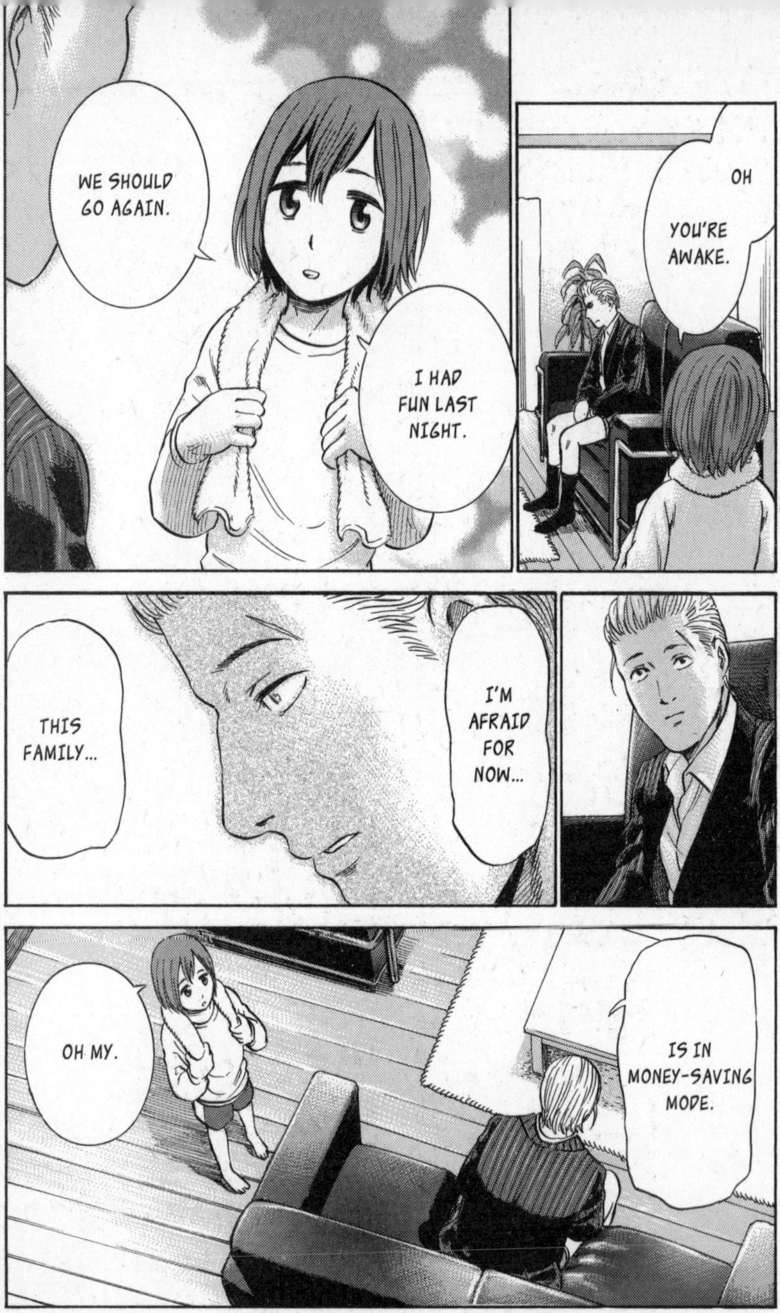
OH
YOU'RE AWAKE.
I HAD FUN LAST NIGHT.
WE SHOULD GO AGAIN.
I'M AFRAID FOR NOW...
THIS FAMILY...
IS IN MONEY-SAVING MODE.
OH MY.

CHAPTER 4 END

EXTRA 1

THOSE TASTEBUDS OF YOURS ARE CLUELESS

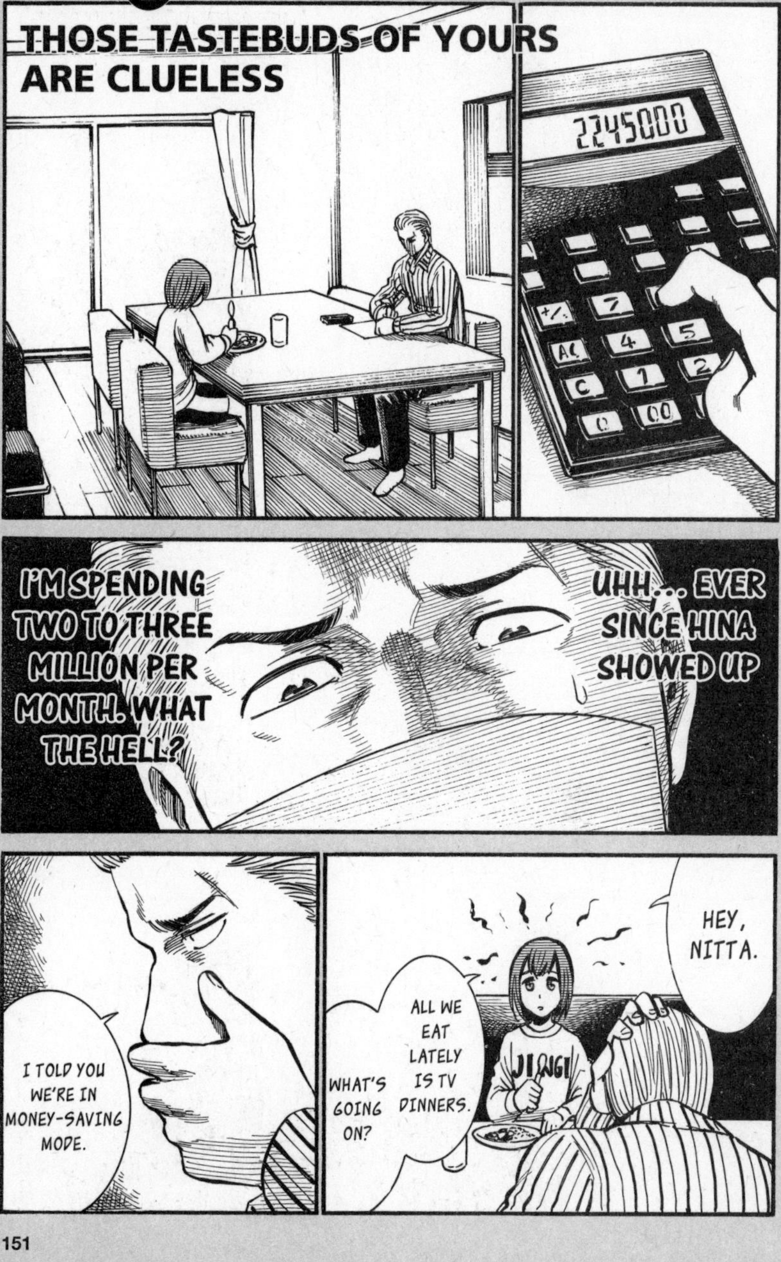

2245000
UHH... EVER SINCE HINA SHOWED UP
I'M SPENDING TWO TO THREE MILLION PER MONTH. WHAT THE HELL?
HEY, NITTA.
ALL WE EAT LATELY IS TV DINNERS.
WHAT'S GOING ON?
I TOLD YOU WE'RE IN MONEY-SAVING MODE.

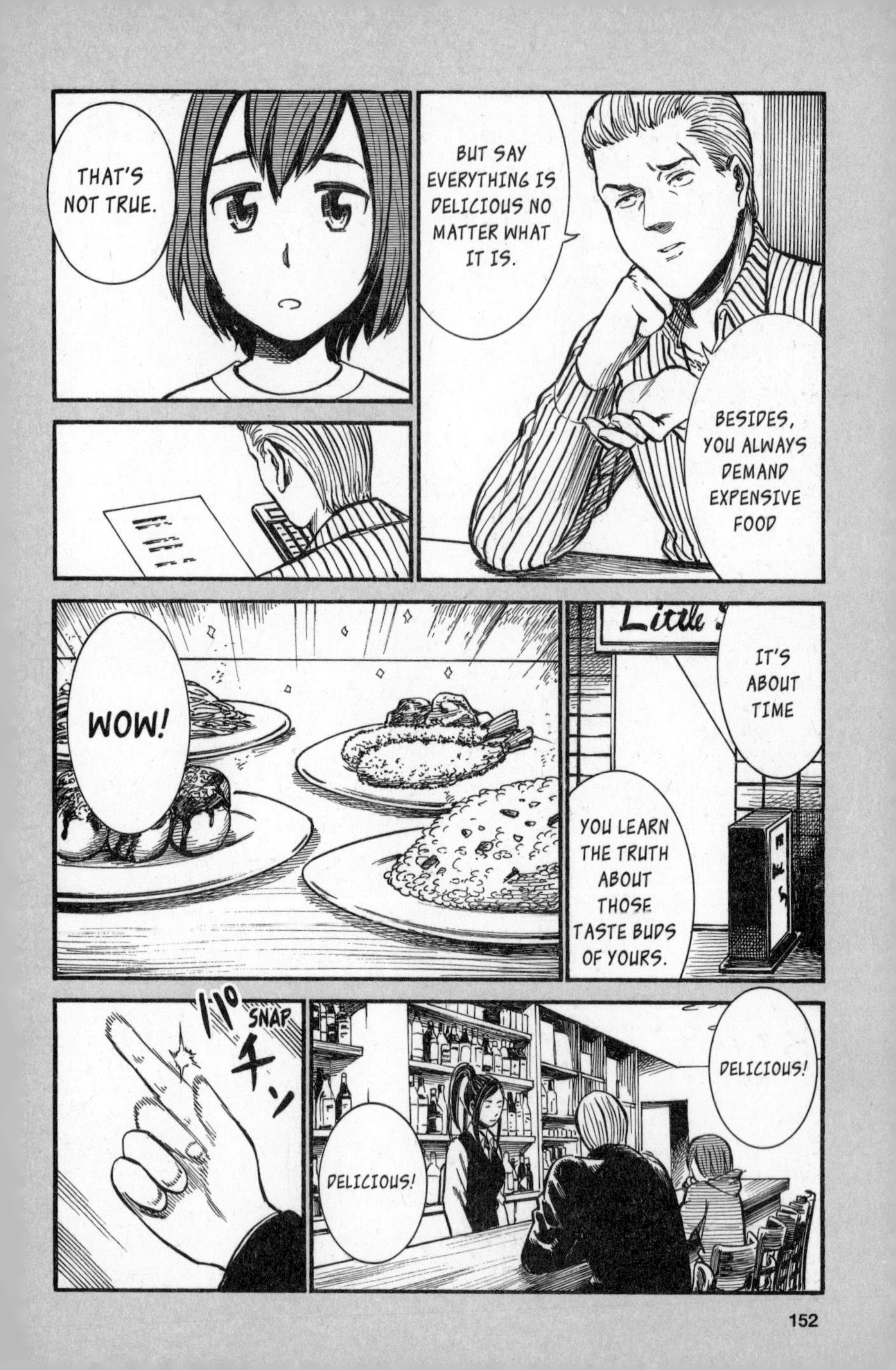
BUT SAY EVERYTHING IS DELICIOUS NO MATTER WHAT IT IS.
BESIDES, YOU ALWAYS DEMAND EXPENSIVE FOOD
THAT'S NOT TRUE.
Little
IT'S ABOUT TIME
YOU LEARN THE TRUTH ABOUT THOSE TASTE BUDS OF YOURS.
WOW!
DELICIOUS!
DELICIOUS!
SNAP

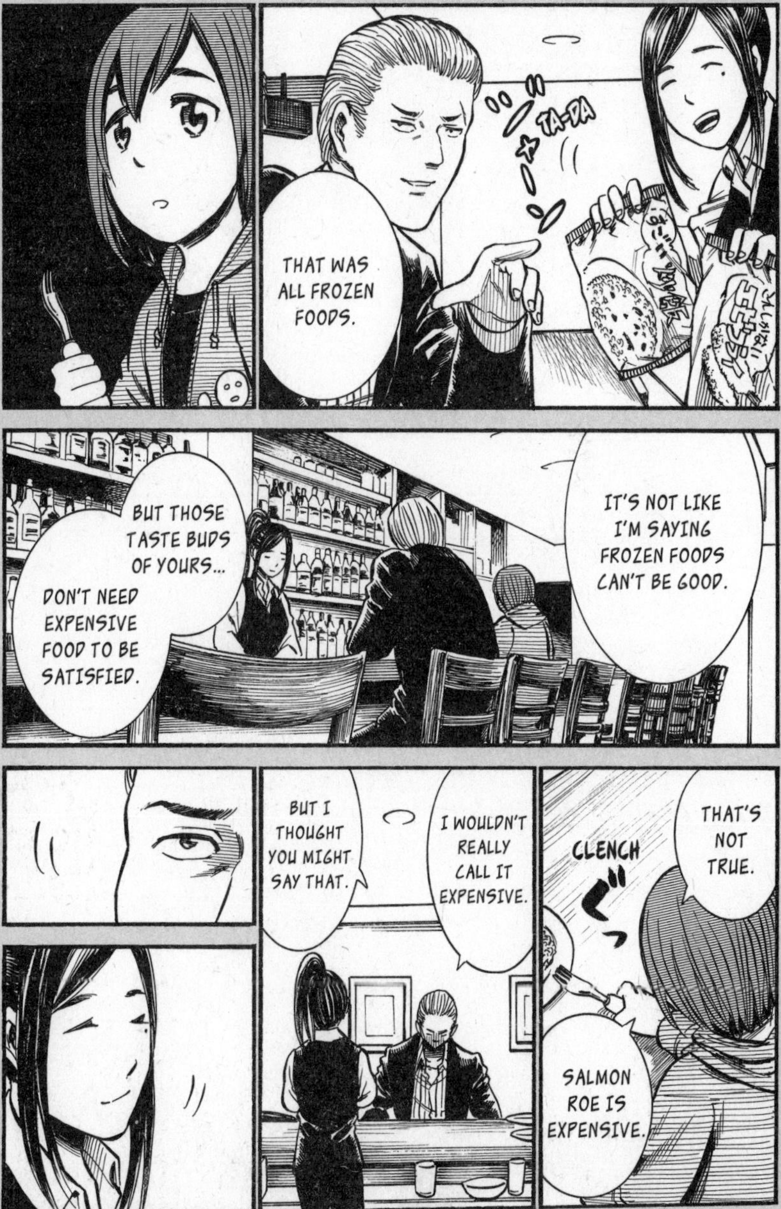
TA-DA
THAT WAS ALL FROZEN FOODS.
IT'S NOT LIKE I'M SAYING FROZEN FOODS CAN'T BE GOOD.
BUT THOSE TASTE BUDS OF YOURS...
DON'T NEED EXPENSIVE FOOD TO BE SATISFIED.
THAT'S NOT TRUE.
CLENCH
SALMON ROE IS EXPENSIVE.
I WOULDN'T REALLY CALL IT EXPENSIVE.
BUT I THOUGHT YOU MIGHT SAY THAT.

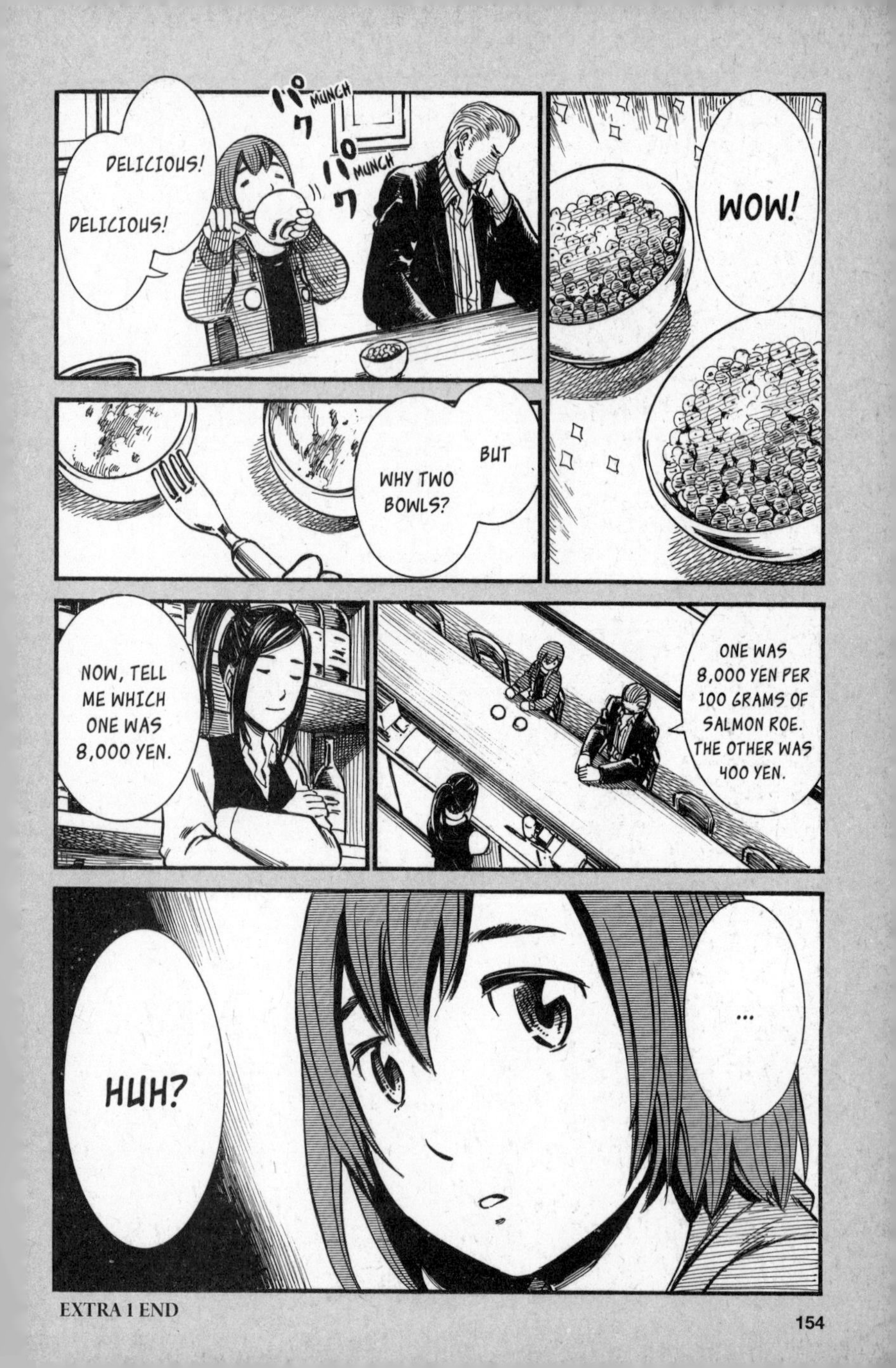
WOW!
パク
MUNCH
パク
MUNCH
DELICIOUS!
DELICIOUS!
BUT
WHY TWO BOWLS?
ONE WAS 8,000 YEN PER 100 GRAMS OF SALMON ROE. THE OTHER WAS 400 YEN.
NOW, TELL ME WHICH ONE WAS 8,000 YEN.
...
HUH?

EXTRA 1 END

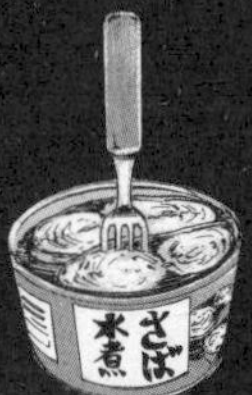
さば水煮

CHAPTER 5

THIS IS REALLY NO TIME FOR FISHING

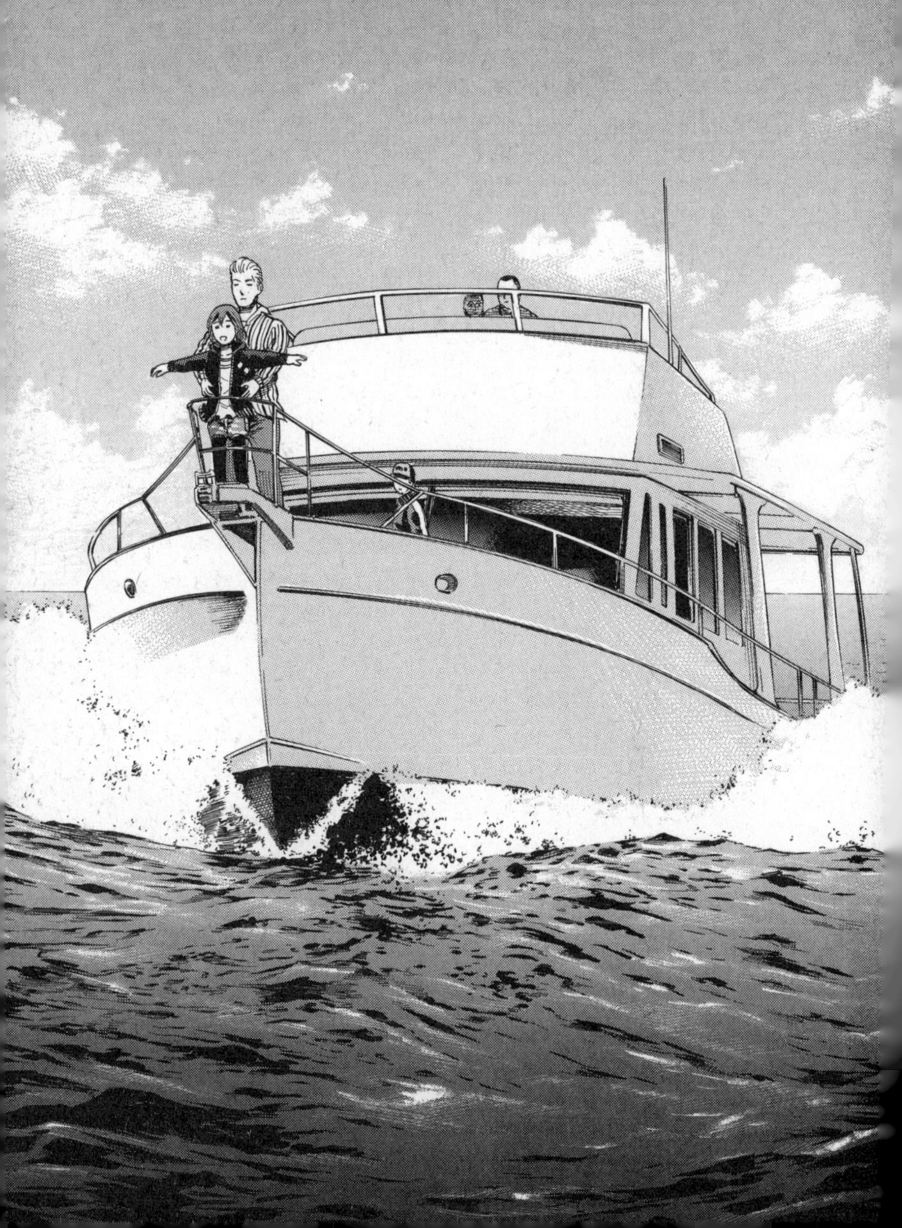

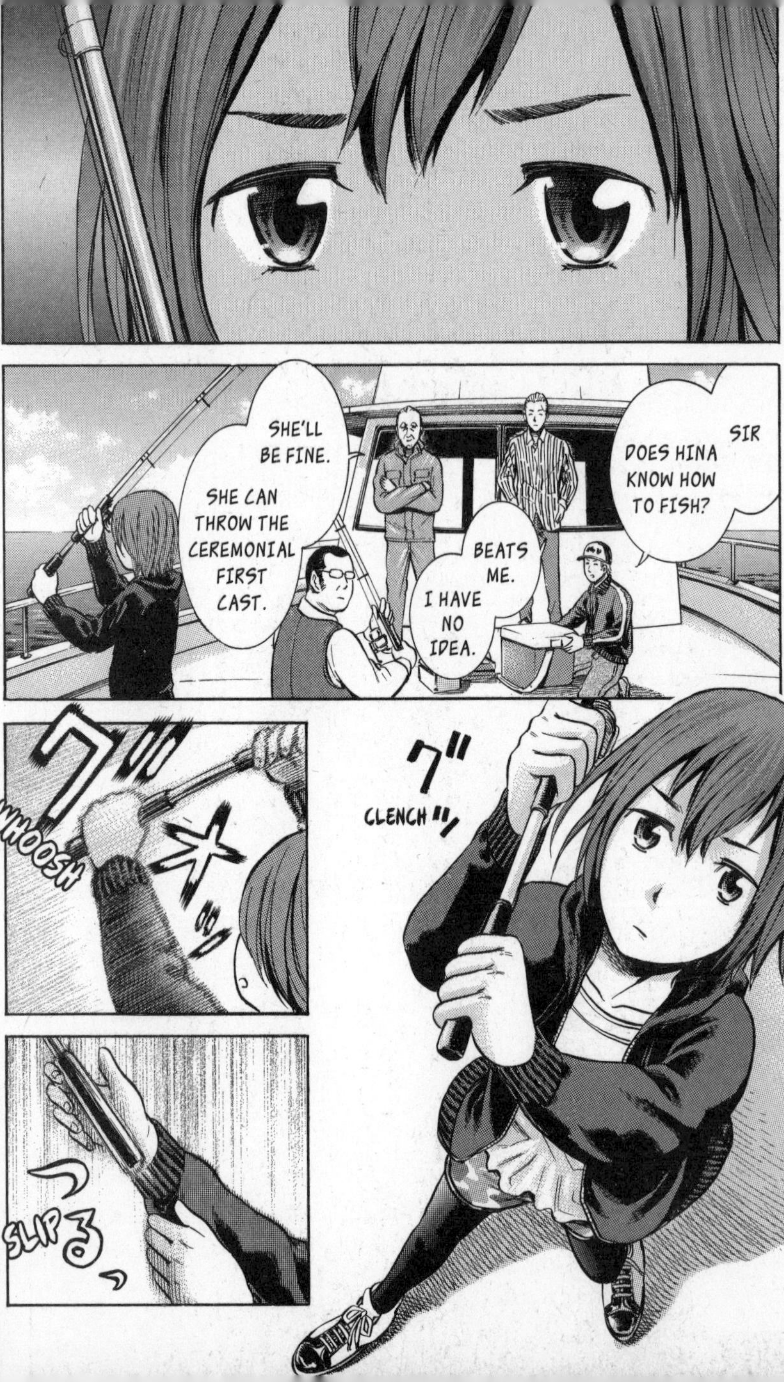
SIR
DOES HINA KNOW HOW TO FISH?
BEATS ME.
I HAVE NO IDEA.
SHE'LL BE FINE.
SHE CAN THROW THE CEREMONIAL FIRST CAST.
CLENCH
WHOOSH
SLIP

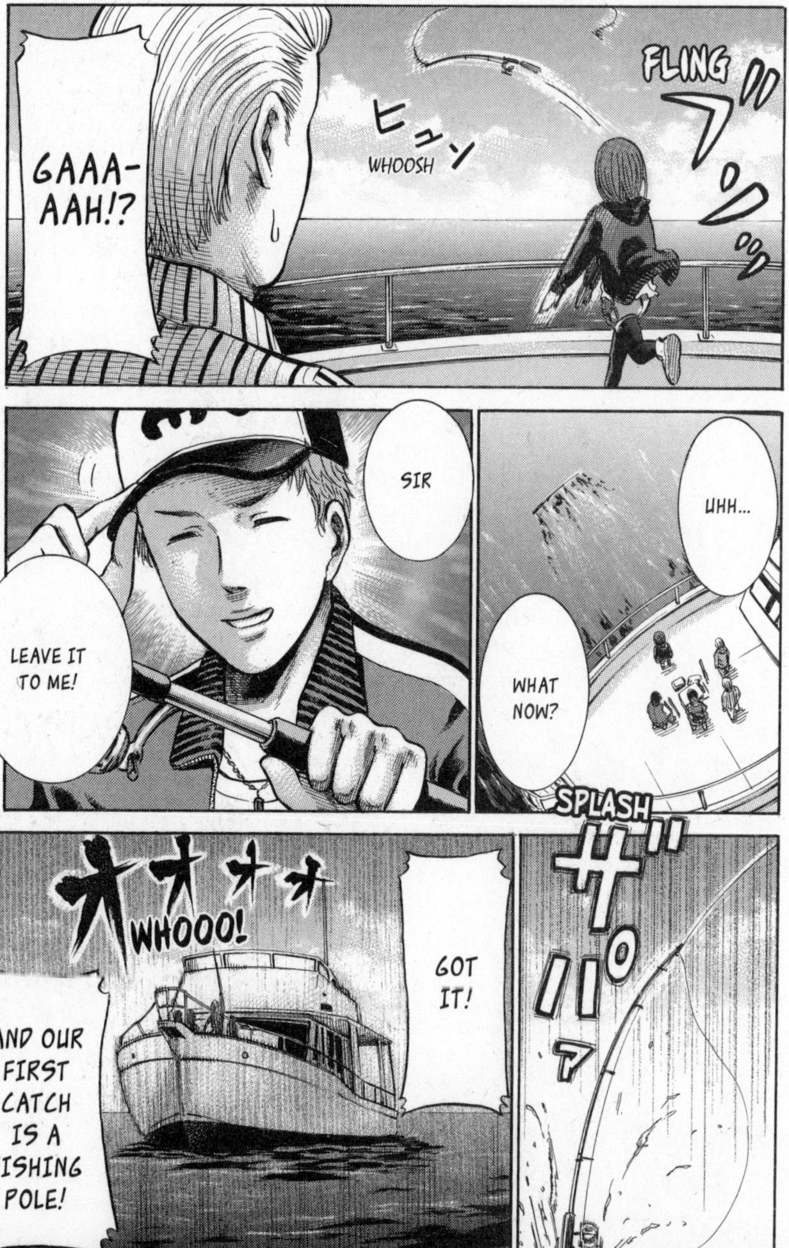
FLING
ヒュン
WHOOSH
GAAAA-AAH!?
UHH...
WHAT NOW?
SIR
LEAVE IT TO ME!
SPLASH
GOT IT!
WHOOO!
AND OUR FIRST CATCH IS A FISHING POLE!

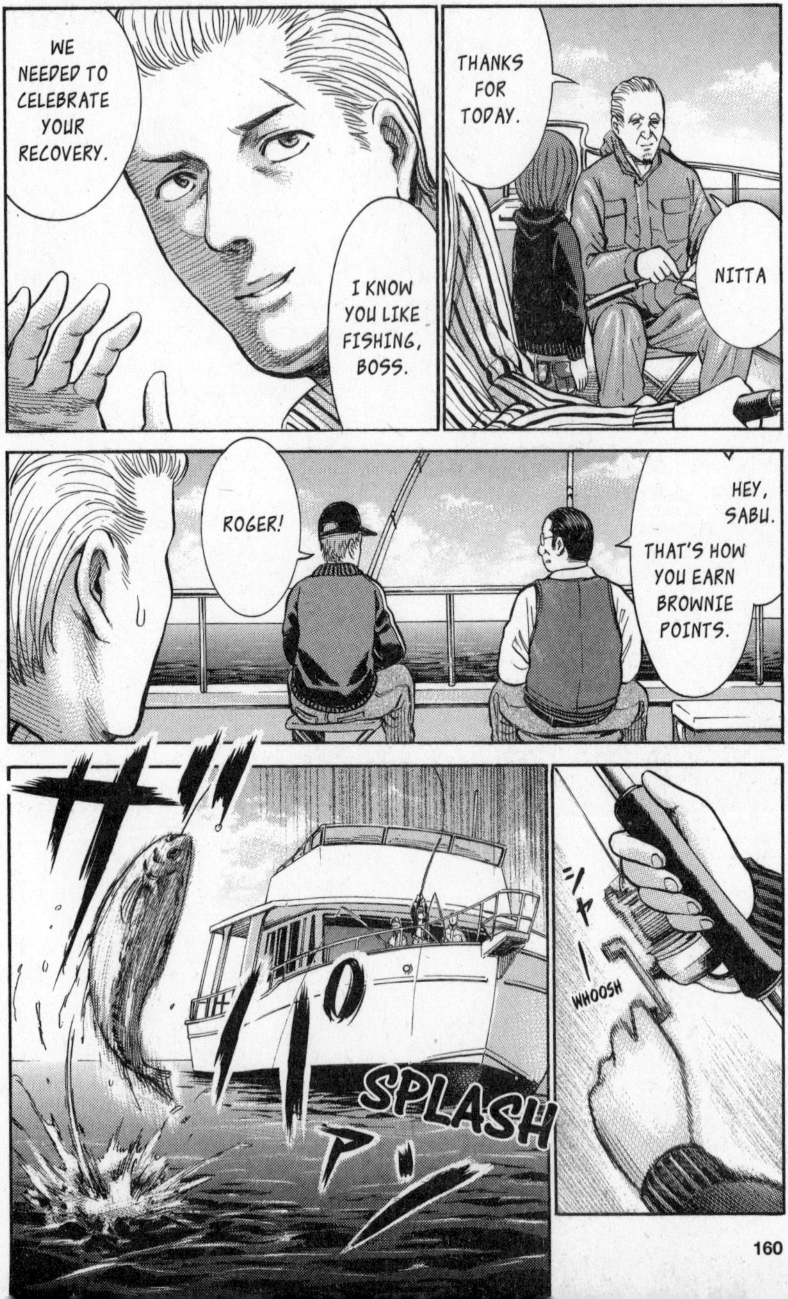
THANKS FOR TODAY.
NITTA
WE NEEDED TO CELEBRATE YOUR RECOVERY.
I KNOW YOU LIKE FISHING, BOSS.
HEY, SABU.
THAT'S HOW YOU EARN BROWNIE POINTS.
ROGER!
WHOOSH
SPLASH

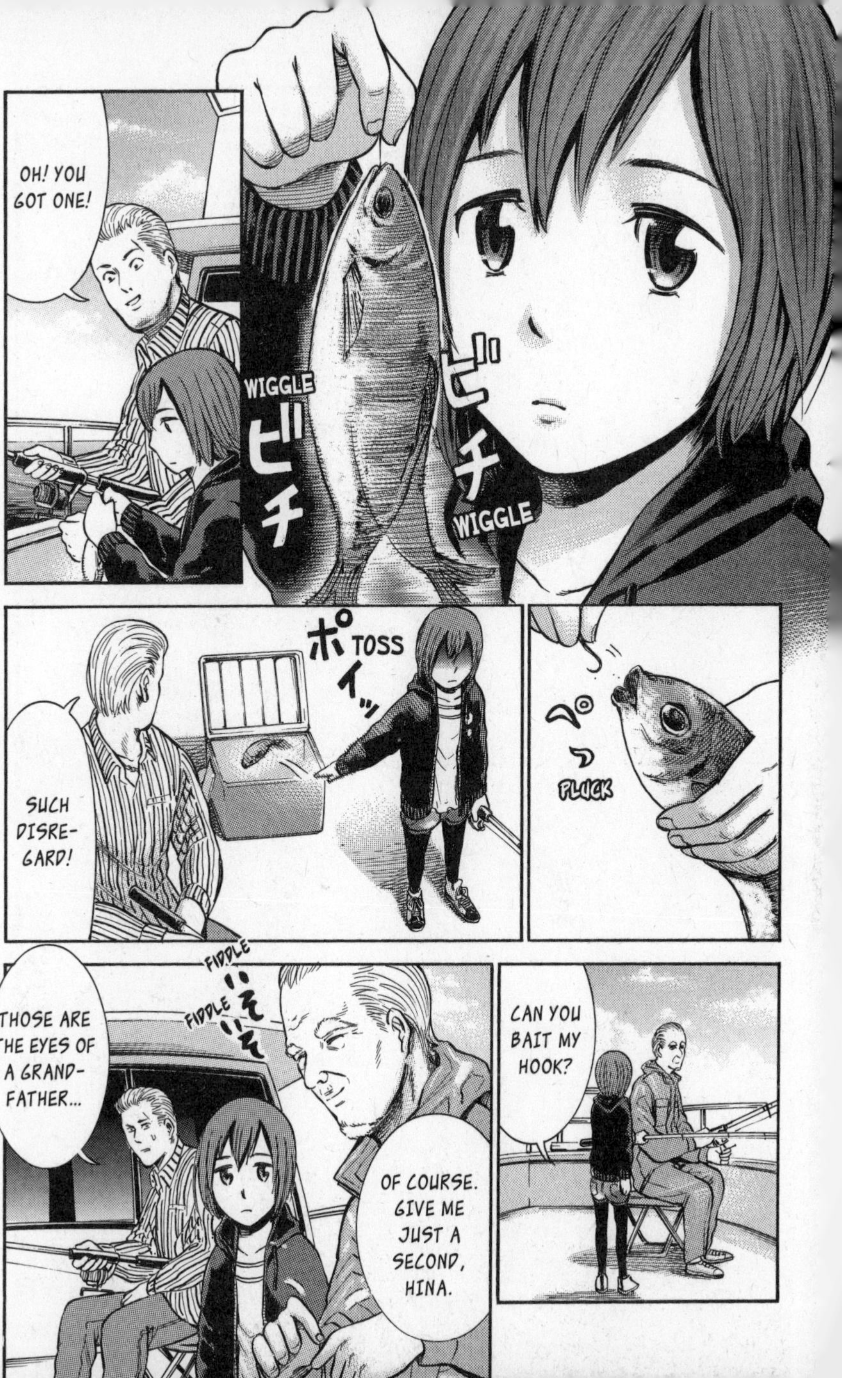
ビチ
WIGGLE
WIGGLE
ビチ
OH! YOU GOT ONE!
ペっ
PLUCK
ポイッ
TOSS
SUCH DISREGARD!
CAN YOU BAIT MY HOOK?
いそいそ
FIDDLE FIDDLE
OF COURSE. GIVE ME JUST A SECOND, HINA.
THOSE ARE THE EYES OF A GRANDFATHER...

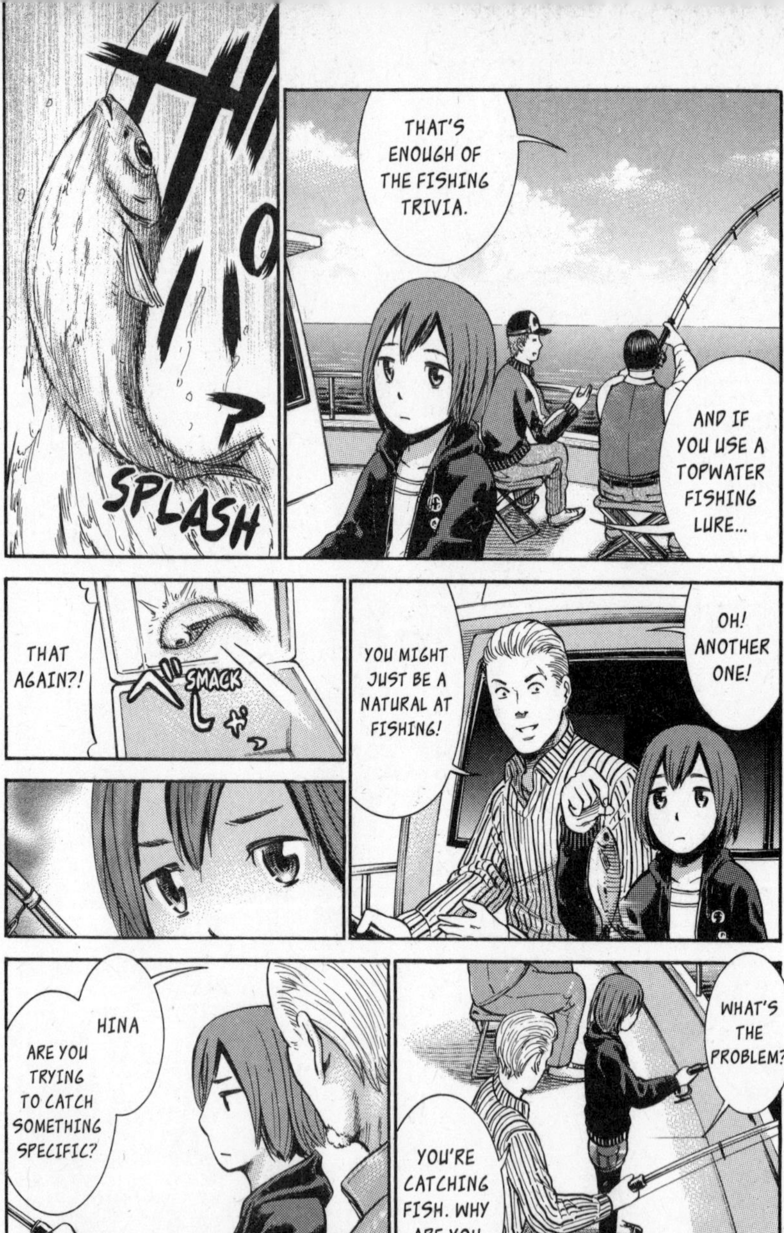
AND IF YOU USE A TOPWATER FISHING LURE...
THAT'S ENOUGH OF THE FISHING TRIVIA.
SPLASH
OH! ANOTHER ONE!
YOU MIGHT JUST BE A NATURAL AT FISHING!
THAT AGAIN?!
SMACK
WHAT'S THE PROBLEM?
YOU'RE CATCHING FISH. WHY ARE YOU UPSET?
HINA
ARE YOU TRYING TO CATCH SOMETHING SPECIFIC?

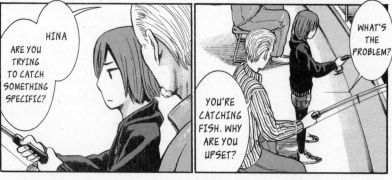

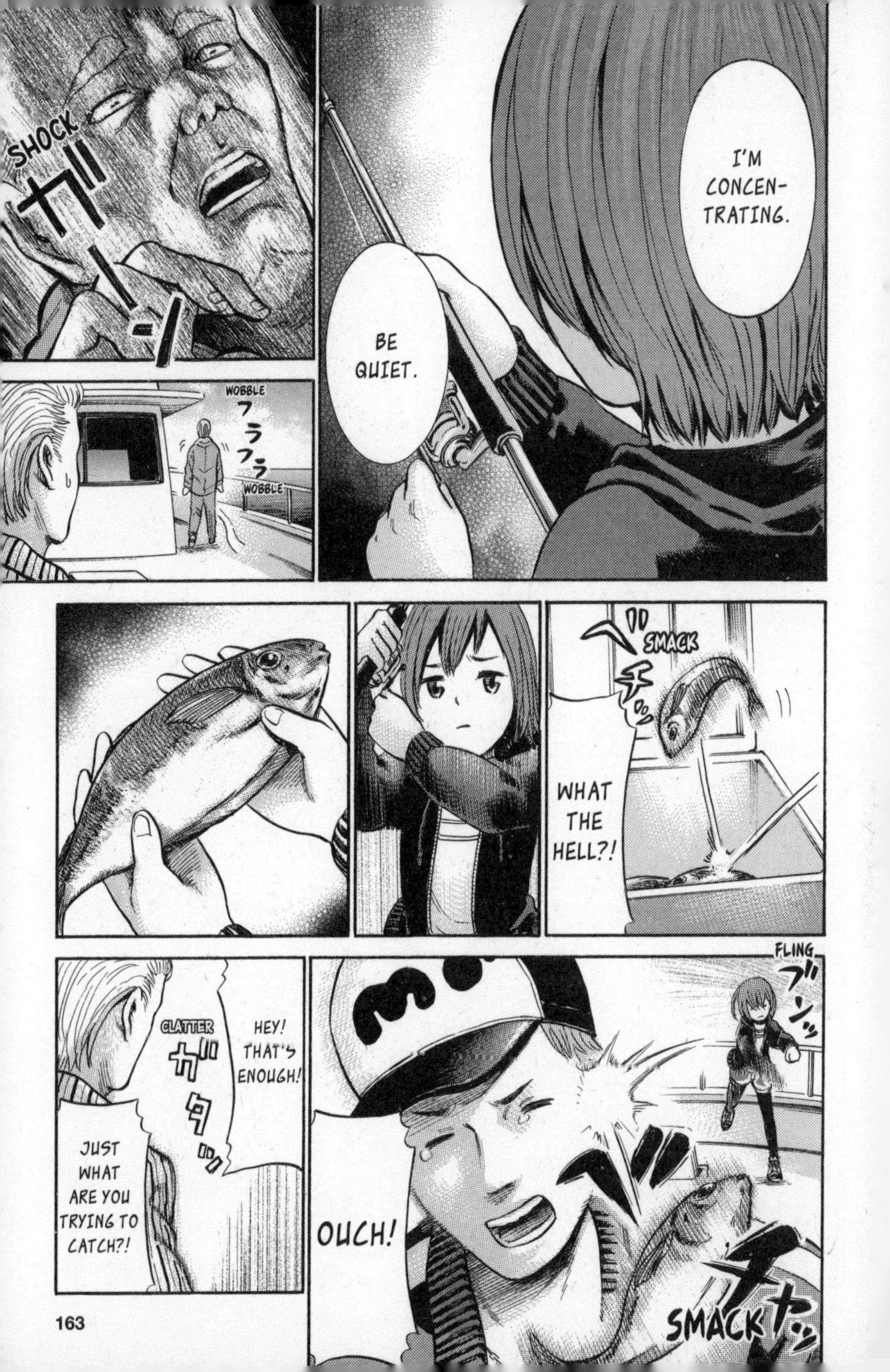
I'M CONCENTRATING.
BE QUIET.
SHOCK
WOBBLE
WOBBLE
SMACK
WHAT THE HELL?!
FLING
OUCH!
SMACK
CLATTER
HEY! THAT'S ENOUGH!
JUST WHAT ARE YOU TRYING TO CATCH?!

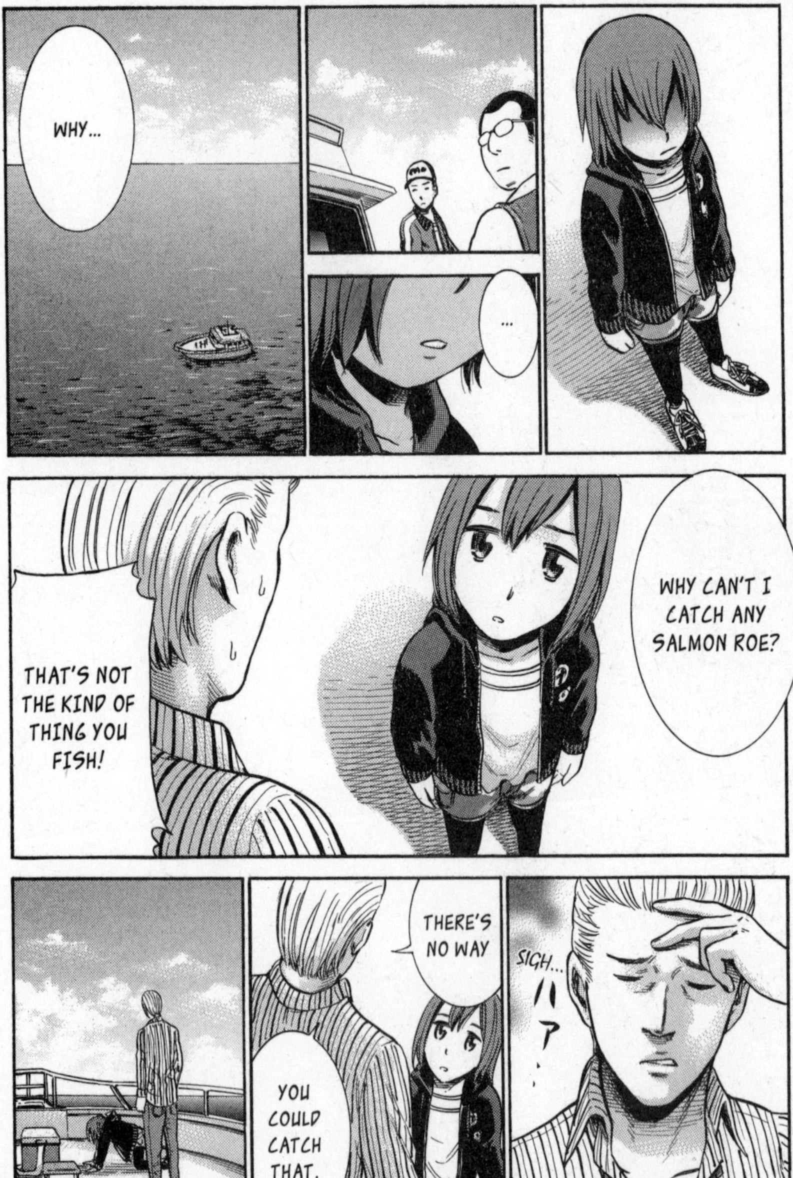
...
WHY...
WHY CAN'T I CATCH ANY SALMON ROE?
THAT'S NOT THE KIND OF THING YOU FISH!
SIGH...
ハア
THERE'S NO WAY
YOU COULD CATCH THAT.

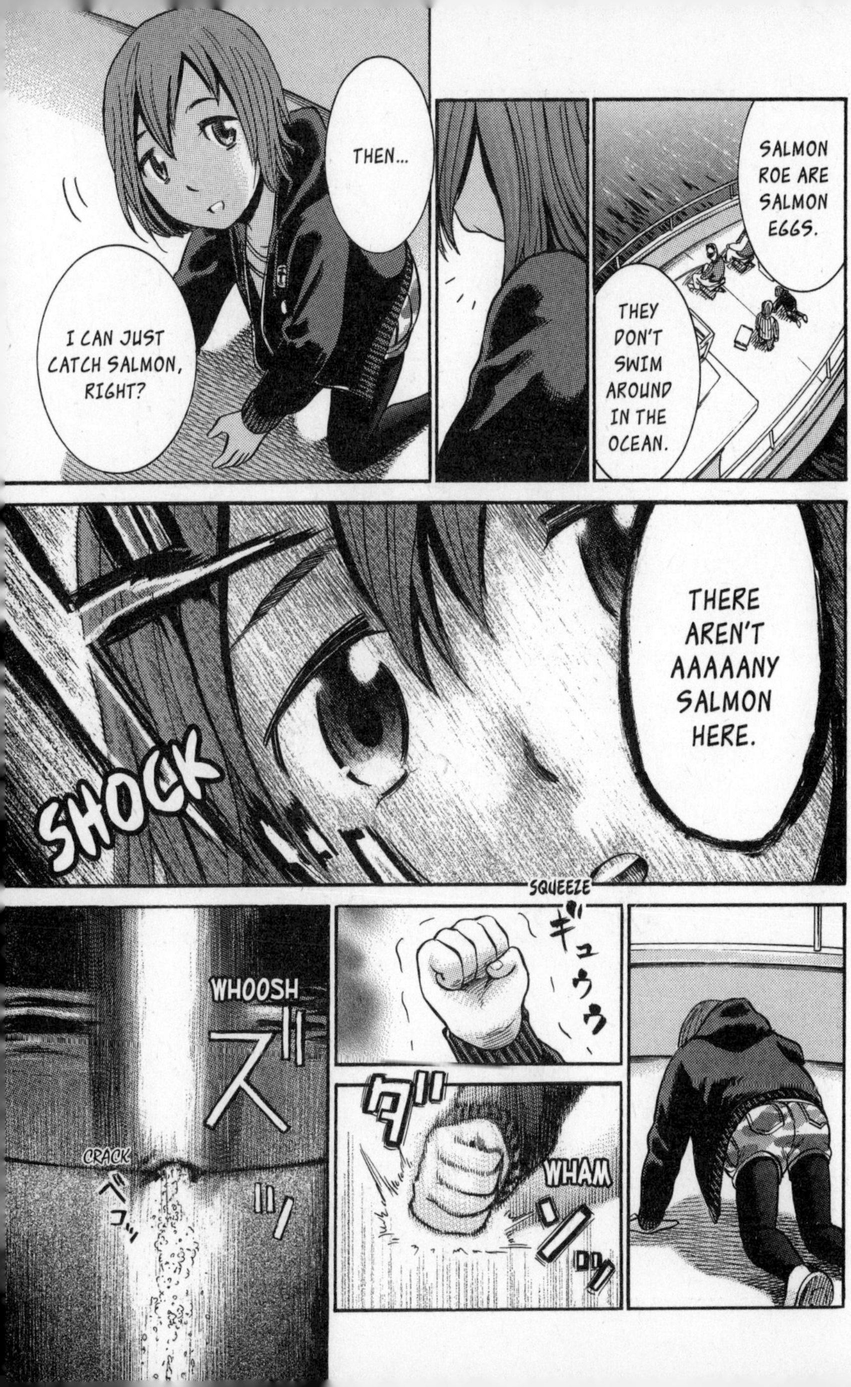

SALMON ROE ARE SALMON EGGS.
THEY DON'T SWIM AROUND IN THE OCEAN.
THEN...
I CAN JUST CATCH SALMON, RIGHT?
THERE AREN'T AAAAANY SALMON HERE.
SHOCK
SQUEEZE
ギュウウ
WHAM
WHOOSH
CRACK

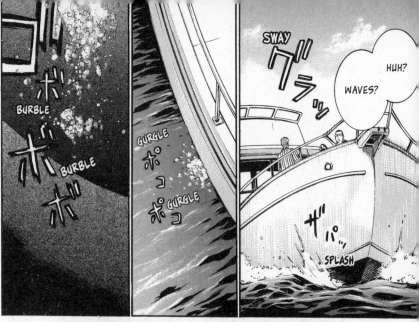

BURBLE

BURBLE

GURGLE

GURGLE

SWAY

HUH?

WAVES?

SPLASH

...

OH...

SHAKE

SHAKE

WHAT IS IT? ARE YOU THAT SURPRISED?

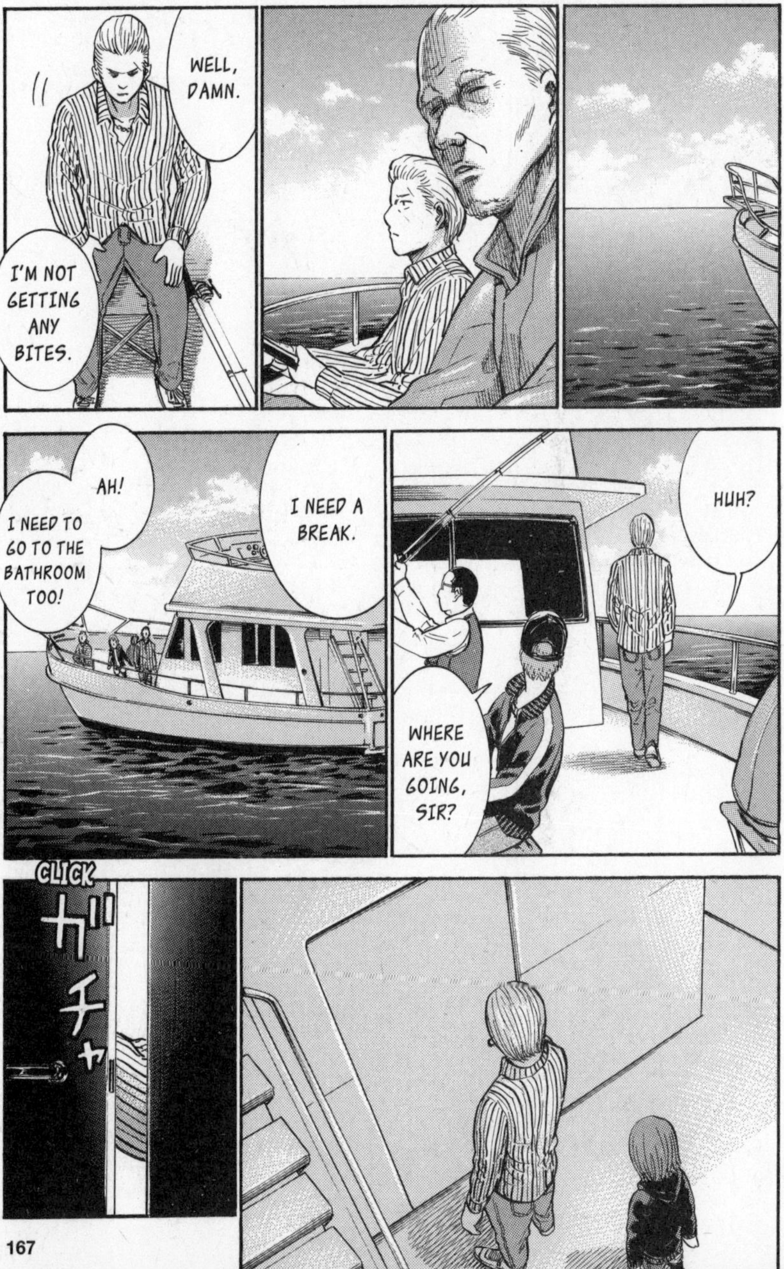
WELL, DAMN.
I'M NOT GETTING ANY BITES.
HUH?
WHERE ARE YOU GOING, SIR?
I NEED A BREAK.
AH!
I NEED TO GO TO THE BATHROOM TOO!
CLICK
ガチャ

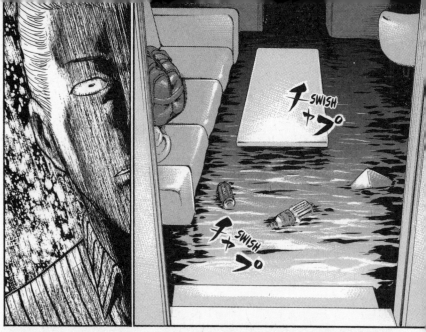

SWISH
ヤプ

SWISH
ヤプ

バタン
SLAM

168

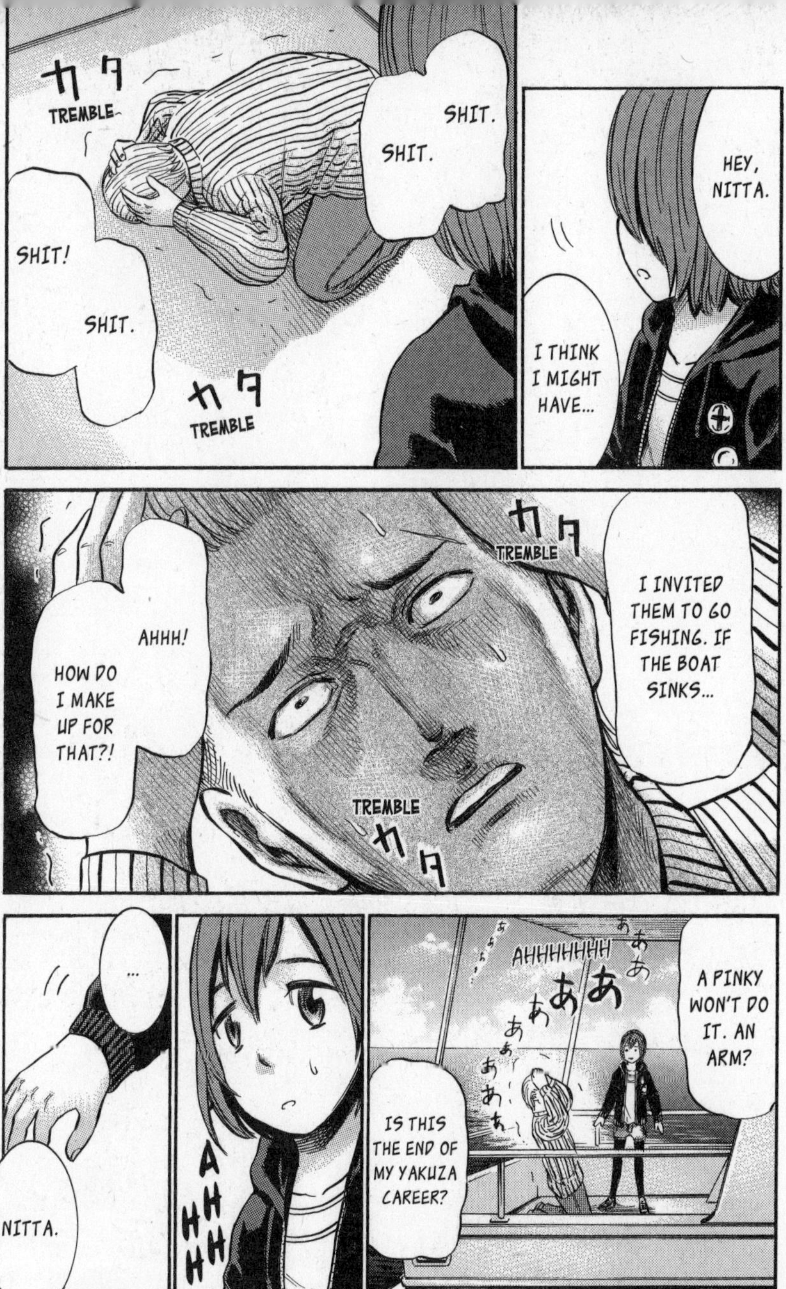
HEY, NITTA.
I THINK I MIGHT HAVE...
SHIT.
SHIT.
カタ
TREMBLE
SHIT!
SHIT.
カタ
TREMBLE
カタ
TREMBLE
I INVITED THEM TO GO FISHING. IF THE BOAT SINKS...
AHHH!
HOW DO I MAKE UP FOR THAT?!
TREMBLE
カタ
A PINKY WON'T DO IT. AN ARM?
AHHHHHHH
ああ
ああ
IS THIS THE END OF MY YAKUZA CAREER?
AHHHHHH
...
NITTA.

REALLY? REALLY?

ほんとに？

LEAVE IT TO ME.

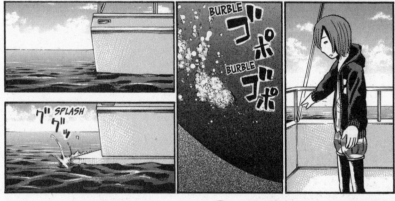

BURBLE

BURBLE

SPLASH

PHEW.

WE'RE SAFE FOR NOW.

170

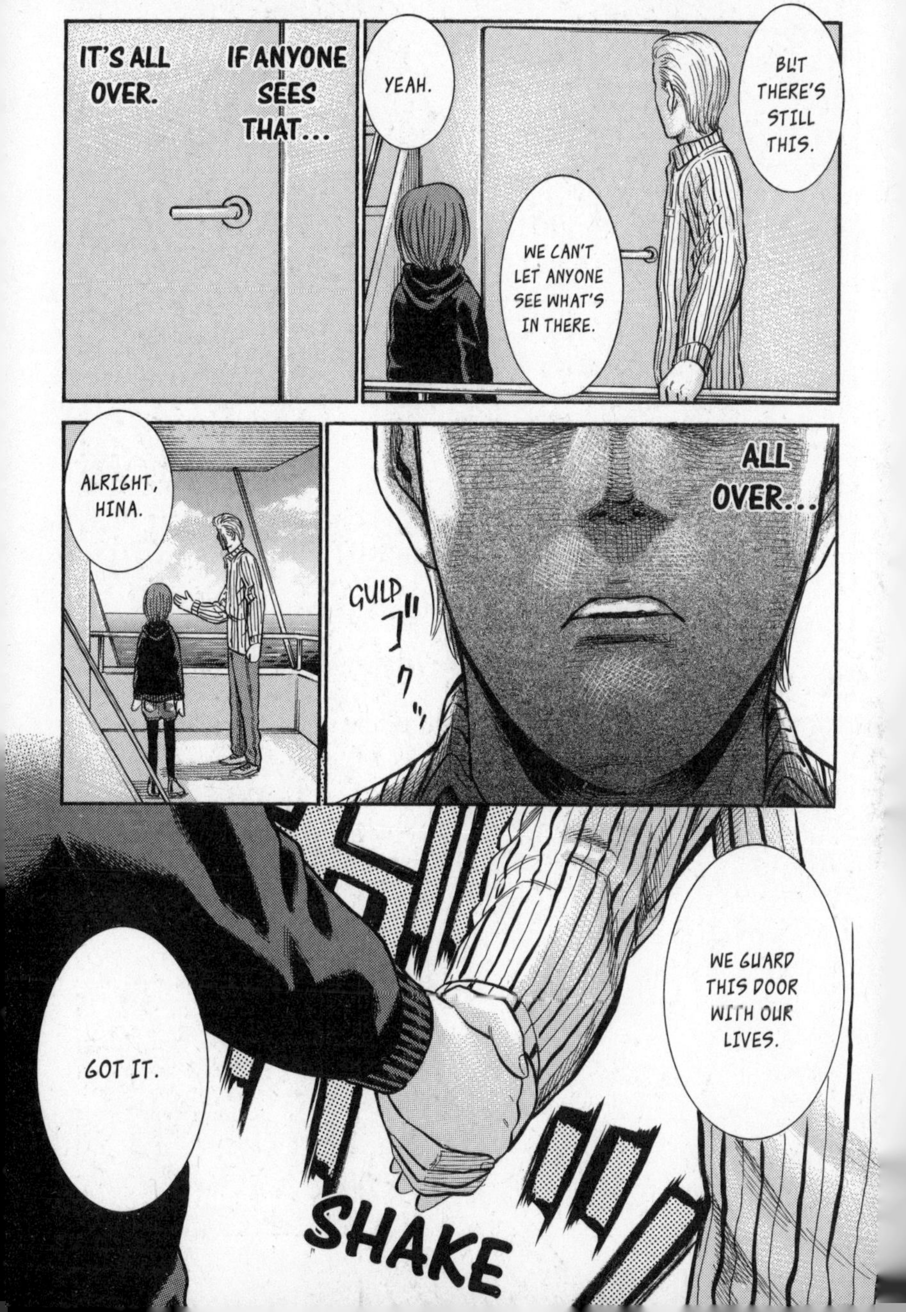
BUT THERE'S STILL THIS.
YEAH.
WE CAN'T LET ANYONE SEE WHAT'S IN THERE.
IF ANYONE SEES THAT...
IT'S ALL OVER.
ALL OVER...
GULP
ゴクッ
ALRIGHT, HINA.
WE GUARD THIS DOOR WITH OUR LIVES.
GOT IT.
SHAKE

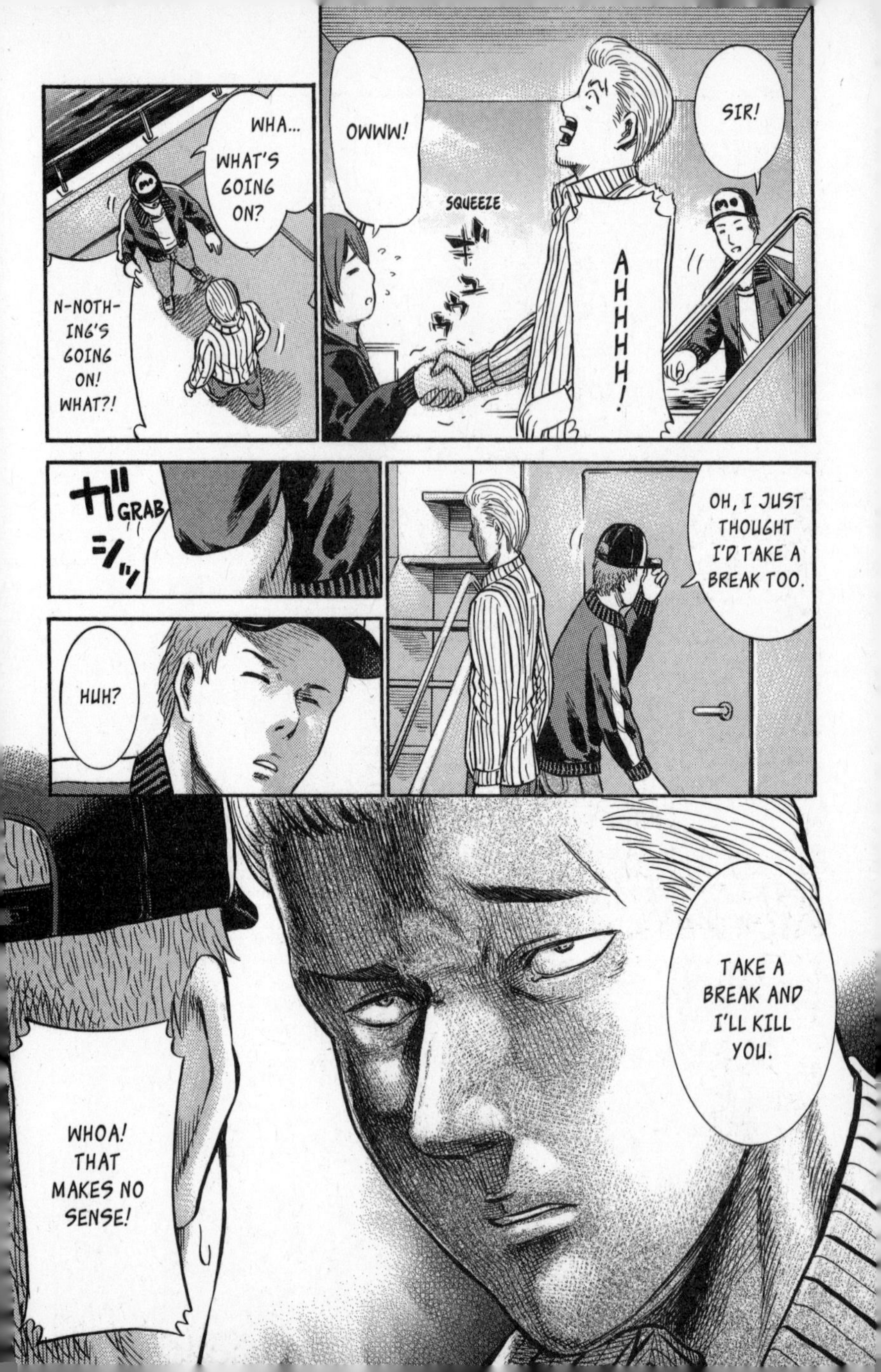
SIR!
AHHHHH!
SQUEEZE
OWWW!
WHA...
WHAT'S GOING ON?
N-NOTHING'S GOING ON! WHAT?!
OH, I JUST THOUGHT I'D TAKE A BREAK TOO.
GRAB
HUH?
TAKE A BREAK AND I'LL KILL YOU.
WHOA! THAT MAKES NO SENSE!

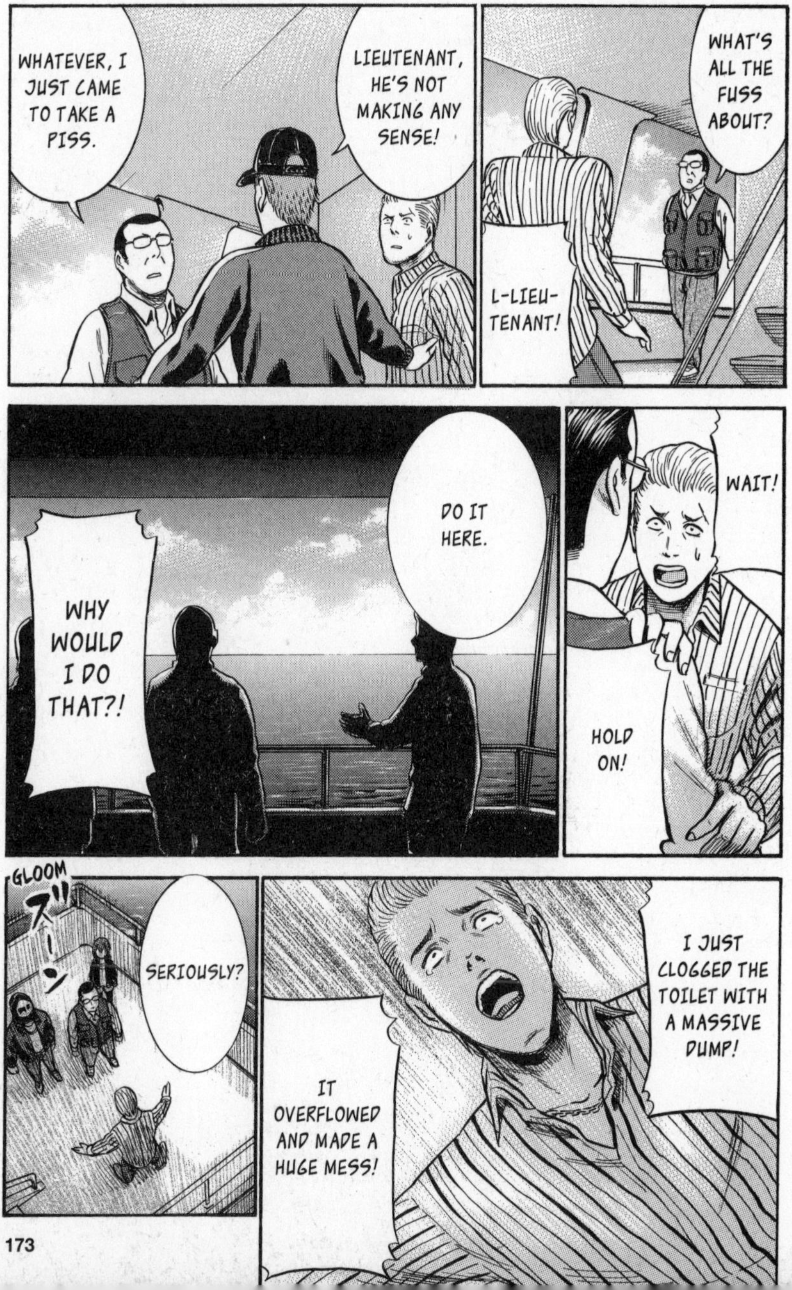
WHAT'S ALL THE FUSS ABOUT?
L-LIEU-TENANT!
LIEUTENANT, HE'S NOT MAKING ANY SENSE!
WHATEVER, I JUST CAME TO TAKE A PISS.
WAIT!
HOLD ON!
DO IT HERE.
WHY WOULD I DO THAT?!
I JUST CLOGGED THE TOILET WITH A MASSIVE DUMP!
IT OVERFLOWED AND MADE A HUGE MESS!
SERIOUSLY?
GLOOM

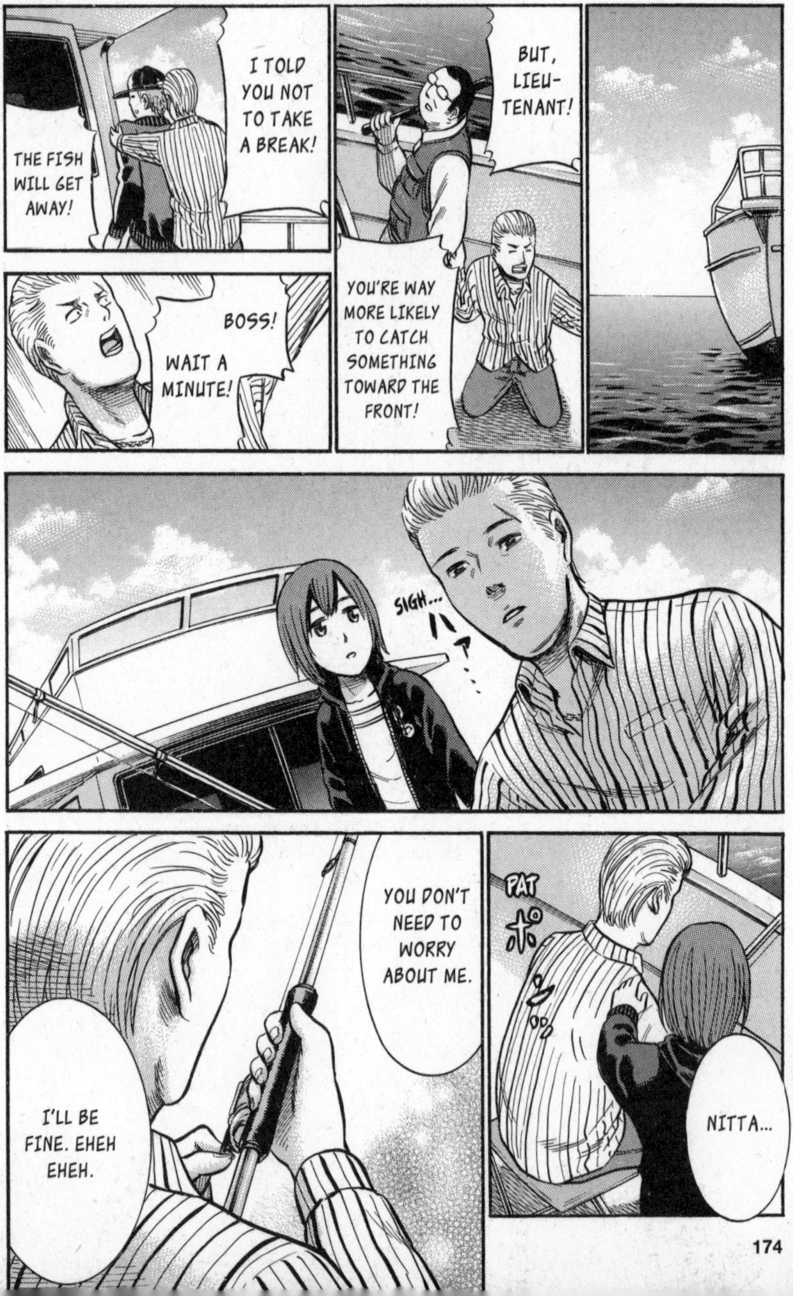
BUT, LIEU-TENANT!
YOU'RE WAY MORE LIKELY TO CATCH SOMETHING TOWARD THE FRONT!
I TOLD YOU NOT TO TAKE A BREAK!
THE FISH WILL GET AWAY!
BOSS!
WAIT A MINUTE!
SIGH...
ハァ…
PAT
NITTA...
YOU DON'T NEED TO WORRY ABOUT ME.
I'LL BE FINE. EHEH EHEH.

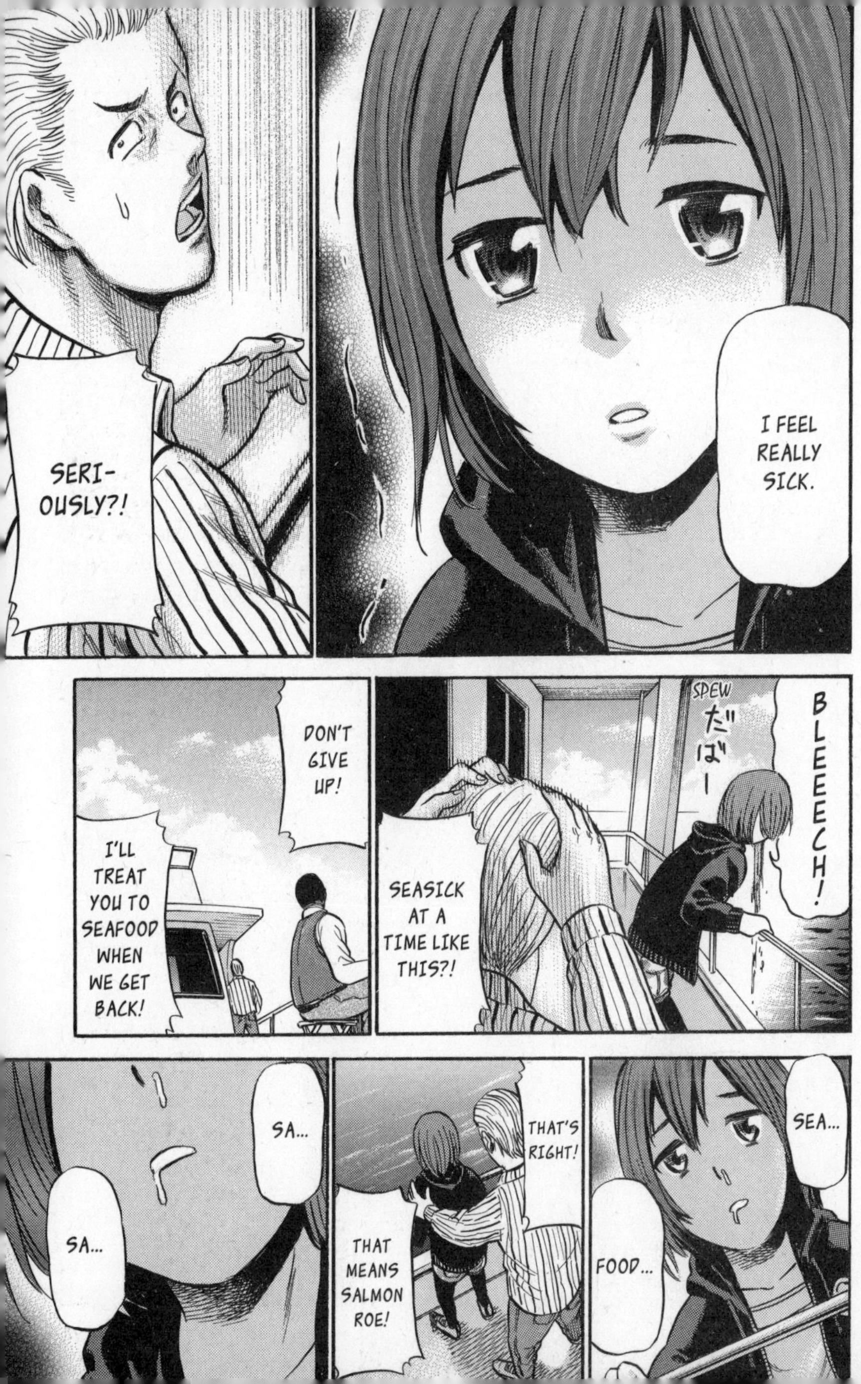
I FEEL REALLY SICK.
SERI- OUSLY?!
BLEEEECH!
SPEW
だばー
SEASICK AT A TIME LIKE THIS?!
DON'T GIVE UP!
I'LL TREAT YOU TO SEAFOOD WHEN WE GET BACK!
SEA...
FOOD...
THAT'S RIGHT!
THAT MEANS SALMON ROE!
SA...
SA...

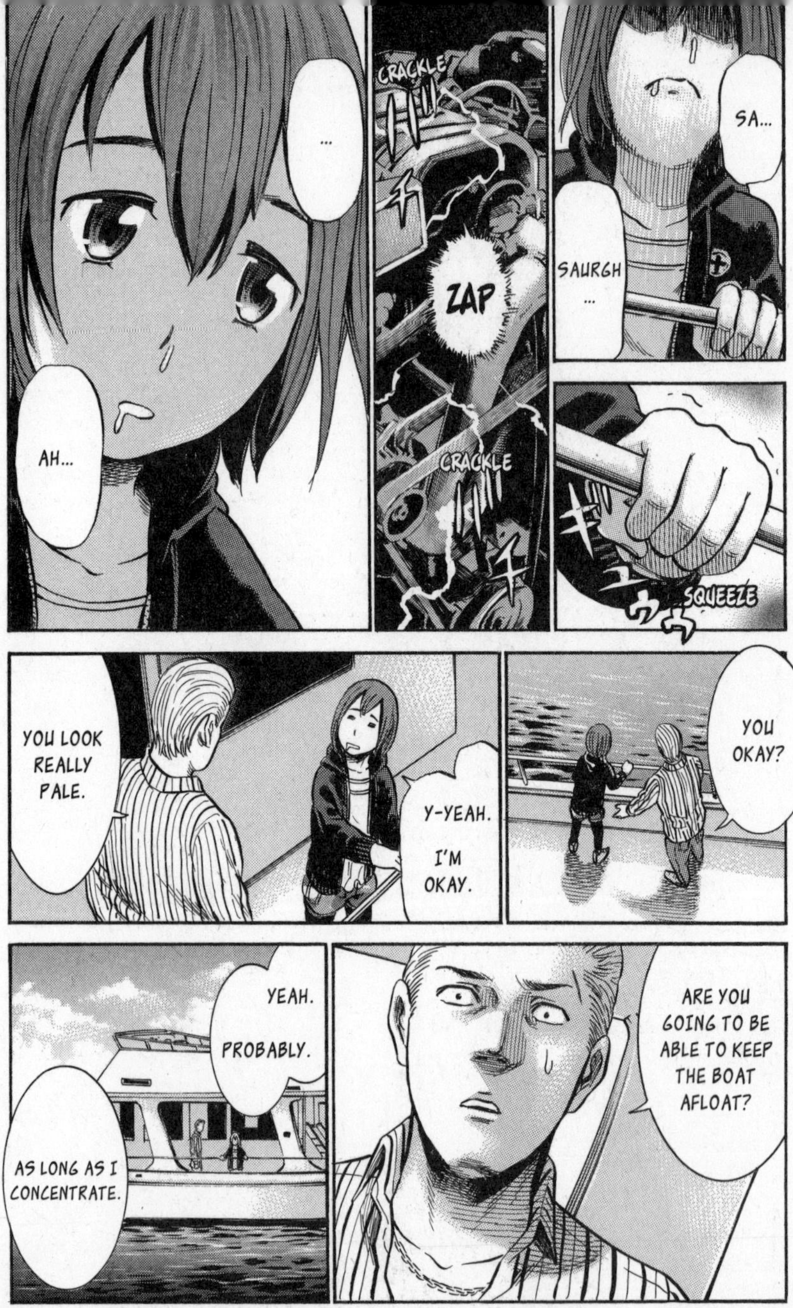
SA...
SAURGH ...
SQUEEZE
CRACKLE
ZAP
CRACKLE
...
AH...
YOU OKAY?
Y-YEAH.
I'M OKAY.
YOU LOOK REALLY PALE.
ARE YOU GOING TO BE ABLE TO KEEP THE BOAT AFLOAT?
YEAH.
PROBABLY.
AS LONG AS I CONCENTRATE.

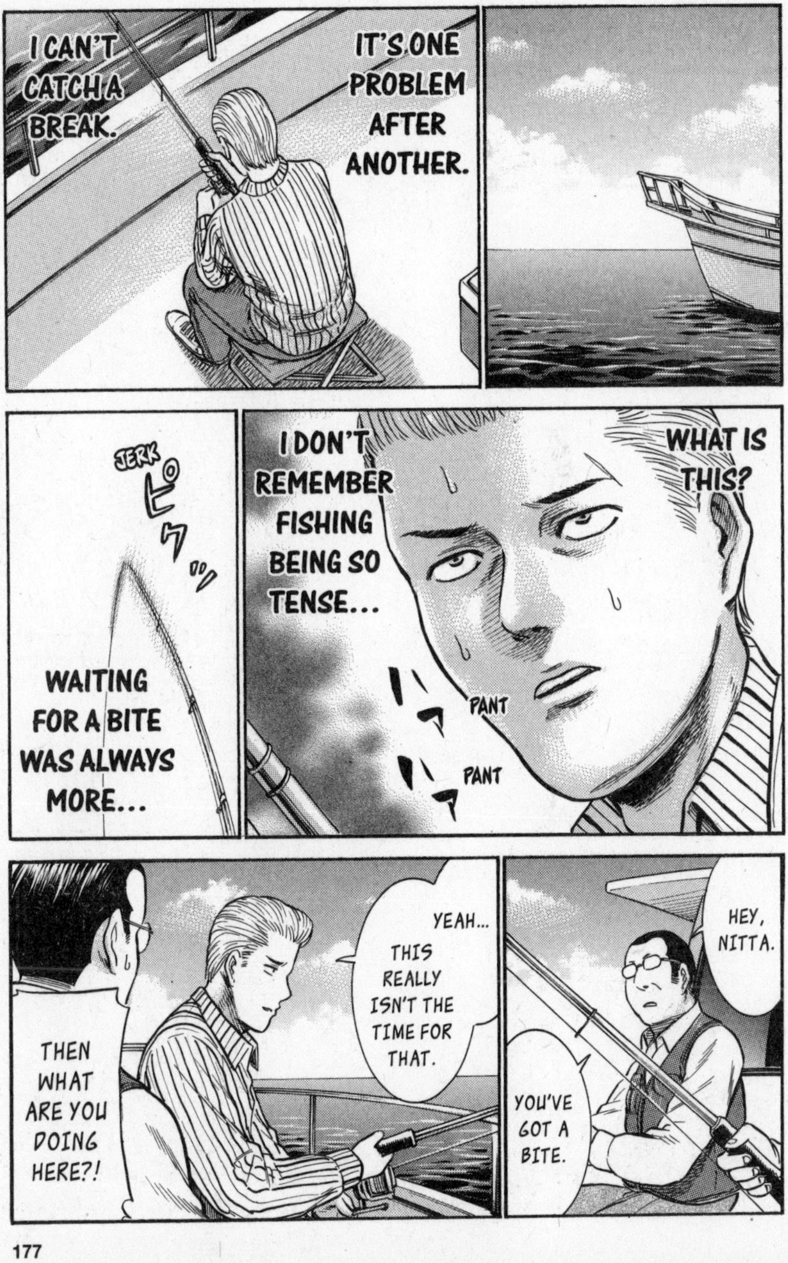
IT'S ONE PROBLEM AFTER ANOTHER.
I CAN'T CATCH A BREAK.
WHAT IS THIS?
I DON'T REMEMBER FISHING BEING SO TENSE...
ハァ
PANT
ハァ
PANT
JERK
ピクッ
WAITING FOR A BITE WAS ALWAYS MORE...
HEY, NITTA.
YOU'VE GOT A BITE.
YEAH... THIS REALLY ISN'T THE TIME FOR THAT.
THEN WHAT ARE YOU DOING HERE?!

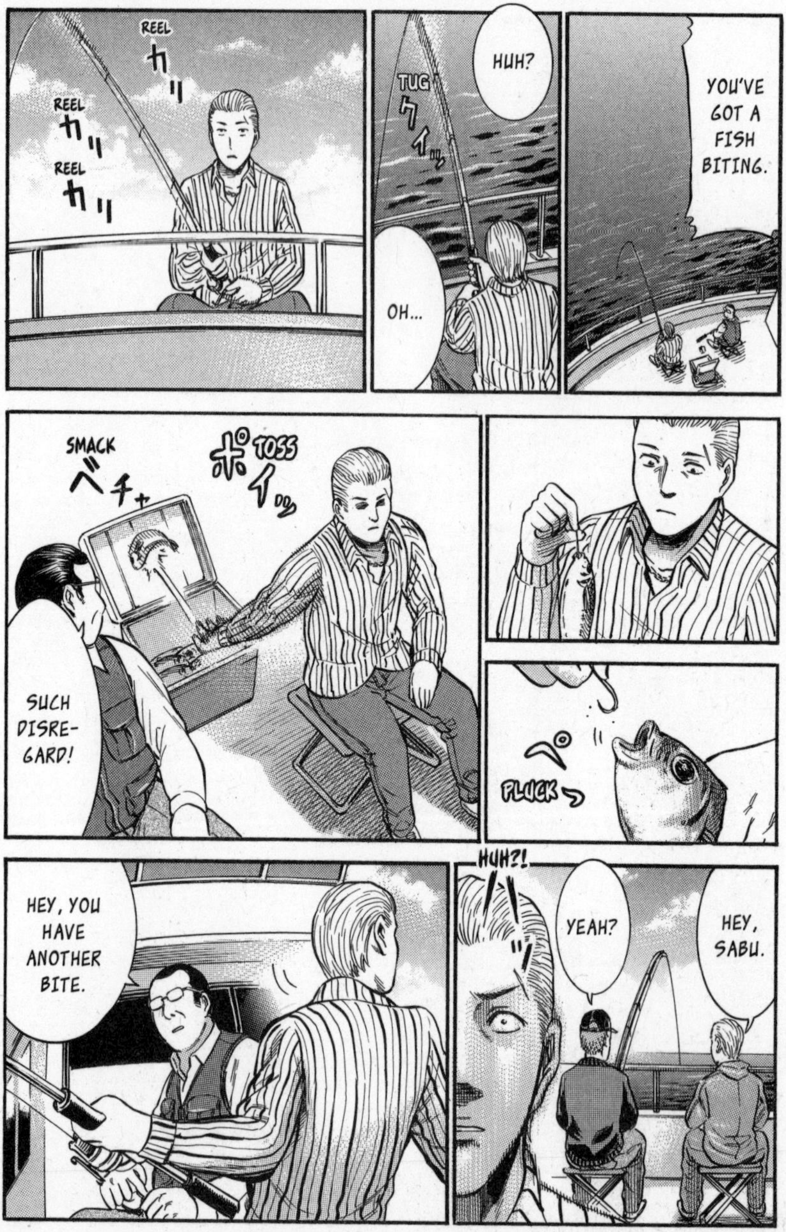

YOU'VE GOT A FISH BITING.
HUH?
TUG
クイッ
OH...
REEL
カリ
REEL
カリ
REEL
カリ
ペ
PLUCK
TOSS
ポイッ
SMACK
ベチャ
SUCH DISRE-GARD!
HEY, SABU.
YEAH?
HUH?!
HEY, YOU HAVE ANOTHER BITE.

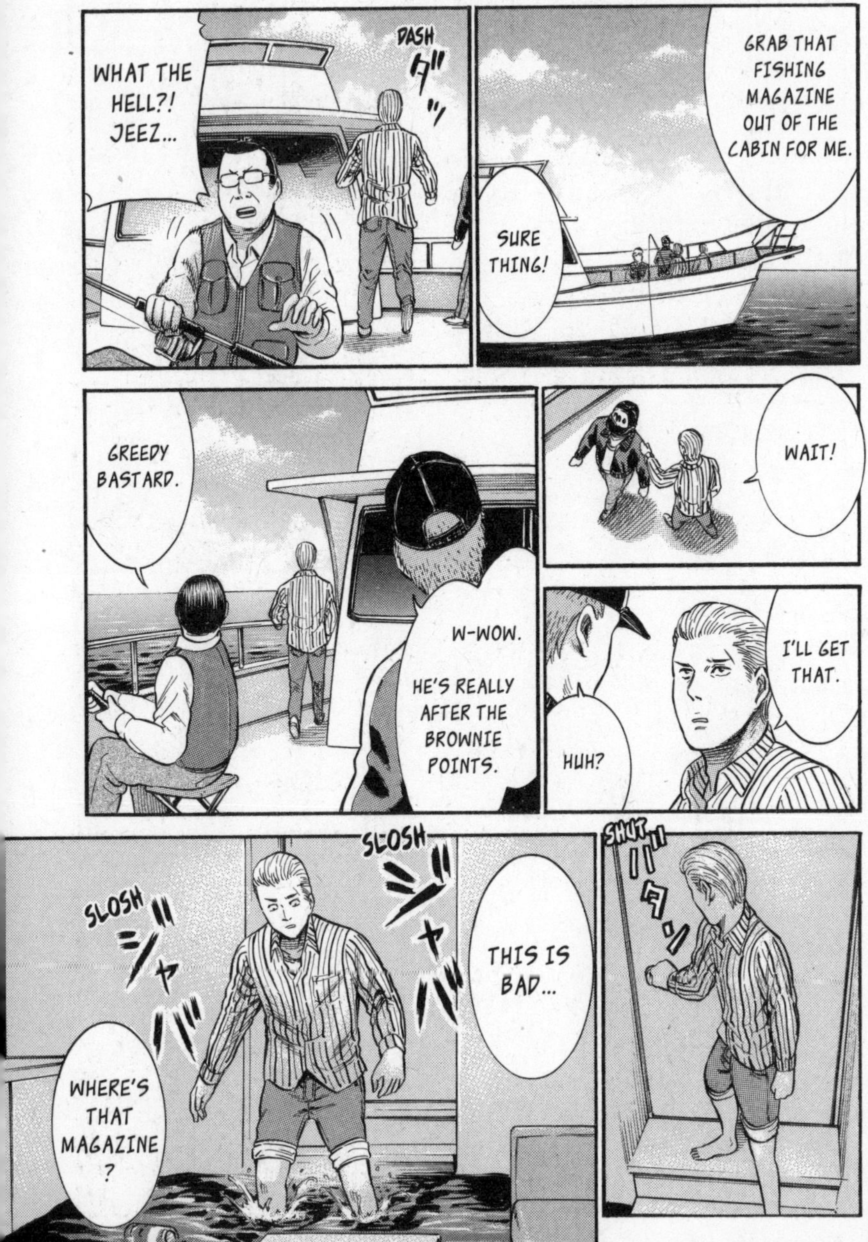
GRAB THAT FISHING MAGAZINE OUT OF THE CABIN FOR ME.
SURE THING!
DASH
ダッ
WHAT THE HELL?! JEEZ...
WAIT!
I'LL GET THAT.
HUH?
GREEDY BASTARD.
W-WOW.
HE'S REALLY AFTER THE BROWNIE POINTS.
SHUT
バタッ
SLOSH
ジャバ
THIS IS BAD...
SLOSH
ジャバ
WHERE'S THAT MAGAZINE?

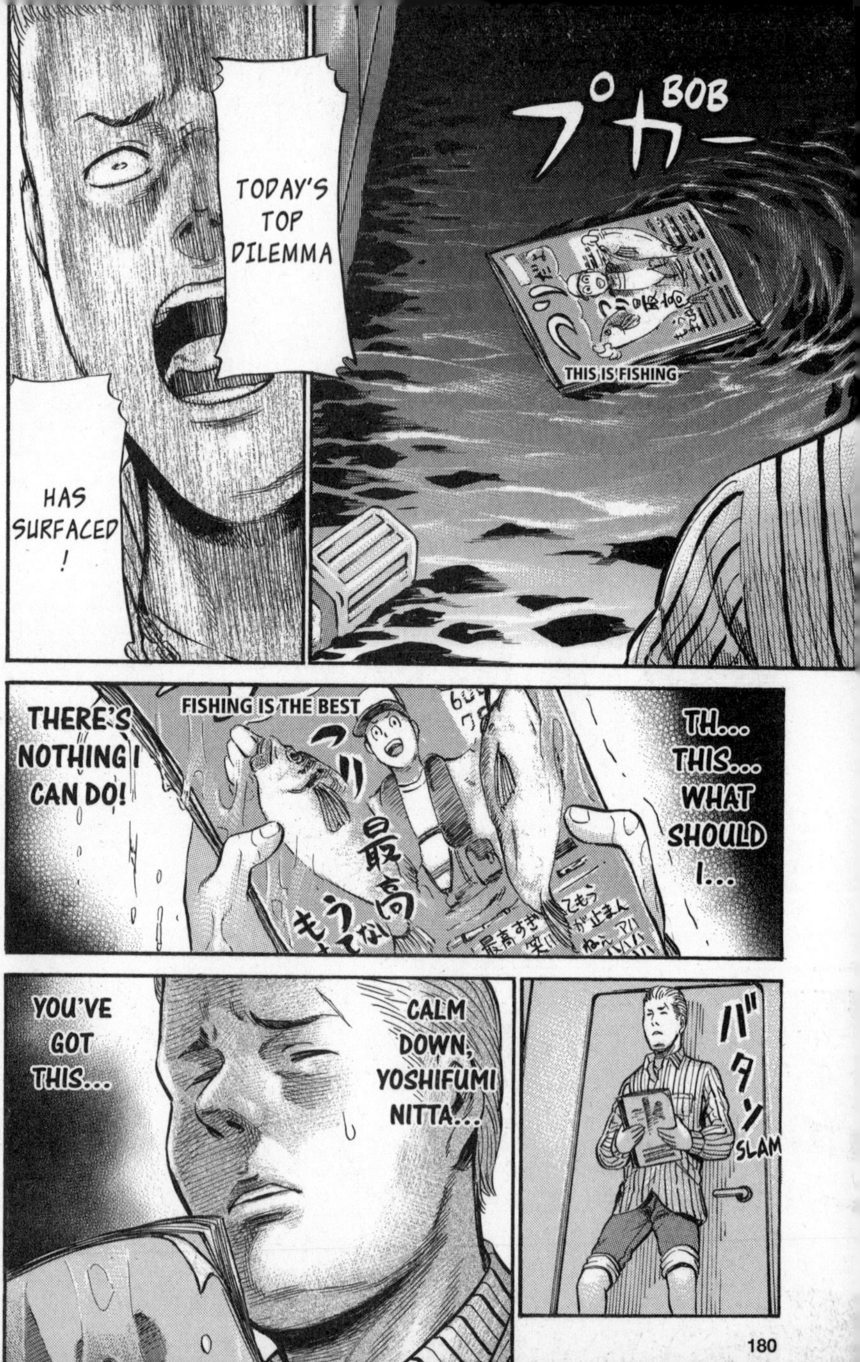
プカー
BOB
THIS IS FISHING
TODAY'S TOP DILEMMA
HAS SURFACED!
TH... THIS... WHAT SHOULD I...
FISHING IS THE BEST
つり
最高
THERE'S NOTHING I CAN DO!
バタン
SLAM
CALM DOWN, YOSHIFUMI NITTA...
YOU'VE GOT THIS...

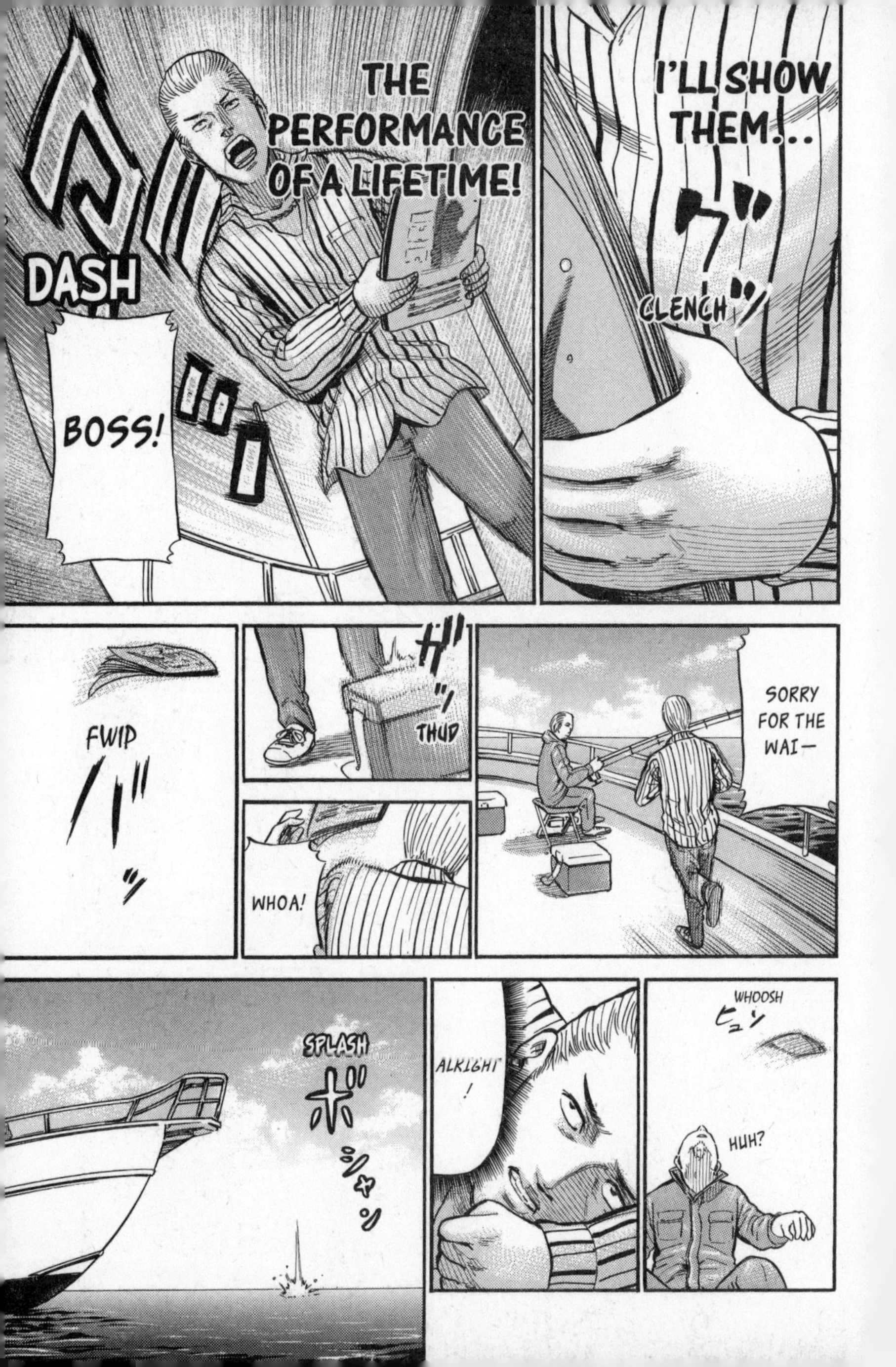
I'LL SHOW THEM...
CLENCH
THE PERFORMANCE OF A LIFETIME!
DASH
BOSS!
SORRY FOR THE WAI—
THUD
WHOA!
FWIP
WHOOSH
HUH?
ALRIGHT!
SPLASH

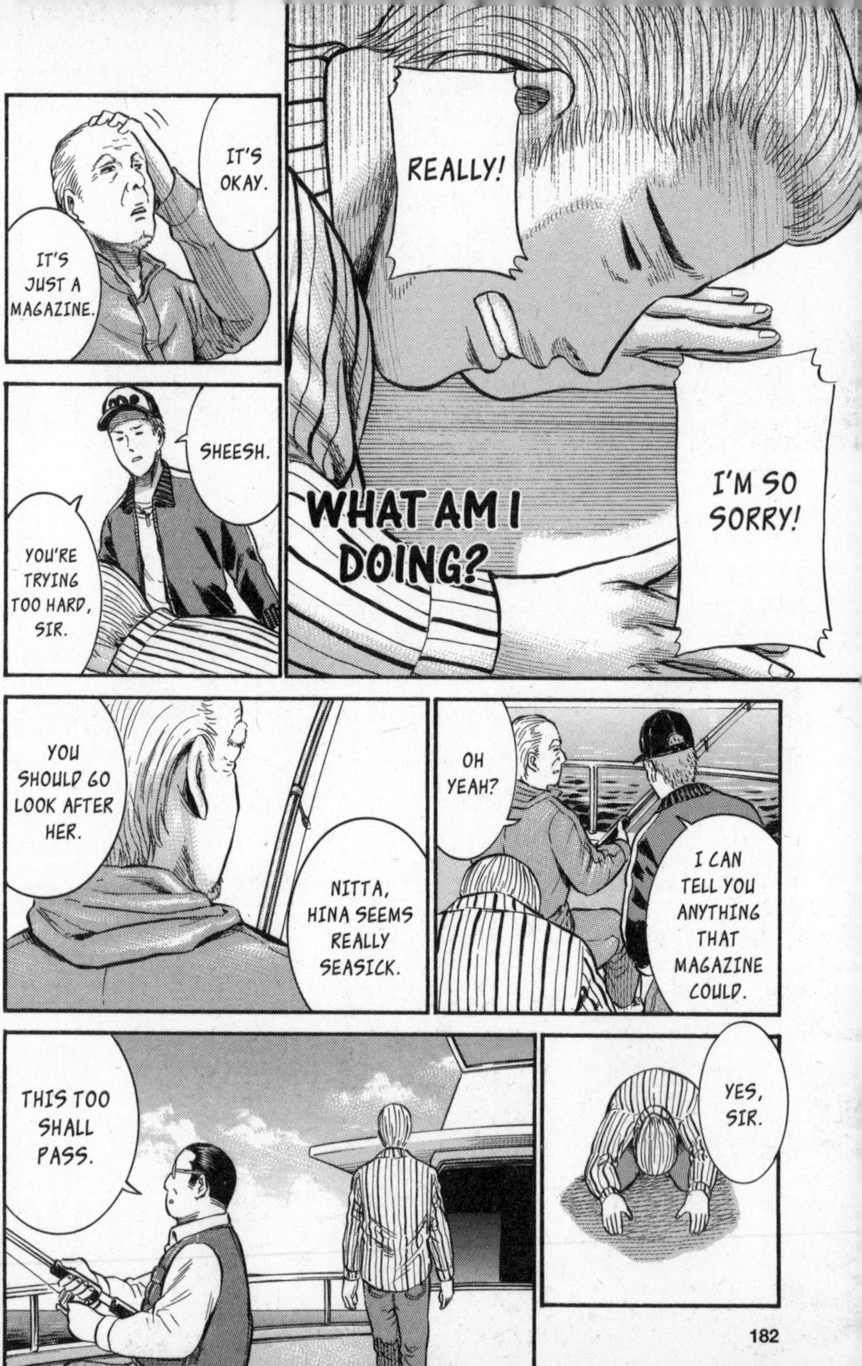

REALLY!
I'M SO SORRY!
WHAT AM I DOING?
IT'S OKAY.
IT'S JUST A MAGAZINE.
SHEESH.
YOU'RE TRYING TOO HARD, SIR.
OH YEAH?
I CAN TELL YOU ANYTHING THAT MAGAZINE COULD.
NITTA, HINA SEEMS REALLY SEASICK.
YOU SHOULD GO LOOK AFTER HER.
YES, SIR.
THIS TOO SHALL PASS.

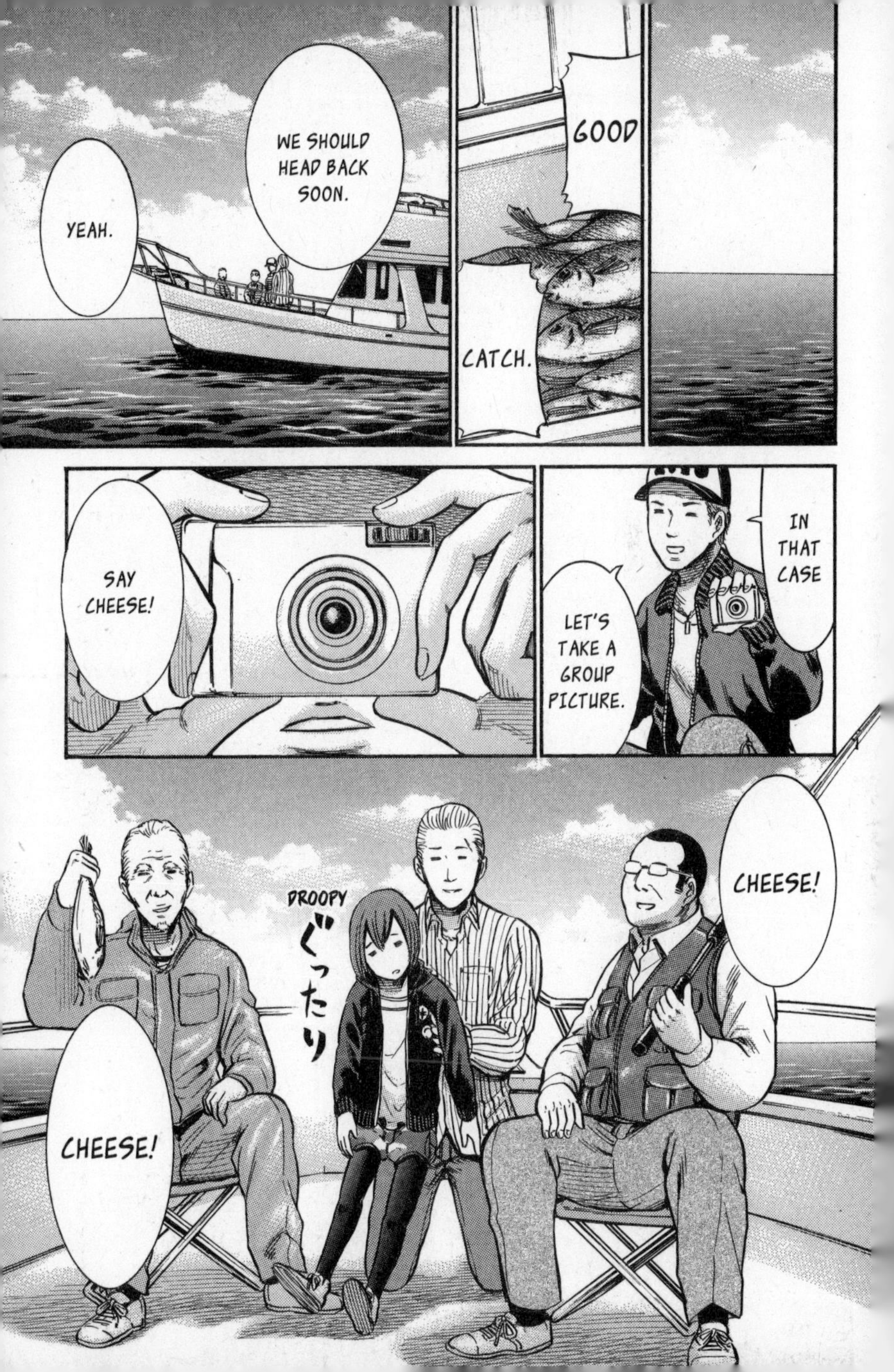
GOOD
CATCH.
WE SHOULD HEAD BACK SOON.
YEAH.
IN THAT CASE
LET'S TAKE A GROUP PICTURE.
SAY CHEESE!
CHEESE!
DROOPY
ぐったり
CHEESE!

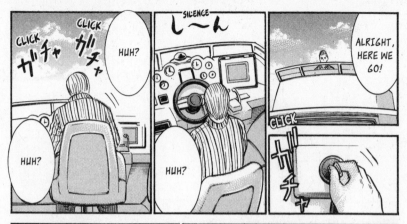

CLICK ガチャ

CLICK ガリチャ

HUH?

HUH?

SILENCE し〜ん

HUH?

ALRIGHT, HERE WE GO!

CLICK

ガリチャ

TAP ・

SORRY, I KNOW YOU'RE EXHAUSTED

BUT CAN YOU GET THE BOAT BACK TO PORT?

UGH...

UGHHH...

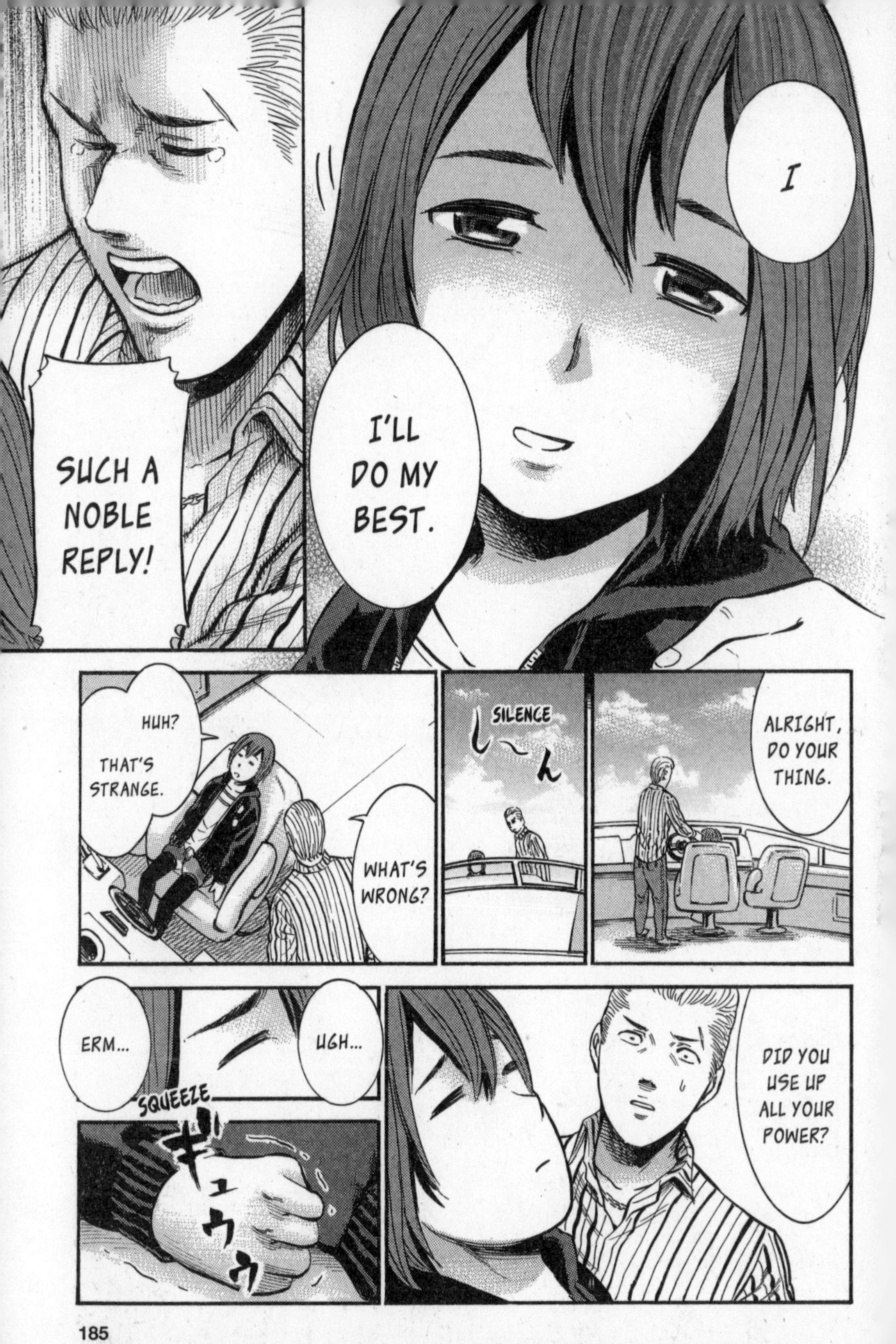
I
I'LL DO MY BEST.
SUCH A NOBLE REPLY!
ALRIGHT, DO YOUR THING.
SILENCE
しーん
HUH?
THAT'S STRANGE.
WHAT'S WRONG?
DID YOU USE UP ALL YOUR POWER?
UGH...
ERM...
SQUEEZE
ギュウウ

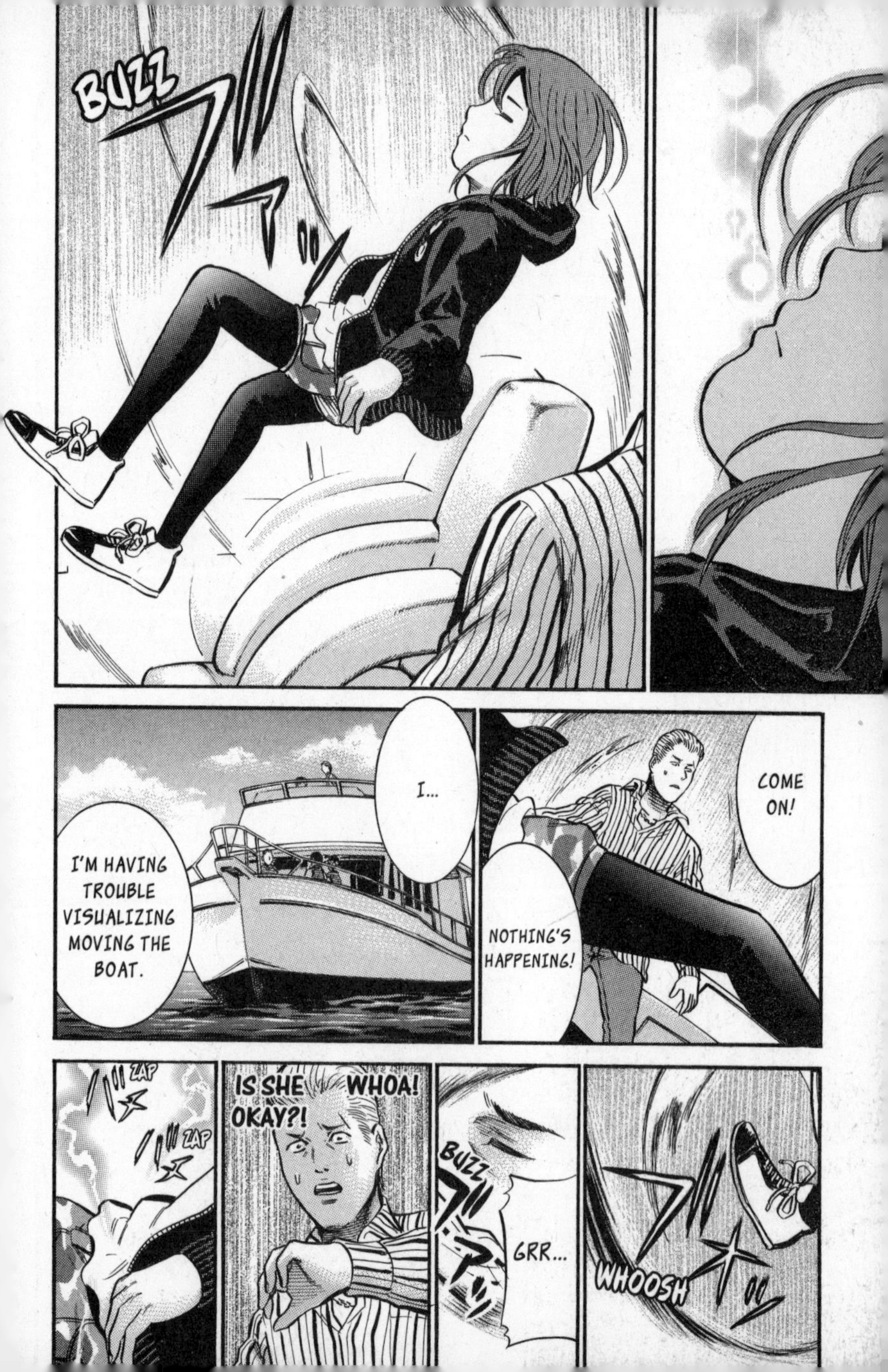

BUZZ
COME ON!
NOTHING'S HAPPENING!
I...
I'M HAVING TROUBLE VISUALIZING MOVING THE BOAT.
WHOOSH
BUZZ
GRR...
WHOA!
IS SHE OKAY?!
ZAP
ZAP

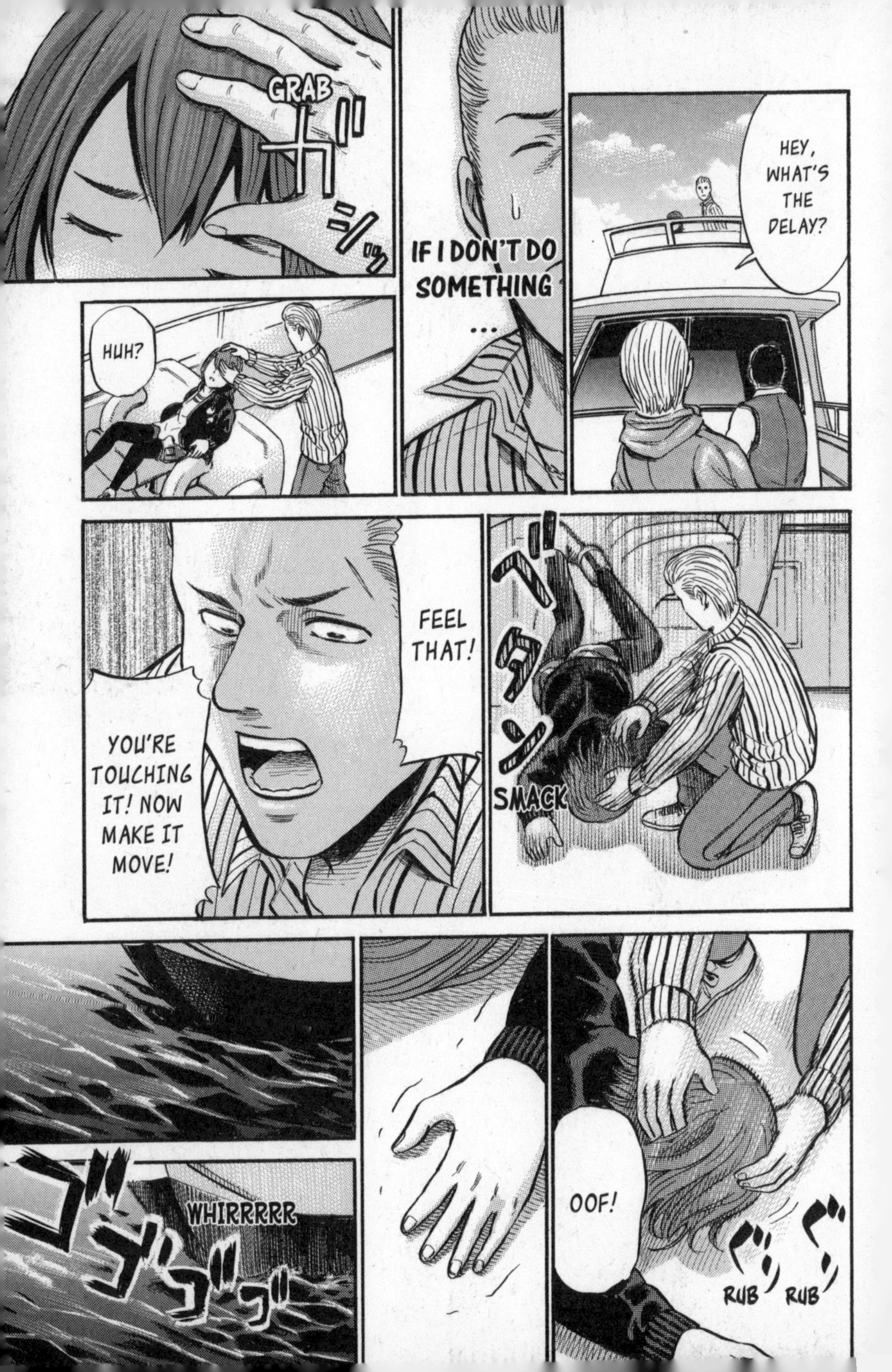
HEY, WHAT'S THE DELAY?
IF I DON'T DO SOMETHING
...
GRAB
HUH?
SMACK
FEEL THAT!
YOU'RE TOUCHING IT! NOW MAKE IT MOVE!
OOF!
RUB RUB
WHIRRRRR

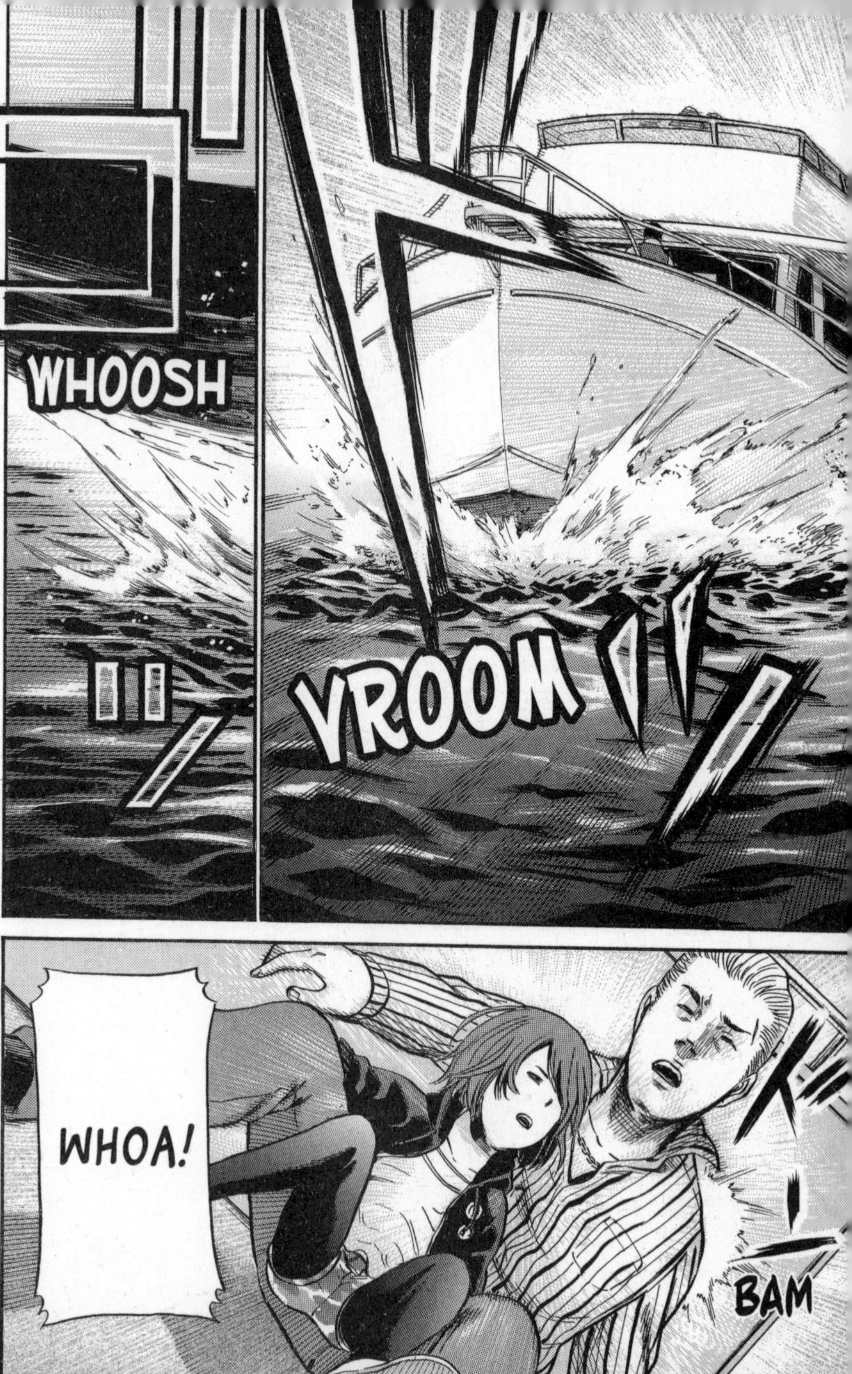
VROOM
WHOOSH
BAM
WHOA!

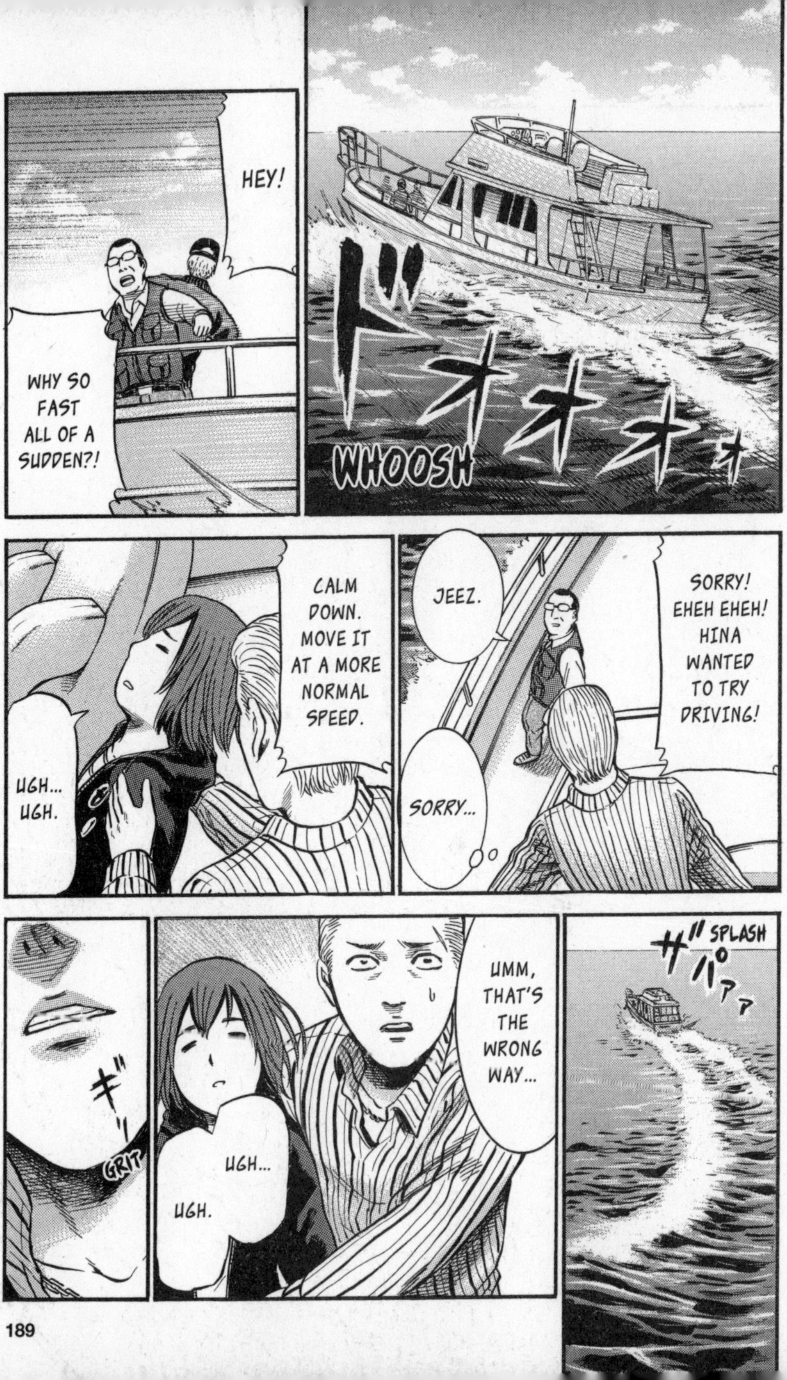
ドオオオォ
WHOOSH
HEY!
WHY SO FAST ALL OF A SUDDEN?!
SORRY! EHEH EHEH! HINA WANTED TO TRY DRIVING!
JEEZ.
SORRY...
CALM DOWN. MOVE IT AT A MORE NORMAL SPEED.
UGH... UGH.
ザパァァ
SPLASH
UMM, THAT'S THE WRONG WAY...
UGH...
UGH.
ギリ
GRIT

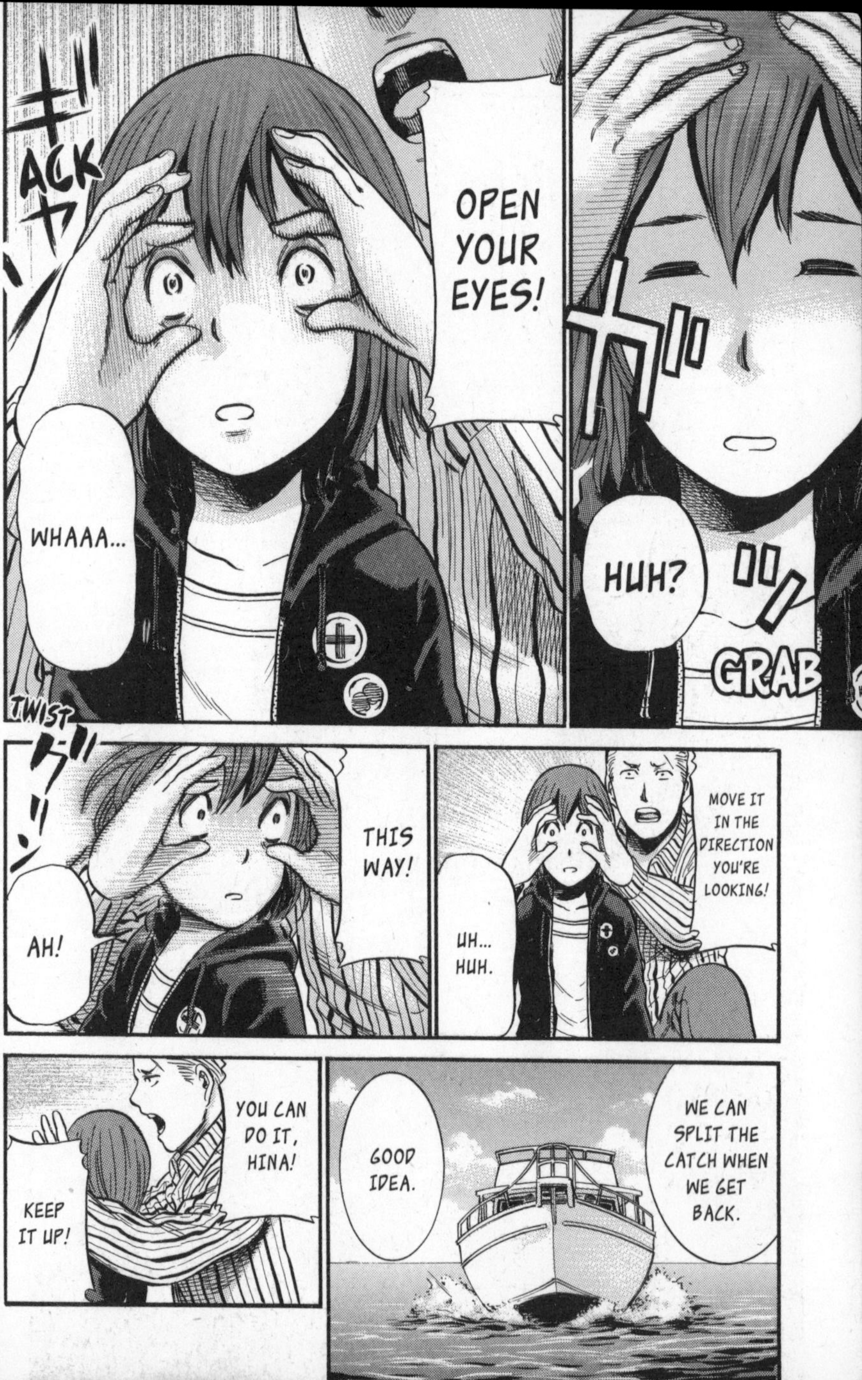
HUH?
GRAB
OPEN YOUR EYES!
ACK
WHAAA...
TWIST
MOVE IT IN THE DIRECTION YOU'RE LOOKING!
UH... HUH.
THIS WAY!
AH!
WE CAN SPLIT THE CATCH WHEN WE GET BACK.
GOOD IDEA.
YOU CAN DO IT, HINA!
KEEP IT UP!

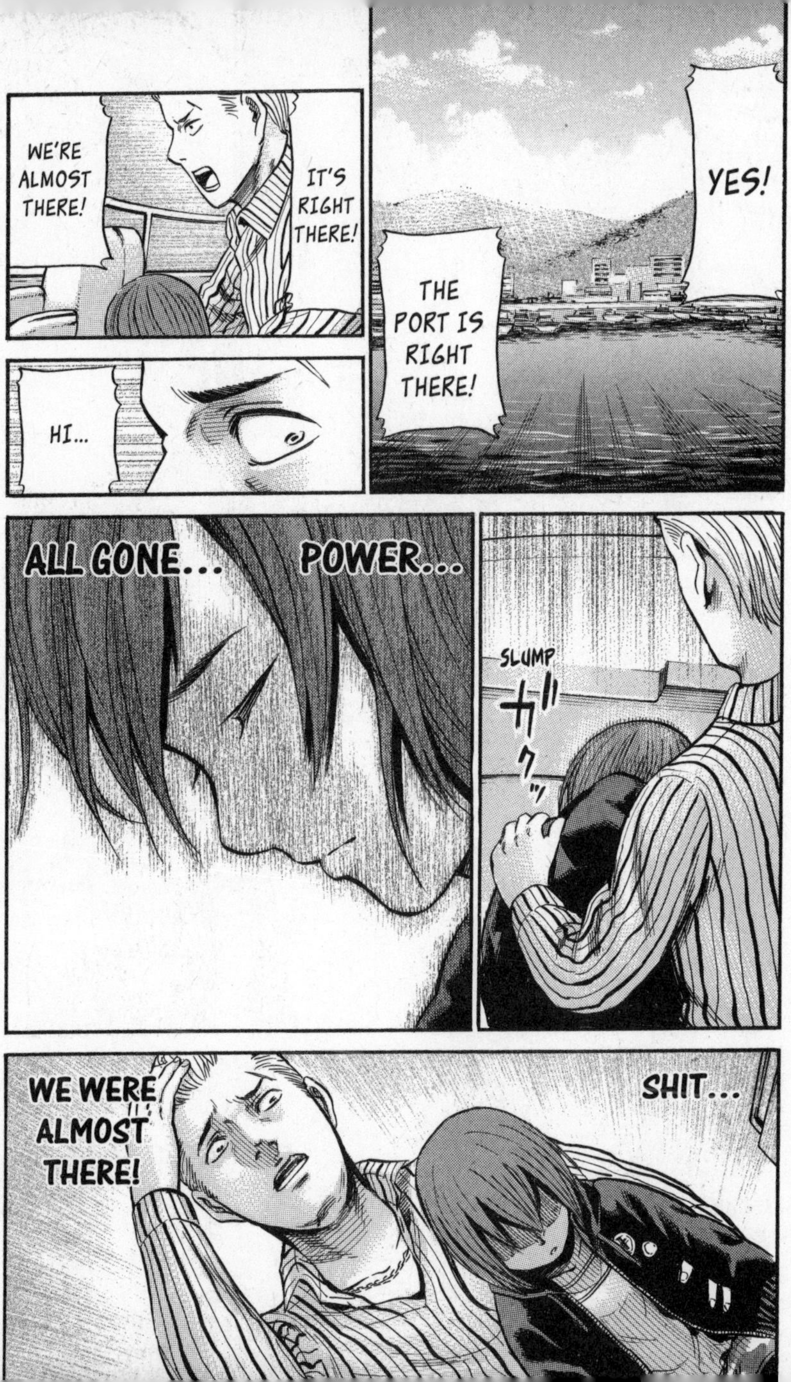
YES!
THE PORT IS RIGHT THERE!
IT'S RIGHT THERE!
WE'RE ALMOST THERE!
HI...
SLUMP
ガクッ
POWER...
ALL GONE...
SHIT...
WE WERE ALMOST THERE!

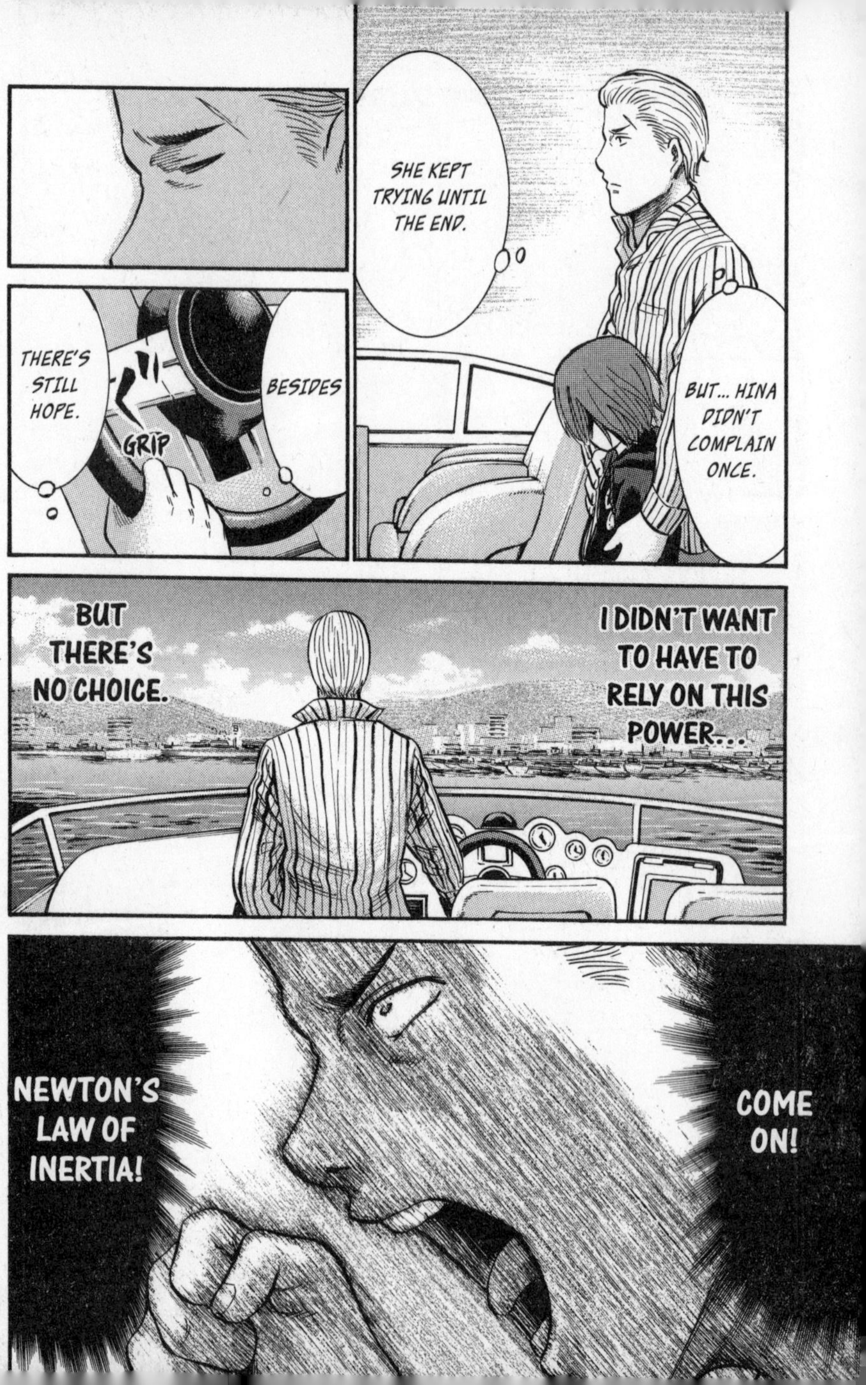
BUT... HINA DIDN'T COMPLAIN ONCE.
SHE KEPT TRYING UNTIL THE END.
BESIDES
GRIP
THERE'S STILL HOPE.
I DIDN'T WANT TO HAVE TO RELY ON THIS POWER...
BUT THERE'S NO CHOICE.
COME ON!
NEWTON'S LAW OF INERTIA!

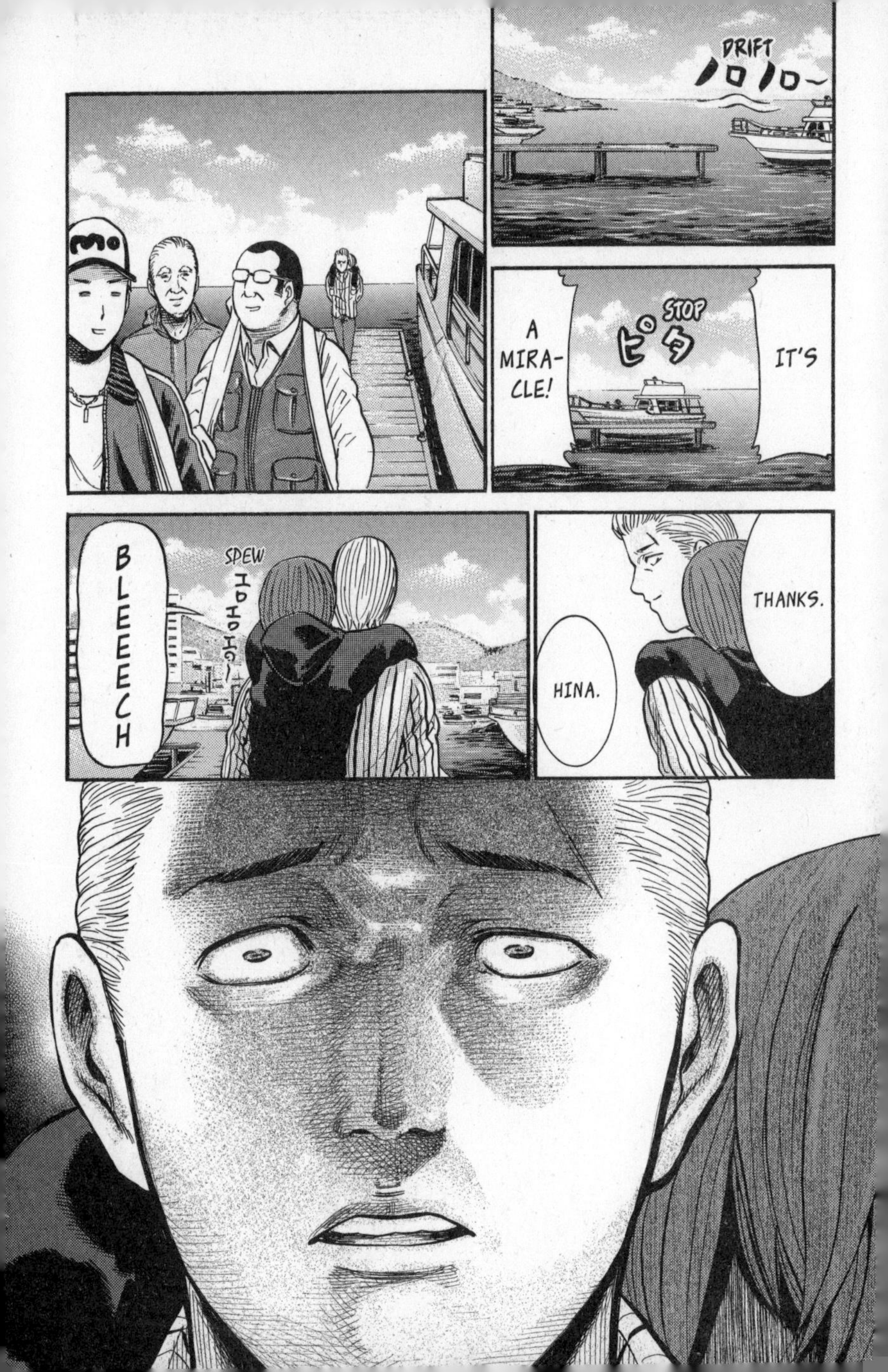
DRIFT
ノロノロ~
STOP
ピタ
IT'S
A MIRA-CLE!
THANKS.
HINA.
SPEW
ゲロゲロ~
BLEEEECH

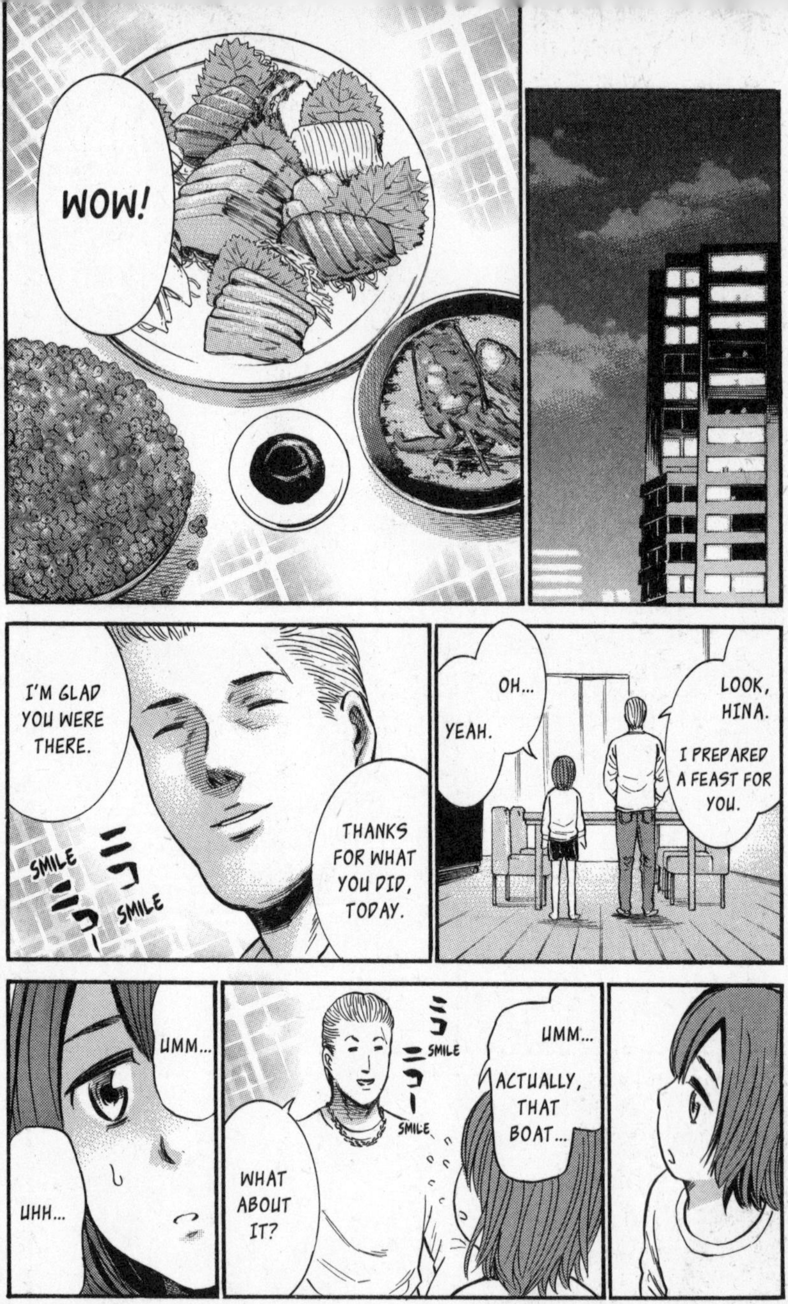
WOW!
LOOK, HINA.
I PREPARED A FEAST FOR YOU.
OH...
YEAH.
THANKS FOR WHAT YOU DID, TODAY.
I'M GLAD YOU WERE THERE.
SMILE
SMILE
UMM...
ACTUALLY, THAT BOAT...
SMILE
SMILE
WHAT ABOUT IT?
UMM...
UHH...

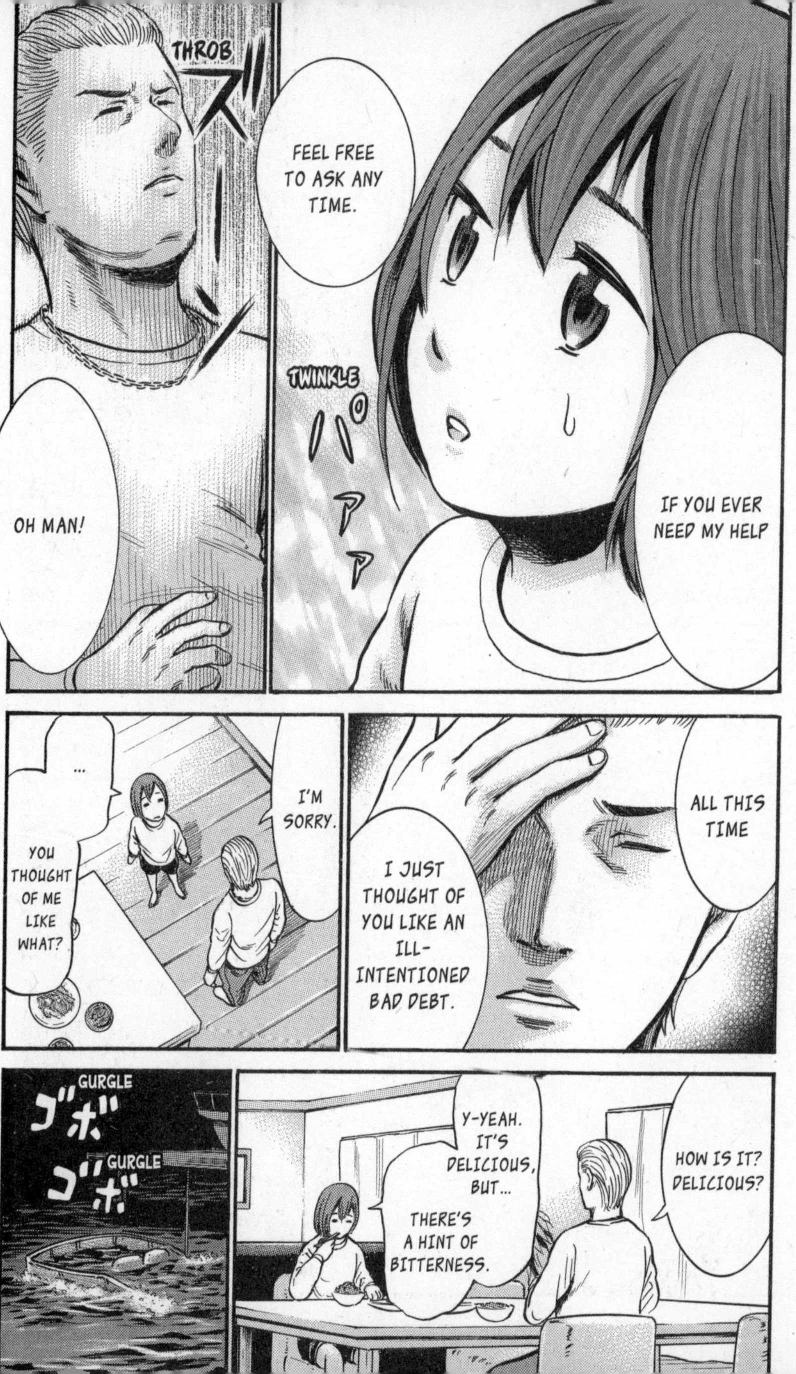
IF YOU EVER NEED MY HELP
FEEL FREE TO ASK ANY TIME.
TWINKLE
THROB
OH MAN!
ALL THIS TIME
I JUST THOUGHT OF YOU LIKE AN ILL-INTENTIONED BAD DEBT.
I'M SORRY.
...
YOU THOUGHT OF ME LIKE WHAT?
HOW IS IT? DELICIOUS?
Y-YEAH. IT'S DELICIOUS, BUT...
THERE'S A HINT OF BITTERNESS.
GURGLE
GURGLE

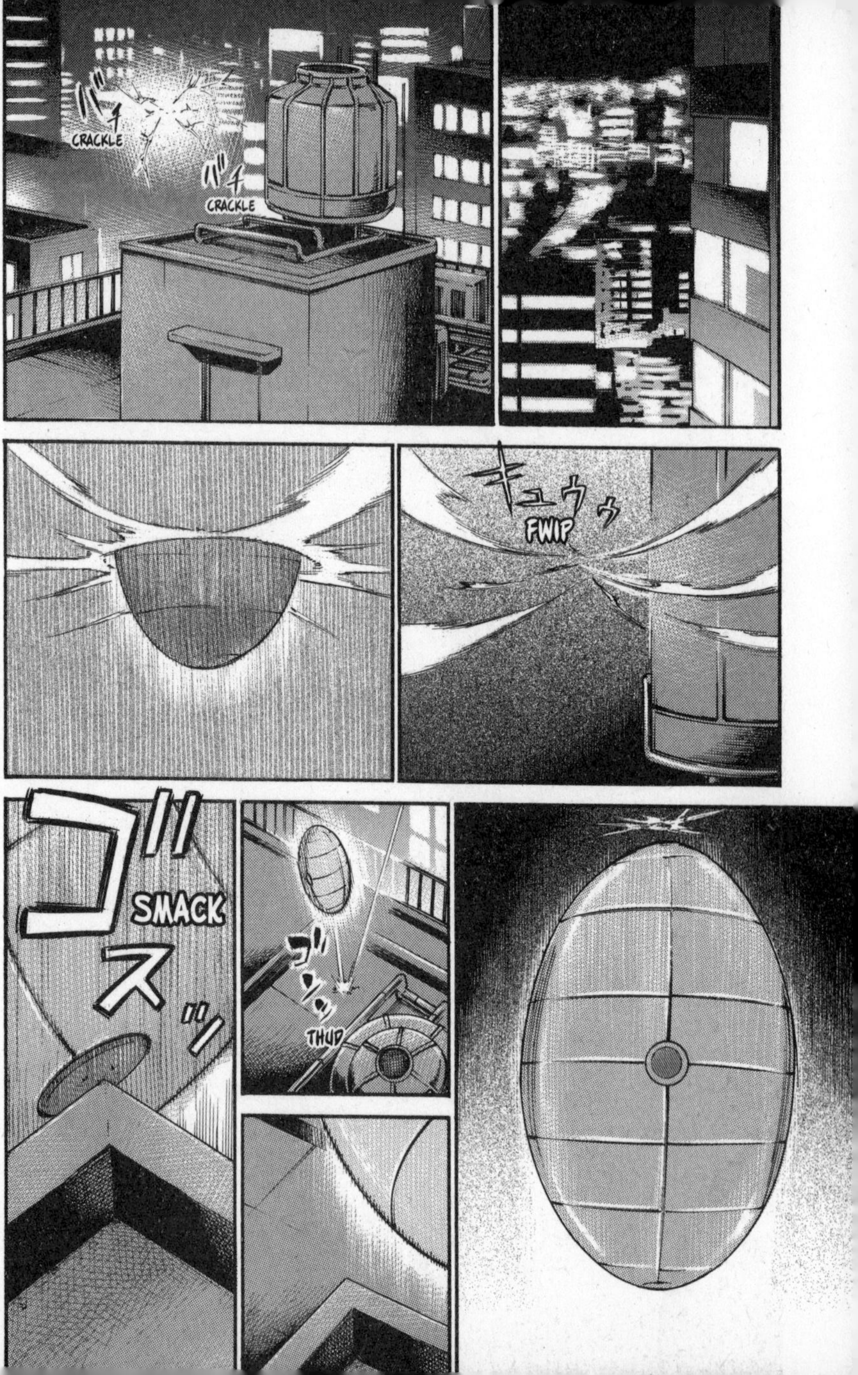
バチ
CRACKLE
バチ
CRACKLE
キュウゥ
FWIP
ゴンッ
THUD
ゴスッ
SMACK

GAH!

PLUNK

THUD

WHOOSH

THIS THING! THE DESIGN IS DEFINITELY FLAWED!

OWW...

MY SIDE...

CREAK

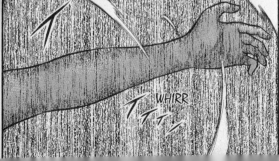

WHIRR

CRACK

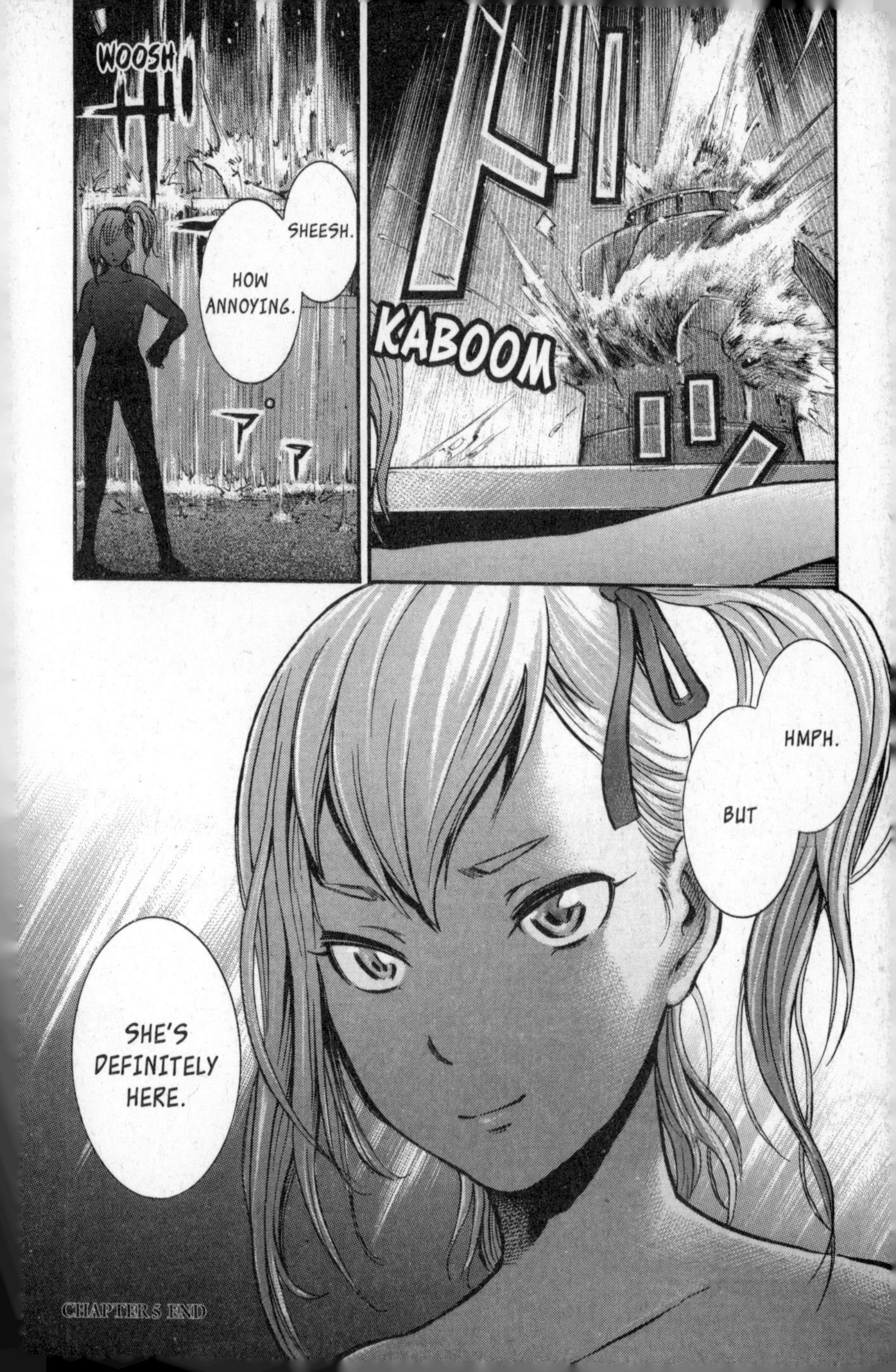
KABOOM
WOOSH
SHEESH. HOW ANNOYING.
HMPH. BUT
SHE'S DEFINITELY HERE.

CHAPTER 5 END

EXTRA 2 DADUM DUM DADUM

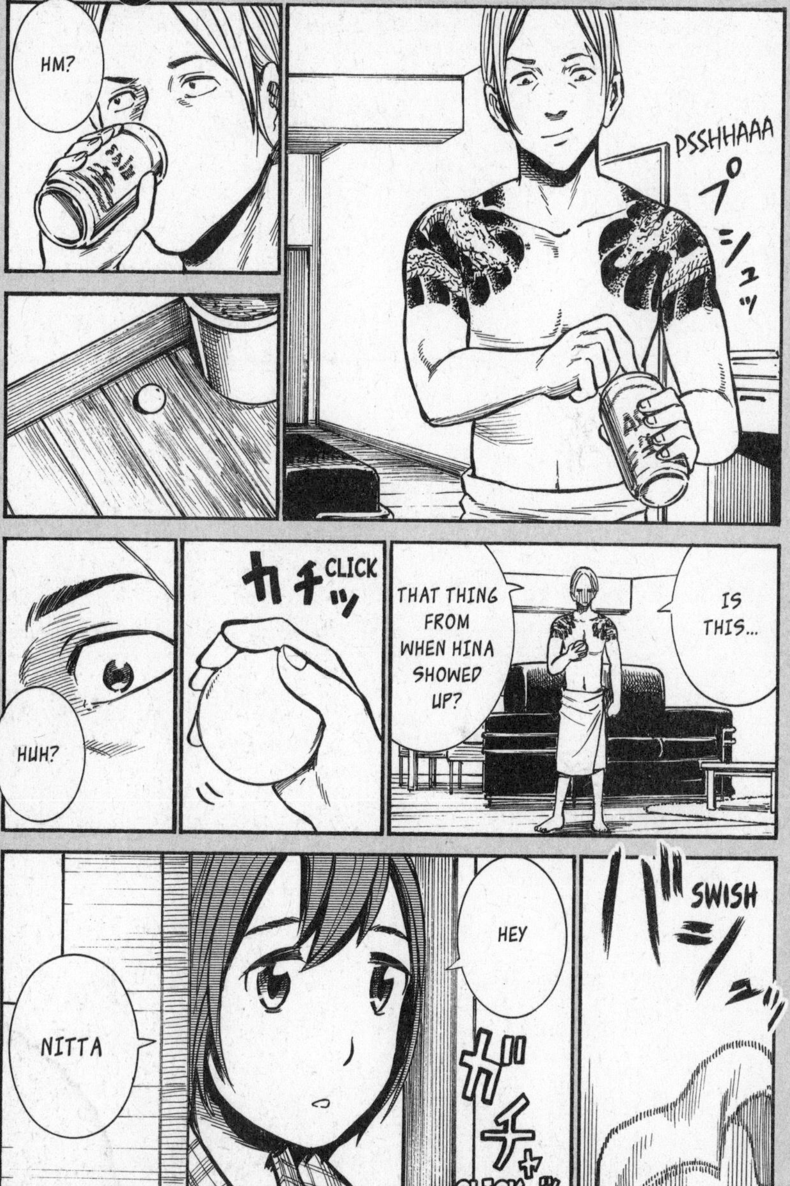
PSSHHAAA
プシュッ
HM?
IS THIS...
THAT THING FROM WHEN HINA SHOWED UP?
カチッ
CLICK
HUH?
バシュッ
SWISH
HEY
ガチャッ
CLICK
NITTA

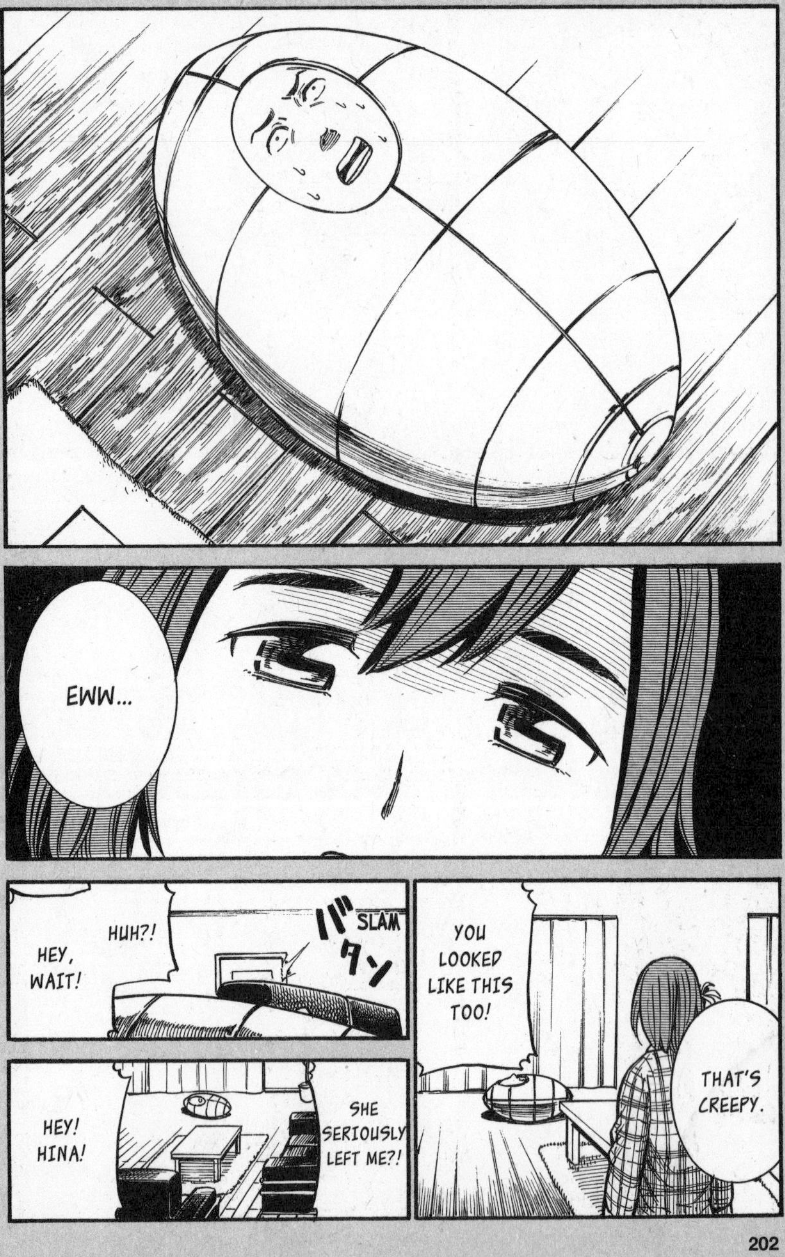
EWW...
YOU LOOKED LIKE THIS TOO!
THAT'S CREEPY.
バタン SLAM
HUH?!
HEY, WAIT!
SHE SERIOUSLY LEFT ME?!
HEY! HINA!

WOBBLE
WOBBLE
IT'S NO GOOD.
MY STRENGTH...
I CAN DO IT.
BINGO!
MUSTER UP THE LAST OF YOUR STRENGTH!
RAHHH!
グワン
WOBBLE
グワン
WOBBLE
YES! HERE IT COMES!
HERE IT COMES!

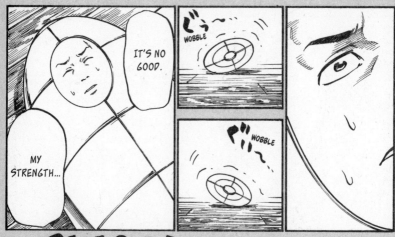

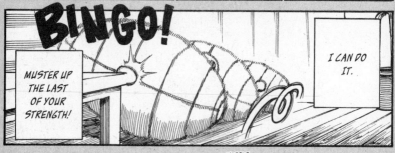

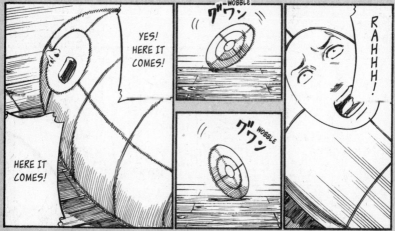

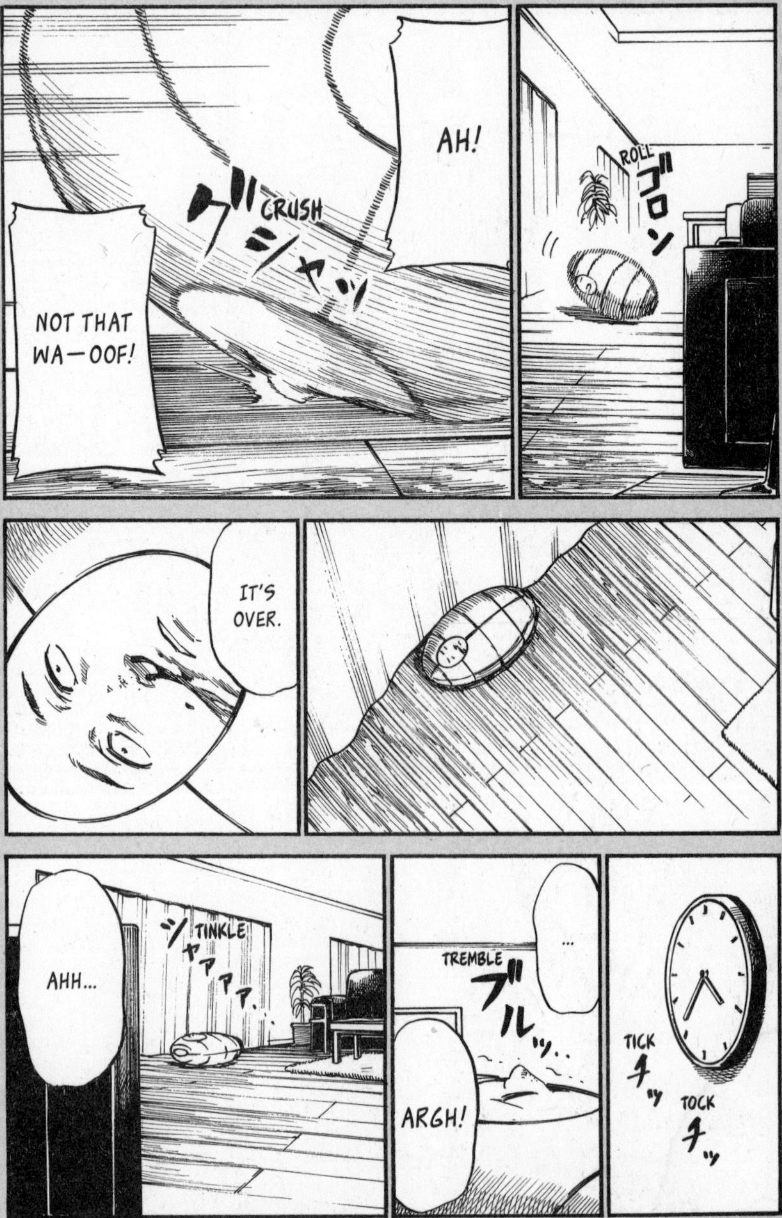
ROLL
ゴロン
AH!
CRUSH
グシャッ
NOT THAT WA—OOF!
IT'S OVER.
TICK
チッ
TOCK
チッ
...
TREMBLE
ブルッ..
ARGH!
TINKLE
シャアアア..
AHH...

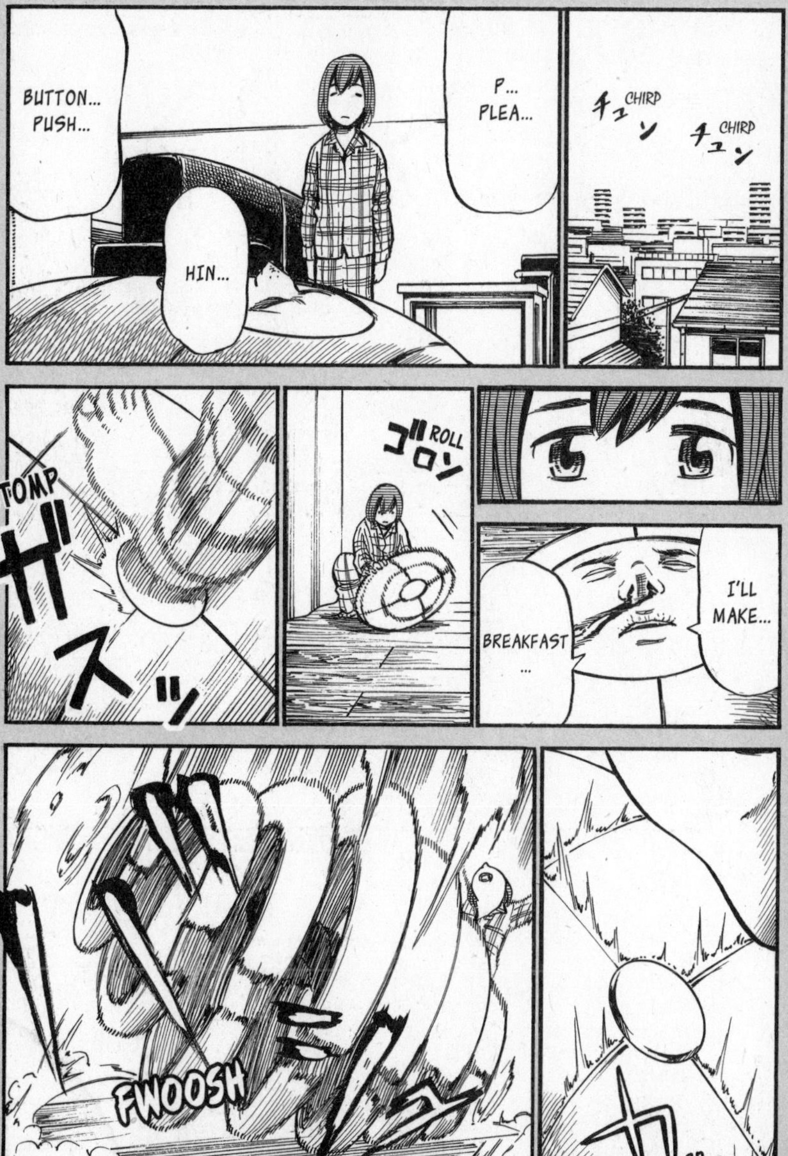
チュン CHIRP
チュン CHIRP
P... PLEA...
BUTTON... PUSH...
HIN...
I'LL MAKE...
BREAKFAST ...
ゴロン ROLL
STOMP
ザスッ
カッ
CLICK
FWOOSH

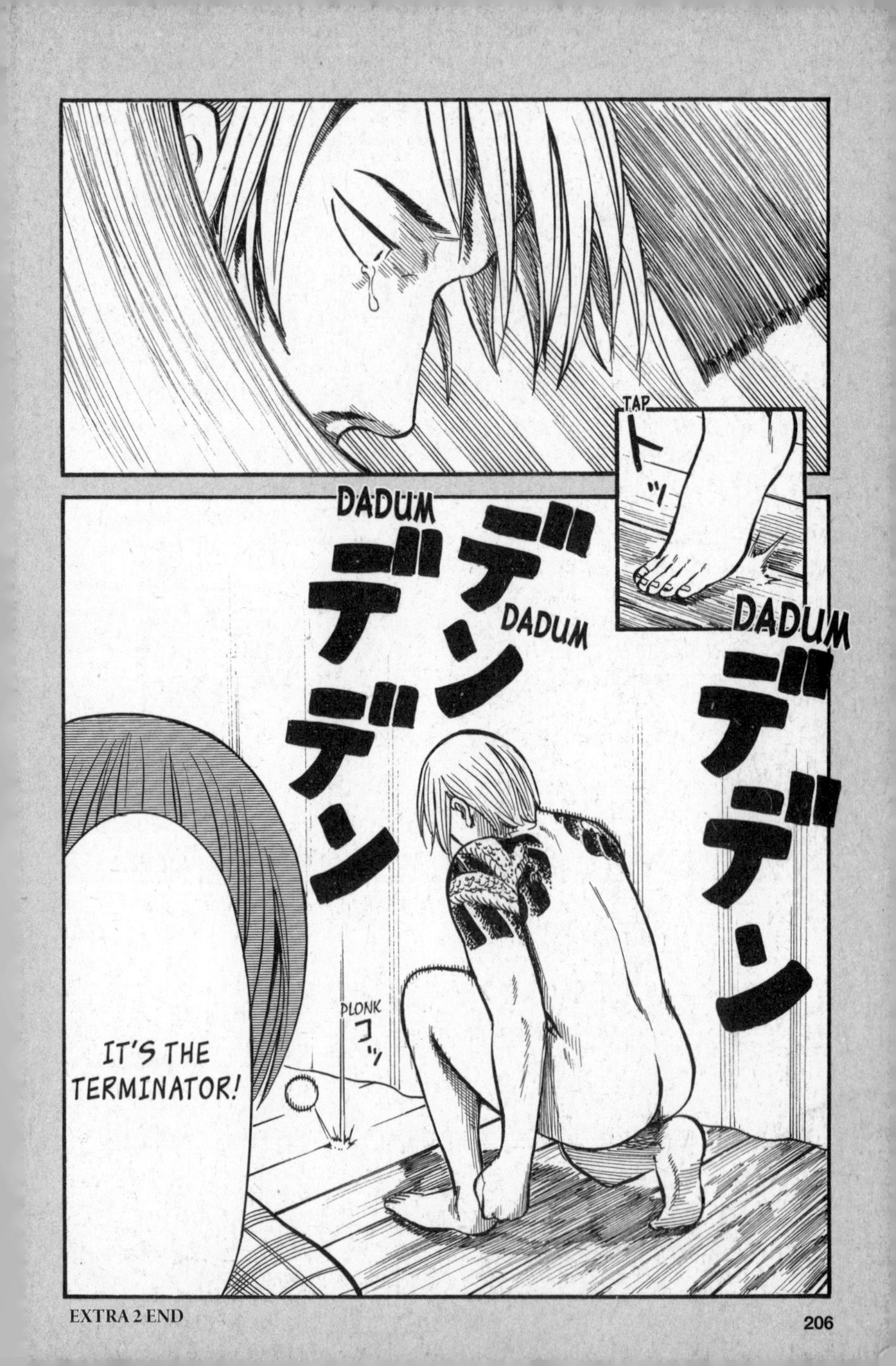
TAP
トッ
DADUM
デデン
DADUM
デデン
DADUM
デデン
PLONK
コッ
IT'S THE TERMINATOR!

EXTRA 2 END

TO BE CONTINUED
IN HINAMATSURI
VOLUME 2.

HINAMATSURI Volume 1

Copyright © 2011 Masao Ohtake
All Rights Reserved.
First published in Japan in 2011 by KADOKAWA CORPORATION
ENTERBRAIN
English translation rights arranged with KADOKAWA CORPORATION
ENTERBRAIN

ISBN: 978-1-64273-005-0

Written and illustrated by Masao Ohtake
Translated by Nathan Takase
English Edition Published by One Peace Books 2018

Printed in Canada

2 3 4 5 6 7 8 9 10

One Peace Books
43-32 22nd Street STE 204 Long Island City New York 11101
www.onepeacebooks.com